BEYOND THE SHADOW
OF THE SENATORS

BEYOND THE SHADOW OF THE SENATORS

THE UNTOLD STORY OF THE HOMESTEAD GRAYS
AND THE INTEGRATION OF BASEBALL

BRAD SNYDER

Contemporary Books

Chicago   New York   San Francisco   Lisbon   London   Madrid   Mexico City
Milan   New Delhi   San Juan   Seoul   Singapore   Sydney   Toronto

Library of Congress Cataloging-in-Publication Data

Snyder, Brad.
    Beyond the shadow of the Senators : the untold story of the Homestead Grays and the integration of baseball / Brad Snyder.
        p.   cm.
    Includes bibliographical references (p.   ).
    ISBN 0-07-140820-7
    1. Homestead Grays (Baseball team)—History.   2. Baseball—Washington (D.C.)—History—20th century.   3. African American baseball players—Washington (D.C.)—History—20th century.   4. Washington Senators (Baseball team : 1899–1960)—History.   5. Discrimination in sports—United States.   I. Title.

GV875.H59 S69   2003
796.357'64'09753—dc21
                                                2002031335

1 2 3 4 5 6 7 8 9 0   AGM/AGM   1 0 9 8 7 6 5 4 3 2

ISBN 0-07-140820-7

McGraw-Hill books are available at special quantity discounts to use as premiums and sales promotions, or for use in corporate training programs. For more information, please write to the Director of Special Sales, Professional Publishing, McGraw-Hill, Two Penn Plaza, New York, NY 10121-2298. Or contact your local bookstore.

This book is printed on acid-free paper.

For Harry, Linda, and Ivan Snyder

CONTENTS

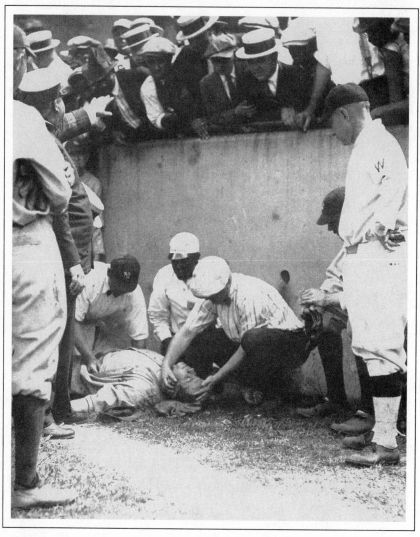

Babe Ruth knocks himself unconscious running into a wall next to Griffith Stadium's right-field pavilion, the cheering section of the Senators' loyal black fans. The July 5, 1924, Yankees-Senators contest was Buck Leonard's first major league baseball game. (TRANSCENDENTAL GRAPHICS)

INTRODUCTION

Between the Babe and Jackie

July 5, 1924

Griffith Stadium is packed for a doubleheader between the Washington Senators and the New York Yankees. The two teams are battling for first place, and the atmosphere at the stadium, located in the heart of Washington's black community, is electric. In the first game, while chasing a foul ball off the bat of Senators first baseman Joe Judge, Yankees legend Babe Ruth knocks himself unconscious running into the right-field retaining wall—directly in front of the pavilion reserved for the Senators' black fans.

A photographer perched in foul territory captures a classic image of the black fans peering down at the sprawled-out slugger. Trainers rush from both dugouts with water buckets and black medical bags. Players from both teams look on anxiously. Police Captain Doyle, a caricature of an Irish cop, stretches out a white hand to keep a sea of black faces at bay.

Buck Leonard, a husky, sixteen-year-old railroad worker, almost certainly stands among the multitude of concerned fans. A future Negro League star, Leonard is attending his first major league baseball game. Sam Lacy, an eighteen-year-old stadium vendor and future sportswriter, is selling soft drinks and making comparisons between the white players in major league baseball and the black players in the Negro Leagues whose teams play at Griffith Stadium when the Senators are out of town. Two decades later, Leonard emerges as the star first baseman of the Homestead Grays, Lacy as a crusading black journalist campaigning for the integration of major league baseball, and the Grays as the best baseball team, black or white, playing at Griffith Stadium.

In 1940, seventeen years before the Dodgers moved to Los Angeles and the Giants moved to San Francisco, the greatest baseball dynasty that most people had never heard of moved the bulk of its home games from Pittsburgh to Washington, D.C. Behind their home-run-hitting catcher Josh Gibson and slugging first baseman Buck Leonard, the Homestead Grays dominated black professional baseball, known as the Negro Leagues, by capturing eight of nine Negro National League titles from 1937 to 1945. Historians dubbed Gibson the "Black Babe Ruth" and Leonard the "Black Lou Gehrig" and compared the Grays to the great New York Yankees teams of the 1920s and '30s.

Although the Grays originated in the steel town of Homestead, Pennsylvania, they reached the peak of their popularity by playing their home games at Washington's Griffith Stadium. From 1940 to 1950, the Grays played at Griffith Stadium when the Washington Senators—one of the worst teams in the major leagues during that period—were out of town. The Grays outclassed the Senators (also known as the Nationals or, as headline writers often referred to them, the Nats) on the field and often outdrew them at the box office. When sportswriter Charley Dryden quipped that Washington was "first in war, first in peace, and last in the American League," he wasn't referring to the Grays. During World War II, the Grays fielded one of the best professional baseball teams of any color, capturing Negro National League titles and competing against Satchel Paige and the Kansas City Monarchs in showdowns that electrified Griffith Stadium the way Ruth's Yankees once did. The big difference was that nearly all the fans at Grays games were black.

During the first half of the twentieth century, Washington, D.C., was a segregated Southern town. Racial discrimination in the nation's capital prevented blacks and whites from attending the same schools, living on the same streets, eating in the same restaurants, shopping in the same stores, playing on the same playgrounds, and frequenting the same movie theaters. As a result, black and white Washingtonians lived in separate social worlds.

Those worlds collided at Senators games. Griffith Stadium was one of the few outdoor places in segregated Washington where blacks could enjoy themselves *with* whites. The ballpark, located at Seventh Street and Florida Avenue in northwest Washington, stood in the heart of a thriving black residential and commercial district. It also was just down the street from Howard University, the "Capstone of Negro Education." The educational opportunities at Howard and the job opportunities in the federal government had lured many of the country's best and brightest black residents to the nation's capital. Many of them lived near the ballpark in neighborhoods such as LeDroit Park, which was just beyond Griffith Stadium's right-field wall.

With an affluent black population in their own backyard, the Senators boasted one of major league baseball's largest and most loyal black fan bases. The Senators' black fans sat in the right-field pavilion—Griffith Stadium was one of only two segregated major league ballparks (Sportsman's Park in St. Louis was the other). Segregated seating, however, did not deter the Senators' black fans from attending games. On the contrary, black Washingtonians were so enamored of the Senators that they refused to support any of the Negro League teams that played at Griffith Stadium during the 1920s and 1930s. The Senators enjoyed unprecedented success during this period—winning the World Series in 1924 and returning to the Fall Classic in 1925 and 1933—as well as unwavering support from their black fans.

Only one player during the 1920s and '30s tested the loyalty of the Senators' black fans—Babe Ruth. The Babe's big lips and broad, flat nose often triggered racial epithets from white players and fans but endeared him to black ones. "Ruth was called 'nigger' so often that many people assumed that he was indeed partly black and that at some point in time he, or an immediate ancestor, had managed to cross the color line," wrote Ruth biographer Robert W. Creamer. "Even players in the Negro baseball leagues that flourished then believed this and generally wished the Babe, whom they considered a secret brother, well in his conquest of white baseball."[1]

With their "secret brother's" retirement in 1935 and the Senators' nosedive after the 1933 season, the calls for a "real brother" on the Senators came from the team's black fans. One of those fans was a Washington native and young journalist named Sam Lacy. During the mid-1930s, Lacy began lobbying Senators owner Clark Griffith to integrate his team. But from Ruth's retirement until Jackie Robinson's debut with the Brooklyn Dodgers in 1947, Lacy and other black Washingtonians waited in vain for another major league hero.

During World War II, the Homestead Grays ended the long-standing love affair between black Washingtonians and the Senators. Blacks flocked to Grays games, not out of some social obligation but because they thirsted for recreational outlets during the war and they loved good baseball. While such major league stars as Ted Williams, Joe DiMaggio, Hank Greenberg, and the Senators' Cecil Travis were off serving in the military, the Grays maintained a team of talented yet aging players led by Gibson and Leonard. Satchel Paige, the star pitcher for the Kansas City Monarchs, also was too old to serve in the military, but not too old to compete. The Grays-Monarchs clashes were the best show in town. Although white fans never caught on, more than twenty-eight thousand black fans attended a 1942 Grays-Monarchs game at Griffith Stadium. They sat wherever they wanted. And they saw top-notch professional baseball.

The Grays' popularity and on-field success transformed Washington into the front lines of the campaign to integrate major league baseball. The city was a natural forum for social protest. Segregation thrived in the nation's capital while the United States fought a war against Nazi white supremacy. The city's sophisticated black population was ready to embrace a black major league player. The best team in the Negro Leagues played in the same ballpark as one of the worst teams in the major leagues, highlighting the illogic of maintaining separate leagues. And no major league team was more desperate for an influx of new talent than the Senators, who could have been instant contenders by signing Grays sluggers Gibson and Leonard.

Recognizing all of these factors in Washington's favor, Lacy and other black journalists initially thought that the best chance of integrating the major leagues lay with Griffith. As a young manager with the 1911 Cincinnati Reds, Griffith had pioneered the passing of olive-skinned Cubans as "white" major leaguers. As the owner of the Senators, he continued his practice of plucking players out of Cuba with the help of his primary scout, Joe Cambria. Griffith also forged a healthy relationship with Washington's black community and encouraged the development of the Negro Leagues. The Senators owner, however, was set in his ways, and he made so much money by renting his ballpark to the Grays that he refused to sign Gibson and Leonard. Griffith also had a secret ally—Grays owner Cum Posey—in maintaining separate leagues. Over time, Griffith became one of the most outspoken supporters of segregation.

Two leading black sports columnists, Lacy of the *Baltimore Afro-American* and Wendell Smith of the *Pittsburgh Courier*, made Washington, D.C., one of the focal points of their efforts to integrate baseball and Griffith the target of their most biting criticism. Had it been up to Lacy, blacks would have played on the Senators closer to Ruth's time than to Robinson's.

This is the story of the lost era between the Babe and Jackie, of a crusading journalist named Sam Lacy, an immensely talented black ballplayer named Buck Leonard, and a stubborn major league owner named Clark Griffith. It's the story of why the fight to integrate major league baseball began in Washington and not in Brooklyn, why black Washington ultimately lost the fight, and why the Senators were not the first team to integrate. And it's the story of the greatest baseball dynasty that most people have never heard of, the Homestead Grays, whose wartime popularity at Griffith Stadium moved them beyond the shadow of the Senators.

Sam Lacy's 1924 Armstrong High School yearbook photo. Lacy pitched for Armstrong's championship baseball teams for three seasons. (CHARLES SUMNER MUSEUM AND ARCHIVES)

ONE

SAM, BUCK, AND GRIFFITH STADIUM

The day the Babe crashed into the right-field pavilion at Griffith Stadium was one of many afternoons Sam Lacy spent at the ballpark. The eighteen-year-old stadium vendor had grown up five blocks from the ballpark—it was his second home. An aspiring young ballplayer, Lacy would shag balls in the outfield for the Senators while they took batting practice. He befriended several players, including first baseman Chick Gandil, shortstop George McBride, and center fielder Clyde Milan, and, after batting practice, he would run errands for them such as picking up their laundry and taking their shirts to the cleaners. Even after these players left the team, the Senators rewarded Lacy for his pregame work with the most profitable items to sell in the stands: coffee in the spring, cold drinks in the summer, and scorecards when the Senators defeated the New York Giants in the 1924 World Series.[1]

Lacy discovered an added benefit from shagging flies and selling scorecards: He learned how to make comparisons between the white major leaguers and the black professional players who took the field at Griffith Stadium when the Senators were out of town. Lacy knew that Babe Ruth and Ty Cobb were good, but the future Hall of Fame sportswriter also knew that contemporary Negro League stars Oscar Charleston and John Henry Lloyd should be playing on the same teams as Ruth and Cobb.

Racial segregation wasn't confined to the playing field; it also was in the stands. In 1924, the right-field pavilion was reserved for the Senators' black fans. There were no signs or rigid seating policy as in St. Louis (which did not lift its racially segregated seating policy until 1944).[2] There was even some debate as to whether segregated seating at Griffith Stadium existed at all,[3] in part because black fans occasionally sat in the left-field bleachers. Blacks rarely, if ever, sat in box seats or the grandstand. "There were black people around from time to time, but you used to do almost a double take when you saw them," recalled baseball author Bill Gilbert, who had grown up going to Senators games. "You just thought they were going to be sitting out in the right-field pavilion or the bleachers."[4]

Calvin Griffith, who assumed ownership of the team upon his Uncle Clark's death in 1955, confirmed that his family segregated black fans in the right-field pavilion. "That was because of the colored preachers coming in there and asking Mr. Griffith to put aside a section for the black people," Calvin recalled, respectfully referring to his uncle. "Mr. Griffith gave them practically down from first base to the right-field fence. That's what they wanted. They got what they asked for."[5]

The segregated seating rankled Lacy. "There were places I couldn't go, places my friends couldn't go, places my family couldn't go. At that time, by nature of being raised here, you have to know where they had segregated seating at Griffith Stadium . . ." Lacy recalled. "They required you to sit in the right-field pavilion up against the fence almost, and [there was] no being able to sit anywhere else in the stadium."[6]

Segregation—the separation and exclusion of blacks through laws and local customs—thrived in the nation's capital, but in an idiosyncratic way. It existed in the public schools, housing, and employment, but not transportation. It existed on most playgrounds, but not ones controlled by the Department of the Interior. It existed in all parts of downtown Washington, but not in public buildings, such as the White House, the Capitol, the Smithsonian museums, art galleries, public libraries, or the Library of Congress. It existed in downtown restaurants, department stores, and movie theaters, but to varying degrees. Some offered blacks a full range of services; others served blacks in limited ways; however, most refused to serve them at all.

The inconsistency arose from the Northern and Southern characteristics Washington inherited as a border city and from the presence of the federal government.[7] It is therefore not surprising that there were no "white" and "colored" signs at Griffith Stadium. Washingtonians often refused to advertise their discriminatory practices.[8] Segregation developed through local custom, in part because the city had passed "lost laws" in 1872 and 1873 that actually prohibited discrimination in public accommodations.[9] The laws were never repealed, but they were usually ignored. As historian C. Vann Woodward observed, "Laws are not an adequate index of the extent and prevalence of segregation and discriminatory practices in the South."[10] The off-the-books segregation at Griffith Stadium proved that Washington was no different from the rest of the Jim Crow South.

Griffith Stadium, however, was different from other public places in Washington by virtue of its location—the ballpark at Seventh Street and Florida Avenue was a white island in the heart of the black community. The center-field wall detoured around five houses in the upscale black neighborhood known as LeDroit Park. Howard University, one of the nation's finest historically black colleges, lay on a hill just north of the ballpark. Another black institution, Freedmen's Hospital, stood between Howard and Griffith Stadium.

It was not always a black neighborhood. Professional baseball had been played on the site of Griffith Stadium since 1891. That year the Washington Nationals of the American Association cut down about 125 oak trees, filled in the holes from the stumps, and built a single-level wooden grandstand and baseball diamond known as Boundary Field.[11] At the time, Seventh Street and the Boundary (Florida Avenue) marked the end of the horse-drawn trolley line and the beginning of farmland.[12] During the late nineteenth century, the neighborhood around the ballpark was a white suburb.

Griffith Stadium itself was built in 1911, during the golden age of baseball's concrete and steel ballparks. Comiskey Park opened in

3

1910, followed by the Polo Grounds in 1911, Fenway Park and Tiger Stadium in 1912, Ebbets Field in 1913, and Wrigley Field in 1914. Although a contemporary of these other classic ballparks, Griffith Stadium was an architectural blight.[13] In 1911, the ballpark was born out of a fire started by a plumber's blowtorch, which destroyed the old wooden ball yard less than a month before Opening Day. The Senators' then-owners pledged $125,000 toward a state-of-the-art twelve thousand–seat concrete-and-steel structure and vowed to have it ready for the opener.[14] Only a roofless, single-decked grandstand was completed in time.[15] The *Washington Star* reported of the ball-park's hasty construction: "Day and night the chanting of the negro laborers has been heard in the vicinity, like Aladdin's palace, the structure rose as if by magic."[16]

Piecemeal additions over the next two decades gave the ballpark a perpetually unfinished feel. The roof of the double-decked grand-stand stood about ten to twenty feet lower than the roof of the dou-ble-decked grandstands subsequently erected down the foul lines.[17] In 1923, concrete bleachers were installed in left field, and the ball-park, then known as American League Park, was renamed Clark Griffith Stadium after the team's majority owner.[18] Soon people sim-ply referred to the ballpark as Griffith Stadium.

Despite its flaws, Griffith Stadium possessed a certain charm. Fans gathered on the promenade in front of Seventh Street and bought tickets at small booths with stucco roofs. The smell of freshly baked bread frequently wafted into the ballpark from nearby bakeries. Every U.S. president from William Howard Taft to John F. Kennedy threw out a ceremonial first pitch there on Opening Day.[19] The com-mander in chief had access to a field-level presidential box whenever he wanted to take in a game.

The ballpark's seating capacity of twenty-seven thousand to thirty-two thousand was among the lowest in the major leagues. The play-ing field was one of the largest—405 feet to left field, 420 to 457 in straightaway center, and 320 to right backed by a thirty-one-foot-high wall. The right-field wall contained a hand-operated scoreboard (one young operator was future major league commissioner Bowie Kuhn). The center-field wall jutted inward at a right angle to avoid five row houses and a giant oak known as the Tree. "I'll meet you by 'the Tree,'" young fans often told their friends.[20]

The Tree, which was more than five hundred feet from home plate and behind a thirty-one-foot wall, was no match for Babe Ruth, who hit a ball into the top of the Tree in 1922. Senators center fielder Sam Rice, who saw the Yankee slugger's blast leave the park that day, later commented that Yankee Stadium wasn't the only "House That Ruth Built." Ruth's popularity among Washington's black and white fans led the Senators' management to increase the ballpark's seating capacity during the early 1920s. "[Ruth] built all these stands," Rice declared in David Von Sothen's 1964 documentary *The Last Out*, about Griffith Stadium. "He drew all the people."[21]

By the 1920s, the neighborhood around Griffith Stadium was increasingly black; by World War II, it was almost all black. Seventh Street, which ran just west of the ballpark, served as the playground of the black masses. The pool halls, barbershops, and storefront churches reminded recent migrants from Virginia and the Carolinas of the Southern ways of life that they had left behind.[22] They frequented movies at the Dunbar Theater and after-hours nightspots like the Old Rose Social Club, Off-beat, Little Harlem Cafe, Dreamland, and Cafe De Luxe.[23]

The Howard Theater, the oldest of the live, black theaters known as the "Chitlin Circuit," anchored the neighborhood just off Seventh and T Streets.[24] The fifteen hundred–seat venue featured the finest musicians, comedians, and entertainers for more than half a century, influencing local artists from Duke Ellington to Marvin Gaye. "The Howard was my real high school. I studied the singers like my life depended on it," Gaye told his biographer, David Ritz. "When I saw Sam Cooke and Jesse Belvin I'd try to avoid friends and family for days. I didn't want to talk or be talked to 'cause I was busy practicing and memorizing everything I heard those singers do."[25] Ellington received a high school equivalency degree of sorts on Seventh Street, studying the techniques of the city's top piano players who hung out at Frank Holliday's pool hall next to the Howard Theater.[26] Ellington wrote: "Guys from all walks of life seemed to converge there: school kids over and under sixteen; college students and graduates, some

5

starting out in law and medicine and science; and lots of Pullman porters and dining-car waiters."[27]

Seventh Street's grittiness also captured the imaginations of several Harlem Renaissance artists. During Langston Hughes's fourteen unhappy months amid the city's black elite, he delighted in Seventh Street's simple pleasures. "Seventh Street was always teemingly alive with dark working people who hadn't yet acquired 'culture' and the manners of stage ambassadors," Hughes wrote in 1927, "and pinks and blacks and yellows were still friends without apologies."[28] Jean Toomer, a less heralded Harlem Renaissance writer who had grown up amid Washington's black upper class, found Seventh Street an inspiring source of poetry and prose. "Seventh Street is a bastard of Prohibition and the War," Toomer wrote. "A crude-boned, soft-skinned wedge of nigger life breathing its loafer air, jazz songs and love, thrusting unconscious rhythms, black reddish blood into the white and whitewashed wood of Washington."[29]

Just a few blocks west of the Seventh Street ball yard people strolled up and down the bustling U Street corridor known as "Black Broadway" and the "Colored Man's Connecticut Avenue." On U Street, blacks wore their finest clothes to movie theaters such as the Lincoln and the Booker T, dance halls such as the Lincoln Colonnade and the True Reformers Hall, and black businesses such as the Murray Brothers Printing Company and Addison Scurlock's Photography Studio.[30] Like Beale Street in Memphis, Auburn Avenue in Atlanta, and Lenox Avenue in Harlem, U Street presented the best that segregation could offer Washington's black residents.

Yet what distinguished the neighborhood near Griffith Stadium from other large African-American communities was the size and influence of the black elite.[31] Black doctors, lawyers, college professors, schoolteachers, and civil servants flocked to the nation's capital because of the educational opportunities at Howard University and the job opportunities with the federal government. They prized educational and professional achievement, multiple generations of local ancestry, and light skin color. They included an upper echelon that the *Washington Bee* referred to as the "Black 400" (after New York City's white aristocratic "400"), though in 1900 the Black 400 con-

6

sisted of about one hundred families out of seventy-five thousand black residents. The Black 400's influence on Washington's economic, social, and intellectual life extended far beyond their actual numbers and far beyond the area near Griffith Stadium. According to historian Willard Gatewood, "From the end of Reconstruction until at least World War I, Washington was the center of the black aristocracy in the United States."[32]

Sociologist E. Franklin Frazier labeled the black elite "the old black middle class," likening their economic status and social behavior to that of middle-class whites: "They wanted to forget the Negro's past, and they have attempted to conform to the behavior and values of the white community in the most minute details. Therefore, they have often become, as has been observed, 'exaggerated' Americans."[33] Frazier derided Washington's black elite as living in a "world of make believe."[34]

The grandson of the first black detective on the D.C. police force, Samuel Harold Lacy was born into Washington's world of make-believe on October 23, 1905, as the youngest of four surviving children.[35] From his mother, Rose, a Shinnecock Indian, Lacy inherited a long, thin face, high cheekbones, an angular nose, a prominent forehead, and a caramel-colored complexion.[36] Lacy should have felt comfortable in this exclusive social world—his family was professionally accomplished, he was a third-generation Washingtonian, and he was fair-skinned.

Lacy's family, however, struggled to make ends meet. He recalled wearing the shoes of his older brother, Erskine, "with paper inside the soles to cover the holes where he had worn them out."[37] Lacy's father, a notary and legal researcher, moved the family several times.[38] They rented houses just a few blocks south of U Street on Tenth and Thirteenth Streets and frequently took in boarders.[39] His mother, the family disciplinarian, worked as a hairdresser, raised her children as devout Catholics, and refused to allow alcohol in her home.[40]

Lacy found release from Washington's class-divided black community on the vacant lot next to the Twelfth Street YMCA. The nation's first full-service YMCA for blacks, the Twelfth Street Y opened only a block and a half away from Lacy's home on Thirteenth Street.[41] Lacy spent hours on the Y's vacant lot playing baseball. Although right-handed, Lacy learned how to hit left-handed to avoid breaking windows in the adjacent Y building that served as the third-base line.[42]

Lacy's childhood in some ways paralleled Duke Ellington's, though Ellington was several years older than Lacy. Ellington's family moved around Washington as many as fourteen times, often within a block or two of Lacy's Thirteenth Street home.[43] Ellington's father worked as a chauffeur, a butler, and a caterer. His mother worked as a laundress and a domestic. Yet his parents inculcated him with middle-class values, experiences, and habits and the belief that he could accomplish anything.[44] Families like the Ellingtons and the Lacys constituted the majority of Washington's growing black middle class—not rich professionals, but lower-middle-class black families striving for education, social refinement, and a better life.

Lacy attended and then rejected the black middle class's crown jewel, Dunbar High School. The first black public high school in the United States, Dunbar boasted a faculty with Ivy League educations, law degrees, and Ph.D.s.[45] They taught at Dunbar in part because the federal government paid all of Washington's black teachers the same salaries as white teachers.[46] Dunbar churned out future generations of Ivy League graduates and a who's who of black America. Lacy's classmates included William Hastie, the first black federal appeals court judge; W. Montague Cobb, a Howard professor of anatomy and medicine for forty years; Charles Drew, the founder of the American Red Cross Blood Bank and early developer of blood plasma; William George, a diplomat under President Truman; and Allison Davis, a University of Chicago professor.[47] Other famous Dunbar graduates included the first black general in the U.S. Army, Benjamin O. Davis; the first black member of a presidential cabinet, Dr. Robert C. Weaver, the Secretary of Housing and Urban Development under Lyndon Johnson and one of the leaders of Franklin D. Roosevelt's "black cabinet"; the first black U.S. Senator since Reconstruction,

Senator Edward Brooke of Massachusetts; and two of the city's delegates on Capitol Hill, Rev. Walter Fauntroy and Eleanor Holmes Norton.[48]

The black masses, however, resented Dunbar as a club run by and for the privileged class. They accused Dunbar of funneling students to Ivy League schools based not only on their academic records but also on their family backgrounds and lighter skin color.[49] Dr. Kenneth B. Clark, a black social psychologist whose studies contributed to the U.S. Supreme Court's school desegregation decisions, told writer Jervis Anderson that Dunbar "is the only example in our history of a separate black school that was able, somehow, to be equal. But this was possible only because of the class distinctions among blacks. . . . It could scarcely have existed in any other part of the country."[50]

Lacy hated his time at Dunbar. He seldom mentioned it in interviews, perhaps because of his abrupt departure. During his sophomore year, he had made first sergeant on the school's prestigious drill team. The principal, however, caught Lacy ditching drill team practice in favor of playing sports and took away Lacy's sergeant stripes.[51] "Thus, it might be said that my younger days were spent among the elite, but not as one of them. I was the stray," Lacy wrote in his autobiography, *Fighting for Fairness*. "Actually, I have been considered antiestablishment. Maybe stubborn and impulsive would be a better description. I resented authority figures who behaved in autocratic fashion."[52]

Lacy was so angry about his demotion from the drill team that he transferred to Dunbar's rival, Armstrong Technical High School.[53] If Dunbar embodied W. E. B. DuBois's "Talented Tenth," then Armstrong reflected Booker T. Washington's emphasis on vocational education.[54] "I went to Armstrong because my buddies at the YMCA were going to Armstrong," Lacy recalled. "We went to Armstrong en masse."[55]

At Armstrong, Lacy helped lead the baseball team to three straight city championships from 1922 to 1924 as the star pitcher, part-time third baseman, and eventual team captain.[56] Although too short and

9

slender to play a leading role on the football and basketball teams, Lacy shined on the pitcher's mound.[57] On one afternoon, he struck out seventeen Dunbar hitters; as he later wrote in his autobiography, he "got a kick out of beating Dunbar when the two teams squared off."[58]

A few years later, Lacy bolted from the black middle class's other educational pillar, Howard University. Founded by white Congregationalists in 1867 and named after Gen. Oliver O. Howard, the head of the Freedmen's Bureau, Howard University boldly referred to itself as the "Capstone of Negro Education."[59] The university enjoyed its halcyon years under its first black president, Mordecai W. Johnson.[60] During Johnson's tenure from 1926 to 1960, Howard boasted a dream team of black intellectuals: E. Franklin Frazier in sociology; Alain Locke in philosophy; Sterling Brown in English; Rayford W. Logan in history; Ralph Bunche in political science; Charles Drew in medicine; Ernest Just in biology; Abram Harris in economics; Percy Julian in chemistry; and William Hastie, Charles Hamilton Houston, and James Nabrit in law.[61] At that time, Howard offered some of the few graduate and professional programs, particularly in law, medicine, and dentistry, open to people of color.[62]

In 1926, Lacy placated his mother by briefly enrolling at Howard.[63] He lasted only a year there. He had never wanted to be a doctor or a lawyer; he wanted to be a professional baseball player.[64] And his childhood experiences among the black intelligentsia—growing up near U Street and briefly attending Dunbar and Howard—taught him that as an adult he did not want to join their crowd.

Instead Lacy drifted into trouble. He tried to pattern himself after his older brother, Erskine, who had quit his government printing job because he could make more money as a pool shark.[65] During his twenties, Lacy took to betting on horse racing, but with less financial success. His gambling debts eventually forced him to write several bad checks for ten or twenty dollars apiece. In his autobiography, Lacy said he "came close to becoming a jailbird instead of a journalist. It took all my wits to keep one step ahead of the police until I could manage to satisfy the various holders."[66] Much like Griffith

Stadium, Lacy stood at the crossroads of the upper- and working-class black communities, and he didn't fit into either one.

For Lacy and many other black residents, Griffith Stadium was an oasis. Despite the subtle segregation, Senators owner Clark Griffith made blacks feel welcome inside his ballpark. Griffith opened his stadium to the black public schools and regularly rented the ballpark for black sporting and other community events.[67] "Griffith Stadium was sort of like outdoor theater for the black community," recalled local historian Henry Whitehead, who has lived in Washington since the late 1940s. "It was important to the black community that we had that venue in our neighborhood."[68]

Griffith Stadium was host to events that appealed to blacks of all occupations and social classes. The black elite flocked to the annual high school drill team competition and the Howard-Lincoln football game. The drill team competition, a precursor to modern-day step shows that featured Dunbar and Armstrong students dressed in uniforms, toting rifles, and performing syncopated military maneuvers, was so important that students were let out of school to attend.[69] The Howard–Lincoln University football game, a Thanksgiving affair between two of the nation's top historically black colleges, attracted as many as twenty thousand fans, with some of them elegantly dressed in "their raccoons, chinchillas, and sable skins."[70]

The black working class preferred the baptisms of Elder Solomon Lightfoot Michaux. A fish peddler from Norfolk, Virginia, Elder Michaux opened his Church of God in 1928 directly across from Griffith Stadium. He united his flock through a weekly radio show and prided himself on his theatrical stadium appearances. In 1938, he made Clark Griffith an honorary deacon. That same year, Michaux baptized new followers at Griffith Stadium in a large canvas tank with water allegedly imported from the River Jordan.[71] Six years later, with help from a 156-person "Happy Am I" choir, Michaux baptized 135 people before 25,000 spectators.[72] A writer for *Tomorrow* magazine reported: "Perhaps the supreme bit of showmanship occurs when

Michaux urged several former invalids whom he has apparently cured to make a spirited dash around the bases in a 'home run for Jesus.'"[73]

Black Washingtonians witnessed many historic events at Griffith Stadium. They saw slinging Sammy Baugh quarterback the Redskins beginning in 1937, Joe Louis retain his heavyweight title in 1941 despite getting knocked through the ropes by Buddy Baer, an unforgettable riot during a 1942 battle of the bands between Louis Armstrong and Charlie Barnett, professional wrestling matches, the circus, and, most frequently of all, Washington Senators games.

Blacks considered Griffith Stadium their ballpark and the Senators their team. In 1920, Washington had the third-largest black population (behind New York and Philadelphia) and the most passionate black fans.[74] "For years we have been trying to fathom this mania Negroes have for white professional baseball," the *Washington Tribune*'s H. Scott wrote in 1924. "We believe it is spurred by the desire to see the best in the sport."[75]

Senators fans included some of the city's most prominent black residents. Dr. William McNeill, the chief of obstetrics at Howard University, set his office hours around Senators games.[76] Before the Great Migration began to send Southern blacks streaming into Washington during the mid-1930s, the black upper class dominated the city's segregated social scene. Its members possessed the time and money to spend on recreational activities, and elite participation provided certain activities with an aura of respectability.

Working class blacks also embraced the Senators. One of the right-field pavilion's most conspicuous fans was a leather-lunged bench jockey named "Greasy." Greasy walked up and down the aisles insulting opposing players and ringing a cowbell.[77] "Greaseball, too bad he's not around today with a mike," Calvin Griffith recalled. "He would have all the comics. Funny. God, he was funny. All baseball, too. It was all about baseball."[78]

Despite their loyalty, the Senators' black fans endured other racial slights in addition to segregated seating. One of the Senators' most loyal rooters was Sam Lacy's father, Samuel Erskine Lacy. Before the 1924 World Series, the Senators and the Giants marched in a parade

12

down U Street and Florida Avenue toward the ballpark. The elder Lacy stood at the curb, waving a Senators pennant and wearing a white ribbon saying, "I Saw Walter Pitch His First Game—1907," which he had received in 1918 from the Senators' ace pitcher, Walter Johnson. As the Senators rode by, pitcher and future on-field comedian Nick Altrock gave the old man a nasty look and spit in his face.[79] "One thing I never quite figured out about my father was why he refused to go see the all-white Redskins play but was a regular in the Jim Crow pavilion to take in games of the all-white Senators," Lacy wrote in his autobiography.[80]

The Senators discriminated against their black fans in numerous ways. After a nearly violent incident in his ballpark in the fall of 1920 during an exhibition game between a black professional team and its white counterpart, Griffith instituted a twenty-plus-year ban on interracial baseball games. In 1925, the team rejected a disproportionate number of written requests for World Series tickets from addresses in black neighborhoods.[81] That same year, the local NAACP chapter criticized Griffith for failing to include black children in a ballpark promotion.[82]

Black Washingtonians were so enamored with the Senators that they not only overlooked these slights but also snubbed black professional baseball. Black baseball thrived in other major league cities such as New York, Philadelphia, and Chicago, but not in Washington. In 1921, Washington was home to two independent black professional baseball teams, the Black Sox and the Braves, which quickly closed up shop because of lack of support. In 1923 and 1924, the Washington Potomacs were the first black professional team to rent Griffith Stadium on a regular basis. The Potomacs, led by player-manager Ben Taylor, found it impossible to turn a profit there. In 1923, Griffith charged Taylor 25 percent of gross profits to rent the ballpark, reaped all the profits from the concession stands, forced Taylor to hire Griffith's stadium ushers, and refused to allow him to play against white semipro teams.[83] "Colored baseball fans in Washington are more interested in the opening of Clark Griffith's Nationals on April 15 than Ben Taylor's Potomacs on April 26th," the *Washington Tribune* reported in 1924.[84] The Potomacs finished last in

13

the Eastern Colored League in 1924, the year the Senators won their only World Series. The following year, the Potomacs relocated to Wilmington, Delaware, rather than return to Griffith Stadium to watch the Senators repeat as American League champions. In 1932, the Washington Pilots of the East-West League met a similar fate.[85] Lacy blamed the lack of support on the instability of the teams themselves. "The Washington Potomacs and the Washington Pilots and these other teams were fly-by-night teams," Lacy recalled. "They'd come in, maybe, and you never knew when they were going to play another game. They'd play another game maybe a month later."[86]

Yet even Lacy could not deny that the Elite (pronounced E-Light) Giants brought a better, more stable brand of baseball to Washington in 1936. The Elites moved to Washington from Nashville to be closer to the other East Coast teams. They won the first half of the 1936 Negro National League title, finished tied for last in the second half, then canceled the playoffs.[87] Despite their first-half success, the Elites fared no better at the box office than the Potomacs or the Pilots had. In 1937, the Elites began splitting their home games between Baltimore and Washington. After drawing twice as many fans in Baltimore, where their only competition was the Triple-A Baltimore Orioles, the Elites moved all their home games there. "Last year we lost money with the club operating from Washington," Elites owner Tom Wilson said. "I sincerely feel Baltimore [is] far superior to Washington as a baseball town."[88] Dick Powell, the Elites' public relations director who had lured the team from Washington, saw the problem as being less with the city than it was with the Senators: "Washington, that is the black population, was set on the Senators."[89]

Negro League historian Donn Rogosin has argued that Washington "felt keenly the stigma of being a teamless city."[90] On the contrary, black Washingtonians did not seem to care. "Black baseball was a nonentity," recalled black photographer Robert McNeill.[91] After the Elites moved to Baltimore, two more black teams owned and managed by Ben Taylor tried to make Griffith Stadium their home. In 1938, the Washington Black Senators joined the Negro National League but folded after half a season. The following year, the semi-pro Washington Royal Giants played at Griffith Stadium in hope of joining the Negro National League, but they relinquished their final two home dates to the Newark Eagles and the Baltimore Elite Giants.[92]

Underlying the failure of numerous black baseball teams in Washington was the belief among the Senators' black fans that "white baseball is superior to that of our group."[93] Black Washingtonians flocked to Senators games under the assumption that this was the best baseball the city had to offer. They delighted in Babe Ruth's regular visits and the Senators' two-straight World Series appearances and overlooked the exclusion of black players. Before the 1924 season, the *Washington Tribune* commented on the black community's lack of interest in its own teams: "Why, then, should we continue to support, foster, and fill the coffers of a national enterprise that has no place or future for men of color, although they have ability to make the grade? No white man has yet done anything with a baseball and bat that a Negro can not do."[94] Yet black stars such as John Henry Lloyd and Oscar Charleston did not come to Washington often enough to prove that latter assertion to be true. It would take the arrival of the Homestead Grays in 1940 to demythologize for black Washingtonians the superiority of the Senators and the inferiority of black baseball.

The shock of seeing Babe Ruth knocked unconscious, the vastness of Griffith Stadium's playing field, and the sights and sounds on Seventh and U Streets must have dazzled the sixteen-year-old railroad worker named Buck Leonard. The day that Ruth crashed into the right-field pavilion, Leonard saw his first major league baseball game. He remembered Senators Hall of Famer Walter Johnson pitching against Yankees ace Herb Pennock. He remembered Ruth hitting a double. And he even remembered seeing the player he later adopted as his idol, Yankees first baseman Lou Gehrig.[95] Human memory is an imperfect archive. Gehrig played only ten games in 1924, none of them in Washington.[96]

On that July Fourth weekend in 1924, Leonard had taken the train to Washington from his hometown of Rocky Mount, North Carolina, to see the Senators-Yankees doubleheader. He didn't care about sitting in the right-field pavilion. He didn't care about the lack of black players on the field. Years later, the future star first baseman for the Homestead Grays described his first afternoon in a major league ballpark as "the thrill of my life until that time."[97]

Leonard recaptured his lost childhood that weekend at Griffith Stadium. Five years earlier, his father, John, had died of influenza and pneumonia at age thirty-six. John Leonard's death had thrust his eleven-year-old son into the role of "Mr. Man."[98]

Walter Fenner "Buck" Leonard was born on September 8, 1907, the great-grandson of slaves who had toiled in the cotton and tobacco fields of Franklin County in eastern North Carolina.[99] A stocky, broad-shouldered young man, Leonard was not averse to hard work. He had quit school after the eighth grade to help support his mother and five siblings. He sewed stockings at a hosiery mill and shined shoes at the railroad station before finding steady employment with the Atlantic Coast Line Railroad.[100]

In 1885, the Atlantic Coast Line Railroad—owners of track from New York to Florida—had turned Rocky Mount into a thriving industrial town by building a repair shop there.[101] Although the trains eventually took many of Rocky Mount's most ambitious black residents north during the Great Migration, the trains initially provided others, like Leonard's father, with employment.

John Leonard worked as a railroad fireman shoveling coal into the steam engines of freight trains as they traveled from Rocky Mount to Washington, North Carolina.[102] It was hard, physical labor, but it bought the Leonard family a four-room wooden house. They lived near other families of black railroad workers in a west Rocky Mount neighborhood known as Little Raleigh.[103]

After his father's death, Buck Leonard started in the rail yard picking up trash for less than two dollars a day. Soon, he landed a job as an office messenger because he could read and write. After two years, he persuaded the foreman to allow him to work in the repair shop as a mechanic's helper. For the next seven years, he cleaned brake cylinders and installed them on boxcars for about four dollars a day. He worked as a mechanic but received a helper's salary because blacks could not belong to the shop union.[104]

As his family's primary breadwinner, Leonard asserted his authority at home. He ordered his younger sister, Lena, home from the playground. He bossed around his younger brothers, Herman and Charlie. He bought the family's first radio, an Atwater-Kent, the kind that sat on the family mantel.[105] He raised hogs to make extra money.[106] In his spare time, he liked to do crossword puzzles and to take apart household appliances.[107] An introspective young man who rarely got into trouble, Leonard had a dark brown complexion, a round face, and a brilliant smile.

One of Leonard's younger brothers who had been learning how to talk kept trying to call him "Buddy," but it came out as "Bucky" instead.[108] Everyone in Rocky Mount began referring to Walter Leonard as Buck or Bucky. One person refused to call Buck by his nickname—his mother, Emma. A short, educated woman with Native-American features, Emma Leonard always called her son "My Walter." He, in turn, called her "Miss Emma." The other children simply referred to them as Buck and Mama. They acted like husband and wife. She helped support the family by taking in white people's laundry.[109] He worked for the railroad and presided as head of the household. "He made the big decisions, and my mother went along with it," Leonard's sister, Lena Cox, recalled. "So what could we do?"[110]

Leonard relinquished his father-figure role on the baseball diamond. Although not very tall, he was strong, coordinated, and a good hitter. He had joined the Lincoln Junior High School baseball team while he was still in grade school.[111] At that time, there was no black public high school in Rocky Mount. Lincoln Junior High was Leonard's first and last scholastic baseball experience.

After graduating from the eighth grade in 1921, Leonard joined the local black sandlot team known as the Rocky Mount Elks. Sandlot teams organized by amateur players served as the unofficial breeding ground for black professional baseball.[112] For most players, sandlot baseball was the place where working men blew off steam. On the Elks, Leonard played center field while holding down his job at the repair shop. After work, he would ride his bike from the rail shop to the ballfield, change into his baseball uniform at a house across the street, and then play in that afternoon's game.[113]

Leonard emerged as the king of the Rocky Mount sandlots. A left-handed batter, he smashed fastballs into the trees behind the right-field wall at Rocky Mount's Mary Talbott Park. After the team's manager died in 1925, Leonard, seventeen, assumed the dual role as the Elks' captain and field manager. He switched from center field to first base to be in a better position to argue with the umpires.[114]

Buck's youngest brother, Charlie, also joined the Rocky Mount team. In contrast to his other brother, Herman, the town pool shark and drunk, Charles Delmonte Leonard was Buck's pride and joy. Charlie never missed a day of school at the newly opened Booker T. Washington High School.[115] He received straight A's in his first year at nearby Brick Junior College, where he was president of the freshman class and a member of the football, basketball, and baseball teams. The *Brick Bugle* described Charlie as a "pitcher of great ability."[116]

Charlie, however, chafed under his oldest brother's leadership. Rather than play for Buck, Charlie agreed to pitch, manage, and play shortstop for the Wilson Braves, a rival team in the town of Wilson fifteen miles away. Buck rejected an offer to join his younger brother on the Braves.[117] During the fierce rivalry that developed between the two brothers, Buck continued to look after Charlie. In a memorable Rocky Mount–Wilson encounter, Charlie broke his ankle sliding into second base. Buck carried his brother into the stands. Although a doctor determined that the ankle was broken, Charlie steadfastly refused to go to the hospital until after the game. And Buck wouldn't let anybody else touch him.[118]

In 1931, Buck took his management of the Elks more seriously after a record-high twenty-three men came out for spring practice. That April, he placed a notice in the *Norfolk Journal and Guide*, one of the nation's largest black newspapers, inviting sandlot and semipro teams from Virginia and the Carolinas to contact him about playing the Elks. "Bucky Leonard, captain, is holding down his customary position at the initial sack," the notice said.[119]

Leonard's aspirations, however, did not extend beyond managing and playing for the Elks. He had a decent job at the rail shop, a steady girlfriend, and a big reputation on the ballfield. Weekend trips to Washington, D.C., Philadelphia, and New York City to see an occasional major league game satiated any desire to leave town permanently. The twenty-four-year-old sandlot king planned to live in Rocky Mount forever.[120]

Sam Lacy saw baseball as his escape from class-divided black Washington, from the intellectual world of make-believe, and from his mounting gambling debts. He yearned to leave Washington and to make his mark in the world as Duke Ellington did with his music and Langston Hughes did with his poetry.

Lacy's road to professional success was on the sandlots. In 1923, during the summer after his junior year at Armstrong, he pitched for one of the worst teams in Washington's six-team black sandlot league, the Buffalo A.C. Against stronger teams, such as the Piedmonts and the Teddy Bears, he mostly struggled on the mound.[121]

Near the end of the 1923 campaign, however, Lacy led the lowly Buffaloes to an 11–10 victory over the mighty LeDroit Tigers.[122] Named after the upscale LeDroit Park neighborhood just south and east of Griffith Stadium's right-field wall, the Tigers were the black champions of the D.C. sandlots. In 1922, they nearly beat the all-black professional Lincoln Giants at Griffith Stadium. The Tigers loaded the bases in the ninth inning, forcing the Giants to bring in their six-foot five-inch Hall of Fame pitcher, Smokey Joe Williams, to salvage a 2–1 victory.[123] The Tigers served as Washington's unofficial farm team for the black professional ranks.[124]

The *Washington Tribune*, the local black weekly, proclaimed Lacy's 11–10 victory over the Tigers the "Season's Biggest Upset." Lacy "pitched effective ball," and his triple was "the longest clout of the day."[125] A year-end review of the sandlot season described him as "another star in the making."[126]

This effusive praise may have come from Lacy's own pen. During his sophomore year of high school, he had begun covering sports for

19

the *Tribune*.[127] As far as his career aspirations were concerned, however, journalism was an afterthought.[128] Baseball was Lacy's ticket—especially because the LeDroit Tigers invited him to pitch for them the next season.

In 1924, Lacy graduated from Armstrong High to the LeDroit Tigers. By late June, he had pitched a six-inning no-hitter and led all league pitchers with a 4–0 record. Although his fastball could barely break a pane of glass, he possessed a wicked curve that bedeviled the sandlot hitters. He didn't lose his first game for the Tigers until late July. A career in the black professional ranks was seemingly within his grasp.[129]

Lacy's professional baseball career purportedly peaked with a stint with the Atlantic City Bacharach Giants. The Bacharachs were one of black baseball's best professional teams during the mid-1920s.[130] Lacy was an above-average sandlot pitcher. Yet in numerous interviews and in his autobiography, he claimed to have spent a season and a half with the Bacharachs as a second baseman. None of the Negro League encyclopedias, team histories, or rosters has included Lacy as a member of the Bacharachs. Nor is Lacy mentioned in any contemporary newspaper accounts, box scores, or modern oral histories with black players from the 1920s and the 1930s.

During interviews, Lacy gave hazy accounts of his experiences with the Bacharachs. He claimed to have played "professionally or semi-professionally" with the Bacharachs when he was seventeen.[131] He named the Hall of Fame shortstop–second baseman John Henry "Pop" Lloyd as one of his teammates. He said he quit because, "I was younger than everybody else, and when they finished, they'd go to these boarding houses, and smoke, drink, carouse, have women, and all that. . . . That's when I went back to school and got my degree in journalism."[132] At age seventeen, Lacy had just arrived on the Washington, D.C., sandlot scene. In June 1923, the *Washington Tribune* published an article about seventeen former D.C. sandlotters playing in the black professional ranks; Lacy wasn't mentioned.[133] Nor is Lacy pictured in the Bacharachs' 1923 team photo published in the *Atlantic City Daily Press*.[134] Finally, Lacy never got a journalism degree from

Howard or anywhere else, though he graduated from Armstrong High in 1924.[135]

Lacy's autobiography, which he wrote with Moses J. Newson when he was more than ninety years old, only exacerbates the confusion. Lacy claimed to have played for the Bacharachs before graduating from Armstrong in 1922 (he graduated in 1924) and described them as a "semipro team" (it was a top-flight professional team).[136] Two pages later, he claimed to have played for the Bacharachs *after* finishing high school, attributing his departure to "boozing and bawdy-house carousing" and homesickness.[137] Finally, he claimed to have played *against* Negro League stars such as Pop Lloyd and Dick Lundy.[138] But if Lacy were on the Bacharachs in 1924 or 1925, he would have played with these players, not against them.

If Lacy ever played for the Bacharachs, he probably would have joined them in 1925. He had just come off his best season with the LeDroit Tigers. Tigers business manager Andrew Allen, according to Lacy, scouted for the Bacharachs.[139] Lacy was absent from the Tigers' box scores in the *Washington Tribune* during the second half of the 1925 season. Finally, Lloyd, whom Lacy recalled as a teammate, managed the Bacharachs in 1925 and played second base.[140] Lacy could have spent the 1925 season as Lloyd's seldom-used backup.

Did Lacy embellish his sandlot pitching career with a Walter Mitty fantasy about having played for the Bacharachs? Several aspects of his story are troubling. First, he spent his entire career on the Washington sandlots as a pitcher, occasionally catching and playing outfield. Yet with the Bacharachs, he claimed to have spent a season and a half as a second baseman. Second, the *Washington Tribune* religiously tracked Lacy's athletic career, but the *Tribune* never mentioned his having played with the Bacharachs. Third, Lacy's career as a sportswriter spanned more than seventy-five years and roughly three thousand columns, and yet he wrote nary a word about his sojourn in black professional baseball.[141] Finally, the *Atlantic City Daily Press* (along with its Sunday counterpart) was one of the few white daily newspapers that covered black baseball and in particular the Bacharachs, publishing box scores of every home game and many away games and reporting on roster changes. Yet he never showed up in the *Daily Press* stories about the Bacharachs in 1924, 1925, or 1926.[142]

Lacy's recollections should be given some leeway. He was between eighty and ninety-five years old when he gave the interviews and wrote his autobiography. The lack of written documentation also is understandable because of black baseball's sketchy statistics, schedules, and record keeping. Historians are only beginning to augment important oral histories from the 1970s and 1980s by mining black newspapers and archival sources. Seldom-used players, such as Lacy, moreover, would have been completely excluded from contemporary box scores and newspaper accounts. Finally, his failure to discuss the Bacharachs in any of his columns may have been an effort to block out a painful memory.

Even if he were on the team, Lacy would not have left the Bacharachs because of the drinking, womanizing, and carousing; he would have left because as a professional baseball player he couldn't cut it. Lacy's two documented pitching performances in exhibitions against top-flight black baseball teams were disastrous. The Baltimore Black Sox of the Eastern Colored League hammered Lacy for seven runs in 1926 (with the LeDroit Tigers) and in relief in 1927 (with the Washington Black Sox).[143] A pitcher with a pretty fair curve and no fastball would not last against black professional competition. The most significant aspect of this mysterious chapter of his life is not whether Lacy actually played for the Bacharachs, rather it is his almost certain failure. Lacy learned firsthand about the level of talent required to play black professional baseball.

Lacy, however, would not give up on his baseball dreams. In 1926, he played for the LeDroit Tigers for a few months before spending the remainder of the summer on a team of baseball-playing hotel waiters in Water Hill, Rhode Island.[144] Although he returned in time to help the Tigers clinch the city sandlot title, that fall (and probably earlier that spring) he was enrolled at Howard University.[145]

In October 1926, Lacy left Howard for his first full-time newspaper job. Above a picture of Lacy in a tank top and sporting a flattop haircut, the *Washington Tribune* announced the latest addition to its sports staff: "Lacey [sic] to Write Local Sports for the Tribune." Below the headline, the *Tribune* explained:

Samuel H. Lacey [sic], Armstrong Technical High School graduate will write local sports for The Tribune. Mr. Lacey [sic] has had wide experience in athletics, having been a member of the Armstrong Tech football, basketball, and baseball teams. He is also a pitcher on the LeDroit Tigers. His articles will especially cover high school and amateur sports, including football, basketball, track, and baseball.[146]

Two months later, the twenty-one-year-old Lacy was named the paper's sports editor.[147] He also began writing two regular sports columns: "Sam Scripts" and "The Reflector." He made fifteen dollars a week.[148] The following year, Lacy married a waitress two years his junior named Alberta Robertson.[149]

Not even marriage and a steady job could kill Lacy's baseball obsession. During the summer of 1927, Lacy led a massive defection from the LeDroit Tigers to the Washington Black Sox and suffered through what his own newspaper described as the "the poorest season of his career."[150] The following summer, he pitched sparingly and served as the president of the local sandlot league.

During the summer of 1929, the twenty-three-year-old Lacy abdicated his position as the *Tribune's* sports editor to play baseball in Connecticut.[151] He may have left Washington to escape the mounting gambling debts that troubled him while he was in his early twenties. More likely, he embarked on a last-ditch effort to make it as a professional baseball player.[152]

Lacy soon realized that "the dream of a baseball career [was] no longer a realistic option."[153] In 1930, he returned to reporting for the *Tribune*.[154] Two years later, he worked as a local mail carrier for the U.S. Post Office, played outfield on a team of black postal workers, and pitched for and managed several local sandlot clubs.[155] In July 1933, he regained his position as the *Tribune* sports editor. His "Looking 'Em Over with the Tribune" column regularly appeared in the sports section.[156] During the next several years, his dreams began to change.

On July 1, 1932, Buck Leonard got laid off by the railroad. During the Great Depression, blacks were generally the "last hired, first fired."[157] Initially, the railroad demoted Leonard from a mechanic to a helper, replacing him with a white worker. Eventually, it let him go after nine years and four months of service.[158] He was twenty-four. Leonard spent the rest of 1932 working part-time for the local undertaker and playing on Rocky Mount's black sandlot team, which had changed its name from the Elks to the Black Swans.[159]

At the beginning of the 1933 baseball season, opportunity knocked on Leonard's door. Abram Daughtry arrived at the Leonard family home and asked if Leonard wanted to play for Daughtry's Portsmouth, Virginia–based semipro team for fifteen dollars a week plus room and board. Although he preferred to stay in Rocky Mount, Leonard needed to support his family. He reluctantly left for Portsmouth in Daughtry's car.[160]

Leonard played in Portsmouth for only about two and a half months. The team, previously known as the Portsmouth Firefighters, was called Daughtry's Black Revels.[161] Daughtry had plucked several players off the North Carolina sandlots and put them on salary.[162] Although the Black Revels were one of the better semipro teams in Portsmouth, they often lost to top-flight sandlot teams. In 1933, for example, the LeDroit Tigers traveled to Portsmouth and pummeled the Black Revels.[163] As the LeDroit Tigers proved, the distinction between a sandlot team like the Tigers and a semipro team like the Black Revels was often meaningless.

In Leonard's first two games with the Black Revels, the *Norfolk Journal and Guide* referred to him as "Lennox."[164] Leonard, however, befriended the sports editor, E. B. Rea, by buying him a box of his favorite Tampa Nugget cigars. The paper never got Leonard's name wrong again.[165] People quickly took notice of his ability as a hitter. It took a month before an opposing pitcher struck him out—and that was on a called third strike.[166]

24

Despite his success in Portsmouth, Leonard missed his girlfriend and longed for Rocky Mount. So the Black Revels found Leonard a new girlfriend in Portsmouth and returned to Rocky Mount to play his old team, the Black Swans.[167] Leonard's sister, Lena Cox, recalled the Black Revels arriving at Rocky Mount's Union Station with a full band. All the children headed down to the train station and waited for the band to play its trademark song, "Blue Heaven." "They'd play 'Blue Heaven' from the time they got off that train 'til the time they got to the park," Cox recalled. "And we'd follow 'em."[168]

As much as Lena liked Portsmouth's band, she still rooted for Rocky Mount out of loyalty to her younger brother, Charlie. In Buck's absence, Charlie had become the Black Swans' manager, pitcher, and shortstop. Charlie ruined his older brother's homecoming as the Black Swans cruised to an 8–0 victory.[169] The following week at Portsmouth's Washington Street Park, Buck exacted revenge with his younger brother on the mound. Buck knocked four hits off Charlie in four at-bats, scoring three runs, driving in two, and stealing four bases to lead the Black Revels to a 9–0 victory.[170] In the rubber match in Rocky Mount, Buck's team won again, 6–5. In the first inning, Buck smacked a double off Charlie that the center fielder misplayed, resulting in an inside-the-park home run.[171]

Charlie was not discouraged about losing to Buck. By the summer of 1933, Charlie had graduated from Brick Junior College and received scholarships of $100 and $73 to Alabama's Talladega College. The local news clipping described him as the former manager of the Wilson Braves and an honors graduate of Brick Junior College who is "known throughout the state as well as surrounding states for his athletic ability."[172]

In late June 1933, Charlie joined a traveling black professional team known as the Baltimore Stars.[173] Ben Taylor, the former Washington Potomacs manager and the finest black first baseman of his era, was the Stars' owner, manager, and best player.[174] The Stars had split two games with the Black Swans in Rocky Mount and were making their way to Portsmouth.

Taylor hoped to sign Buck as his heir apparent at first base. Buck had recently switched teams, leaving Daughtry's Black Revels for

their local rivals, the Berkley Black Sox.[175] Playing first base and batting cleanup for the Black Sox, he managed one of his team's three
hits off the Stars. The following day, he joined his younger brother's
new team.[176] "Ben Liked Them So He Took Two," the *Journal and
Guide* declared above tobacco-card sized photographs of Charlie
and Buck and a caption that said:

> Charley [sic] Leonard, top left, and Walter "Buck" Leonard, two
> brothers hailing from Rocky Mount, N.C., who impressed Ben Tay-
> lor, bottom, left, pilot of the Baltimore Stars, to the extent that Ben
> took them back to Baltimore this week, as members of his team.
> Charley [sic] formerly hurled for the Black Swans of Rocky Mount,
> while "Buck," one of the most colorful first sackers ever to perform
> in this section, started the season with Daughtry's Black Revels,
> later transferring to the Berkley Black Sox.[177]

Taylor promised Buck more than the fifteen dollars a week plus
the room and board he currently earned. The Stars were an independent traveling team—they didn't have a home ballpark or belong
to an established league, and the players shared the profits rather than
collect monthly salaries. Several Portsmouth players warned Buck
that traveling teams did not make money and often stranded their
players in distant places. For Buck, it wasn't about the money or playing for Ben Taylor; it was about looking after Charlie.[178]

The dire predictions of the Portsmouth players came true. In the
Carolinas, Charlie and Buck wanted for food. In Baltimore, they
lived with a few other players at Taylor's house. After Taylor took out
money for expenses, such as room and board, each player received
between three and six dollars a week. Buck tried to remedy his ten-
uous financial situation by jumping to the Baltimore Black Sox, a
more established black professional team that paid its players a regular salary. Taylor, however, instructed his wife to hide Buck's
clothes.[179]

On the field, Taylor taught Leonard the fundamentals of playing
first base. Although nicknamed "Old Reliable" in his prime because
of his fielding, the forty-five-year-old Taylor was too old to play every

day. He made Leonard, at that time the Stars' regular right fielder, his understudy.[180] Taylor turned Leonard from a converted outfielder into a solid first baseman—not flashy, but sure-footed and sure-handed.[181]

Leonard already had earned a fearsome reputation at the plate. In the first game of an August doubleheader, the Winston-Salem (North Carolina) Black Twins intentionally walked him four straight times. In the second game, he "hit a drive to the fence with such force that the ball bounced fifteen yards, scoring two runs that tied the score."[182]

Taylor took the Stars to New York City in the hopes of improving their financial fortunes. But Taylor's refusal to pay notorious New York booking agent Nat Strong his mandatory 10 percent fee left the Stars bereft of competition. When the Stars couldn't pay their bill at the Dumas Hotel, the owner auctioned off the team's cars on the street. Taylor told Buck, Charlie, and the rest of the players that the team was finished; the players were on their own.[183]

At that point, Buck's primary goal was getting Charlie back to college. Despite playing sparingly with the Stars, Charlie wanted to stay in New York with Buck and keep playing baseball. Buck, however, didn't think Charlie had what it took to be a professional ballplayer. "When he was playing with us, I didn't think he was physically strong enough to play that caliber of ball," Buck recalled. "And I didn't want him to play because I wanted to him to finish his education. I used to talk to Mama about that, and tell her to not let him play."[184]

On the streets of New York City, Buck ran into Randolph Armstrong, a former coach at Rocky Mount's Booker T. Washington High School. Armstrong agreed to give Charlie a ride back to Rocky Mount. From there, Charlie headed back to Talladega College.[185]

At the end of the 1933 season, Leonard hooked up with the Brooklyn Royal Giants. He wandered over to a Harlem bar where players and coaches usually hung out and asked Royal Giants manager and former pitcher "Cannonball" Dick Redding for a job. Redding agreed despite having never seen Leonard play.[186] The Royal Giants, once one of black baseball's stronger teams, had devolved into an underfinanced, unaffiliated outfit stocked with flashy-fielding veterans, such as first baseman Robert "Highpockets" Hudspeth and third

27

baseman Elias "Country" Brown, and two prospects in Leonard and future Philadelphia Stars center fielder Gene Benson.[187] Leonard played out the year in right field.[188]

After the season, Leonard stayed in New York City because he had arranged to play on an All-Star team in Puerto Rico. At the last minute, however, the organizer of the trip informed Leonard that the roster had been cut from fifteen to thirteen players. Jobless, penniless, and transportation-less, Leonard duped an old girlfriend into giving him enough money to get home to Rocky Mount.[189]

In April 1934, Leonard returned to New York City to play again for the Brooklyn Royal Giants. One night, Smokey Joe Williams, the pitcher who had shut down the LeDroit Tigers in 1922, told the players to send Leonard over to the Harlem Grill, a Lenox Avenue bar near 135th Street.[190] Williams, who had recently retired and was tending bar, offered Leonard some sage advice: "Look, Buck, don't you want to get with a good team?"

"What are you talking about?" Leonard replied.

Williams said: "The Homestead Grays."

Williams, who had capped off his career with a seven-year run as the Grays' ace pitcher, had seen Leonard play several times and believed that the first baseman could make his former team. Williams called Grays owner Cum Posey, who instructed Williams to give Leonard a bus ticket and five dollars spending money. Along with an old catcher named Tex Burnett, Leonard hopped on an overnight bus to West Virginia to try out for the Grays.[191]

Buck Leonard (seated third from right) poses with his family in 1918 in front of their home in the Little Raleigh section of Rocky Mount. His brother, Charlie, is standing in front of his father. (WILLIE B. COX PRATHER)

Sam Lacy (seated far right) with the 1924 Armstrong High School football team at Griffith Stadium. Griffith regularly allowed the public schools, black and white, to use his stadium for their athletic events. (CHARLES SUMNER MUSEUM AND ARCHIVES)

Sam Lacy (second row, second from left) and the Armstrong High School basketball team lost in the finals of the black high school championship in Chicago. (Charles Sumner Museum and Archives)

Grays manager and outfielder Vic Harris is pictured in the Griffith Stadium dugout with several of his players behind him. A mean, fiery player who liked to slide hard into opposing infielders, Harris initially played for the Grays in 1925. (ROBERT H. McNEILL)

TWO

THE HOMESTEAD GRAYS

The Homestead Grays are the greatest baseball dynasty that most people have never heard of. Most people have never heard of them because from 1884 to 1947 major league baseball excluded black players. Instead, many would-be major league stars played in the relative obscurity of the black professional ranks known as the Negro Leagues. Yet until 1920, there was no official black league at all.

Black professional teams emerged during the 1880s, more than a dozen years after the first black sandlot teams and during the era when the last black players competed in white professional leagues. During the 1880s, major league baseball consisted of the National League and the American Association. As a catcher with the Toledo club in the American Association in 1884, Moses Fleetwood Walker was the last American-born black player to compete on the major league level until Jackie Robinson officially broke the color barrier in 1947.[1] In 1887, more than a dozen blacks competed on white minor league teams.[2] Three years later, there were none. With the end of Reconstruction and the rise in discrimination and repression against blacks, historian Rayford W. Logan labeled this period of African-American history from 1877 to 1901 "the Nadir."[3]

Not surprisingly, the onset of segregation during the Nadir coincided with the formation of all-black professional teams. In 1885, the Cuban Giants formed from three black sandlot teams: the Keystone

Athletics and the Orions, both of Philadelphia, and the Manhattans of Washington, D.C. The Argyle Hotel in Long Island, New York, hired this new team of American-born blacks, which probably called itself the Cuban Giants to mitigate racial prejudice, to entertain the hotel's guests.[4] Between 1900 and 1920, other famous black professional teams emerged including the Lincoln Giants of New York, the Atlantic City Bacharach Giants, the Indianapolis ABCs, the Philadelphia-based Hilldale Club, and the Chicago American Giants.[5]

In 1920, Rube Foster, the owner and star pitcher of the American Giants, founded what is today referred to as the Negro Leagues. He organized eight Midwestern teams, including the ABCs, American Giants, and Kansas City Monarchs, into the Negro National League (NNL). The NNL sought to circumvent white booking agents (principally New York's Nat Strong), to create a black professional organization that rivaled the white major leagues, and to keep its players from jumping to other NNL teams or their Eastern rivals. Black players often jumped to other teams because of the absence of written contracts. In 1923, Eastern-based teams, including the Bacharach Giants, the Baltimore Black Sox, the Brooklyn Royal Giants, the Lincoln Giants, and the Hilldale Club, formed the Eastern Colored League (ECL).[6]

They were not leagues in the modern sense. Black teams played unbalanced league schedules of anywhere from fifty to eighty games a season, depending on each team's exhibition schedule. They traveled the country playing exhibition games, which was known as barnstorming, competing in small towns against all-white (and sometimes black) semipro teams. These exhibition games were more lucrative than league games because black teams could play two games a day, could command a larger portion of the gate, and did not have to pay booking agents a large stadium rental fee. Thus, even at the height of the popularity of the Negro Leagues, teams such as the Grays played 50 to 80 league games but 100 to 120 exhibition games a season against white and black semipro teams.[7]

The Grays initially preferred to play only exhibition games and did not join either league, both of which failed during the Depression.

In 1933, the Negro National League re-formed around Eastern teams owned mostly by black men who operated illegal lotteries known as the numbers. The Grays eventually joined the new NNL. In 1937, Midwestern and Southern teams formed the Negro American League.

Negro League teams rarely kept accurate statistics, played sporadic league schedules, and relied almost exclusively on black newspapers for publicity. When the mainstream press deigned to cover black teams, it usually depicted them as minstrel performers. Negro League teams toured the country playing more than two hundred games a season, their athletic gifts underappreciated and their financial survival depending on barnstorming dates against white semipro teams and on the availability of major league ballparks, such as Griffith Stadium.

Of these teams, the Grays were the greatest dynasty in the history of the Negro Leagues. There were better individual clubs, such as the Pittsburgh Crawfords of 1934, 1935, and 1936. There were teams that produced more future major leaguers, such as the Kansas City Monarchs. But in terms of putting the strongest teams on the field year after year, the Grays had no equal. Of the eighteen people elected to the Baseball Hall of Fame based on their Negro League careers, nine played for the Grays at some point. Opposing teams respected, feared, and admired the Grays. They dominated black baseball in the late 1920s and early 1930s and again in the late 1930s and early 1940s. While the New York Yankees were winning championships in the major leagues, the Grays were winning championships in the Negro Leagues. They won eight of nine Negro National League titles from 1937 to 1945 and another in 1948. Their last seven titles came in Washington, where the Grays restored Griffith Stadium to its former glory and put most of the Senators teams of that era to shame.

People who have heard about the Grays and their success at Griffith Stadium usually mention Negro League legends Josh Gibson and Satchel Paige. Tall tales about Gibson and Paige make them seem more like mythological figures than real men trying to make a living in Jim Crow America. Gibson and Paige were integral to the Grays' popularity in Washington, but they represent only part of the story. It's a story that began in Pittsburgh with a wealthy local black basketball star named Cum Posey.

The Grays started in 1910 as a recreational activity for black steelworkers in Homestead, Pennsylvania. Homestead was a steel town across the Monongahela River from Pittsburgh and the home of the Homestead Works of the Carnegie-Illinois Steel Company. Black workers flooded into Homestead after the famous steel strike of 1892.[8] They worked in the mills, and many lived in boardinghouses in a rough, immigrant neighborhood close to the river known as "The Ward."[9] For recreation, black steelworkers formed baseball teams because they were excluded from white steelworker teams. In 1900, some young black steelworkers organized a sandlot team known as the Blue Ribbons and later the Murdock Grays. A decade later, the team changed its name to the Homestead Grays.[10]

In 1911, an outfielder named Cum Posey joined the Grays and changed the team's fortunes forever. Cumberland "Cum" Willis Posey Jr. wasn't a steelworker. He was the son of one of the richest black men in Homestead. His father, Cumberland "Cap" Willis Posey Sr., earned an engineering license, supervised the construction of ships, and ran the largest black-owned business in Pittsburgh, the Diamond Coke and Coal Company.[11] His father also served as the first president and one of the founding incorporators of the *Pittsburgh Courier*, the nation's largest black newspaper.[12] His mother, Anna, was said to be the first black graduate of Ohio State University.[13]

Cum Posey was one of Pittsburgh's most famous basketball players. Although only five feet nine and 140 pounds, the quick, intelligent guard played for and managed the famous semipro Monticello basketball team and its professional counterpart, the Loendi Club. Posey's win-at-all-costs attitude, which he instilled in players on the Grays, initially earned him fame on the basketball court. "No 'all time' floor quintet would be complete without him," sportswriter W. Rollo Wilson wrote in 1934.[14] The light-skinned Posey played basketball at Penn State and studied chemistry and pharmacy at the

University of Pittsburgh. He played college basketball again in 1916 at Holy Ghost (later called Duquesne) under the assumed name "Charles Cumbert."[15] Journalist Merlisa Lawrence wrote of Posey/Cumbert: "His skin was pale, his eyes were hazel, his hair slick and wavy—he passed for white."[16]

Posey brought his athleticism to the Grays' outfield and his experience promoting basketball games to the team's business operations. Five years after joining the Grays, he had taken over as the team captain, field manager, and booking agent. In 1920, he quit his job with the Railway Mail Service to own and manage the Grays full time. He replaced the steelworkers with Pittsburgh's best sandlot players including pitchers Oscar Owens and Charles "Lefty" Williams, second baseman Raymond "Mo" Harris, outfielder Elander "Vic" Harris (Mo's brother), and third baseman Jasper "Jap" Washington. He even put his star players on salary to prevent rival teams from stealing them away. With Posey scheduling games against white semipro teams and managing the team on the field, the Grays dominated the baseball scene in Pennsylvania, Ohio, and West Virginia.[17]

Black professional baseball came into its own just as Posey began to groom the Grays for greatness. In 1920, Andrew "Rube" Foster established the original Negro National League. A large, barrel-chested pitcher, Foster had earned his nickname by defeating white major league ace Rube Waddell in 1904.[18] Seven years later, Foster had started one of the most successful black professional teams, the Chicago American Giants. Unlike other teams that traveled by car or bus, the American Giants traveled by train in private Pullman cars. "If the talents of Christy Mathewson, John McGraw, Ban Johnson, and Judge Kenesaw Mountain Landis were combined in a single body, and that body were enveloped by black skin," Negro Leagues historian Robert Peterson wrote, "the result would have to be Andrew (Rube) Foster."[19]

During the 1920s, Posey rebuffed Foster's entreaties to join the NNL. Rather than be tied down by a league schedule, Posey preferred that his team traverse both sides of the Allegheny Mountains playing white semipro teams. He also enjoyed the luxury of raiding both leagues of their best players. In 1925, Posey lured Hall of Fame pitcher Smokey Joe Williams from the Lincoln Giants. Although thirty-nine years old when he joined the Grays, the six-foot five-inch Williams towered over the competition in stature and talent. The part–Native American pitcher from Texas threw so hard that some opposing hitters called him "Cyclone." In a 1952 *Pittsburgh Courier* poll of black baseball aficionados, Williams edged Paige as the greatest pitcher of all time.[20]

Over the next seven years, Williams helped Posey make history with the Grays. The Grays finished 130–23–5 in 1925 and 106–6–6, including forty-three straight wins, in 1926.[21] The following year, Posey quit playing, continued managing, and installed outfielder Vic Harris as team captain. Harris—a notoriously hard slider and ruthless competitor—embodied Posey's ideal ballplayer.[22] Posey sought out tough guys like Harris who refused to back down from the opposition and who hated to lose, fighters like Posey himself. In 1928, Posey added pitchers Sam Streeter and Webster McDonald, power-hitting shortstop John Beckwith, and jack-of-all-trades Martin Dihigo. A Hall of Famer, the Cuban-born Dihigo pitched and played the other eight positions on the diamond.

The 1930 edition of the Grays is one of Posey's greatest teams. Hall of Famer Oscar Charleston held down first base. Regarded as the best all-around black player of his generation, Charleston once roamed center field like Willie Mays and brought to the plate both speed and power. The rest of the infield included George Scales at second base, Jake Stephens at shortstop, Hall of Famer Judy Johnson at third base, and Josh Gibson, an eighteen-year-old catcher plucked off the Pittsburgh sandlots.

Gibson, even more than Paige, is black baseball's Paul Bunyan. The Negro Leagues' incomplete statistics, the Grays' barnstorming schedule, and Gibson's early demise facilitate the tall tales about his home-run-hitting prowess. Some credit him with more than eight hundred career home runs and seventy-five in a season. These incredible numbers, however, obscure known facts about Gibson the man, the teammate, and the ballplayer—and how his career changed the fortunes of the Grays.

Born in Buena Vista, Georgia, on December 11, 1911, Gibson grew up in the Pleasant Valley section of Pittsburgh's Hill district as the oldest of three children and the son of a Carnegie–Illinois Steel worker. He dropped out of school after the ninth grade to become an apprentice electrician at an air brake company. Standing six feet one and 210 pounds, he looked as if he had been carved from stone. In 1940, Sam Lacy asked Gibson if he had acquired his incredible physique through manual labor. "Naw, man, you can't put that down there," Gibson replied. "I never had but two jobs in my life and they were soft. I got paid for them only because the people liked me."[23]

Gibson's Negro League career allegedly began on a July night in 1930 as a spectator. The story goes that Posey pulled Gibson—already an eighteen-year-old sandlot legend with the semipro Crawford Colored Giants—out of the stands after the Grays' only catcher had busted his finger.[24] More likely, Posey simply signed Gibson midway through the 1930 season and found a hitter for the ages.

In September 1930, Gibson smacked one of the longest home runs ever hit at Yankee Stadium. He hit it off Lincoln Giants pitcher Connie Rector in the ninth game of a ten-game playoff series for the eastern championship of black baseball. In a contemporary account of that game, black sportswriter W. Rollo Wilson reported that "Gibson made the longest home run wallop of the year in Yankee Stadium when he hit into the left field bleachers, a distance of over four hundred thirty feet. . . ."[25] Another contemporary account, in the *New York Age*, stated that "Gibson hit a home run that went into the left bleachers, a distance of 460 feet. It was the longest home run that was hit at the Yankee Stadium, by any player, white or colored, all season."[26]

Over the years, people have dubiously claimed that Gibson hit the ball clear out of Yankee Stadium. In 1934, Wilson wrote that "[e]ven Babe Ruth has hit no home run further" at Yankee Stadium and described Gibson's blast as clearing "the extreme left wing of the grandstand."[27] In 1938, Gibson appeared to set the record straight: "I hit the ball on a line into the bullpen in deep left field."[28] Posey added that Detroit Tigers first baseman Hank Greenberg was the only other player who had hit a ball there—Greenberg accomplished the feat in 1938 while Gibson was in the Dominican Republic.[29] Years later, however, eyewitnesses from both teams debated whether Gibson's home run cleared the stadium's left-field grandstand or merely hit the back wall of the left-field bullpen 505 feet from home plate.[30] The consensus, especially in light of the two eyewitness accounts, is that Gibson's home run landed more than 450 feet away in Yankee Stadium's old left-field bullpen.

The 1930 Grays were so good that on the day Gibson blasted the ball into the Yankee Stadium bullpen, he batted sixth. Gibson hit behind left fielder Harris, third baseman Johnson, first baseman Charleston, center fielder Chaney White, and second baseman Scales.[31] In fact, Gibson hit sixth that entire series against the Lincoln Giants, in which the Grays captured black baseball's Eastern championship. With Smokey Joe Williams pitching, Gibson catching, Charleston playing first base, and Johnson manning third, the 1930 Grays featured four future Hall of Famers.

In 1931, the Grays' roster got even better. Posey added Hall of Fame pitcher Willie Foster (Rube's half brother), catcher/pitcher Ted "Double Duty" Radcliffe, outfielder Ted Page, and third baseman Jud "Boojum" Wilson. Gibson later said the 1931 Grays were the best team he ever played on, better than the Crawford teams of the mid-1930s.[32] Posey agreed, five years later describing the 1931 Grays as "the strongest club the Grays ever assembled and the strongest club of modern Negro baseball as far back as we can remember."[33] The following year, in 1932, Hall of Fame outfielder James "Cool Papa" Bell, second baseman Newt Allen, pitcher/outfielder Ray Brown, catcher/outfielder Quincy Trouppe, and Hall of Fame shortstop Willie Wells joined the Grays. During the 1930s and 1940s, nearly every great black ballplayer suited up for the Grays at one time or another.

Financially, however, Posey could not afford to pay his abundance of talented players. The Depression destroyed the Grays' profits, as well as the rest of black baseball. From 1912 to 1929, the Grays boasted that they had made a profit every year.[34] But after 1929 many people could no longer afford to attend Negro League games, and profits dried up. After the ECL folded in 1927, its brief successor, the American Negro League, lasted until 1931. The NNL, leaderless after Rube Foster's mental illness in 1926 and death in 1930, also disbanded after the 1931 season.

In 1932, Posey tried to fill Foster's shoes by forming the East-West League. Posey's plans for the new league were too ambitious—he hired the Al Munro Elias Bureau to keep statistics, drew up a 112-game split-season league schedule, and obtained the use of several major league parks. Travel was impossible with teams in both the Midwest and on the East Coast. Posey owned at least two of the franchises, the Grays and the Detroit Wolves, and maybe even a third.[35] The Wolves folded in June, and the East-West League quickly followed suit.[36]

Posey's biggest problem in 1932 came from the Pittsburgh Crawfords. Started in 1928 as a local sandlot team, the Crawfords gained the financial backing of William A. "Gus" Greenlee, the king of Pittsburgh's North Side numbers racket. Greenlee was one of many brilliant black entrepreneurs of that era who made their fortunes through underworld activities. As the operator of the city's illegal lottery, Greenlee attempted to gain legitimacy in the world of sports and entertainment. In addition to owning the Crawfords, Greenlee sponsored a stable of championship-caliber boxers and owned a popular nightclub—the Crawford Grill—in Pittsburgh's Hill district.[37]

Greenlee capitalized on Posey's financial woes and preoccupation with keeping the East-West League afloat by persuading many of the Grays' players to jump ship.[38] Gibson joined a contingent of former Grays on the Crawfords that included Cool Papa Bell, Judy Johnson, Ted Page, and Oscar Charleston. Satchel Paige headlined as the star. With Paige pitching and Gibson catching, the Crawfords of 1932 to 1936 featured the game's two best players and rivaled the Grays of 1930 and 1931. The mass defections prompted sportswriter W. Rollo Wilson to state: "If there is room for only one team in that district— I am very much of the opinion that the Grays are closing their books."[39]

More than a businessman with extra money to throw around, Greenlee revolutionized black baseball. During the 1932 season, he

41

opened Greenlee Field, a seventy-five hundred–seat, lighted ballpark on Bedford Avenue in the heart of Pittsburgh's black Hill district. Greenlee Field was one of the few ballparks owned by a black team. The Grays played their home games there and at the Pirates' Forbes Field.

In 1933, Greenlee inaugurated the annual East-West All-Star Game at Chicago's Comiskey Park. The East-West Game developed into black baseball's biggest moneymaker and in its heyday attracted more than fifty thousand fans.[40] It was far more profitable than the Negro League World Series, which suffered from black teams' uncertain schedules, poor access to home ballparks, and geographically scattered fan bases.

During the 1933 season, Greenlee reorganized the Negro National League around Eastern teams, including the New York Black Yankees, the New York Cubans, the Philadelphia Stars, the Baltimore Elite Giants, and the Newark Eagles. The Grays initially joined the new NNL in 1933, dropped out after a dispute over raiding players, and then rejoined a year later as an associate member.[41] As an associate member, the Grays played a reduced league schedule that freed them up to play more profitable barnstorming dates. In 1935, the Grays became full-fledged NNL members. Two years later, the Negro American League (NAL) formed around Midwestern and Southern teams, eventually including the Kansas City Monarchs, the Chicago American Giants, the Birmingham Black Barons, the Memphis Red Sox, the Indianapolis Clowns, and the Cleveland Buckeyes.[42] The kings of the numbers rackets dominated the Eastern clubs with Greenlee's Crawfords, Ed Semler's Black Yankees, Alex Pompez's Cubans, Tom Wilson's Elite Giants, and Abe and Effa Manley's Eagles.

Posey recruited his own black underworld booster, Rufus "Sonnyman" Jackson. The king of the Homestead numbers racket, Jackson rented hundreds of jukeboxes to area bars and soon owned a Homestead nightclub called the Sky Rocket Cafe. Posey, by contrast, belonged to exclusive clubs, wrote a baseball column for the *Pittsburgh Courier,* and served on the Homestead School Board. Posey was the team's chief decision maker; Jackson was the bankroll.[43]

Jackson paid off the Grays' 1933 payroll and bought the team a new bus—all the 1934 Grays needed now were some ballplayers. Smokey Joe Williams had retired after the 1932 season, the forty-six-year-old pitcher trading in his mound duties for a Harlem bartending job. Gibson had left for the Crawfords in 1932. Even fiery team captain Vic Harris defected to Greenlee's Crawfords in 1934 after putting up with Posey's inability to meet the payroll in 1933.[44] Other Grays players found work with rival teams.

Help arrived at the Grays' 1934 spring training camp when a twenty-six-year-old first baseman stepped off the overnight bus from New York City. Buck Leonard was greeted by half a foot of West Virginia snow and a chilly reception from Posey. The Grays' owner turned up his nose at the five-foot ten-inch first baseman that his former pitcher-turned-bartender had sent him. "I was looking for a bigger man than you," Posey told Leonard. "Can you play first base?"[45]

Posey informed Leonard that the Grays were waiting on a six-foot two-inch first baseman from Fort Wayne, Indiana, named Joe Scott. "The Homestead Grays liked big men," Leonard explained in his autobiography, "just like the [New York] Yankees did."[46] When Joe Scott arrived in camp, Leonard would be out of a job. As Leonard relished telling the story, "Joe Scott never did come."[47]

Once the snow cleared, Leonard demonstrated that his advanced age and small size did not detract from his extraordinary ability as a hitter. No fastball was too fast for Leonard, a left-handed batter who smashed line drives and rarely struck out. Posey gave Leonard several helpful batting tips: he instructed Leonard to grip the bat with his hands together rather than spread apart and to open his stance against left-handed pitchers to hit curveballs better.[48] A week after touting Joe Scott as the team's starting first baseman, Posey changed his tune in his *Pittsburgh Courier* column:

43

> Leonard, a first baseman who started the 1933 season as one of Ben Taylor's protégés and came so fast he was rated as the equal of any in the East when he finished the season with the Brooklyn Royal

Giants, joined the Grays in time for Sunday's game. The Grays were hot after Leonard last season but were unable to get him until a few days after practice sessions had started for the 1934 season.[49]

Posey recognized Leonard—still mastering the fundamentals of first base but a natural hitter—as the Grays' potential star. A month into the season, Leonard broke a 3–3 tie against the Philadelphia Stars with an eleventh-inning home run.[50] Local baseball observers, such as W. Rollo Wilson, who doubled as the NNL commissioner that season, began to take notice: "Leonard, a first baseman who is a ringer for the Ben Taylor of two decades ago, proved that he could field and hit in big-league fashion."[51]

Even with Leonard, however, the Grays were no match for the Crawfords. On July 4, Satchel Paige no-hit the Grays and struck out seventeen before an overflow crowd of 7,500 at Greenlee Field. He walked only one hitter, Leonard, in the first inning. It was the first reported no-hitter thrown against the Grays in the team's twenty-five-year history.[52] The Grays defeated the Crawfords, 4–3, later that same night despite a relief appearance by Paige. From 1934 to 1936, however, the Grays played second fiddle to the Crawfords.

At the end of the 1934 season, Leonard finally met up with his phantom first-base competition. August 5 was "Smokey Joe Williams Day" at Forbes Field, with Williams returning to pitch two scoreless innings for the Grays against an interracial team sponsored by the Berghoff Beer Company of Fort Wayne, Indiana. Fort Wayne's first baseman was Joe Scott.[53]

Joe Scott finally did come to Pittsburgh, but he was an afterthought in light of Leonard's terrific first season. Posey installed Leonard as the team's captain and even tried to make him the Grays' field manager on the road. Leonard lacked the experience and edginess to manage—he couldn't stand up to the veteran players who balked at his decisions.[54] Posey, who resumed his job as the full-time field manager, placed Leonard on his year-end All-American Team: "I take it for granted there is no diversion of opinions in Gibson, Paige, [left-handed pitcher Slim] Jones, [and] Leonard in their positions."[55] W. Rollo Wilson agreed: "Cum Posey had the greatest find

44

of the year in Buck Leonard, his first baseman, whose fielding and hitting rate him above any performer I saw this season."[56] In an article for *Crisis* magazine titled "They Could Make the Big Leagues," Wilson wrote that Leonard "is a certain fielder and a hard, steady hitter who would mace as many four-masters in the big circuits as Jimmie Foxx and Lou Gehrig."[57]

Despite these accolades, Leonard barely survived his first season with the Grays. He initially lived in Pittsburgh with several other players, but Posey forced them to move to Homestead so that he could keep an eye on them. Leonard hated Homestead, a bleak industrial town that was famous for its steel mills and its vices.[58] He was homesick. His only contact with Rocky Mount came through weekly letters and financial support that he sent home to Miss Emma. The likelihood of his running into someone from Rocky Mount in Homestead, in contrast to Washington, D.C., or New York City, was practically nil.

The Grays' grueling travel schedule also didn't agree with him. Life in the Negro Leagues was hard, but it was even harder with the Grays because of their hectic itinerary. Players couldn't take it for more than a year or two. The Grays played one and usually two games every day from early April to mid-September. In 1934, they were an "associate" NNL member because they did not play a full league schedule and did not have a home ballpark. They often played white semipro teams in Pennsylvania and West Virginia towns on the same day they took on Negro National League teams like the Philadelphia Stars. The players spent the whole summer riding in a "specially made" small Ford bus that seated eighteen, didn't have a back door, and was derisively referred to as the "Blue Goose."[59] Leonard passed the time by singing four-part harmonies with several other players. They tried to sound like Leonard's favorite group, the Mills Brothers, and often sang themselves to sleep.[60]

After a summer of living in Homestead and riding in the Blue Goose, Leonard decided that the 1934 season would be his last. "As the season went on, I said, 'Well, I don't like it out here in this steel-mining town,'" Leonard told author John Holway. "'I'm going to finish the season here and then I'm not coming back.'"[61]

In 1935, the Grays came to Leonard by holding spring training practically in his backyard, in nearby Wilson, North Carolina.[62] The *Pittsburgh Courier* described Leonard as "Rocky Mount, N.C.'s gift to the Grays. He is almost without a peer at the initial sack, playing an aggressive game at all times."[63]

The 1935 season was even better than 1934 for Leonard. He flew in an airplane for the first time in August, playing in the 1935 East-West All-Star Game in Chicago before twenty-five thousand fans.[64] During the spring of 1936, he joined the Brooklyn Eagles in the Winter League in Puerto Rico, facing the Cincinnati Reds in exhibition games and improving his fielding skills.[65] In 1936, Leonard remained the Grays' captain, but Vic Harris (who had returned the previous season) took over as the field manager. During the second half of the 1936 season, Leonard competed on a black All-Star team that included Gibson and Paige and won the Denver Post Tournament, a national semipro tournament awarding the winning team five thousand dollars.[66] Leonard made Posey's All-American Team both seasons.[67]

Although Leonard led a glamorous life of flying to Chicago, Puerto Rico, and Denver to play baseball, it was not the life he wanted for his younger brother, Charlie. In a brief article at the end of the 1935 season, headlined "'Young Buck' Named Best in the 'Tarheel' State," the *Pittsburgh Courier* wrote:

> Charles "Pop-eye" Leonard, the "kid" brother of "Buck" Leonard, star Homestead Grays first-baseman, has been voted by fans as the best all around shortstop in the Old North State. Leonard is manager of the Wilson Braves during the summer and spends the fall and winter months as a student and athlete at Talladega College, down Alabama way.[68]

At Talladega in 1935, Charlie lettered in track, tennis, and football.[69] With the Newark Dodgers training in Rocky Mount and the Grays training in Wilson in the spring of 1935, Charlie's Negro League audition with Newark was not far behind.

After graduating from Talladega in 1936, Charlie hooked up with the renamed Newark Eagles.[70] In early August 1936, Newark played a weekend series against the Washington Elite Giants at Griffith Stadium.[71] The night after the Eagles and the Elites played a Sunday doubleheader, Charlie ate dinner with his younger sister, Lena, and spent the night at her apartment. Only eleven months apart, Charlie and Lena had grown up getting bossed around by their oldest brother. Amid this lack of personal autonomy, they bonded and often rebelled against his authority. Charlie's playing for Newark was part of the rebellion.[72]

The next morning, Charlie returned to the Whitelaw Hotel, where the Eagles had been staying, only to find out that he was out of a job. The previous week, Buck had instructed the Eagles manager—who happened to be Buck's tryout companion and former Grays catcher Tex Burnett—to release Charlie in Washington because it was not far from Rocky Mount.[73] About an hour after leaving Lena's house, Charlie returned with his gear in his hands and anger in his heart. "He just cried he was so mad," Lena recalled. "Ooh, he was mad at Buck."[74]

The two brothers did not cross paths for months. Buck had just left the Grays to play in the Denver Post Tournament and did not return to Rocky Mount until the end of the season. Charlie left for Hollister, North Carolina, to become a schoolteacher. "When the season was over and Buck went home, Charlie was in Hollister," Lena recalled, "but he was still mad with him."[75]

Leonard did not tell the Eagles to release Charlie out of selfishness. Leonard did not want his younger brother to have to experience the long bus rides, hard-drinking teammates, and itinerant lifestyle. He knew that his younger brother's talent lay elsewhere. Ending Charlie's dreams of playing black baseball was an act of love.

The Eagles would not have released Charlie if they had thought he was a stellar shortstop. Rube Foster had forbidden his younger half-brother, Willie, from playing black baseball, but Willie defied Rube and ended up a Hall of Fame pitcher. Just as when Leonard sent Charlie home from New York City rather than allow him to play for the Brooklyn Royal Giants, Leonard correctly observed that in

47

1936 Charlie wasn't "physically strong enough to play that caliber of ball."[76]

Leonard wanted Charlie to enjoy an educated, professional life.[77] After graduating from Brick Junior College and Talladega College, Charlie taught elementary school and served as the school's principal for three or four years in Hollister, North Carolina. Charlie then moved back to Rocky Mount to become the head of the black unemployment board; he later accepted a similar position in Kinston, North Carolina.[78] As the person in charge of finding employment for Kinston's black residents, Charlie became a pillar in his community while his oldest brother developed into a full-fledged Negro League star.

In 1937, the Grays returned to the pinnacle of black baseball by reacquiring their home-run-hitting catcher, Josh Gibson. In a deal that had been rumored for weeks leading up to the 1937 season, the Grays received Gibson from the Crawfords in exchange for third baseman Henry Spearman, catcher Lloyd "Pepper" Bassett, and $2,500 cash.[79] While Gibson was playing for the Crawfords, the Grays had formed a solid nucleus around Leonard, pitcher/outfielder Ray Brown, center fielder Jerry Benjamin (Leonard's roommate and close friend), and left fielder/manager Vic Harris. Gibson's return not only brought his big bat into the lineup but also added his ebullient personality to team bus rides. "That's when we started winning," Leonard wrote. "Josh made the whole team better. He put new life into everybody. Before that we were just an ordinary ballclub. Josh made the difference."[80]

The greatest hitter in the history of black baseball, Gibson feasted on off-speed pitches. A short, compact batting stroke, a small stride, and a long, heavy bat allowed him to adjust to breaking balls at the last minute and to knock them out of the park because of his strong hands and wrists. "You could get him out with a fastball, but if you threw him a curveball, he'd hit it a mile," Leonard wrote.[81] Whereas Leonard, a left-handed pull hitter, banged line drives to right field, Gibson, a right-handed hitter, smashed laser shots to all fields. Gibson would hit the ball so hard that opposing infielders played him on the outfield grass.[82] In his younger days, Gibson even ran well for a big man. Although no one questioned the strength of his throwing arm, he initially needed work on fielding different pitches and blocking balls in the dirt. His only enduring weakness was an inability to catch pop-ups. As a hitter, however, he was unmatched.[83]

Leonard benefited the most from Gibson's return to the Grays lineup. With Gibson initially hitting fourth and Leonard hitting third, Leonard saw better pitches to hit. Playing one of their first exhibition games together in Miami, Gibson homered twice and doubled; Leonard homered and tripled.[84] By mid-July, Leonard led the Negro National League with a .500 batting average; he and Gibson tied for the team lead with seven home runs apiece.[85] Gibson became known as the "black Babe Ruth" and Leonard as the "black Lou Gehrig." Together they formed black baseball's best one-two punch. The black press dubbed them the "Thunder Twins."

Gibson left the Grays in mid-June of 1937 to play for dictator Rafael Trujillo's team in the Dominican Republic. Over the years, many black players jumped at midseason offers from Latin American teams because of promises of big paydays and to escape the South's Jim Crow laws that often made life difficult for them on the road. Gibson's leaves of absence in Latin America became a recurring pattern. Although Gibson played out the 1938 and 1939 seasons, he bolted for Venezuela in 1940 and for Veracruz, Mexico, in 1941. In Latin America, Gibson made more money (Trujillo reportedly paid him $2,200 for seven weeks of work in 1937), played fewer games, and received first-class treatment at restaurants and hotels. Gibson also may have been running away from his inner demons. In 1930, Gibson's wife, Helen, had died while giving birth to twins. The babies' survival burdened Gibson with financial responsibility, and his wife's death haunted him. Gibson may have found release traveling the world playing baseball. Every time he left the country, however, Gibson returned to finish the season with the Grays. In 1937, for example, other black players who had jumped to the Dominican Republic formed an All-Star team that played in the Denver Post Tournament, but Gibson returned to the Grays by the end of July.[86]

49

Leonard, a company man ever since his days as a young railroad worker, never deserted the Grays for greener pastures. He continued to enjoy success stateside, homering and singling in the 1937 East-West Game before twenty thousand fans at Comiskey Park. After the All-Star Game, Leonard swung such a hot bat that he began protecting Gibson in the batting order by hitting fifth. Leonard finished the 1937 season with a league-leading .383 batting average and thirty-six home runs.[87] In 1938, Leonard picked up where he left off, leading the league on July 2 with a .480 batting average.[88] Praising Leonard's hitting while poking fun at Washington's black elite known as the "Black 400," *Pittsburgh Courier* columnist Wendell Smith wrote:

> We have always wanted to mingle with individuals who are classified within the most exclusive circle known as the "Four Hundred." Although we have never had a burning desire to "join up" with that contingent of select personalities, it has always been a yen of ours to see what makes them tick. We've always been interested, more or less, in the other half. . . . Even though he's a member of the ".400," we found that there was nothing snooty about him.[89]

Smith concluded that Leonard's .480 midseason batting average "makes him 80 points better than the '.400.'"[90]

In his private life, Leonard continued to strive for what education had bestowed on his younger brother, Charlie: middle-class respectability. On December 30, 1937, Leonard married one of the most prominent, educated members of Rocky Mount's black community, Sarah Wroten Sorrell.[91] The daughter of a wealthy farmer, Sarah grew up in the eastern North Carolina coastal town of Jarvisburg, about 150 miles from Rocky Mount.[92] Sarah's first husband, Rocky Mount's black undertaker, Heathen Sorrell, had died in 1935. In addition to inheriting her late husband's business, Sarah graduated from the University of Michigan with a master's degree in speech education.[93] An olive-skinned woman, Sarah was mistaken as Hispanic when she visited Leonard in Latin America while he was playing winter ball.[94] "He was the athlete and she was *the* lady in Rocky Mount," Charlie's son, C. D. Leonard, recalled.[95]

Buck and Sarah exhibited strong wills and independent spirits. Every Sunday they attended separate churches, and yet they formed a solid partnership. Before they got married, Buck had persuaded Sarah to sell the undertaker business. Leonard agreed to augment his initial $125 monthly salary with the Grays by playing winter ball. Sarah taught first grade, with her monthly salary eventually increasing from forty-eight dollars to seventy-eight dollars. "If she hadn't been teaching school," Leonard admitted in his autobiography, "I would have had to quit playing baseball."[96]

Leonard's continued presence and Gibson's return transformed the Grays into champions, but losing Gibson spelled disaster for the Crawfords. Before the 1937 season, Greenlee had fallen on hard times. Pittsburgh's ward politics had turned against him, leading to more frequent police raids on his numbers operation. Leonard claimed that Grays co-owner Sonnyman Jackson had acquired Gibson in return for helping Greenlee pay off a big hit in the numbers lottery.[97] In trading Gibson to the Grays, the Crawfords conceded his worth as a ballplayer but questioned his ability as a drawing card.[98] The Crawfords figured as long as they held onto Satchel Paige, they could attract large crowds and continue to rival the Grays. Before the 1937 season, however, Paige initiated a mass exodus of Crawfords to Trujillo's team in the Dominican Republic. Greenlee must have been out of money because his best players never came back. The Crawfords limped through the 1937 and 1938 seasons in Pittsburgh. Greenlee Field was demolished after the 1938 campaign.[99]

Posey reaped the greatest rewards from the demise of Greenlee and the Crawfords. Although the NNL named him only the secretary in 1937, the Grays' owner ruled black baseball. His team captured the 1937 and 1938 NNL titles. Some Negro League historians claim that the Grays won nine consecutive NNL titles from 1937 to 1945, but that statistic overstates the team's accomplishments. Although the Grays are generally credited with winning eight of nine during this period, 1939 being the lone exception, league titles were often hard to measure. Like most black teams, the Grays based their league schedule on the availability of major league ballparks; they also played an inordinate number of exhibition games during a typical season—these two factors rendered the official league schedules meaningless.[100] To complicate matters further, the league divided its season into halves. At the end of each season, the first-half and second-half winners competed in a playoff. In 1939, for example, the Grays won both halves of the "regular" season but lost a three-game series to the Baltimore Elite Giants in an unusual four-team playoff. Not even the Grays' own letterhead boasted the 1939 championship, although it sometimes included 1939 as one of nine-straight "pennants."[101] The Grays won both halves of the regular season and the playoff every year from 1937 to 1945, except 1939 (when the Elites won the playoff) and 1941 (when the New York Cubans won the second half, but the Grays won the first half and the playoff). The first-half and second-half champion, however, was not always evident. Each team played a different number of league games, and the determination of what constituted a league game was critical.

Rival teams often accused the Grays of using their nebulous schedule and Posey's power over league matters to manipulate their won-loss record. Dick Powell, the Elite Giants' public relations director, denied that the Grays won nine-straight titles. "Sure it's an inaccuracy," Powell said. "They would be declared winners because they could show that they won more games than they lost because they either had accessibility to a ballpark or there were instances where we played each other in an exhibition game or a league game."[102] Leon Day, a Hall of Fame pitcher for the Newark Eagles, agreed that the determination of a game's status rested with the Grays. "They'd play a game and they'd call it an exhibition if they lost," Day recalled. "If they won, it was a league game."[103]

The best measure of the Grays' dynasty is not their NNL titles but their decades of great teams and players. To their nucleus of Leonard, Gibson, Harris, Benjamin, and Brown, the 1938 Grays added pitchers Roy Partlow, Roy Welmaker, and Edsall Walker; second baseman Matthew "Lick" Carlisle; and shortstop Norman "Jellylegs" Jackson. Few could argue that the Grays did not possess black baseball's best team. In a 1938 column describing the Grays as the new Gas House Gang, a reference to the great St. Louis Cardinals teams of the 1930s, Wendell Smith wrote: "Not only are the Grays champions of Negro baseball, but they are a cocky bunch of ballplayers.

They do not believe that any team can beat them. They don't give a hoot for umpires, fans, newspaper men, or anything else. Baseball is all they care about—it is their life."[104]

Posey cared about winning, first and foremost, but he also cared about making money. And in the late 1930s the Grays weren't making any money in Pittsburgh. The demise of the Crawfords and the demolition of Greenlee Field left the Grays without a home ballpark and without a convenient rival. The Grays were not sad to see Greenlee Field go. The seventy-five hundred–seat ballpark was too small, and, in Posey's words, it "had been a financial stumbling block in the path of the Grays since 1932."[105] The Grays were forced to schedule all of their home games at Forbes Field. Posey's team did not draw well there because, unlike Greenlee Field, Forbes Field was not conveniently located near the black communities on the Hill or in Homestead.[106] Pittsburgh's black population, moreover, never exploded during the 1930s to the same degree as in East Coast cities like New York, Philadelphia, Baltimore, and Washington. By 1940, Washington's black population (187,266) was three times Pittsburgh's (62,216).[107]

Losing money while playing at Forbes Field, the Grays announced in July 1939 their interest in moving their home games to Washington. The main headline in the *Pittsburgh Courier*'s sports section blared: "Grays May Shift Home Park to D.C."[108] Barring an increase in fan support in Pittsburgh, Sonnyman Jackson declared that he would begin negotiations with Clark Griffith about renting Griffith Stadium for 1940.[109] A few weeks later, the *Pittsburgh Courier* published a letter from an ardent Grays fan: "It is the duty of every colored baseball fan of Pittsburgh to give the Homestead Grays his whole-hearted support. . . . The Grays belong to this city. It is a great team and a credit to our community. Let us, as a race, give this great team our full measure of appreciation and support. It is our duty. . . ."[110]

The 1930 Grays was the second-greatest team in Grays history. Pitcher Smokey Joe Williams (fourth from right) and outfielder Oscar Charleston (kneeling far right) have been inducted into the Hall of Fame. Josh Gibson, who joined the team at midseason, is not pictured in this March 1930 photo. (NATIONAL BASEBALL HALL OF FAME LIBRARY)

Josh Gibson (standing fourth from right) says the 1931 Grays was the greatest team he ever played on, better than the Pittsburgh Crawfords teams of the mid-1930s. In 1936, Cum Posey (standing at left) said the 1931 Grays was the best Grays team ever and the best in the history of black baseball. (ART CARTER PAPERS, MOORLAND-SPINGARN RESEARCH CENTER, HOWARD UNIVERSITY)

Buck Leonard displays the batting stance that helped him rocket balls over Griffith Stadium's right-field wall. Grays owner Cum Posey taught Leonard to open his stance against left-handed pitchers in order to see curveballs better. (ROBERT H. MCNEILL)

Clark Griffith chats with his nephew and heir apparent, Calvin, in Clark's office at Griffith Stadium. These two men ran the Senators from 1911 to 1960. (NATIONAL BASEBALL HALL OF FAME LIBRARY)

THREE

THE OLD FOX

By 1935, major league baseball was in trouble. The game's cash cow, Babe Ruth, retired as an active player two months into the 1935 season. Attendance was down during the Great Depression, when people had little money to spend on recreation and those with decent-paying jobs could ill afford to take off work to attend daytime games. Larry MacPhail, the general manager of the Cincinnati Reds, tried to boost his team's flagging attendance by introducing night baseball. On May 24, 1935, at Crosley Field, the Reds and Phillies played major league baseball's first night contest. Other major league magnates derided MacPhail for ruining the grand old game.[1]

Washington Senators owner Clark Griffith was among MacPhail's biggest detractors. "Baseball," Griffith said, "was meant to be played in God's own sunshine."[2] No team was hurting more than Griffith's. Although just two years removed from the World Series, the Senators quickly slid into the abyss of the American League's second division. Griffith lacked both the money and the desire to invest in baseball's other latest innovation, the farm system. Stockpiling a multitude of major league prospects on minor league teams was beyond his financial means. He was so deep in debt (owing a Washington, D.C., bank $125,000) that in 1934 he had sold shortstop Joe Cronin—the team's manager and best player, not to mention Griffith's own son-in-law—to the Boston Red Sox for shortstop Lyn Lary and

$250,000.[3] The Senators' attendance the following season, 255,011, was their lowest since 1919.[4] They missed the Babe's eleven appearances at Griffith Stadium each season.

Griffith envisioned a cheaper solution to his team's woes than investing in a farm system or playing night games—Cuban players. For years, he had been plucking a few players off the island of Cuba and turning them into major leaguers. Now he began employing them in even greater numbers. Although some of these Cubans may not have been "white" according to American definitions of race, their ambiguous racial heritage did not seem to matter to Griffith as long as they could play ball.

Sam Lacy had other ideas about how to improve the Senators. A few months after MacPhail unveiled his lights in Cincinnati, Lacy challenged Griffith and his cohorts: "Why Not Give Baseball a Little 'Color'?"[5] "If baseball club-owners are really anxious to come to their own rescue," Lacy argued in the August 3, 1935, edition of the *Washington Tribune*, "they should put a little 'color' in the game." Lacy insisted that the great Negro Leaguers of the 1920s and 1930s were every bit as good as Senators players past and present. "I can almost hear the snickering now in some quarters as I go on to say that Oscar Charleston, of the Pittsburgh Crawfords CAN PLAY AS MUCH FIRST BASE TODAY AS JOE JUDGE EVER PLAYED," he wrote. " 'Showboat' Thomas of the New York Black Yankees is deadly on ground balls to either side, possesses hands like the immortal Chick Gandil and has foot-work that would make a composite of Joe Kuhel and Mule Shirley look like a lumbering zoo elephant." Lacy concluded:

Talking through my hat, eh? Now I'll laugh. No truer saying was ever mumbled or scribbled than 'one-half of the world doesn't know what the other half is doing.' Have you ever seen Stevens or Lundy or Harris field? Have you ever watched Bell or Crutchfield run base? Or Scale or Perkins throw? Or Gibson or Mackay [sic] or Beckwith hit? Or Matlock [sic] or Tianti [sic] or Brewer pitch? No? Well there's your TONIC.[6]

Washington, D.C., seemed like the natural place for the twenti-eth century's first black major leaguer. It had a major league team that desperately needed players. It had an owner who seemed some-what racially sympathetic, given his signing of Cubans and the way he permitted the black community to use his stadium. And it had a large and affluent black population that not only embraced the local major league team but also had the wherewithal to attack the city's racial segregation. All the city needed was an instigator.

During the mid-1930s, Lacy found his voice as a race man who "took on anybody involved in any way with sports."[7] He criticized the pro-moter of a three-team doubleheader (the winner of the first game plays the third team) at Griffith Stadium between the Baltimore Black Sox, Homestead Grays, and Bacharach Giants.[8] He attacked the Senators' Southern-born radio announcer, Arch McDonald, for suggesting that the Negro Leagues were some sort of minstrel show (McDonald commented on the air: "They are funny things, these colored baseball games. . . .").[9] He encouraged African Americans to follow the Jews in using the 1936 Berlin Olympics to highlight that "American history is dotted with such injustices perpetuated on Negroes."[10] He lashed out at white writers for their coverage of the Joe Louis–Max Baer heavyweight championship fight.[11] And he chas-tised performer Bill "Bojangles" Robinson for joining Louis's entourage and tarnishing the boxer's image (and even published a let-ter of reply from Robinson's wife).[12]

Lacy's big break involved a 1937 football game between Syracuse University and the University of Maryland and the racial identity of Syracuse's star passer and running back, Wilmeth Sidat-Singh. A week before the October 23 contest, Lacy discovered that Syracuse's "Hindu halfback" was actually an American-born black. Wilmeth Sidat-Singh was born Wilmeth Webb to Elias and Pauline Webb of Washington, D.C. His father had died when Wilmeth was just a boy. His mother remarried a Howard University doctor from South Asia, Samuel Sidat-Singh, and Wilmeth took his second father's last name.

59

During the 1930s, no black college football players competed against whites in stadiums below the Mason-Dixon line. Instead, Northern teams agreed to hold their black players out of these games. Lacy decided to challenge this so-called gentlemen's agreement.[13]

In a front-page article headlined "Negro to Play U. of Maryland: Boy Called Hindu by Papers," Lacy revealed Sidat-Singh's true story. A *Tribune* editorial said:

> The joke will be on staid University of Maryland, with its background of Southern tradition, next week when officials learn that a colored youth is a prominent member of the Syracuse football team which clashes with its own boys this Saturday. . . . There is much speculation as to what the University will do when and if it learns that its lily White team must rub shoulders with a Negro.[14]

After the publicity from Lacy's scoop, Syracuse and Maryland agreed to keep Sidat-Singh out of the game. Sidat-Singh practiced with the team all week, traveled to Maryland, and even suited up to play.[15] At the team's pregame chalk talk, however, Syracuse coach Ossie Solem informed his team that "school officials" had decided that Sidat-Singh would sit out.[16] Syracuse, which had been previously undefeated, lost without its star player. Lacy wrote on the *Tribune*'s front page: "An unsoiled football record went by the boards here today as racial bigotry substituted for sportsmanship and resulted in the removal of the spark-plug from the machine which was Syracuse University's football team."[17] Although neither team's coach responded to Lacy's postgame inquiries, Lacy wrote that Sidat-Singh "was denied the privilege of playing in today's 'contest' when Maryland University officials learned his nationality and demanded removal. . . ."[18]

Some *Tribune* readers directed their anger at Lacy for exposing Sidat-Singh's racial background. Threatening a massive boycott of the paper, a subscriber wrote: "Negroes like you that like to dig up such on your race to help the White man keep you down are the cause of the Negro race being where they are today." Others, such as Edwin B. Henderson, the director of physical education for the black public schools and a longtime racial activist, applauded Lacy's efforts: "These southern intolerants will save face anytime by recognizing a colored man as an Indian, Cuban or some kind of foreigner, but draw the line if he is classified as an American Negro."[19]

In response to his critics, Lacy rejected the notion that he should have waited to reveal Sidat-Singh's racial identity until after the game. Lacy agreed with Henderson that "passing" was not a means of achieving racial progress: "To me such a contention seems only to be a weak-livered admission that we are willing to see our boys progress using any kind of masquerade: that we agree with the Nordic observation that ANYTHING BUT A NEGRO is okay." Although praising Sidat-Singh's athletic gifts, Lacy recognized that the issue was about "more than a mere game between two schools. It was NOT a question involving the playing of ONE Negro boy in ONE college football game. But it was one which reached out and embraced the whole of colored America."[20]

Lacy was not the only one butting heads with the University of Maryland. Charles Hamilton Houston, the dean of Howard University's law school, and Thurgood Marshall, Houston's protégé and a recent Howard law graduate, began their legal assault on segregation by challenging the University of Maryland's refusal to admit black students to its law school.

In a lawsuit known as *Murray v. Maryland*, Houston and Marshall championed the case of Donald Murray, a twenty-year-old Amherst graduate and the grandson of a bishop in Baltimore's African Methodist Episcopal Church. They argued that Maryland's rejection of Murray because of his race and the lack of a state-sponsored law school for black students violated the Supreme Court's mandate of "separate but equal" facilities.[21] In June 1935, the trial judge ordered Murray's admission to Maryland law school that fall. In January 1936, the Maryland Court of Appeals, the state's highest court, agreed that absent a separate law school for blacks, equal treatment compelled Murray's continued enrollment.[22]

While Houston and Marshall fought for racial justice in the courts, other lawyers and Howard faculty members had taken to the streets. In 1933, they formed the New Negro Alliance, which organized mas-

61

sive consumer boycotts against white-owned businesses that refused to hire black employees.[23] Its 1934 "Call to Arms" stated:

> If the Negroes in Washington alone would organize 137,000-strong they could make and break at their will the businesses of Washington and change the economic condition of the masses. The white man may not want you to sit in the same theatre with him, he may not want you to work in the same room with him, he may not want you to go to the same school with him, but in order for him to live you must buy the goods he produces.[24]

More than twenty years before the Montgomery bus boycott, the New Negro Alliance turned mass protest into a social and economic movement for racial justice.

The Alliance picketed a small U Street hot dog stand, People's Drug Store, High's Ice Cream, A&P, the Sanitary (Safeway) Grocery Co., and Kaufman's Department Store—with mixed results. Although People's refused to hire blacks or to serve them at its soda fountains, A&P hired eighteen black clerks, and Sanitary hired eleven. The Alliance claimed in 1934 that its boycotts had resulted in more than fifty new black employees, a number that eventually rose to three hundred.[25] It also received a boost from the United States Supreme Court, which in 1938 reaffirmed the Alliance's right to picket stores engaging in racially discriminatory employment practices.

Rank-and-file members of Washington's black community did not always support the boycotts. When the principal of Armstrong High School, G. David Houston, broke the picket line at People's Drug Store to buy Ping-Pong balls, one of the protesters confronted Houston and called him "a hell of a teacher."[26] Howard University history professor Harold Lewis recalled going door-to-door to obtain signatures for a petition against a downtown department store: "No, indeed I'm not going to sign any petition," one woman told Lewis. "They are the only ones that sell the type of shoe I wear."[27] Sometimes the Alliance's rallying cry—"Don't buy where you can't work. . . . Buy where you work—buy where you clerk"[28]—failed to be heard.

Lacy must have been listening. Emboldened by the Sidat-Singh controversy and encouraged by the black community's nascent racial activism, he focused his energies on another Seventh Street employer who catered to blacks yet refused to hire them—Senators owner Clark Griffith.

Obviously, Griffith was the key if the Senators were going to be the first major league team to sign a black player. He would prove to be Lacy's most complex adversary. On the one hand, Griffith segregated the seating in his ballpark and forbade interracial exhibition games between white and black teams. On the other, he regularly opened his ballpark to the black community and frequently rented it to Negro League teams. Most black Washingtonians considered Griffith—in contrast to the virulently racist Redskins owner George Preston Marshall—a friend. And though Griffith loathed changes in baseball, such as night games and the farm system, he had pioneered the signing of Cuban players and even helped found the American League. A magazine profile of Griffith captured these paradoxes, describing him as a "red-eyed radical and archconservative."[29]

Clark Calvin Griffith entered the world during America's post–Civil War struggles with race. Born November 20, 1869, in a log cabin in Clear Creek, Missouri, Griffith experienced the Reconstruction-era struggles with law and justice. "Missouri was sort of half and half during the war," Griffith told writer Ed Fitzgerald. "Some of the boys went to service for the North and some for the South. And some didn't go for either side. Bushwhackers, they were called. They stayed home and robbed and pillaged and abused the women." Griffith recalled awakening as a young boy to the sight of one of these Bushwhackers hanging from a tree. Life in Missouri imbued Griffith with an outlaw spirit. He once saddled the horse of Jesse James, and his lifelong hero was the radio personality, the Lone Ranger.[30]

Griffith grew up poor and fatherless. His father, Isaiah, died in the Missouri cornfields after a seventeen-year-old neighbor mistook him for a deer and shot him. Griffith was two years old at the time and the youngest of five children (the sixth was on the way). His family

63

subsisted on a forty-acre farm, where "the medium of exchange was apple butter." Griffith was so small and sickly as a child that the neighbors speculated he had malaria. When he was thirteen, his mother, Sarah Ann, moved the family closer to her relatives in Bloomington, Illinois, and opened a boardinghouse in the nearby town of Normal.[31]

In Illinois, Griffith developed into a star sandlot pitcher. In 1887, at age seventeen, he signed with the Bloomington (Illinois) Reds of the Inter-State League, where his tutor was Bloomington resident and nineteenth-century pitching star Charles "Old Hoss" Radbourn. Griffith jumped to Milwaukee's Western League team in June 1888 for $225 a month. Three years later, he departed for the major leagues with the American Association's St. Louis Browns. Although he made a lifelong friend in Browns manager Charles Comiskey, Griffith developed arm trouble, finished the 1891 American Association season with Boston, and bounced around the minors for much of the next two seasons.

In 1894, Griffith's arm recovered and he returned to the majors for good with the National League's Chicago Colts (later the Cubs). Only five feet six and a half inches and 156 pounds, Griffith succeeded on his wits and nerve. He threw an array of curveballs, screwballs, and change-ups. He also was willing to do whatever it took to win—scuffing the ball with his spikes, badgering umpires, and bad-mouthing opposing players. With bushy eyebrows, sparkling eyes, and a keen intelligence, the twenty-four-year-old Griffith earned the nickname "the Old Fox." The young pitcher developed into the "pet" of Chicago manager Adrian "Cap" Anson. Sportswriters Bob Considine and Shirley Povich wrote of Anson: "From the picturesque master [Griffith] picked up the sulphuric vocabulary, the pugnacious disposition and the umpire and crowd baiting tactics which made him enthusiastically hated and feared and admired."[32]

Griffith may have absorbed Anson's ignominious enforcement of baseball's color barrier. During the 1880s, Anson reigned as one of baseball's best players and its most prominent bigot.[33] In 1887, he refused to play in an exhibition game against International League pitcher George Stovey, and he had pulled similar stunts against

64

American Association catcher Moses Fleetwood Walker.[34] Although Anson did not single-handedly institute the color line, as some have insisted, he stood out as an enthusiastic enforcer of it.[35]

At the dawning of the twentieth century, the red-eyed radical in Griffith had more important things on his mind than racial issues, such as the meager salaries of National League players. When the league refused to increase the minimum annual salary from $2,400 to $3,000, Griffith responded by joining Comiskey and Western League president Ban Johnson in founding the American League.[36] Griffith was entrusted with persuading his fellow National Leaguers to join him. Of the forty top players targeted by Griffith, thirty-nine, including second baseman Napoleon Lajoie, switched leagues. The lone holdout, Pittsburgh Pirates shortstop Honus Wagner, resisted Griffith's entreaties by barricading himself in a second-story pool hall. Griffith's reward was to serve as player-manager of Comiskey's new team, the Chicago White Sox.

From his new boss, Griffith learned how other teams tried to skirt baseball's color line. During spring training in Hot Springs, Arkansas, Baltimore Orioles manager John McGraw spotted a bellhop nimbly fielding grounders on a baseball diamond near the team's hotel. The bellhop was Charlie Grant, a second baseman with the Columbia Giants, a Negro League team from Chicago. McGraw tried to pass off the light-skinned, angular-featured Grant as a "full-blooded Cherokee" named Charlie "Chief" Tokahoma. Before Tokahoma ever played second base for the 1901 Orioles, Comiskey exposed McGraw's ruse. Griffith's boss bellowed: "If McGraw really keeps this 'Indian' I will put a Chinaman on third base. This Cherokee is really Grant fixed up with war paint and feathers. His father is a well-known Negro in Cincinnati where he trains horses."[37]

Griffith pitched and managed the White Sox to the 1901 American League title and managed the New York Highlanders (later the Yankees) from 1903 to 1908. After his first four seasons with the Highlanders, Griffith drastically curtailed his mound appearances and finished with a lifetime pitching record of 237–146. With the Highlanders on their way to a last-place finish in 1908, Griffith found himself looking for a new job.

Embittered that as a league founder he had not been given an ownership stake in an American League team, Griffith returned to the only place he could find work—the National League. Managing the Cincinnati Reds from 1909 to 1911 in the despised rival league may have been the nadir of Griffith's major league career, but Cincinnati proved to be fertile ground for testing the lessons that Griffith had learned during the Chief Tokahoma incident.

At the end of his stewardship in Cincinnati, Griffith signed the first two Cuban players in the modern major leagues, third baseman Rafael Almeida and outfielder Armando Marsans. Griffith later claimed that signing Almeida and Marsans in 1911 was the idea of the Reds' business manager who had returned from a winter cruise in Cuba gushing about a fleet-footed outfielder. The business manager's original prospect, Almeida, failed to impress Griffith (though Almeida played 102 games for the Reds from 1911 to 1913). Griffith, however, raved about the ability of Almeida's interpreter, Marsans, a major league outfielder for eight seasons.[38] Whoever's idea it was to sign Almeida and Marsans, Griffith knew how to execute it. Griffith informed Reds president Garry Herrmann, "We will not pay any Hans Wagner price for a pair of dark-skinned islanders." Thus, the Reds received documentation from Cuban officials that the two light-skinned players were of "Castilian and not Negro heritage." The Cincinnati press described Almeida and Marsans as "two of the purest bars of Castilian soap ever floated on these shores."[39]

Griffith left the Reds after the 1911 season when his opportunity to own an American League team finally arrived. The Washington Senators offered Griffith the positions of field manager and largest single stockholder. Griffith mortgaged his Craig, Montana, ranch and borrowed from a Helena bank to purchase a 10 percent interest in the team for $27,500. The team, known as the Senators or Nationals, was no great prize. During its first eleven seasons in the American League, Washington had never finished in the first division.[40]

Griffith turned things around by discarding all of the team's veteran players except future Hall of Fame pitcher Walter Johnson, center fielder Clyde Milan, and shortstop George McBride. Griffith also paid twelve thousand dollars for a young first baseman from Montreal, Arnold "Chick" Gandil. Seven years before fixing the World Series as a member of the 1919 Black Sox, Gandil led the Senators to seventeen straight wins and a miraculous second-place finish.[41]

Griffith made another key acquisition in Montreal: his nephew and unofficially adopted son, Calvin. After marrying Anne Robertson in 1900, Clark raised two children from Anne's brother, Jimmy Robertson, a failed ballplayer and alcoholic. Calvin and Thelma Robertson, ages ten and nine, respectively, arrived in Washington in 1922 for a summer vacation with Uncle Clark, and they never left. Upon their father's death a year later, their mother and five siblings joined them in Washington. Only Calvin and Thelma took the Griffith name.

Calvin was the apple of Griffith's eye and Griffith's eventual successor. Over the years, Calvin served as the team's batboy ('23–'26); custodian of the concession stand ('27); batting practice pitcher, locker-room attendant, and general manager of the team's Charlotte farm club ('35–'37); president and general manager of the Chattanooga farm club ('38–'39); and then back to Washington as the head of the concessions business and Griffith's right-hand man.[42] Calvin idolized the man he always referred to as his Uncle Clark. "I did everything in the world to make that man happy. Everything," Calvin told writer Gary Smith while admiring Griffith's picture. "His eyes could pierce right through you. Look at those goddamn bushy eyebrows. When he got mad at you, it was like they were coming out and pointing at you. Next to God, Clark Griffith was it."[43]

After the 1919 season, Griffith purchased a majority interest in the team with the help of Philadelphia grain exporter William Richardson and a $100,000 loan from a Washington bank. He stopped managing after the next season. As an owner and general manager, Griffith proved himself to be an adept trader and a shrewd judge of talent. The Senators won their only World Series in 1924 behind their twenty-seven-year-old "boy manager," shortstop Bucky Harris. They made two more unsuccessful appearances in the Fall Classic in 1925 and 1933.

Then Griffith's days of nickel-and-diming his way to the World Series through a few nifty trades came to an abrupt halt. As Fred Lieb

67

has pointed out, Griffith's association with the Senators can be divided into two parts: from 1912 to 1933, the Senators finished in the first division sixteen out of twenty-two times; from 1934 to 1955, the Senators finished in the first division only four out of eighteen times.[44] Griffith increasingly relied on only a handful of minor league teams, one or two scouts, and more Cubans.

During Griffith's glory years, the Senators roster included only a handful of Cuban players.[45] As the Senators fell in the standings, however, Griffith signed more and more Cubans through his chief scout, Joe Cambria.

A former minor league ballplayer whose career ended after he broke a leg, Cambria owned a Baltimore laundry business known as the Bugle Coat and Apron Supply Company. But his real business was baseball. During the Depression, Cambria owned the local Negro League team, the Baltimore Black Sox. In 1932, Cambria built the team its own ballpark, Bugle Field. The team, however, disbanded two years later as a professional club because of Cambria's penury. "They began to deteriorate under his direction because he was labeled a cheapskate," recalled Dick Powell, the Baltimore Elite Giants' former business manager who had grown up watching Black Sox players such as shortstop Dick Lundy and pitcher Slim Jones. "He didn't want to pay top players what they demanded, so as I said they went elsewhere."[46]

Cambria's penny-pinching proved more successful with minor league teams. He bought about a dozen minor league clubs on the cheap, stocked them with high school players whom he had signed for peanuts, and then sold the players to major league clubs.[47] Minor league baseball proved to be so lucrative that in 1938 Cambria sold his laundry business.

Griffith got first crack at Cambria's best players because he had saved Cambria from the wrath of baseball commissioner Judge Kenesaw Mountain Landis. A flamboyant yet frequently reversed federal judge from Chicago, Landis had been best known for leveling $29,240,000 in fines against John D. Rockefeller's Standard Oil Company. In 1915, he had earned favor with major league baseball's powers-that-be by refusing to rule for nearly a year on an antitrust lawsuit brought by the rival Federal League. The Federal League, which at that time operated as a third major league, had settled out of court during Landis's delay.

After eight members of the 1919 White Sox had been accused of fixing the World Series, the owners sought to repair baseball's image by making Judge Landis the game's first commissioner. He wielded absolute power, and he wasted no time in using it. He banned for life the eight Black Sox, even though they had been acquitted in court of conspiring with gamblers. During the 1920s, Landis banished eleven additional active players who either had consorted with gamblers or had engaged in other conduct that tarnished baseball's image.[48] He exonerated others, such as Ty Cobb, Tris Speaker, and Smokey Joe Wood, of gambling charges. In 1921, he fined Babe Ruth and suspended him for forty games for violating Landis's edict against postseason barnstorming by members of a World Series team.

Landis also abhorred the advent of the farm system. During the 1930s and 1940s, he freed more than two hundred minor league players who had been buried on their teams' massive farm systems and had been bound contractually to those teams under baseball's reserve clause. In 1938, he released ninety-one players from the St. Louis Cardinals, whose general manager, Branch Rickey, had invented the farm system idea, and two years later Landis released 106 players from the Detroit Tigers.[49] He also imposed fines on various teams for hiding players by signing them to bogus contracts.

Judge Landis struck the fear of God into a small-time operator like Cambria. Before the 1941 season, Landis banned major league scouts from owning minor league teams.[50] Although Cambria was forced to sell his teams, Griffith hired Cambria as the Senators' primary scout. "Griffith, being a good friend of Landis, stepped in to save [Cambria's] life in that respect," *Washington Post* sportswriter Shirley Povich recalled.[51] Over the years, Cambria signed some of the Senators' best players—Mickey Vernon, Eddie Yost, George Case, Pete Runnels, Early Wynn, Dutch Leonard, Walt Masterson, Camilo Pascual, Pedro Ramos, and Zoilo Versalles.

Cambria is best remembered as Griffith's source of Cuban players. An Italian who spoke only "pidgin" Spanish, Cambria practically lived on the island of Cuba. During the 1930s and 1940s, he owned a Cuban apartment, bar, and minor league team, the Havana Cubans of the Florida International League. His exploitation of Cuban players—signing them to blank major league contracts, burying them on his minor league teams, and subjecting them to racially unfriendly atmospheres in Southern spring training sites and minor league affiliates—exposed him to frequent criticism. A Cuban journalist referred to the Italian-born Cambria as "the Christopher Columbus of baseball." The American press referred to him as an "Ivory Hunter."[52] The Cuban players called him "Papa Joe." Cambria passed off the Cubans, whether light-skinned or dark, as "white" major leaguers. Some of these darker-skinned players raised eyebrows, particularly in the case of Roberto "Bobby" Estalella.

Slipping onto the scene about a dozen years before Jackie Robinson, Estalella is regarded by many as modern baseball's first black major leaguer. "Bobby Estalella definitely was black," recalled former *Washington Star* sportswriter Burton Hawkins. "I can't go into their heritage, but to look at them, Estalella was black."[53] Povich, who heard "a great many rumors that [the Cuban players] were suspiciously black or indeed black," regarded Estalella as one of the players "I would characterize as black or seemed to me as black."[54] John Welaj, an outfielder with the Senators from 1939 to 1941, told author Donn Rogosin that "most of the Senators considered Robert Estalella black."[55]

During the course of a two-day interview at his home in Indiatlantic, Florida, Calvin Griffith contributed to the rumors about Estalella's black heritage. Calvin and Estalella crossed paths during the late 1930s on the Senators' minor league teams in Charlotte and Chattanooga and during the early 1940s in Washington. "We used to call him the Black Snake. He had a penis that goes half the distance between here and here," Calvin said, holding his hands at the ends of a square table about three feet wide while eating lunch at the Eau Gallie Yacht Club. "And he could hit, goddamn he could hit that ball."[56]

Before his death in Hialeah, Florida, in 1991, Estalella denied having any black roots. He told writer Robert Heuer that the notion of his breaking baseball's color barrier was "absurd. . . . It was only an issue for the Americans."[57] In Latin America, Estalella—who had a yellowish complexion and thin lips, but a flat, wide nose and kinky hair—would have been called a *"mulato,"* referring to someone of mixed black and white ancestry. Cuban players, such as Rodolfo Fernandez, referred to Estalella as a *"mulato capirro,"* or a very light mulatto.[58] As long as Estalella spoke Spanish, however, he fell below Judge Landis's radar screen.

A five foot eight, 180-pound hitter from Cardenas, Cuba, Estalella was nicknamed "El Tarzan" because of his strong, stocky build and massive home-run power.[59] Estalella broke in with the Senators as an outfielder/third baseman in September 1935 and spent parts of four seasons with the team. Known for his bat but not his glove, Estalella played nine seasons overall, including stints with the St. Louis Browns and the Philadelphia Athletics. He was a minor league star whose major league career, according to baseball historian Bill James, should have "take[n] off sooner and last[ed] longer."[60] His grandson, also named Bobby, is a major league catcher who has played for the Philadelphia Phillies, the San Francisco Giants, and, of late, the Colorado Rockies.

Estalella was not the only darker-skinned foreigner considered by many to be a "black Senator." Venezuelan Alejandro "Alex" ("Padron" or Big Foot) Carrasquel, a Senators pitcher from 1939 to 1945, was another of Povich's prime suspects.[61] Describing Carrasquel's face as "swarthy" and "pock-marked," Povich wrote in his book about the Senators: "With a cutlass in his hand and a knife in his mouth, he could have doubled as any respectable pirate boarding a victim ship."[62] Other teams passed off darker-skinned Latins as "white" major leaguers as well. Baseball historians have argued that Reds pitcher Tom de la Cruz ('44) of Cuba and Cubs pitcher Hi Bithorn ('42–'43, '46) of Puerto Rico quietly integrated the game before Jackie Robinson.[63]

But the Senators imported dusky-skinned Cubans in the largest numbers. They brought at least eleven Cubans to spring training in

College Park, Maryland, in 1944, housing an additional six in Williamsport, Pennsylvania. Even Calvin admitted that the Senators bent, if not broke, the color line. "You had to have 'em mixed up," he told biographer Jon Kerr. "You got a Cuban and you got a Castilian, they were white—true Spanish. There's no question that some of the ballplayers Mr. Griffith signed had black blood. But nobody said anything about it. Nobody said nothing about it. So why bring up questions about something that nobody asked about."[64]

Opposing players showered Estalella and his Cuban teammates with racial insults and abuse. Estalella endured more than his fair share of beanballs and brushback pitches.[65] "Perhaps you didn't know it, but there are many 200 per cent Americans among the pitchers in the big leagues and they resent the presence of the Cuban ballplayers, particularly the *swarthy ones* like Estalella," *Washington Post* columnist Shirley Povich wrote in 1938.[66] But it didn't seem to bother the power-hitting Estalella. "[Senators manager Bucky Harris] had a hunch Estalella would reap more than a just crop of mean pitches and he'd be knocked down plenty," the *Washington Daily News* reported. "Just how the stumpy little gent would take it was an itching question. So far, Senor Estalella's courage is holding up remarkably well."[67]

During the 1944 season, the St. Louis Browns "insisted on expressing the opinion audibly and volubly that the Cuban players on the Washington roster were of African, rather than Latin, descent."[68] The race-baiting reached a boiling point when the Browns' third-string catcher, Tom Turner, physically threatened the Senators' diminutive, 150-pound catcher, Mike Guerra. Senators outfielder Roberto Ortiz, six foot four and 200 pounds, challenged Turner, six foot two and 195 pounds, to a fight. Ortiz won the brawl, but he broke his thumb.[69]

The Senators' Cuban players protected each other because they could not expect much help from most of their white teammates or from their manager. Some white Senators ostracized their Cuban teammates, according to a 1940 *Washington Daily News* article, and manager Bucky Harris "nursed a deep-seated grudge against the chattering monkeys from Gen. Bautista's game preserve."[70] Harris, who described the Senators' Cuban players at their 1940 spring training as "trash," said, "If I have to put up with incompetents, they must at least speak English."[71] During one spring training, Harris tried to confine the weak-fielding Estalella to the outfield. When Estalella, an aspiring third baseman, playfully protested, Harris chased Estalella into the outfield by threatening him with a bat.[72] Others, however, insisted that Estalella got along well with his teammates. "Bobby was a pudgy, happy-go-lucky fellow who struck people the right way," Ossie Bluege, the Senators' longtime third baseman who replaced Harris as manager in 1943, told writer Robert Heuer.[73]

For Estalella and other Cuban players, life on the Senators was hard. During spring training and on their Charlotte and Chattanooga minor league affiliates in the segregated South, the Senators often found alternative housing and eating arrangements for their darker-skinned Cubans. "The Cuban ballplayers, some of them were as black as your tape recorder," Calvin Griffith recalled. "We had to find places for them to stay across the railroad tracks."[74] Although the Senators' Cuban players faced the added handicaps of a language barrier and cultural disorientation, they never experienced the degree of public scrutiny, racial harassment, and isolation thrust upon Jackie Robinson when he officially integrated the minor leagues in 1946 and the major leagues in 1947. The Cubans had their own means of communication, and, as the Turner-Ortiz fight illustrated, they had each other.

Griffith also searched for unclaimed baseball talent within U.S. borders. At the end of the 1934 season, Cambria signed Allen Benson, a pitcher for the House of David, a barnstorming team that had been affiliated with a Michigan-based religious sect and whose players sported long hair and beards. Although Benson got hammered in his first start with the Senators, Griffith wanted him to pitch again as long as Benson kept his beard. The beard, Griffith believed, was a gate attraction. Benson, however, wanted to shave it off. "Nothing doing," Cambria said. "You're staying only if the beard stays."[75] Benson made one more disastrous start, and then he quietly left the scene. In 1935, Cambria signed Edwin "Alabama" Pitts to a minor league contract; Pitts had just been released from Sing Sing prison.

73

Although Judge Landis shockingly reversed minor league president William G. Bramham's ban of Pitts, the convicted robber fared less well at the plate in the Triple-A International League, where he batted .233 in forty-three games, than he did in the prison yard.[76] Griffith recognized that Cubans were easier to find, cheaper to sign, and more reliable on the field. "They were good ballplayers," Calvin told Jon Kerr. "They could play and they were eager to play because $400 or $500 a month was like a million dollars to them. That's where Mr. Griffith got in with those Cubans way back in those days."[77]

Where else could Clark Griffith find top-notch ballplayers, not signed by other major league teams, who were willing to play for the Senators for four hundred and five hundred dollars a month? Lacy confronted him with the obvious answer.

In early December 1937, shortly before the start of baseball's winter meetings, Lacy wrote separate letters to Clark Griffith and Judge Landis. Lacy urged Griffith to discuss with his fellow owners the prospect of "the Negro baseball player as a potential big league performer." Lacy requested that Judge Landis grant "a committee of three colored newspaper men" an audience with the owners "to plead the cause of Negro representation in major league baseball." He argued that "it was time for organized baseball to keep apace with the spirit of the times."[78] Landis never responded personally. After Griffith brought the matter to Landis's attention, Landis instructed Griffith to talk to Lacy as soon as the Senators owner returned to Washington.

On the Monday morning after the winter meetings, Griffith invited Lacy to the Senators' offices at Griffith Stadium. The former stadium vendor established a professional tone with Griffith. "I told him that I was approaching him in a new role as sportswriter, rather than as an employee," Lacy told author Peter Sheingold. "I brought the proposition to him that he should try to get out of the cellar, or improve his team, by using some of the black players that he was seeing on Thursday nights when the Senators were out of town."[79]

Griffith's optimistic reply grabbed headlines in the black press: "[T]he time is not far off when colored players will take their places beside those of other races in the major leagues. However, I am not so sure that time has arrived yet. . . . A lone Negro in the game will face rotten, caustic comments. He will be made the target of cruel, filthy epithets. I do not try to win your opinion when I say I certainly would not want to be the one to have to take it."[80]

Griffith also rejected the immediate integration of baseball because of the black athlete's alleged inferiority: "The economic stress through which the American Negro race has been forced to grow has so hindered their athletes that the group itself is not to be blamed for their shortcomings in certain phases of athletic life," he said. "It is unreasonable to demand of the colored baseball player the consistent peak performance that is the requisite of the game as it is played in the big leagues."[81]

Lacy acknowledged that the first black major leaguer would face "caustic comments" from Southern ballplayers and fans, but he rejected Griffith's inferiority argument. Lacy believed that though some of the Negro League stars could not make the majors, others could. Lacy asked Griffith to offer a long-term solution.[82]

The solution, according to Griffith, "is one that will not be realized in one year, or two, or maybe five. It will take time. My belief is that the answer lies in the setting up of a single league of eight REAL, bona-fide clubs. A league that is going to be run on the level, one that is going to completely remove any and all forms of shady goings-on." Griffith envisioned a Negro League so professional and well run that it "cannot be ignored when world's series time comes around."[83] According to his nephew Calvin, Griffith desired a World Series in which "the black boys play the white boys."[84] On the basis of its professionalism, he argued that the Negro Leagues would force the major leagues to integrate.

For several years, Griffith had been encouraging black professional teams to build up their own leagues. While watching an August 1932 night game between the Washington Pilots and the Pittsburgh Crawfords at Griffith Stadium, Griffith praised Crawfords outfielder Rap Dixon ("How that boy can sock em") and Pilots first baseman Mule Suttles ("Mule, that is worth anybody's money"). Although opposed to night baseball for the Senators, Griffith favored night games for black teams. He also urged these teams to re-form the Negro National League, which had folded after the 1931 season. "Negroes no longer are willing to pay to see just any kind of ball, and least of all, here in this section of the country and where they can see Babe Ruth, Lou Gehrig and other stars on regular big league teams instead," Griffith told the *Pittsburgh Courier*. "You must give them a comparative brand of ball."[85]

Five years later, Griffith's argument about a comparative brand of ball rang hollow. By 1937, the Senators were terrible, Ruth had retired, and Gehrig tragically followed him a few years later. Griffith's Cubans could not fill the void. The Senators' black fans no longer had as much incentive to sit in the right-field stands.

After Lacy's December 1937 interview with Griffith, Grays owner Cum Posey exhorted his fellow Negro National League owners to read the interview before their annual meeting. Posey wanted them to form a committee in order to create "a sound constitution, workable contracts, and start off on such a solid base that all affected will have the confidence to sell the League as it should be sold—to the Fans."[86] Posey shared Griffith's goals of building up the Negro Leagues. In short order, Posey and Griffith formed an alliance that benefited both men as the Grays exclusively rented Griffith's ballpark. They envisaged the same "bright future for Negro Baseball," a future that contravened Lacy's goal of integrating the Senators.[87]

Lacy initially agreed with Griffith's argument about improving the professionalism of the Negro Leagues. For the next five years, Lacy served as the Negro Leagues' watchdog and biggest critic. Lacy viewed black baseball's shortcomings—numbers kings who owned the teams, booking agents who controlled them, star players who ignored their contracts and jumped to other teams, and teams that ignored league schedules in favor of more lucrative barnstorming dates—as obstacles to integration. Lacy failed to realize in 1937 that the biggest obstacle to integration was not the Negro Leagues but traditionalist white major league owners such as Griffith himself.

The 1937 interview with Griffith marked the beginning of Lacy's campaign to integrate baseball in Washington. For the next seven months, Lacy ran a column in the weekly *Washington Tribune* titled "Pro and Con on The Negro in Organized Baseball." He reprinted letters of support from prominent black Washingtonians. He also quoted the mixed reactions of prominent white sportswriters. Washington-based writers initially gave Griffith the benefit of the doubt. Bob Considine of UPI said: "I think Griffith is sincere and that his paramount interest is in merit, rather than in color." Vincent X. Flaherty of the *Washington Herald* said: "If the colored man isn't playing big-league baseball, it's not the fault of the major leagues. It's the fault of the colored race, for not until colored baseball is thoroughly organized will the colored player break into the scheme." New York–based writers were generally more sympathetic to integration. John Kieran of the *New York Times* said: "There can be no logical, intelligent, and unprejudiced objection to permitting Negroes to play in organized baseball." Jimmy Powers of the *New York Daily News*, a frequent advocate of integration, said: "Football is a much more vicious body-contact sport than baseball, yet there are not 'cruel epithets' hurled at the Negroes who play all over the country."[88]

The Senators' black fans were getting just as worked up as Lacy about baseball's discriminatory practices. Letters of support streamed into the *Tribune* offices. During the late 1930s, black Washingtonians no longer reacted to racial bigotry with indifference (as they had with the New Negro Alliance boycotts); they reacted with indignation.

The first public display of discontent from the Senators' black fans arose from a Griffith Stadium appearance by New York Yankees outfielder Jake Powell. During a July 1938 pregame radio interview in Chicago, a WGN reporter asked Powell how he stayed in shape during the off-season. Powell, a police officer in Dayton, Ohio, during the winter months, responded that he wielded a police club "cracking niggers over the head." Chicago's black leaders demanded that Powell be banned for life. Judge Landis immediately suspended Powell for ten days.[89] Shirley Povich quipped of the .254-hitting Powell that "Negroes on Powell's off-season beat have little to fear if he is no more effective with a police club than he is with his bat this season."[90]

Alvin "Jake" Powell grew up just outside of Washington, D.C., in Silver Spring, Maryland, and broke into major league baseball with the Senators. Signed by Joe Cambria, Powell initially played with the Senators in 1930 and then again from 1934 to 1936. Playing center field for Washington at the end of the 1934 season, Powell caught the final out of Babe Ruth's American League career.[91] In 1936, Griffith traded Powell to the Yankees for outfielder Ben Chapman—a bigot-for-bigot swap. Three years earlier, Chapman had incited a bench-clearing brawl by spiking and tackling the Senators' Jewish second baseman, Buddy Myer. (Shirley Povich wrote that Chapman "cut a swastika with his spikes in Myer's thigh."[92]) As the Philadelphia Phillies' manager during the late 1940s, Chapman earned eternal infamy as Jackie Robinson's most vocal tormentor. Powell, for his part, deliberately had run into Detroit Tigers first baseman Hank Greenberg while still with the Senators in 1936, breaking the Jewish slugger's wrist. Powell's run-ins with opposing players of all colors and ethnic backgrounds are too numerous to mention.[93]

In 1938, Powell was the poster boy of baseball's racial bigotry. Although he attempted to rehabilitate his image by touring Harlem's nightspots and buying rounds of drinks (in part because black New Yorkers threatened to boycott the beer sold by Yankees owner Col. Jacob Ruppert), the goodwill gesture failed to mollify Washington's black fans.

Over the years, the Senators' black fans sat in the right-field pavilion and passed judgment on sympathetic and unsympathetic players. They loved Babe Ruth and treated him like one of their own. They hooted and hollered at perceived racists. During an interracial exhibition game in the fall of 1920 against the Brooklyn Royal Giants, Senators outfielder Frank Brower had punched a black umpire in the face. Black rooters heckled Brower so badly that Griffith eventually traded Brower to Cleveland and banned interracial exhibitions for more than twenty years. In 1933, Senators relief pitcher Bill McAfee punched a black heckler in Cleveland. When the Senators returned for a game at Griffith Stadium and McAfee began warming up in the bullpen located in right field, the black fans in the pavilion showered McAfee with boos. The following season, McAfee was pitching for the St. Louis Browns.[94]

Powell's first game back from his suspension just happened to be an August 16 doubleheader at Griffith Stadium. The game drew the largest crowd of the season, twenty-three thousand fans. Before the game, Washington fans, calling themselves the National Constitution Defense League, wrote a letter to the Yankees' owner, Col. Ruppert, urging him not to play Powell when the Yankees came to Washington.[95] Their urgings went unheeded.

A pop bottle greeted Powell, who played left field during the second game of the doubleheader, as he walked to first base after his first at-bat. The glass grenade was a prelude of things to come. Pop bottles rained down on Powell in the sixth inning as he left the Yankees' dugout and took his position in left field. After a ten-minute delay in which the grounds crew cleaned up the bottles, the fans flung more bottles at Powell in the seventh. There was no mistake where the bottles came from—the right-field pavilion and left-field bleachers. Shirley Povich wrote: "From the right-field pavilion, favorite section of colored fans, came loud and insistent shouts of 'Take him out!' At one point during the turmoil, a pop vender's bucket came hurtling out of the stands and fell perilously close to the Yankee outfielder."[96] This wasn't a few drunken fans (Griffith refused to sell beer in those days, though one of his biggest advertisers was the National Bohemian beer company). This was a full-scale rebellion. The artillery, according to the *Washington Herald*'s Vincent Flaherty, included thirty-eight pop bottles, a pop bottle bucket, a peanut vendor's bucket, two straw hats, a slightly worn shoe, and "3,967 coarse remarks."[97] Unaware of the pregame warning, Povich blamed Yankees manager Joe McCarthy for returning Powell to the lineup in Washington: "In Washington, unlike other league cities, colored fans are congregated chiefly in one sector of the park. They could have been expected to work up a fury against Powell. They did, too."[98] Griffith responded to the anger from the Senators' black fans by announcing that ballpark soda vendors would serve beverages in paper cups.[99] The following year, the city's black fans improvised by pelting Powell with vegetables.[100]

In 1939, black Washingtonians proved to be less violent but more organized when the Daughters of the American Revolution (D.A.R.) barred an Easter performance at Constitution Hall by black opera

79

singer Marian Anderson. The Howard University School of Music
had invited Anderson to give the concert in Washington. A fire had
destroyed the theater where Anderson originally was supposed to
sing.[101] Anderson's agent, Sol Hurok, attempted to book Anderson's
concert at the D.A.R.-controlled Constitution Hall, the city's largest
auditorium. To this day, the D.A.R. says that the Washington Sym-
phony already had reserved Easter and that Hurok failed to request
another date.[102] Hurok, however, inquired about the days before and
after Easter but was told that those dates were open only to "white
artists."[103] That applied to just about every day at Constitution Hall,
where blacks attended concerts but could not perform. In fact, the
D.A.R. board voted thirty-nine to one to deny Anderson a special
exception.[104]

Charles Houston, James Nabrit, and Mary McLeod Bethune—
three of the city's most prominent black leaders—formed the Marian Anderson Citizens Committee (MACC).[105] They rallied the
black community through a series of church-based protest meetings.
On February 26, Houston spoke at Mt. Pleasant Congregationalist
Church. That same day, Nabrit discussed the legal implications of the
D.A.R.'s segregated practices at Lincoln Congregationalist Church,
with a benediction from the Church of God's Elder Michaux. Houston and Nabrit reached out to Washington's black middle class at the
Congregationalist churches while Elder Michaux attracted Southern
migrants. They also generated support among Howard University
students, who demonstrated March 7 in front of Constitution Hall.[106]

As the architect of the NAACP's legal campaign, Houston used the
Marian Anderson controversy to call national attention to the
nation's capital's segregated schools. Houston petitioned the District
of Columbia School Board to use one of the city's largest public
auditoriums at all-white Central High School for Anderson's performance. The school board, consisting of five whites and three blacks,
initially rejected Houston's request outright.[107] In the face of "national
indignation," the board reconvened March 9 and agreed to allow
Anderson to use the auditorium, "provided colored people did not
take advantage of this situation to try to get the auditorium again."[108]
Houston rejected the "back door" offer. On March 26, he spoke at

another protest meeting at the Metropolitan African Methodist Episcopal Church, this time with Bethune and Assistant Secretary of the Interior Oscar L. Chapman.[109]

Government support was critical to Anderson's cause. Bethune, as the director of the Negro division of the National Youth Administration, had ties to the Roosevelt administration. After the D.A.R. denied Anderson's request to play at Constitution Hall, first lady Eleanor Roosevelt renounced her D.A.R. membership in her nationally syndicated Scripps-Howard newspaper column.[110] But it was Chapman who lobbied his racially sympathetic boss, Secretary of the Interior Harold Ickes, to allow Anderson to perform an outdoor concert at the Lincoln Memorial.[111]

On a cold Easter late afternoon, Anderson, dressed in a long, black mink coat and a mink hat and wearing white gloves, stood on the steps of the Lincoln Memorial in front of seventy-five thousand people. The symbolism of Anderson standing in front of the statue of the Great Emancipator was not lost on Ickes, who movingly introduced the great contralto singer to the crowd. "Genius draws no color line," Ickes said in a performance of his own.[112] The day, however, belonged to Anderson. The enduring moment of Anderson's performance was her opening rendition of "America." "I will never forget that vast audience and this woman got out there and sang, 'My country 'tis of thee, sweet land of liberty,'" recalled Robert Weaver, a member of Roosevelt's unofficial "black cabinet" who was in the audience. "If ever there was irony, that was it."[113]

Anderson performed six additional songs: two opera tunes, including her trademark, "Ave Maria," and four Negro spirituals, including an encore number by request, "Nobody Knows the Troubles I've Seen." Black and white bigwigs in attendance included Houston, Bethune, William Hastie, Mordecai Johnson, NAACP President Walter White, Chief Justice Charles Evans Hughes and his wife, Associate Justice Hugo Black (a former member of the Ku Klux Klan), and numerous U.S. senators and congressmen.[114] Millions more listened to Anderson's performance on NBC's national radio broadcast.

Lacy covered Anderson's concert that day. Having switched papers in 1939 from the *Washington Tribune* to the Baltimore-based *Afro-*

81

American chain, Lacy wrote about how Anderson's performance had brought together a city divided by both race and class: "The venture turned out to be one of those rare occasions when caste is forgotten, when dignitaries rub elbows with street urchins, and when milady and her servant meet in the same social sphere."[115] A day after the performance, Bethune wrote Houston a congratulatory and emotion-filled letter:

> History may and will record it, but it will never be able to tell what happened in the hearts of the thousands who stood and listened yesterday afternoon. Something happened in all of our hearts. I came away almost walking in the air. My hopes for the future were brightened. All fear had vanquished. We are on the right track—we must go forward.[116]

Things were moving forward in Washington.

Clark Griffith sits at his Griffith Stadium office in front of pictures of U.S. presidents throwing out the first ball on Opening Day. Griffith's friendship with FDR was a major reason that Roosevelt wrote the "Green Light" letter allowing professional baseball to continue during World War II. (AP/WORLDWIDE)

Buck Leonard and wife Sarah Wroten Sorrell, "the lady" of black Rocky Mount, having earned a master's degree in speech education from the University of Michigan. While Leonard played ball, she taught in the Rocky Mount public school system. (Art Carter Papers, Moorland-Spingarn Research Center, Howard University)

Sam Lacy (seated fourth from right) covers a Howard University football game. Lacy's good friend, Grays promoter Art Carter (third from right), is seated next to him. (Art Carter Papers, Moorland-Spingarn Research Center, Howard University)

Buck Leonard slams a home run over Griffith Stadium's right-field fence during a 1938 game against the New York Cubans. (NATIONAL BASEBALL HALL OF FAME LIBRARY)

The Homestead Grays, pictured in midgame, played at Griffith Stadium when the Senators were out of town. Howard University, known at that time as the "Capstone of Negro Education," is in the background. (Robert H. McNeill)

FOUR

THE GRAYS COME
TO WASHINGTON

Washington, D.C., seemed like the ideal fit for the Grays. The city had a growing, educated black population that loved baseball, a major league stadium in the heart of the black community, and a convenient location on the rail lines to Philadelphia and New York. Every Negro League team playing on the Eastern seaboard passed through Washington.[1] The Grays had played at Griffith's ball yard — then known as American League Park — as early as 1921 against the Washington Braves.[2] Sixteen years later, Josh Gibson's return had transformed the Grays into Negro National League champions. To this day, Washington remains a transient, political town that treats its sports teams like it treats politicians — the nation's capital likes winners.

Events during the late 1930s made Washington even more attractive as a black baseball town. Senators owner Clark Griffith had expressed strong support for the Negro Leagues in his December 1937 interview with Lacy. Jake Powell's comments in 1938 had infuriated many of the Senators' loyal black fans. A year later, Marian Anderson's concert had united black Washingtonians across the economic and social spectrum.

In February 1940, the Grays announced that they would play some of their home games at Griffith Stadium. They rented the ballpark when the Senators were out of town and wore Ws on the sleeves of their uniforms to connote their new status as the *Washington* Homestead Grays. In Pittsburgh, the Grays donned uniforms with Hs on their sleeves. During their first few seasons, the Grays divided their home games evenly between the two cities.[3]

The Grays introduced themselves to black Washington primarily through Sunday doubleheaders. After playing Saturday at Forbes Field, they would leave Pittsburgh well after midnight, drive 263 miles from Pittsburgh to Washington, and arrive in Washington about 11:00 A.M. Most of the players would grab sandwiches before heading into the ballpark around 11:30 A.M. The players referred to weekend doubleheaders, usually the most profitable days of the week for a black baseball team, as "'getting-out-of-the-hole' days."[4]

Black Washington, however, greeted the Grays with indifference. Only four thousand people attended the team's official home opener, a Sunday sweep of the Cuban Stars (also known as the New York Cubans).[5] The following week, a rematch of the 1939 playoff series between the Grays and the Baltimore Elite Giants garnered only fortyeight hundred fans.[6] In 1940, the Grays' attendance hovered between three thousand and four thousand a game. The following season, it dwindled to fifteen hundred to three thousand in June and July.[7]

Other cities kept the Grays afloat. A 1940 Grays-Elites doubleheader at Forbes Field drew seven thousand fans, and a similar contest at Yankee Stadium attracted eight thousand to ten thousand.[8] The 1940 NNL playoffs at Yankee Stadium featured four teams and fetched fifteen thousand fans.[9] The following season, eleven thousand people ventured to Brooklyn's Dexter Park to see the Grays play the white semipro Brooklyn Bushwicks, and two Yankee Stadium doubleheaders against the Cubans drew twelve thousand people each.[10] After fifty thousand people witnessed the 1941 East-West All-Star Game at Chicago's Comiskey Park, twenty-eight thousand fans flocked to a Grays-Elites doubleheader at Detroit's Briggs Stadium.[11] At the end of the 1941 season, the Grays announced that they had made a profit for the first time in more than eight years—despite their poor attendance in Washington.[12]

The Grays failed to catch on in Washington in 1940 and 1941 in part because they hired a white publicity agent. The agent—former

88

Washington Times-Herald sportswriter Joe Holman—knew how to promote events at Griffith Stadium, but he could not get the city's white daily newspapers to cover the Grays.[13] White papers occasionally devoted one or two paragraphs to the Grays but usually did not bother covering them at all.

Hiring a white publicity agent also alienated the Grays' biggest source of free publicity—the black press. When the Grays announced their intention to play home games in Washington, Lacy wrote: "It was generally known Homestead officials were considering the move when one of them asked a downtown (ofay, if you please) sportswriter to do their publicity. Ho hum! Incidentally, it was the same scribe who only a few minutes before had told me he thought the best chance for colored players to break into the big leagues lay in their ability to 'clown.'"[14] (*Ofay* means white person.) In that same edition, Lacy's *Afro-American* gave the Grays' big announcement just two paragraphs.[15] During the 1940 and 1941 seasons, however, the weekly *Afro-American* (and Lacy in particular) covered the Grays' games at Griffith Stadium more extensively and more critically than any other media outlet in the country.

The Grays' biggest problem in 1940 and 1941 was the absence of their top drawing card, Josh Gibson. Gibson spent almost the entire 1940 season playing in Venezuela, where he made six hundred dollars a month (one hundred dollars more than his salary with the Grays, plus all expenses paid) for playing one or two games a week. Upon returning to the Grays in late August 1940, Gibson barely saw the inside of Griffith Stadium. Banned from all league games (and the All-Star Game) for jumping to South America, Gibson played only in exhibitions. While Buck Leonard competed in the 1940 East-West Game in Chicago, Gibson was in Washington with the Grays. Gibson smacked a 450-foot homer in the first game of a doubleheader against Philadelphia, catching the first game and playing first base in the second. That was Gibson's only recorded appearance at Griffith Stadium in 1940.[16]

Gibson abandoned the Grays and Griffith Stadium altogether in 1941, playing the entire eight-month season in Veracruz, Mexico, for about eight hundred dollars a month.[17] Because Gibson already had signed a contract for five hundred dollars a month with the Grays,

Posey sued the catcher for breach of contract and received a ten thousand dollar lien on Gibson's house.[18] In both 1940 and 1941, a handful of the Grays' better players, such as shortstop Sam Bankhead and left-handed pitcher Roy Partlow, followed Gibson to Latin America.

In addition to losing Gibson as an everyday gate attraction in 1941, the Grays failed to arrange a Griffith Stadium contest featuring Satchel Paige. Pitching for the Kansas City Monarchs in the Southern and Midwestern Negro American League, Paige single-handedly kept black baseball out of the red. His three-inning appearance at the 1941 East-West Game in Chicago was the major reason fifty thousand people showed up. In 1941, Paige drew crowds between ten thousand and twenty thousand in major league ballparks from Chicago to St. Louis to New York City. "Sir Posey is still dreaming of bringing him to Washington on a night date at Griffith Stadium . . ." *Washington Afro-American* sportswriter Ric Roberts wrote. "It may attract 20,000 fans."[19] In 1941, however, Paige's Monarchs wouldn't cooperate.

As a drawing card, Leonard paled in comparison to Gibson and Paige. Near the end of the 1940 season, a *Pittsburgh Courier* columnist dubbed Leonard "the least colorful."[20] Perhaps the best description of Leonard came from Newark Eagles pitcher Max Manning, who played with Leonard in Mexico later in their careers. Manning told John Holway:

> Two people who reminded me of each other were Buck Leonard and Pop Lloyd; their characters were so similar — the quiet humbleness, the spartan-like kind of living. Buck never cursed, never drank. You'd always find him with a paper in his hand. In Mexico, if I wanted to find him, I'd go to the park, and he'd be sitting on a bench reading the paper, doing his crossword puzzle. He'd be in bed by nine o'clock.[21]

Leonard's "Black Lou Gehrig" moniker was apt, not only as a fellow first baseman and line drive–hitting RBI man, but as a more easygoing, bland personality compared with his home-run-hitting counterpart. Two qualities stood out about Leonard: his free and easy smile that Wendell Smith described as revealing "a set of teeth that would take a dentist's breath away"[22] and his introspectiveness that masked an intense competitiveness and a fertile mind absorbing everything around him. Leonard was as reliable as Gibson and Paige were unreliable.

Leonard emerged as the Grays' quiet, dependable star. Defensively, he had developed into the best first baseman in the league. He played far and deep off the first-base bag, enabling him to catch sharp grounders that otherwise would have gone into right field for base hits. Although he occasionally experienced trouble with underhand tosses to Grays pitchers covering first base, Leonard's defensive lapses were overshadowed by his fielding gems. H. G. Salsinger of the *Detroit News* raved in 1941 about "a play that we have never seen matched by an American League first baseman. He ran almost to the extreme end of the bullpen in right-field foul territory and caught a fly ball over his shoulder."[23] After watching Leonard play first base at the 1939 East-West All-Star Game, Frankie Mastro of the *Chicago Tribune* gushed: "Buck Leonard is the greatest first baseman I have ever seen on any club, black or white."[24]

Offensively, Leonard stood out as one of the most feared hitters in the Negro National League. A dead fastball hitter, Leonard regularly rapped line drives up and over Griffith Stadium's thirty-foot-high right-field wall. He also mastered curveballs, especially after Posey had taught him to open his stance against left-handed pitchers. If Leonard had any weaknesses as a hitter, it was the change-up. Every pitcher knew this. Unfortunately for them, so did Leonard. At the 1941 East-West Game, he knocked Ted "Double Duty" Radcliffe's change-up 368 feet into Comiskey Park's right-field bleachers. The fans accused Radcliffe of serving up a fat pitch. Posey wrote: "After the game 'Double Duty' came all the way to the Braddock Hotel on 126th street to tell this writer that Leonard was a 'sucker' for a slow ball, and as long as he lived 'Double Duty' would not throw Leonard another fastball."[25]

Some opposing pitchers preferred to pitch to Gibson instead of Leonard. "The toughest one for me to get out was Buck Leonard," longtime Kansas City Monarchs pitcher Chet Brewer told John Holway. "I don't ever remember pitching a game against Buck he didn't get two hits off me. I could get Josh Gibson out, but by golly, that Buck Leonard hit me like he owned me."[26] Having grown up thirty-eight miles from Rocky Mount in Greenville, North Carolina, New York Cubans ace Dave Barnhill had been trying to throw his blazing fastball by Leonard since Barnhill's days as a member of the rival Wilson (North Carolina) Braves. "You could put a fastball in a 30-30 rifle, and you couldn't shoot it by him. That's right," Barnhill told John Holway. "Later on Josh was the toughest hitter I ever faced. But you could strike Josh out; you might throw a fastball by him. But not Buck."[27]

Everybody began noticing the quiet star in 1940 and 1941, when Leonard (along with pitcher-outfielder Ray Brown) led the Gibson-less Grays to two straight Negro National League titles. Moving into Gibson's cleanup spot, Leonard turned into the league's leading offensive threat. During mid-August 1940, Leonard was second in the Negro National League with a .376 average in twenty-three league games and unparalleled as a power hitter.[28] During the 1940 East-West Game, he walked twice, singled three times, and narrowly missed a fourth hit in his final at-bat. "Buck Leonard proved his right to be heralded as the greatest first-baseman in sepia baseball," the *Washington Tribune* wrote.[29] In selecting his 1941 year-end All American Team, Posey described Leonard as "the most valuable player in Negro baseball."[30]

From 1937 to 1941, Leonard provided the backbone for the Grays' success. He—not Gibson or Paige—was responsible for bringing championship black baseball to Washington. Wendell Smith suggested Leonard as the logical replacement if Vic Harris ever stepped down as manager:

> When Josh Gibson was playing with the Grays, the assumption was that "as Gibson goes, so goes the Grays." But now that Josh has been away for two years, and the Grays have continued to win pennants, diamond critics discovered that the man behind the Grays' gun wasn't Gibson after all, but Leonard, the likeable slugger from

North Carolina. Like Paige, he is worth a million bucks to a major league club.[31]

In 1939, the *Pittsburgh Courier* juxtaposed two large photos of the left-handed-hitting Leonard and the right-handed-hitting Gibson above the headline: "If the Majors Opened the Doors to Sepia Players, These 2 Stars Could Make the Grade!"[32]

Lacy made the case for Leonard with Griffith, the owner with the most frequent opportunity to see Leonard play and with the team most in need of an All-Star first baseman. Lacy was brutally honest in comparing Leonard with Senators first baseman Zeke Bonura, who hit .273 with three home runs in 1940 and whose team finished second to last:

> [Griffith] is probably telling the truth when he says that we have got to go a long way in organizing our own game before we can hope to crash the gates of major league baseball as players. But he cannot deny that we don't have to go far to see the difference between his own first baseman, whom nobody wants judging from the fact that waivers have been obtained on him from two leagues in as many seasons, and a little colored boy who holds down the initial sack on alternate Sunday [sic], when the Senators are not at home. . . .
>
> Most of us are in accord that Griff "is a good guy." My answer to that is "he oughta be." And if he really is, I say, he should be able to realize that right here in Washington, under his very nose, is a situation that presents an unusual comparison between a white player, getting in the neighborhood of $10,000 a year, and a colored player whom he could hire for $400 a month.[33]

Lacy treated Griffith with kid gloves in 1940 and 1941 because the strident sportswriter still thought that the Senators would be the first team to sign a black player. He believed Griffith during their 1937 interview that the "time was not far off" for integration. He agreed with Griffith's argument about building up the Negro Leagues. Thus, he gave the Senators owner deference and respect. So did other black Washingtonians. Dr. Claude Carmichael, "the city's unofficial historian on colored baseball," wrote in 1938: "Mr. Griffith has, so as I know, been fair-minded, or rather liberal in so far as treatment of our group is concerned, especially the fans who attend games in his stadium."[34] In April 1939, Lacy rejected the idea of picketing and boycotting Griffith's ballpark because of his refusal to hire black players. "It appears that there is a better chance to win the fight here than in any place in the country," Lacy wrote. "Pickets at Griffith Stadium, therefore, would be misplaced, to my way of thinking."[35]

During the early 1940s, Griffith seemed increasingly amenable to change. In 1942, Griffith secretly lobbied his good friend and ardent Senators fan, President Franklin Delano Roosevelt, to keep baseball going during the war. In January 1942, Judge Landis had written Roosevelt inquiring about the status of the upcoming season. A rabid anti–New Dealer, Judge Landis despised Roosevelt. The enmity was mutual. "Landis," Griffith told sportswriter Shirley Povich, "wasn't much more welcome at the White House than the Japanese ambassador."[36]

Griffith, however, was one of President Roosevelt's favorite people. Roosevelt had been coming to Griffith Stadium since his days as the assistant secretary of the navy. Griffith's contact with Roosevelt increased during his multiple presidential terms. Before every season, Griffith would visit the White House to present Roosevelt with two season passes. FDR delighted in talking baseball with the Old Fox, phoning Griffith for advice in order to bet on games with aides and cabinet members. The president's crippling bout with polio had made it increasingly difficult for him to attend games (despite a special ramp installed at the ballpark that allowed Roosevelt to reach his box). On Opening Day in 1941, President Roosevelt stood up in Griffith Stadium's presidential box by clutching the arm of a military aide. As Griffith looked on just behind them, Roosevelt tossed out the first ball. Declining health and preoccupation with the war prevented Roosevelt from coming back again. But he heeded Griffith's advice about saving wartime baseball.

Griffith took credit for Roosevelt's initial "Green Light letter," which allowed professional baseball to continue during World War II.

Although Roosevelt refused to exempt baseball players from war-time service, he concluded that professional baseball should continue because it was good for American morale. "And, incidentally," Roosevelt's letter said, "I hope that night baseball can be extended because it gives an excellent opportunity to the day shift to see a game."[37]

Roosevelt's plug for night baseball revealed the depth of Griffith's influence. In 1941, Griffith spent $230,000 on a 1,140,000-watt lighting system, the first of its kind in the American League. Griffith's capital outlay—aided by a $125,000 interest-free loan from the league—was nonetheless remarkable considering that in 1935 he had lambasted Larry MacPhail's introduction of night baseball with the Cincinnati Reds.[38] Griffith changed his tune when he realized that night baseball got the Reds out of debt in two years and the Brooklyn Dodgers in three years.[39] In 1941, the Senators played the league-maximum seven night games. Before the 1942 season, Griffith persuaded the other American League owners to allow him to play fourteen night games. Landis, however, opposed night baseball and blocked the measure. After the Green Light letter, Landis backed down and Washington was allowed to play twenty-one night games in 1942, seven more than the new league maximum.

Griffith's lights had paid for themselves after two years of increased attendance.[40] More night games meant more money for Griffith. In March 1943, Griffith wrote Stephen Early, secretary to the president, that night baseball "would be in the best interest of war workers in Washington. . . ."[41] In July, Judge Landis decreed that Griffith's team could play an unlimited number of night games because "[w]artime conditions of employment in Washington make it worthwhile."[42]

Roosevelt's Green Light letter and his support of night baseball also applied to the Negro Leagues. In his *Pittsburgh Courier* column, Posey crowed about the president's pronouncement.[43] Before the 1942 season, Roosevelt had baseball magnates, such as Landis, Griffith, and Posey, at the federal government's mercy. The president could have premised the playing of the 1942 major league season on the immediate integration of professional baseball. Integration would have helped major league teams fill out their depleted rosters with

Negro Leaguers who were physically unable to serve in the military, such as Leonard and Gibson. There could have been dozens of wartime Jackie Robinsons.

Twenty-twenty hindsight belied the racial attitudes emanating from the White House. A presidential-led movement to integrate baseball was incompatible with Roosevelt's (and his wife's) personal philosophy and his New Deal agenda. As Dr. Robert Weaver, who had grown up in Washington, D.C., worked on the New Deal, and served in Roosevelt's informal black cabinet, explained:

> In the first place, he had no real background in this area. Secondly, he had been down in Warm Springs, Georgia, he had respected the southern pattern. Mrs. Roosevelt talked about darkies, Mrs. Roosevelt was anti-Semitic in the beginning, as I told her great-granddaughter, but she changed rapidly. His program was never designed like [Lyndon] Johnson's program, to deal with racial issues. His program was designed to deal with broad, economic, social issues. And because it was concerned with the man further down it did affect the Negro, but the Negro was not affected as a Negro, he was affected as part of the population.[44]

Roosevelt's papers revealed a 1943 letter from a baseball fan in Toledo, Ohio, lobbying for an All-Star Game between black and white teams in support of "the day when Negro baseball players will be permitted to play besides the White man in the major leagues." Roosevelt's White House staff ignored the letter.[45] Yet even without President Roosevelt's assistance, World War II moved major league baseball closer to integration.

Not only was Griffith unwilling to integrate his team in 1940 and 1941, he also hurt the Grays' chances of succeeding at Griffith Stadium by refusing to allow them to play white semipro teams. For more than twenty years, he barred white and black teams from playing each other in his ballpark. His ban arose from an incident in the early 1920s between the black professional Brooklyn Royal Giants and an All-Star team of white major and minor league players formed by Senators first baseman Joe Judge and the black professional Brooklyn Royal Giants.[46] It was the final game of the four-game series (which the teams split two apiece). After a close play at first base, Senators outfielder Frank Brower punched a black umpire in the face. The police escorted Brower out of the ballpark. A near-riot ensued.[47]

Based on the Frank Brower incident, Griffith concluded that interracial contests at Griffith Stadium stirred up violent, pent-up emotions. His opinion was not completely unfounded. An on-field dispute during a July 1940 game between the Grays and the white semipro Brooklyn Bushwicks at Dexter Park triggered a hail of bottles from the stands.[48] In a June 1941 rematch between the two teams, Grays third baseman Jud "Boojum" Wilson reacted to a bad call by pushing a white umpire and accusing the Bushwicks' first baseman of taking a swing at him.[49]

The violence wasn't limited to baseball. In late July 1942, an interracial "Battle of Music" between Louis Armstrong's band and Charlie Barnett's band before twenty thousand fans at Griffith Stadium turned into a battle of the bottle throwers that led to thirteen arrests. Just as Armstrong's band had begun to play, a large group of fans swarmed onto the field, drawing the ire (in the form of glass bottles) of customers who had purchased box seats.[50]

But in general, black and white baseball teams regularly competed against each other without incident. The Grays, like many Negro League teams, often traveled to small towns to play weekday games against white semipro teams. Leonard recalled that the Grays sometimes stopped on their way from Pittsburgh to Washington to play semipro clubs in towns such as Rockville, Maryland.[51] For the Grays and other Negro League teams without their own home ballparks, interracial contests helped black teams survive.

Even if the Grays had hired a black publicity agent, even if Gibson had been with the team for most of 1940 and 1941, and even if Griffith had allowed them to play white semipro teams in his ballpark, the Grays still would not have drawn well in Washington. Their poor attendance at Griffith Stadium before 1940 was further proof of it. During a 1939 Grays–Philadelphia Stars doubleheader, Gibson conquered Griffith Stadium's faraway fences by launching three home runs into the left-field bleachers. He nearly hit a fourth homer that day, but the ball hit a metal railing in front of the bleachers and fell back onto the field for a triple. Yet only two thousand fans turned out for his spectacular performance.[52]

In 1940 and 1941, as in 1939, black Washingtonians were still stuck on the Senators. The black elite, in particular, eschewed Grays games in favor of the Senators' games. *Washington Tribune* columnist Joe Sewall observed in 1940 that members of the city's black upper crust "are seen regularly cooped up in the pavilion of Griff's stadium on the occasions when the Senators are playing here. . . . Looking through the stands during the last appearances made here by the Grays, such a thing as a doctor, lawyer, teacher or student was quite a rarity."[53] The black elite perceived the Negro Leagues as second-rate, and the Grays' white publicity agent lacked the requisite social contacts to change their minds. Sewall appealed to the black intelligentsia, the leaders of the movement to desegregate Washington, in the language of black protest: "Such an omission on the part of Washington's upper strata is obviously inconsistent and makes most of our efforts to improve race conditions here open to attack from the great mass of laymen who make up the strength of any worthwhile movement."[54]

Lacy's coverage of the Grays often reinforced the black elite's notions of inferiority about black baseball. In 1940 and 1941, he adopted Griffith's argument that the only way to integrate baseball was to improve the professionalism of the Negro Leagues. Thus, Lacy assumed the role of watchdog over black baseball—often at the Grays' expense. In a column about the Grays' inaugural game in Washington against the New York Cubans, he characterized the play of both teams as "decidedly amateurish in spots," described three errors on one play as "inexcusable," criticized the players for not catching four foul pop-ups, and chastised them for "between innings loafing."[55] When Gibson broke his 1941 contract with the Grays, Lacy excoriated Gibson for "throw[ing] those of us who are interested in the fight back about five years in the campaign to get colored performers into big-league baseball."[56] In a May 1941 column, he indicted all of Negro League baseball: the players who ignored their contracts, the teams who welcomed them back, the leagues that failed to inform the press and public, and the owners who raided each others' rosters. Lacy concluded: "Perhaps there is something to the contention that we are keeping ourselves down."[57]

Lacy's ally in the integration crusade, the *Pittsburgh Courier's* Wendell Smith, blamed black fans. In 1938, Smith encouraged black fans to boycott major league games in favor of Negro League contests. "Major league baseball does not want us. It never has," Smith wrote. "Still, we continue to help support this institution that places a bold 'Not Welcome' sign over its thriving portal and refuse to patronize the very place that has shown that it is more than welcome to have us. We black folks are a strange tribe!"[58]

In 1941, the Senators and their major league counterparts cast a long shadow over the Gibson-less Grays and their two-straight NNL titles. Despite, and perhaps because of, the absence of black players, 1941 was one of the most memorable seasons in major league history, in which Ted Williams hit .406 and Joe DiMaggio hit safely in fifty-six consecutive games. Indeed, the Griffith Stadium faithful saw DiMaggio break George Sisler's modern record of forty-one games on a day when someone stole Joltin' Joe's lucky bat.[59] At season's end, the Senators' Cecil Travis finished two points ahead of DiMaggio for second place in the AL batting race with a .359 average and a league-leading 218 hits. The Senators finished tied for next to last in the American League.

In another major Griffith Stadium event in 1941, Joe Louis defended his heavyweight championship against a white challenger, Buddy Baer. Nearly twenty-four thousand people paid $105,000 to attend the fight; about 70 percent of the fans were black. Blacks all across America listened to the fight on the radio, cheering on Louis and their race. "If Louis lost, we were back in slavery and beyond help," Maya Angelou wrote in her memoir *I Know Why the Caged Bird Sings*, describing her emotions as a little girl growing up in Arkansas listening to the Louis–Primo Carnera fight. "It would all be true, the accusations that we were lower types of human beings."[60]

The Louis–Buddy Baer fight was marred by controversy. Baer knocked Louis through the ropes early in the fight, then Louis hit

Baer after the bell in the sixth round. Baer was disqualified when he refused to come out for the bell in the seventh. Art Carter of the *Afro-American* advised Louis never to fight in Washington again. "The town is still overburdened with too much of the Southern element," Carter wrote. "The below-the-Mason-Dixon-line whites, even the supposed fair-minded sports scribes, can't stand to see a colored champion beating a white challenger, and to put Louis in Washington again would only jeopardize Joe's prestige."[61]

During the early 1940s, desegregation in the nation's capital occurred in fits and starts. A year before the Louis fight, Kid Cocoa won a unanimous ten-round decision over Wild Bill McDowell at Griffith Stadium in the city's first interracial professional boxing match.[62] In February 1940, Howard University professors and former organizers of the New Negro Alliance picketed the world premiere of the movie *Abe Lincoln in Illinois* at Washington's all-white RKO-Keith theater. Eleanor Roosevelt, one of many prominent government officials who crossed the picket line, commented after the movie: "I think it is particularly tragic that the people whom Lincoln freed should not be allowed to see the show about him."[63] In July 1941, the Department of Interior ordered Washington's East Potomac Park Golf Course opened to all races. Yet a black golfer returned to his car only to find that someone had poured sand in his gas tank and sugar and coffee in his carburetor and oil pump.[64] That same year, newly opened Uline Arena denied admission to more than one hundred blacks who wanted to see the Ice Capades.[65]

The words of Griffith Stadium's public-address announcer at a 1941 football game between the Washington Redskins and the Philadelphia Eagles changed everything. In the middle of the second quarter, he began paging generals, lieutenants, and cabinet secretaries. One by one, government officials made their way out of the stadium. It was December 7. The Japanese had attacked Pearl Harbor.

World War II triggered the events that ultimately turned things around for the Grays in Washington. The war spared many of the players on their aging roster from military service, increased the Grays' Washington fan base, and gave their new fans better jobs and with them disposable income to spend on black baseball. It gradually transformed Washington, D.C., and the Grays into black baseball's biggest financial success story.

The Grays lost fewer players to the war than other NNL teams did. The draft called thirteen members of the Philadelphia Stars and twelve members of the Newark Eagles but only six members of the Grays.[66] Leonard, thirty-five, with a bad back, and Gibson, thirty-two, with aching knees, both received 4-F classifications excluding them from military service.[67] Whereas the Eagles eventually parted with young stars, such as Larry Doby, Monte Irvin, Leon Day, and Max Manning, the Grays retained an aging nucleus consisting of Leonard and Gibson, as well as third baseman Jud "Boojum" Wilson, outfielders Cool Papa Bell and Jerry Benjamin, shortstop Sam Bankhead, and pitchers Ray Brown and Roy Partlow.

The Senators, by contrast, were one of the major league teams hit hardest by the war. Their two best players, shortstop Cecil Travis and right fielder Buddy Lewis, had been drafted before Pearl Harbor. Although Griffith persuaded General Lewis B. Hershey to grant them deferments to play out the 1941 season, Travis and Lewis reported for active duty in 1942.[68] The following season, the Senators lost outfielder Bruce Campbell, as well as starting pitchers Walt Masterson and Sid Hudson.[69] Elsewhere in 1943, American League stars Joe DiMaggio and Ted Williams joined Bob Feller and Hank Greenberg in the military. Even heavyweight champion Joe Louis enlisted. With the best major leaguers and Louis out of action, the Grays were the best show in town.

The war breathed new life into Washington's economy and opened thousands of jobs to blacks and women. It forced the federal government to raise the glass ceiling and to hire blacks in clerical positions traditionally reserved for white males. Before Roosevelt's 1941 Executive Order 8802 outlawing racial discrimination in defense work, blacks represented 8 percent of federal employees, 90 percent of them in "sub-clerical" jobs. By November 1942, blacks made up 17 percent of government employees, about half of them in clerical and professional occupations.[70] Hiring African Americans as clerical workers enlarged Washington's black middle class and gave it more money to spend on Grays games.

The burgeoning federal job market brought the Great Migration to Washington and bolstered the Grays' fan base. From 1940 to 1950, Washington's black population increased from 187,255 to 280,803.[71] This was not the same type of mass migration that compelled Leonard to leave Rocky Mount after he had been laid off by the railroad at the height of the Depression. The "depression migration" of the 1930s had given way to a "boom migration" during the 1940s.[72] Contrary to prevailing stereotypes, many black migrants of the 1930s and 1940s were not uneducated, rural farmers. They came from larger towns and cities, brought experience in skilled or semiskilled jobs, and possessed a high rate of literacy.[73] Many of these boom migrants came from Virginia and the Carolinas.[74]

Some of them hailed from Rocky Mount. A. C. Braxton, who had grown up climbing the trees behind Rocky Mount's ballpark to watch Leonard play baseball, came to Washington in June 1941. By October, Braxton had found a job with the Social Security Administration, commuting five and a half days a week from Washington to Baltimore. Another Rocky Mount native, Eddie Dozier, had arrived in Washington in 1937, found a job in 1941 with the Department of Defense, and worked for the government for thirty-two years.

For recent migrants such as Braxton and Dozier, Grays games at Griffith Stadium reunited them with friends whom they had grown up with in the South but who lived in different parts of the city. The Grays billed an August 5, 1940, Sunday doubleheader against the Cuban Stars as "North Carolina Day: Featuring 'Buck' Leonard."[75] During the war years, Braxton and Dozier would walk to the ballpark together from Fifteenth and T Streets where Braxton lived.[76] Lena Cox, Leonard's younger sister, who had moved to Washington in the early to mid-1930s, recalled attending Grays games with many former Rocky Mount residents who lived in Washington and even nearby Baltimore. "You would see everybody from home when you went to the ball game," she said.[77]

The war also radicalized the efforts of those fighting for racial equality. Blacks were outraged about fighting the Nazis in segregated units and about the American Red Cross maintaining separate blood banks according to skin color. The *Pittsburgh Courier*'s "Double Victory" campaign captured the feelings of protest. The nation's largest African-American newspaper called for a "victory over our enemies at home and victory over our enemies on the battlefields abroad."[78]

A. Philip Randolph, the president of the Brotherhood of Sleeping Car Porters, fought for the victory at home. Randolph planned a 10,000-person march on Washington in July 1941 to protest discrimination in defense-related employment. Ten days before a proposed march that had grown to 100,000 people, Randolph called off his rally in exchange for President Roosevelt's signing of Executive Order 8802. Although Roosevelt's order failed to desegregate the armed forces or specific federal agencies, it outlawed racial discrimination in defense work and created the Fair Employment Practices Committee (FEPC) to address grievances.

Lacy seized on the hypocritical prospect of fighting German white supremacy while maintaining an all-white major league baseball team and a segregated ballpark in the nation's capital. In 1940, Lacy periodically wrote a column in the *Afro-American* titled, "Comrades Tomorrow . . . Why Not Today?" Below the headline, Lacy ran large head shots of Washington Senators players next to those of Negro Leaguers. For example, a June 15, 1940, column sandwiched an image of Newark Eagles ace Leon Day between those of Senators pitcher Dutch Leonard and Senators catcher Rick Ferrell. Lacy wrote: "The battlefields' bullets draw no racial lines; they erase skin pigmentation and spill the same color of blood from white and black alike. . . . The lighter and darker will be found side by side then, why not now?"[79]

103

Lacy's campaign, however, stalled in 1941 because of personal problems with his bosses at the *Afro*. They objected to his promoting and managing a black professional basketball team, the Washington Bruins, while serving as the sports editor of the paper's Washington edition. The owner of the *Afro-American* newspaper chain, Dr. Carl Murphy, ultimately asked Lacy to choose between the newspaper and the basketball team. Lacy—citing commitments to players, opposing teams, and the owner of Turner's Arena where the team played—chose the team. Murphy said that Lacy could return to the newspaper at the end of Lacy's commitment to the team, but only in the *Afro*'s news department in Baltimore.[80]

Lacy's return to the *Afro* after the basketball season proved to be short-lived. Although he occasionally wrote about sports in 1941, he primarily worked in the news department under the direction of one of Murphy's daughters, Elizabeth (Bettye) Phillips Moss. Lacy bristled at some of Moss's story assignments. It didn't take long for him to reach his breaking point. "I was driving on Orleans Street on an assignment from Bettye that made no sense whatsoever to me," he wrote. "I just swung the damn car, made a U-turn, and the next time anyone from the paper heard from me, I was in Chicago."[81]

Before arriving in Chicago, Lacy wrote copy for a Cincinnati radio station, WJLW. In Chicago, he briefly worked for a white daily newspaper, the *Chicago Sun*, for the first and only time in his career. He eventually landed a job as the assistant national editor of the *Chicago Defender*, one of the nation's largest black newspapers, where he worked in 1942 and 1943. During those two seasons, the Grays reached the height of their popularity in Washington while their biggest critic was in exile.

In Lacy's absence, the Grays made amends with the local black press by hiring a black publicity agent, Art Carter. Carter's role in the Grays' success in Washington, D.C., has been overlooked by the traditional histories of the Negro Leagues. As the team's public relations arm and business manager in Washington, he helped the Grays make the transition from Pittsburgh's team to Washington's team. His papers, which are in the manuscript division at Howard University's Moorland-Spingarn Research Center, document his promotional efforts and provide insights into the financial dealings of the Grays in Washington.

Arthur Mantel Carter grew up in a poor neighborhood in Southwest Washington and graduated from the newly opened Cardozo Business High School in 1929.[82] He had met Lacy while playing for the Pleasant Plains basketball team (Lacy was the coach of an opposing team) and soon developed into the first of Lacy's many journal-istic protégés.[83] From 1932 to 1934, he wrote for the *Tribune* sports sec-tion while playing basketball at Howard University.[84] In 1935, Carter joined Lacy's *Tribune* sports staff full-time as a college and high school sports reporter.

Two years later, Carter joined the rival *Afro-American*, where he began writing about Negro League baseball and authoring his "From the Bench" sports column. He soon became the chain's national sports editor in charge of all of its editions. In 1939, Lacy joined his former protégé and close friend as the sports editor of the *Afro's* Washington edition. Lacy promoted the Washington Bruins basket-ball team along with Carter and future *Afro* sportswriter and Grays radio play-by-play man Harold "Hal" Jackson.[85] Only Lacy—perhaps because of his boastful comments in the white *Washington Daily News* about the team's profits—drew the *Afro* management's wrath.[86] Carter kept his job at the *Afro*.

Carter brought his lifelong knowledge of black Washington, his promotional experience with the Bruins, and his status as the *Afro* sports editor to his new part-time job as the Grays' D.C. public rela-tions director. The secret to his success was his aggressive courtship of the black elite. He augmented the Grays' upper-class black fan base by chartering an informal yet exclusive club of fans to whom he gave season passes. Giving out season passes to the "Black 400" made perfect business sense—many of them brought their friends to the games. William B. West, Howard University's dean of men, wrote a glowing letter to Carter thanking him for his free pass for the 1945 season. "To date through your kindness I have not missed a single game and have enjoyed them immensely," West wrote Carter in August 1945. "Further, several of my friends because of my enthusi-asm . . . have fallen into the habit of attending the games and are like myself ardent fans of our Homestead team."[87] West and his friends turned Grays games into well-dressed affairs like Howard-Lincoln football games, where men wore fedoras, jackets, and ties and ladies wore hats and sundresses.

Carter handed out free passes to Howard faculty, wealthy busi-nessmen, prominent black federal employees, and religious leaders.

His original list of sixty-three people included E. B. Henderson, the director of physical education for the city's black public schools; undertaker John T. Rhines; Lemuel Foster, a race relations analyst for the U.S. Army; Dr. Arthur P. Davis, an English professor at Howard University; Dr. Claude Carmichael, the prominent physician and black baseball historian; and, of course, Elder Solomon Lightfoot Michaux.[88]

The most important recipients of Carter's free passes were the black ministers, including Elder Michaux. Michaux probably did not give sermons about the Grays as Kansas City preachers did about the Monarchs, but his followers headed to the ballpark for Sunday doubleheaders after spending their mornings at their place of worship.[89] "People would leave the church across Georgia Avenue and come right to the ballpark," Grays pitcher Wilmer Fields recalled.[90]

Giving free passes to the preachers permitted their followers to attend Grays games on Sunday afternoons. Carter most likely adopted the practice of giving the clergy free season passes from the Senators. "We gave passes to the preachers for the simple reason that Sunday baseball was never legalized in Washington," Calvin Griffith told Jon Kerr. "Mr. Griffith had the foresight to do it and also to sit down with the different denominations and work out hours so they wouldn't interfere with their services. Then we had a chance."[91] In 1945, Carter divided up his free-pass list according to the various denominations: Baptists (most of the free passes went to the Baptists), Congregationalists, Disciples, Episcopalians, Lutherans, African Methodist Episcopals, African Methodist Episcopal Zionists, Christian Methodist Episcopals, Methodists, Presbyterians, Seventh-Day Adventists, and Catholics.[92]

Carter possessed the perfect temperament to be the Grays' public relations man. In print, he fervently supported black baseball. In person, he was affable and charming. His rapid rise at the *Afro* indicated that he had mastered the political skills necessary to navigate a complex chain of command. As the Grays' Washington promoter, Carter answered to the teams' owners, Cum Posey and Rufus "Sonnyman" Jackson, traveling secretary/business manager Seward "See"

Posey, Pittsburgh public relations director John L. Clark, manager Vic Harris, and the Grays' players.[93]

Carter's most important relationship was with Clark Griffith and his adopted son, Calvin. Carter had known the elder Griffith for several years. In 1937, the Senators' owner had given a season press pass to Carter, who was working for the *Washington Tribune*. The following year, Carter, now the *Afro's* sports editor, asked Griffith for another press credential.[94]

As the Grays' promoter at Griffith Stadium, Carter dealt primarily with Griffith's heir apparent, Calvin. In 1942, Clark promoted Calvin from overseeing the Senators' minor league team in Charlotte to running the concessions operations at Griffith Stadium, an important job considering that the Griffiths made most of their money off concessions. Clark also named Calvin the team's vice president so that Calvin could attend major league meetings. Another of Calvin's responsibilities was taking care of the stadium during Grays games. "We used to have wrestling matches, Negro League baseball, and all of these things," Calvin told Jon Kerr. "Someone had to stay around to supervise these things, and I was the low man on the totem pole."[95]

Calvin's equating Negro League baseball with professional wrestling would have strained his relations with Carter, who marketed Grays games as classy affairs tailor-made for an upper-class clientele. Their divergent perspectives about the Grays eventually led to conflict. Bill Scott, the *Afro* photographer in Washington and a close friend of Carter's, related a story that Carter had told him:

> "Scott," he said, "I don't know whether I should get angry at Calvin or not." I said, "What'd he say, Art?" He said that Calvin told him that all the people coming out here on Sundays, they were "nigger rich." Art said he wanted to fight, see. But what the hell? That's the way things were.[96]

Scott laughed as he told the story. When it came to dealing with Calvin, however, Carter put the Grays' interests ahead of his personal pride.

Carter and Grays owner Cum Posey depended on the Griffiths to give the Grays the first crack at the open Sunday dates when the Senators were out of town. Posey went to great lengths to compliment Clark Griffith in his *Pittsburgh Courier* column.[97] In April 1942, Posey wrote: "Clark Griffith, owner of the Washington Senators is in a class with the late [Pirates owner] Barney Dreyfuss of Pittsburgh in his friendliness to N.O.B. [Negro Organized Baseball]. Mr. Griffith allowed the Grays to use Griffith Stadium at Washington to play [sic] Newark Eagles on April 19. By doing so he allowed two Negro clubs to play in his home park before the Senators."[98]

For Griffith, renting his ballpark to the Grays was not an act of altruism. The Senators' owner profited handsomely from the relationship, hiring out the Senators' ticket takers and ushers, reaping all the profits from concessions, and taking 20 percent of the gross gate receipts. For example, the April 19, 1942, exhibition game between the Grays and Eagles drew 4,714 fans. With tickets selling for seventy-five cents and fifty cents, the game grossed $3,176.66. The Senators received 20 percent of the gross profits, or $635.33, for stadium rental, plus $62.50 in expenses for ticket sales, ushers, and cleanup. After subtracting additional expenses and 10 percent of the net profits for promotion, each team that played netted $1,059.84. Thus, the Grays took home $1,000, and Griffith nabbed nearly $700 merely for lending them his ballpark.[99] The relationship, though exploitative, was symbiotic. The larger the crowds at Grays games, the better Griffith and the Grays fared.

Cum Posey's wife, Ethel (left), and two daughters, Ann and Mary (middle and right), sit in the front row of the owner's box at Griffith Stadium. The woman in the third row with the flower hat is Ada Harris, wife of Grays manager Vic Harris. Blacks dressed up to go to Grays games at Griffith Stadium. (ROBERT H. McNEILL)

The Grays stand in front of Griffith Stadium's center-field wall, which juts inward at a 90-degree angle around five row houses and "the Tree." Cool Papa Bell (standing second from left), Josh Gibson (standing far right), and Jud "Boojum" Wilson (kneeling far left) are among those pictured. (ART CARTER PAPERS, MOORLAND-SPINGARN RESEARCH CENTER, HOWARD UNIVERSITY)

Buck Leonard learned how to play first base from the best black first baseman of the 1920s, Ben Taylor. Leonard played far off the first-base bag and took away a lot of would-be base hits. (ROBERT H. McNEILL)

The 1944 Grays pose in the Griffith Stadium outfield. Buck Leonard (standing third from right), Cool Papa Bell (standing fifth from right), pitcher Ray Brown (standing third from left), and Sam Bankhead (kneeling fourth from left) are among those pictured. (Art Carter Papers, Moorland-Spingarn Research Center, Howard University)

The managers and umpires confer before a Grays game at Griffith Stadium. The grandstand is almost full of well-dressed black Washingtonians. (Art Carter Papers, Moorland-Spingarn Research Center, Howard University)

Cecil Travis, Dizzy Dean, and Satchel Paige chat before one of two exhibition games during the 1942 season, the second drawing twenty-two thousand at Griffith Stadium. Pitching for the Grays, Paige defeated Dean's All-Stars, 8–1, and struck out Travis, formerly of the Senators and on leave from military service, much to the delight of black fans sitting in the right-field pavilion. (NATIONAL BASEBALL HALL OF FAME LIBRARY)

FIVE

SATCHEL PAIGE
SAVES THE GRAYS

The Grays' letterhead for 1942 described the team as "black baseball's biggest moneymaker."[1] Yet the 1942 season started out like the first two in Washington. In April and early May, the Grays attracted larger crowds when they were in other cities, such as New Orleans (twelve thousand) and Newark (eighteen thousand).[2] Their attendance at Griffith Stadium averaged only four thousand to five thousand a game.[3] The city's black elite stayed away. "Where were our hordes of civic-minded locals who spend most of their moments ranting high sounding words about race solidarity from any platform that may be available?" the *Washington Tribune's* Joe Sewall wondered after only 4,653 attended a May 21 Grays–Elite Giants doubleheader at Griffith Stadium. "The so-called intelligentsia or literati, many of whom are devout baseball fans whenever the pathetic Washington Senators are in town, were missing from the scene."[4]

The Grays moved out of the shadow of the Senators in late May 1942 because of three factors: the hiring of Carter as the Grays' D.C. public relations man, Griffith's lifting his ban on interracial exhibition games, and, most important, several Griffith Stadium appearances by Satchel Paige.

Satchel saved the Grays. With Joe Louis and most of major league baseball's biggest stars serving their country and the Babe in retirement for the past seven years, the lanky black pitcher emerged during the summer of 1942 as the biggest attraction in sports. He was the Babe Ruth of black baseball. Although many Negro League pitchers could beat him on any given day, Paige possessed the rare combination of superior skill and showmanship. In 1941, he had developed a national following because of magazine profiles and the twenty thousand fans he seemed to draw in every major league ballpark. The Kansas City Monarchs frequently lent Paige to other Negro League teams in need. "Satchel was a lot of franchises," his teammate, first baseman, and friend, Buck O'Neil, told John Holway. "If Memphis needed to make a payroll, Satchel would pitch three innings for them. Babe Ruth made the payroll for a lot of clubs, too."[5]

In Washington, Paige teamed up with the Grays for a May 31 exhibition against a white team led by retired major league pitcher Dizzy Dean. Every bit as colorful as Paige, Dean was once the finest pitcher in the major leagues. Dean, however, had not been the same since his last Griffith Stadium appearance five years earlier. At the 1937 All-Star Game in Washington, Earl Averill's line drive struck Dean, breaking his left big toe. The story goes that Dean returned from the injury too soon, altered his pitching mechanics to compensate for his broken toe, and developed a sore arm.[6] He retired in 1941 to become a broadcaster.

In May 1942, Dean briefly came out of retirement to play wartime exhibitions with a white team consisting of recently drafted major and minor leaguers. Dean had been playing exhibition games against black professional teams for many years and greatly admired the abilities of Paige and Josh Gibson.[7] During a May 24 matchup at Chicago's Wrigley Field, Paige and the Monarchs defeated Dean's All-Stars, 3–1, before a crowd of 29,775.[8] A week later, the Paige-Dean show came to Griffith Stadium, this time with Paige pitching for the Grays.[9]

The Paige-Dean exhibition at Griffith Stadium elicited quite a furor. May 31, 1942, was an unusually warm Sunday afternoon. About ten thousand people stood in sweltering heat in the ballpark's large promenade clamoring for tickets. The large crowd, consisting of many blacks but also many whites, spilled off the promenade and onto Seventh Street.

Although the ticket windows opened at 11:00 A.M., a last-minute surge surprised Griffith's ticket sellers. Temperatures rose, and three thousand people were still waiting for tickets as the game began at 2:00 P.M. "Scalpers," according to the *Afro*, "were getting $3.30 [nearly three times face value] for 'choice' grandstand seats."[10] The black fans had bought up all the tickets in the right-field pavilion where they usually sat for Senators games. Only bleacher seats remained. Tempers flared. Windows broke. Griffith, already edgy about a game between black and white teams at his ballpark, sounded a riot call for additional police protection. The Old Fox, however, had overreacted. As the *Post* observed:

> Although there were so many frenzied calls for additional police help from both official and unofficial sources that some auxiliaries were routed from their homes, there was little disorder. Three windows were broken on the ground floor of the clubhouse. One man, colored, was arrested for creating a disturbance and another man, white, suffered a heart attack but recovered before leaving the stadium.[11]

The last of the twenty-two thousand fans on hand—which the *Post* described as "the largest non-major league crowd in Griffith Stadium history"—did not enter the ballpark until the fourth inning.[12] By that time, the game was effectively over.

Dean's Griffith Stadium return was less than triumphant. He wore his old St. Louis Cardinals uniform but didn't pitch much like a major leaguer. Although the previous week in Chicago he had retired the Monarchs in order in his lone inning, the Grays were a much better hitting team than the Monarchs were.[13] In only one inning, the Grays tagged Dean for two runs on three hits. And it could have been worse.

Leadoff hitter Dave Whatley reached base on an infield hit off Dean's glove, Jerry Benjamin sacrificed Whatley to second, and Howard Easterling walked. Josh Gibson launched a shot to the deepest part of the ballpark, right-center field, more than 422 feet away from home plate—for a very long second out. With both base runners advancing on Gibson's fly ball, Jud Wilson (playing first base for the injured Buck Leonard) drove both runners home with a single to center field. Sam Bankhead singled to left field before manager Vic Harris mercifully popped out to end the inning with the Grays leading 2–0.[14] Dean immediately caught a plane after his inning of work.[15] He was just the warm-up act, as the Grays cruised to an 8–1 victory and Paige took center stage.

Negro League teams traditionally bore down when facing white major leaguers. Even in their primes, Paige had outpitched Dean in postseason exhibition games. In 1934, Paige's Pittsburgh Crawfords won three straight exhibition games against Dean and several members of the World Series champion St. Louis Cardinals (known as the Gas House Gang).[16] According to Negro League historian John Holway, black professional teams won eighty-nine games, lost sixty-seven, and tied one against white major leaguers.[17] "We won the majority of those games—not because we were better. The major league ballplayers couldn't afford to twist an ankle," Buck O'Neil, the star of Ken Burns's nine-part baseball documentary, explained. "We wanted to prove that major leaguers were not superior, and that Negro Leaguers were not inferior. So we'd stretch that single into a double."[18]

Negro League teams probably won too often for the tastes of Judge Kenesaw Mountain Landis. In the early 1920s, a few years after being named commissioner, Judge Landis banned postseason interracial contests involving actual major league teams. He permitted black teams to face only major league All-Star teams, and he limited the number of major leaguers from any particular team.[19] Thus, black professional teams, such as the Grays, could not enjoy the satisfaction of having defeated bona fide major league teams.

116   The extent of Landis's power was evident before and after Paige's May 31 appearance with the Grays. Landis probably prevented Bob Feller, the fastest pitcher in the major leagues, from pitching against Paige and the Grays that day, as had been advertised. Naval officials supposedly forbade Feller from appearing, but the *Afro*'s Ric Roberts blamed Landis.[20] "The Washington Senators are going begging for patrons, and even night ball is not fetching them to Griffith Stadium," Roberts wrote. "Such names as Paige, Feller, and Dean, on

the same Griffith Stadium card, would have been a dangerous expo-sure, in comparison of the shortcomings of the Griffith ensemble, thus far."[21] Indeed, three days after twenty-two thousand saw Paige and the Grays defeat Dean, a night game between the Senators and the lowly St. Louis Browns at Griffith Stadium fetched only five thousand fans.[22]

After the Grays' Griffith Stadium exhibition, Judge Landis con-vinced army officials to thwart a third contest between Dean's All-Stars and Paige's Monarchs scheduled for June 6 in Indianapolis. "A new army regulation forbidding former baseball players to take part in such contests prevented several members of Dean's team, who were stationed at Jefferson Barracks, Mo., from participating," Art Carter wrote. "Landis dislikes seeing those exhibitions outdrawing his major league teams."[23]

Dean's team needed Feller on May 31 against Paige and the Grays. This was a different outfit from the one that Dean had played with the previous week at Wrigley Field. In Chicago, Dean's All-Stars had consisted of past and future major leaguers in the service, including former Senators first baseman Zeke Bonura.[24] In Washington, by contrast, most of Dean's "All-Stars" did not belong on the same field as the Grays. They wore "wretched, ragged uniforms with meaning-less Ls on first-line shirts, and they played in a way that matched their haberdashery."[25] The L's stood for the Lloyd Athletic Club, a sandlot team from Chester, Pennsylvania. It may as well have stood for losers. The team mostly consisted of career minor leaguers and sandlot players, with two pitchers enjoying brief major league stints.[26]

There was one exception to the incompetence of Dean's All-Stars—Senators shortstop–third baseman Cecil Travis.[27] Yes, the same Cecil Travis who finished second in the 1941 American League batting race behind Ted Williams and led the league in hits. The same Cecil Travis, who, according to Williams, belongs in the Hall of Fame.[28] Travis, who also played on Dean's team in Chicago, dis-tinguished himself from the other "All-Stars" in Washington with his "Camp Wheeler" baseball uniform and his professional play. A mod-est, soft-spoken Southerner and a favorite of Washington's white sporting press, Travis was stationed at Camp Wheeler in his home

117

state of Georgia. The army gave Travis a weeklong furlough to play with Dean's All-Stars. Playing once a week at Camp Wheeler, Travis said his timing was so off that he would be lucky to hit .100 in the majors. The slap hitter predicted that he would need at least three weeks to regain his batting stroke.[29] After an 0-for-3 afternoon in Chicago, Travis spent the week in Washington. He went fishing with friends on the Chesapeake Bay, received a gold watch from the *Times-Herald* for being the Senators' most consistent player in 1941, and on Sunday competed against Paige and the Grays.[30]

Reflecting on that exhibition game nearly sixty years later, Travis confessed that at the time he did not even know that the Grays played at Griffith Stadium when the Senators were out of town.[31] Travis's obliviousness about Griffith Stadium's other tenants is not surprising. The Grays had been playing in Washington for only two seasons, they did not break any Griffith Stadium attendance records in 1940 or 1941, and Gibson had been smashing home runs in Latin America during that time. Furthermore, the Senators hit the road when the Grays played in Washington.

Travis's appearance against the Grays marked a new chapter in the Grays-Senators' complex history. During the late 1930s, Griffith allowed the Grays to play exhibition games at the Senators' spring training facilities at Orlando's Tinker Field. Griffith's team also purchased the Grays' batting equipment along with the Senators'. Buck Leonard recalled that if the Senators were ordering eight hundred bats, they would order an additional one hundred for the Grays.[32] Each Grays player, according to historian Donn Rogosin, found a Senator who used the same type of equipment: "Buck Leonard, a lifetime .355 hitter in the Negro Leagues, used Len Okrie's bat. Okrie batted a lifetime .218."[33] Griffith's clubhouse man also purchased uniforms that said "Grays" rather than "Senators." The easiest way to spot a rookie or seldom-used member of the Grays was to look at his uniform—if the front of the uniform said "Grays," he was an integral member of the team; if the uniform had only a W on the left front, then the player never made it into league games because he was wearing an old Senators uniform.[34]

Finally, the Grays' unofficial business manager in Washington was the Senators' ticket manager, John Morrissey. Morrissey would ask the Grays how many people they expected for a particular game. He printed the tickets, hired police protection, and directed the Senators' public-address announcer and play-by-play man to announce the dates of upcoming Grays games. After each Grays game, Morrissey prepared a balance sheet and divided the money among Griffith, the Grays, and the visiting team. Morrissey helped line Griffith's pockets, but he also helped the Grays. "Mr. Morrissey was the greatest help," Buck Leonard told John Holway, "not only for the Homestead Grays, but for Negro baseball, period."[35]

Relations among Grays and Senators players ran from cool to indifferent. The Grays, who boasted playing more than two hundred games during a given season, had neither the time nor the interest to watch the Senators play. "They don't come to see us, we don't go to see them," Gibson told Sam Lacy in 1940. "We can't learn anything from them we don't get from experience, so there's no need to go."[36] Growing up in Pennsylvania, Senators first baseman Mickey Vernon knew all about the Grays. Before Vernon broke in with the Senators in 1939, he had attended games involving Gibson, Paige, and Leonard. But as a member of the Senators, Vernon never saw them play at Griffith Stadium. "I don't recall seeing any of their games in Washington because we were always on the road," Vernon recalled.[37]

Although the Senators heard a lot about the Grays when they returned from road trips, the Senators never felt threatened by their cotenants. After serving in World War II, Vernon won American League batting titles in 1946 and 1953. But playing three full seasons for the Senators from 1940 to 1943, Vernon had never hit .300 or finished with more than nine home runs in a single season. He was a young player with lots of potential but an uncertain future. However, he said he never worried about Leonard taking his first-base job.[38]

Privately, the Grays relished a showdown with the Senators. The *Washington Tribune* reported in August 1940 that "a check of the players on the Grays reveals the game they most desire is that of fac-

119

ing the Washington Senators with Dutch Leonard and [Grays ace pitcher Ray] Brown doing mound duties."[39] "We challenged them, but they wouldn't play us," Grays pitcher Edsall Walker recalled. "They'd say, 'Hey, we ain't got nothing to win. If we beat you, that's what we're supposed to do. But suppose that we lose?' They couldn't take the chance."[40] In June 1942, *Tribune* sports editor Joe Sewall wrote a letter to Griffith proposing a Grays-Senators matchup at Griffith Stadium with all the proceeds to go to "army and navy relief." On June 19, Griffith replied that the major leagues already had sponsored several relief efforts and that "it is my opinion that Negro organized baseball should step out in a program of its own to further the interest of war relief activities."[41] Griffith did not even raise Judge Landis's edicts about barnstorming or the reality that his Senators, who once again finished next to last in the American League, might lose. The Grays never received their showdown with the Senators; they settled for Cecil Travis.

The game against Dizzy Dean's All-Stars on May 31, 1942, had all the feeling of a Senators game. "The whites sat where they wanted to and they dressed where they wanted to," Leonard wrote.[42] Paige and the Grays dressed in Griffith Stadium's visiting locker room. The black fans crammed themselves into the seats in the right-field pavilion. Leonard, based in part on his experiences watching the Senators play the Yankees in 1924, explained:

> When whites were playing they had a black section, usually down the right-field line, and segregated seating was required. When we played exhibition games between blacks and whites, many of them continued to sit in the same place. I think it was just a custom, because it wasn't required. Negroes became accustomed to sitting in certain places while the whites were playing, and when we played, sometimes they would go back to that same section. But we sold tickets for anywhere they wanted to sit and they could have sat anywhere they wanted to sit. We sold box seats, too, for those exhibition games, and if blacks had a box seat ticket, then they could sit in the box seats. But it was a custom in Washington, D.C., not a requirement.[43]

It didn't matter where the fans sat or where their team dressed. The black fans came to see the best of the Senators, Travis, square off against the best of black baseball, Paige and the Grays. Travis won the initial showdown. In the second inning, he ripped Paige's slow curveball up the middle for a single. Grays shortstop Sam Bankhead forced out Travis at second base to end the inning. Back on the bench, Paige didn't even know who had singled off him. "So Cecil Travis got a single, eh?" Paige said to Leonard, who was sidelined with a knee injury. "He took advantage of that slow curve—it came right past me, too; could have knocked it down but was afraid I might have hurt my hand or something."[44]

Paige was notoriously bad with names and even worse on the mound about identifying hitters. He recognized opposing hitters by their batting stances (particularly by the way their knees moved when they swung the bat) but not by their faces. Paige often relied on an infielder, such as his regular first baseman O'Neil, to inform him when a good hitter was coming to bat. Paige also claimed to have less trouble with big hitters, such as DiMaggio or Williams (whom he referred to as simply Joe and Ted), and more trouble with contact hitters, such as Detroit Tigers Hall of Fame second baseman Charlie Gehringer and, on May 31, with Cecil Travis.[45]

Someone must have alerted Paige when Travis returned to the plate. Paige, who wore his Monarchs uniform that day, pitched five innings rather than his usual three. In his final duel with Travis, Paige gave Washington's late-arriving fans a thrill. With the Grays leading 2–0 in the top of the fifth, Grays third baseman Howard Easterling misplayed Claude Corbitt's slow grounder, overthrowing first baseman Jud Wilson and allowing Corbitt to reach second base. With Corbitt on second, Travis came up. The Senators star worked the count to three balls and one strike. Paige threw an inside fastball. Travis swung and missed. Paige threw another inside fastball, this one higher and more inside. Travis swung and missed again. Paige had struck him out.

The crowd, particularly the fans in the right-field pavilion, roared with approval. "The vicarious satisfaction taken in the victories of

Negro athletes who have beaten white competitors has long been observed," Swedish social economist Gunnar Myrdal wrote in 1944.[46] "Satchel Paige," exulted Art Carter, "is the Joe Louis of baseball. Perhaps it is more proper to say Joe Louis is the Satchel Paige of boxing, for Old Satch was tossing 'em plateward long before Joe cut his first wisdom tooth."[47]

The Paige-Travis battle was different from Louis beating up Buddy Baer the previous year at Griffith Stadium. Griffith's refusal to hire black players suggested that black teams such as the Grays were inferior to white teams such as the Senators, that a Paige or a Gibson lacked the requisite skill to play on the same team as a Travis. The black elite's obsession with the Senators only reinforced this racial hierarchy. By striking out Travis, Paige refuted any notions of inferiority and gave people hope that the integration of baseball, as Griffith had prophesied in 1937, was not far off. Robert McNeill, a black photographer who snapped a pregame group picture of Travis, Dean, and Paige that appeared in the *Pittsburgh Courier*, recalled the jubilation of the black fans. He remembered "the gratification that they felt that Josh Gibson and Buck Leonard and others could perform as well as the white players. Even though they didn't feel that blacks would ever play in the [major] leagues, they sort of smugly got satisfaction out of knowing that this may be possible."[48]

On the bench, Paige spoke clinically about making Travis one of his seven strikeout victims. "He went for two bad balls, fast ones inside, up against him," said Paige, who sensed that Travis's timing was off. "He wasn't ready and steady—tried to make up his mind too quick, at the last second. He would have walked if he had looked at the last one."[49] For his five innings, Paige received five hundred dollars plus all travel expenses incurred by him and his personal trainer. Paige, who gave up one unearned run after retiring Travis, failed to make good on his pregame promise to shut out Dean's team. After the game, Paige boasted to a white writer that he could win thirty-five games during a major league season. He also claimed that he could beat the Grays even with Dean's All-Stars behind him.[50] Privately, while riding the train to Pittsburgh with black sportswriter

Wendell Smith, Paige confessed that he was not the same pitcher he had been with the Pittsburgh Crawfords during the 1930s.[51]

Ever gracious in defeat, Travis complimented Paige after the game. "I haven't seen good pitching in a long time," Travis said. "I'm way off my timing. But Paige looked good to me. They say he's been pitching 17 years. I don't doubt [that] he was real good a few years ago."[52] Looking back on that game almost sixty years later, Travis maintained his favorable view of Paige: "He could throw good even at that late year, as far as that goes."[53]

Sadly, Travis never regained his timing as a hitter. After returning to Camp Wheeler and playing a navy relief game in Cleveland in July 1942 featuring—of all people—Bob Feller, Travis was shipped off to France, fought in the Battle of the Bulge, and developed frozen feet.[54] After the war, Travis returned to the Senators for fifteen games at the end of the 1945 season. But the career .314 hitter retired after two disappointing campaigns (.252 in 1946 and .216 in 1947). To his credit, Travis has refused to blame his frozen feet for his demise as a ballplayer. "That didn't have anything to do with it," Travis told sportswriter Dave Kindred. "You didn't have to be off but just a hair and you couldn't play."[55]

Travis, who recalled receiving "a few hundred dollars" plus travel expenses for playing with Dean's All-Stars, did not remember many details about the Grays. But he was notably impressed. "I think they beat us," Travis said from his home in Riverdale, Georgia. "I remember them. They didn't get too much publicity. They deserved a lot, but they didn't get it."[56]

The clash between the Grays and Dean's All-Stars was the only occasion that Washington's white daily newspapers deigned to give the Grays more than a few inches of copy. The *Post*, the *Evening Star*, the *Times-Herald*, and the tabloid *Daily News* usually treated the Grays like a nonentity. May 31, 1942, with Dean, Travis, and Paige on hand, was the exception. The *Post* ran a large photograph of the pregame crowd engulfing the outdoor concourse and another photograph of Travis making an out at second base. The *Post's* game story, however, mistakenly referred to the Grays' outfielders as "Bud"

Whatley and "Bob" Benjamin (rather than as Dave and Jerry, respectively).[57] And the *Post* was the only paper that did not send a columnist. Shirley Povich, who was off covering the Senators, would have put the less progressive white columnists on hand to shame.

Some of the white press coverage of Paige and the Grays—particularly among the columnists—degenerated from mere mistakes into ignorance and racism. Francis Stann of the *Evening Star* described the reaction of the black fans in the right-field pavilion when Paige struck out Travis:

> One had to go back nearly 18 years to find a parallel for the reaction . . . back to that October afternoon when Earl McNeely's grounder hit a pebble and won Washington's first and only world championship. Negro blades in zoot suits stood and filled the air with "yipee," "yay," and "yea boy, yo' got 'im!" Darkies did flip-flops, those sitting close enough to vault over the low wall onto the field. Strangers banged each other across sweaty backs.[58]

Washington, the capital of the free world leading the fight against Nazi white supremacy, exhibited all of the elements of a Southern town—a segregated ballpark; discrimination in downtown stores, restaurants, and movie houses; and a local daily press that refused to give the Grays the same respectful coverage that it gave the Senators.

The black press, by contrast, got the inside scoop from the game's black participants. The *Afro*, recognizing the significance of a reunion of the Paige-Gibson battery, stationed a reporter in the Grays' dugout to record the between-innings banter between Paige and his temporary teammates.[59] Ric Roberts wrote the *Afro* game story and a column while serving as the game's official scorer for an extra $7.50. Art Carter also wrote a column for the *Afro* and kept track of the afternoon's promotional expenses.[60] The *Pittsburgh Courier* sent Wendell Smith to cover the action. Smith, after his train ride back to Pittsburgh with Paige, wrote an insightful column about the ace pitcher. He also wrote a beautiful game story with the following conclusion:

It was a great day for Washington's baseball fandom. They saw the great "Satch" at his best. They saw him uncork his blazing fastball and "blow" it past Cecil Travis in the only "test duel" of the game. They saw the Grays blast Dizzy Dean to the showers and make some of the most amazing catches ever pulled in this American league ball orchard.[61]

Whereas the black press covered the game like professionals, white sports columnists used the exhibition as an excuse to write caricaturish stories about Paige.[62]

Although Paige had not pitched in Washington since the mid-1930s with the Pittsburgh Crawfords, and then only for two innings, he stole the show that afternoon at Griffith Stadium.[63] The twenty-two thousand fans who had witnessed his performance against Dean's All-Stars was a harbinger of things to come. During the early 1940s, Paige led black baseball's renaissance. National magazines such as the *Saturday Evening Post, Life,* and *Time* even stumbled on to his story. Many, like the *Saturday Evening Post* and Washington's white columnists, portrayed him as a clown.[64]

Certainly there were many colorful aspects to Paige's persona. Most writers initially seized on his unusual physical appearance. He looked like a stick figure with his long limbs and six-foot, three-and-a-half-inch, 180-pound frame. They called him "Satchelfoot" because of his big feet (though Paige insisted that he wore only size elevens).[65] They also bestowed on him sage-like qualities through the attribution of amusing aphorisms. Richard Donovan, in a campy 1953 profile of Paige for *Collier's,* turned a few extra quotes from his notebook into Paige's six rules about "How to Stay Young":

1. Avoid fried meats which angry up the blood.
2. If your stomach disputes you, lie down and pacify it with cool thoughts.
3. Keep the juices flowing by jangling around gently as you move.
4. Go very light on the vices, such as carrying on in society. The social ramble ain't restful.

5. Avoid running at all times.
6. Don't look back. Something might be gaining on you.[66]

The last rule became Paige's mantra.

The myths that sportswriters didn't concoct about him, Paige cultivated on his own. His longest-running gag was his refusal to divulge his age, implying that he was ten to fifteen years older than most people believed. He also referred to his pitches by a variety of names: "nothin' ball" (change-up), "wobbly ball" (knuckleball), "be ball" ("'cause it 'be' where I want it"), "Little Tom" (his medium fastball), "Long Tom" (his good fastball), "multiple windmill windup," and, of course, his famous "hesitation pitch" (a delivery writers dubbed "Stepin Pitchit" because his front leg hit the ground well before he released the ball).[67]

"But the main thing is," Paige accurately assessed, "I got control." He performed pregame stunts, such as throwing a ball between two bats that were standing six inches apart at home plate, knocking cigars out of hitters' mouths, and warming up with a matchbox or gum wrapper in front of the catcher instead of home plate.[68]

Whitey Herzog, a teammate of Paige's with the Triple-A Miami Marlins, once bet the fifty-one-year-old pitcher while on a road trip in Rochester that Paige could not throw a ball through a small hole in the outfield fence. Before the game, Herzog had tried to throw the ball through the hole—which was barely the size of a baseball—150 to 200 times. Satchel looked at the hole from the dugout and said, "Wild Child, do the ball fit in the hole?" (Paige called all of the Marlins' young players, including Herzog, "Wild Child.")

"Yeah Satch," Herzog replied. "But not by much. I bet you a fifth of Old Forester that you can't throw it through there."

126

Before the next night's game, Paige came out early for batting practice. He stood sixty feet, six inches away from the little hole in the outfield fence and nearly rifled it through on the first try. On the second try, according to Herzog, Paige "drilled the ball dead center. The ball went right through, and I haven't seen it since."

"Thank you, Wild Child," Satch said, and then went back into the clubhouse."[69]

With his own yen for artful storytelling, Paige often enhanced his reputation by recounting his on-field antics. He usually pulled his most famous stunts—such as guaranteeing to strike out the first nine batters or ordering his outfielders and even his infielders off the diamond—in small towns against white semipro or sandlot teams. He never performed on-field comedy routines, like the Indianapolis Clowns, a Negro American League team owned by Harlem Globetrotters' founder Abe Saperstein, and Paige never dressed in demeaning clothes like the Zulu Giants, whose players wore grass skirts on the field. Facing a top-flight Negro League team, like the Grays, or a team of major league All-Stars, he pitched only one way—to win.

Paige was not a minstrel performer on the mound. He was a complex individual who defied simple racial stereotypes, who entertained sportswriters with his comic personality yet hid his serious side from all but a few close friends, and who overcame a hardscrabble, poverty-stricken childhood. Beneath the myths and legends about Paige, the facts reveal a more dynamic portrait of how he navigated the minefields of poverty, segregation, and discrimination on his way to superstardom.

Leroy Robert "Satchel" Paige was born July 7, 1906, in Mobile, Alabama. His father, John, was a gardener, and his mother, Lula, was a washerwoman. The seventh of eleven children, Paige grew up in a four-room shotgun house. At the age of seven, he worked at the railroad station carrying people's luggage for ten cents a bag. Dissatisfied with his low pay, young Paige rigged a pole with some rope that allowed him to carry numerous bags at one time. The other kids derided his efforts by calling him a "walking satchel tree." In time, everybody in Mobile (except Paige's mother and the local authorities) referred to him as Satchel.[70]

Paige's ingenuity at the railroad station reflected an image antithetical to that of a minstrel performer—the self-assertion and militancy of the "New Negro"—a term coined during the Harlem Renaissance of the 1920s that embodied the assertiveness of a younger, more progressive generation of African Americans.[71] Growing up in Mobile, Paige exhibited the New Negro's race consciousness. "The first few years I was no different from any other kid,"

Paige wrote. "Only in Mobile I was a nigger kid."[72] Engaging in vicious battles with white children on his way home from school, Paige developed his strong, accurate arm by pelting them with rocks. He fought more than he attended school. One afternoon in 1918, he stole some toy rings out of a store. After being apprehended, he was sentenced to five and a half years at the Industrial School for Negro Children at Mount Meigs, Alabama.

Reform school saved Paige. Just as young Babe Ruth had taken to baseball at a Baltimore reform school a decade earlier, Paige was encouraged to develop his pitching talents. After being released from reform school, he played for the semipro Mobile Tigers in 1924. Two years later, he began his professional career with a string of teams: the Chattanooga Black Lookouts, New Orleans Black Pelicans, Birmingham Black Barons, Baltimore Black Sox, Nashville Elite Giants, and Cleveland Cubs. Signing with Gus Greenlee's Pittsburgh Crawfords in 1931 turned Paige into a bona fide superstar. His $250 monthly starting salary climbed rapidly as he teamed with Gibson to form the best battery in the history of black baseball. His fame grew when he defeated Dean and other white major leaguers in 1934 and 1935 during a series of postseason exhibitions.

Paige was a fastball pitcher with impeccable control and an extra hop on his ball as it reached the hitter. In his later years, his command, intelligence, and ability to change speeds on his fastball set him apart from other pitchers. Although Buck Leonard was a dead fastball hitter, Paige befuddled him throughout his career by pitching Leonard, who always tried to pull Paige, on the outside corner. "I'd say Satchel Paige was the toughest pitcher I ever faced," Leonard told John Holway. "All the years I played there, I never got a hit off him. He threw *fire*, that's what he threw."[73]

His fastball may have been reliable, but Paige was not. He drove separately from the team to all of his games and often arrived late. A notoriously bad driver, he claimed to have received speeding tickets in all fifty states. During the 1940s, the Monarchs often sent along another player to make sure that Paige got off the highway at the right exit. The previous decade, Paige had bolted the Crawfords for bigger paydays in places such as Bismarck, North Dakota, in 1935, the

Dominican Republic in 1937, and finally Mexico in 1938. In 1938, Greenlee tried to save his faltering franchise by selling Paige for five thousand dollars to the Newark Eagles. Paige flirted with the Eagles and in particular with their female owner, Effa Manley, but he never signed with them.[74]

Paige's trip to Mexico nearly led to his demise. He developed a sore arm and felt a pop in his shoulder. Doctors informed him that his pitching career was over. So Paige returned to the states and in 1939 signed with the B team of the Kansas City Monarchs. He mostly played first base and outfield and soft-tossed a few pitches while receiving daily treatments on his arm from the Monarchs' trainer, a licensed masseur named Frank "Jewbaby" Floyd. ("I don't know why they called him 'Jewbaby,' because he was as black as I am," Buck O'Neil said.[75]). After about a year and a half of rest, Paige suddenly regained his fastball. His arm felt better. He continued to pitch for the B team until 1941, when he joined the Monarchs.

Paige flourished with the Monarchs, whose owner, J. L. Wilkinson, rented him to other teams. Paige usually pitched three innings (but as many as five) for either a flat fee (like the five hundred dollars for May 31) or a percentage of the gate (as high as 15 percent).[76] During the 1940s, Paige made as much as forty thousand dollars in a given season, while Feller and DiMaggio made only thirty-five thousand dollars.[77] In 1942, by contrast, Leonard and Gibson made only one thousand dollars a month.

Paige's fame and fortune came with a price—the press portrayed him as a minstrel performer, a baseball player in blackface. Paige hated comparisons to "Stepin Fetchit," the famous minstrel show performer, or references to him in print as "Satchelfoot."[78] "'Satchelfoot' sounds like a clown," Paige wrote in his first autobiography, *Pitchin' Man*. "I ain't no clown. I ain't no end man in no vaudeville show. I'm a baseball pitcher and winning baseball games is serious business."[79]

Only Paige's closest friends saw his serious side. Buck O'Neil recounted a car ride with Paige to Charleston, South Carolina, when Paige drove them to nearby Drum Island, an old slave auction site.

"Seems like I been here before," Paige said to O'Neil.

129

"Me, too, Satchel," O'Neil replied.[80]

Quincy Trouppe, who played with Paige in Bismarck, North Dakota, wrote: "I got to know Satch pretty well. As his teammate and friend, I soon learned he could clown one moment and become deadly serious the next. His complex personality made him immensely interesting."[81] The metaphor for Paige's inner turmoil was his bad stomach. Paige often needed to drink bicarbonate of soda while on the mound to get through the game.

Paige clearly understood the racial dynamic of playing against Dean's All-Stars in Washington, D.C. "Washington and Baltimore and those places like that," Paige told Stephen Banker, "was just as bad as Mississippi or Georgia or any of those places down there for a colored man."[82] After an August 1945 Griffith Stadium double-header in which Paige pitched three innings and collected one thousand dollars, Paige made an illegal left turn at Eighth and Florida Avenue. A black police officer, who accused Paige of trying to run him over, socked Paige twice in the eye. Paige was taken to the police station, paid a five dollar traffic ticket, and was released. Paige probably would have quipped that the biggest insult of the whole experience was the police officer's failure to recognize him.[83]

In June 1942, everybody recognized Paige in Washington. Eighteen days after his May 31 performance against Dean's All-Stars, Paige returned to Griffith Stadium with the Monarchs for a showdown against the Grays. People came to see the champions of the East versus the champions of the West, they came to see Gibson versus Paige, and they came in droves. The twenty-eight thousand who saw the Monarchs-Grays matchup was the largest baseball crowd at Griffith Stadium since the Senators' World Series appearance in 1933.[84] The difference was that almost all the fans on the night of June 18 were black. That night, they sat wherever they wanted, instead of gravitating to the Jim Crow pavilion in right field as they had during the game against Dean's All-Stars or being compelled to sit there during Senators games.

The June 18 Grays-Monarchs night contest was billed as the first time two Negro League teams played under major league arc lights.[85] Griffith allowed the Grays to use his new lights for the same reason he had allowed the Louis-Baer fight in 1941 and for the same reason he had lifted his ban on interracial exhibition games for Paige's previous appearance: money. Griffith charged the Grays 20 percent of the gross profits for stadium rental plus expenses for ushers, ticket takers, and stadium vendors. He also reaped 100 percent of the profits from the concession stands. On May 31, when Paige and the Grays played Dean's All-Stars, Griffith made between three thousand and four thousand dollars in rent and expenses alone. On June 18, Griffith took home four thousand to five thousand dollars — even though his grounds crew refused to rake the infield for two black teams — not including concessions and the exorbitant fee he charged for using his new lighting system.[86]

Grays owner Cum Posey had been negotiating with Griffith for nearly a year to use the new lights.[87] In the past, the Grays had tried to illuminate the ballpark's expansive outfield with their own portable lighting system in addition to Griffith Stadium's floodlights. These night games usually turned into error-filled disasters because the players could not pick up the ball.[88] With black Washington teeming with war workers, however, night baseball had become a financial imperative. Estimates about how much Griffith charged the Grays on a per-game basis to use his lights varied from five hundred to fifteen hundred dollars.[89] The *Afro* wrote before the June 18 Grays-Monarchs contest: "The cost of lights, nightly, at Griffith Stadium is enormous and runs well into the hundreds of dollars. . . . However . . . a crowd of 15,000 will be on hand — maybe even more."[90]

When twenty-eight thousand people showed up for the 9:00 P.M. game on June 18, the Grays were not surprised. Carter had advertised the game in *Nite Life*, a Washington weekly newspaper, with ticket prices listed as follows: Box Seats — $1.65, Grandstand — $1.10, Pavilion — 80 cents, and Bleachers — 55 cents.[91] The advertisement from the game against Dean's All-Stars, by contrast, omitted the prices for bleacher seats because no one ever sat there.[92] As early as 1941, Posey knew that he could fill Griffith Stadium with three ingredients: Paige, night baseball, and the Monarchs.

Getting the Monarchs on board was more difficult than negotiating to use Griffith's lights. The Monarchs had been ducking the Grays for the past two seasons. In 1940, after edging the Baltimore Elite Giants for the Negro National League title, the Grays expected to play the Monarchs in a postseason World Series. The Monarchs, however, already had advertised a postseason series with the Elite Giants and refused to play the Grays.[93] In 1941, Posey pined all season for a game with the Monarchs, who drew record crowds in other major league parks with the return of Paige.[94] Both teams won their respective leagues yet once again failed to arrange a World Series. The two teams finally got together in April 1942, when the Grays defeated Paige and the Monarchs in New Orleans before a record-breaking crowd of twelve thousand.[95]

Of all the teams in the Negro Leagues, only the Monarchs matched the Grays in terms of an illustrious history and being a consistently classy outfit. The primary difference between the teams was that the Monarchs were owned by a white man: J. L. Wilkinson. Wilkinson, who previously had owned an interracial team also based in Kansas City known as the All Nations, started the Monarchs in 1920 as one of the charter members of Rube Foster's original Negro National League. When the league folded during the Depression, Wilkinson's Monarchs (like the Grays) survived as an independent club barnstorming against white teams. In 1930, Wilkinson ensured the Monarchs' survival by pioneering the use of a portable lighting system. The Monarchs played independently from 1931 to 1936, when they subsequently joined the Negro American League consisting of Western and Southern teams.[96]

Wilkinson matched Posey as a businessman and evaluator of baseball talent. The Monarchs' owner always made his payroll, even during the Depression. He treated his players with respect and inspired loyalty. In 1939, Wilkinson had signed Paige to the Monarchs' B team when everyone believed that Paige's pitching career was over. Paige remained loyal to Wilkinson (as loyal as Paige could be to any owner) for the rest of his career.[97] Unlike white owners who also doubled as promoters, such as Philadelphia Stars part-owner Eddie Gottlieb and Indianapolis Clowns owner Abe Saperstein, Wilkinson was never accused of exploiting his own players or other black baseball teams. Wilkinson made the Monarchs the class of the Negro American League, the Western equivalent of the Grays.

The Grays-Monarchs matchups of 1942 allowed Paige and Gibson to renew their friendly rivalry. For years, they had robbed black baseball fans of head-to-head battles by playing on the same team—from 1932 to 1936 with the Pittsburgh Crawfords and in 1937 with Trujillo's team in the Dominican Republic. Paige once told Gibson when they were with the Crawfords that the day would come when they would face each other again: "You know what they say, that you're the best hitter in the world? Well I know I'm the best pitcher in the world, and some day we're gonna be on different ballclubs and we're gonna meet up and see who comes out on top."[98]

It was a rivalry predicated on mutual respect. Paige declared years later that Gibson was the best hitter he had ever faced, ahead of Williams, DiMaggio, and Stan Musial.[99] Gibson told anyone who would listen that Paige was the game's best pitcher. Despite this underlying regard for each other's talents, two elements fueled the Paige-Gibson rivalry: both men hated to lose, and both men loved to boast. Gibson and Paige were two of the game's greatest trash talkers. Gibson had started talking about Paige even before the 1938 season had begun. At the end of a lengthy question-and-answer session for Posey's *Pittsburgh Courier* column, Gibson told Posey to ask him how he would do against Paige that season. "Look to get even break, two out of four," Gibson replied to his own question. "One thousand in a pinch, providing [Crawfords manager Oscar] Charleston don't say, 'Put him on.' "[100] Paige, however, had spent the 1938 season in Mexico instead of with the Crawfords and, therefore, never faced Gibson and the Grays. Gibson had to wait four years to show black baseball fans what he could do against Paige.

During the 1942 season, the one-upmanship took place right on the field, sometimes in the middle of an at-bat. On June 18, Paige

133

won the head-to-head battle with Gibson. After retiring the home-run-hitting catcher in the second inning, Paige struck out Gibson to end the fourth. As he walked off the field, Paige gave the Grays' bench some advice: "Say, you guys don't let me ever hear your ranting about Josh Gibson. Against the Monarchs he is just another batter who takes his three and then sits down!"[101]

Before the game, Paige wasn't even well enough to pitch. In the Monarchs' clubhouse, he was doubled over in pain because of his bad stomach. One of his teammates suggested that he see a doctor and stay in bed. "Do you see all those people out there?" Paige asked. "Lot of them came out to see Satch pitch, and Satch has gotta pitch."[102] In the middle of the third inning, Paige's teammates crowded around him when he got sick on the mound. Frank "Jew-baby" Floyd brought out some liquid antacids to soothe his bad stomach. Paige's physical condition did not hurt his pitching. He allowed only one ball out of the infield. In five innings, Paige gave up three hits (two of them infield singles) and no runs. He received fifteen hundred dollars for his performance.[103]

Although he may have lost his individual matchup with Paige, Gibson focused on helping his team win. In the first inning, Gibson's defensive skills may have saved the game. Willie Simms led off the game for the Monarchs with a triple. Newt Allen then hit a fly ball to center field. As Simms began to tag up, Gibson stood at the plate with his arms at his side as if the Grays were conceding the run. But as Simms strode toward home plate, Gibson received a bullet throw from center fielder Jerry Benjamin and tagged out Simms standing up. "All Simms had to do was slide," Paige said later, "and we would have closed the Grays out, then and there."[104]

134   Grays left-hander Roy Partlow held the Monarchs scoreless through nine innings. Partlow, who had spent the previous seventeen months playing in Latin America, was the Grays' surprise starter in lieu of ace right-hander Ray Brown. After Paige threw five scoreless innings, another Hall of Fame pitcher, Hilton Smith, took over for the Monarchs. Smith tied the Grays in knots for the next four innings with his wicked curveball. In a wise move, Smith intentionally

walked Gibson with one on in the sixth inning. Gibson could hit curveballs in his sleep.

In extra innings, the game seemingly favored the Monarchs because of their youth and the freshness of Smith. Partlow, by contrast, began showing signs of fatigue. In the top of the tenth, he walked the leadoff hitter, Joe Greene. Then Buck Leonard, having recently returned from his knee injury, unsuccessfully tried to throw out Greene at second base on a sacrifice bunt by O'Neil. With two on and no outs, Partlow retired the next two hitters. Smith, a notoriously good-hitting pitcher, singled, scoring Greene and giving the Monarchs a 1–0 lead.

The Grays rallied in the bottom of the tenth. Sam Bankhead led off with a walk. Vic Harris hit a grounder to the shortstop that forced out Bankhead at second base. People began heading for the exits. Matthew Carlisle, running for Harris, stole second base when Monarchs shortstop Jesse Williams couldn't handle the throw. Pinch hitter Jud Wilson, the Grays' best contact hitter, lined a 2–2 pitch into left field to score Carlisle. People returned to their seats as Wilson stood on first base with one out and the game tied 1–1.

Partlow, another good-hitting pitcher who, like fellow Grays pitchers Ray Brown and Wilmer Fields, often played the outfield when he wasn't pitching, stepped to the plate. Partlow smacked Smith's first pitch, a "lazy outside curveball," into the left-field corner 405 feet away from home plate for a game-winning triple.[105] Partlow's ten innings of pitching and game-winning hit gave the Grays a 2–1, come-from-behind victory over the Monarchs.

And twenty-eight thousand people couldn't believe it. For a few brief moments, baseball allowed the Grays' black fans to forget about the realities of second-class citizenship. Ric Roberts, writing for the *Afro-American*, described the jubilant postgame scene:

135

> It took the mob fully twenty minutes to stop shrieking and screaming. Partlow, the hero, was carried off the field on the shoulders of a hundred admirers; thousands swarmed onto the field to congratulate the champions of the West, the Kansas City Monarchs, and

the champions of the East, the Washington Homestead Grays, for the most beautifully contested baseball game ever seen on Griffith Stadium sod. It was simply terrific.[106]

The *Washington Tribune* described it as "the greatest baseball treat ever presented anywhere."[107] The *Pittsburgh Courier* called it the "game of the year."[108] Posey declared that it was "the smoothest exhibition of this national game we have yet seen."[109] That night, black Washingtonians accepted a Negro League team originating in Pittsburgh as their own; it was the night the Homestead Grays truly became the *Washington* Homestead Grays.

Even the players—who had ridden buses for weeks and months on end playing games in every two-bit town—found themselves caught up in postgame celebration. The Grays carried Partlow, his jersey unbuttoned, into the clubhouse. Big Ray Brown continued to lift Partlow off the ground as their teammates crowded around the winning pitcher in the locker room. Gratification was just about all they got. "They had thirty-one thousand people there that day, and do you know what the [Grays] owners gave us—an extra ten dollars apiece," recalled Grays pitcher Wilmer Fields, who had rejoined the team after finishing the school year at Virginia State.[110]

Paige, even with fifteen hundred dollars and bragging rights against Gibson to show for his efforts, still took the loss hard. The next morning, while eating ham and eggs with the *Afro's* Ric Roberts, Paige bemoaned the Monarchs' missed opportunities: Willie Simms's failure to slide in the first inning and Jesse Williams's dropping the throw at second base that would have nailed Matthew Carlisle in the tenth. "Gosh, we had that game won," Paige told Roberts. "Every one of those 28,000 fans were sure we were in; even the Grays had but scant hope of recovery when Hilton Smith squared off against them in that crazy tenth."[111] Immediately after the game, Paige's Monarchs teammates boarded the team bus and drove more than one thousand miles back to Kansas City.[112] Paige stayed behind to commiserate with Roberts about the loss.

The rivalry with Paige and the Monarchs helped the Grays catch on in Washington. Black Washingtonians no longer flocked only to

Senators games. "The Poseys have done a beautiful job of promotion in the capital and entrenched the Grays firmly in the hearts of Washingtonians," Roberts wrote. "It has been a very hard task to have the District people embrace the itinerant Homesteaders as their very own but, at long last, it has been done."[113]

The Grays succeeded in Washington by appealing to the black community's different social classes. Of the June 18 game with the Monarchs, Carter wrote: "Ninety per cent of the crowd was colored, and a cross-section ran from Dr. Mordecai W. Johnson, prexy of Howard U., down to Greasy, the rootin' tootin' fan who always brings his cow bell."[114] Carter's strategy of handing out free passes to prominent members of the black elite had worked. The Grays attracted upper-class blacks by promoting the games as classy, well-dressed affairs. Grays management ejected fans who brought bottles of alcohol to the ballpark, refunding the fans' tickets.[115] They also refused to play the Cincinnati (later Indianapolis) Clowns at Griffith Stadium because of a minstrel-type performance by their mascots, lanky first baseman King Tut and the midget Spec Bebop, that many black fans (as well as Clark Griffith) found offensive.[116] With ticket prices as low as fifty-five cents in the bleachers and eighty cents in the right-field pavilion, the Grays also appealed to the city's working-class fans. Grays games continued to serve as a reunion of sorts for recently migrated Southern blacks. "It was a natural," O'Neil recalled. "Those people we drew at Griffith Stadium and other ballparks, they were black. This was an important outlet. It was not only a sports event, it was a social event."[117]

Most people within black baseball credited Carter for turning the Grays into Washington's team. Posey, who marveled at the number of local white daily papers that covered the Grays-Monarchs game, wrote: "The game was advertised better than any in the Grays' history."[118] The day after the game, Newark Eagles owner Effa Manley sent Carter a handwritten note:

> Posey called and told me about the record crowd at Washington last night. I am writing to tell you how happy I am that you had a part in it. I am a great believer in that saying, "You get back out of

life everything you put in it," and you have always unselfishly tried to help Negro Baseball. I hope you have realized something worthwhile from both promotions, and hope you will have more opportunities.[119]

Carter's papers indicate that his promotional efforts earned him as much as 10 percent of the Grays' net profits in Washington.[120] Those profits kept increasing. After the victory over the Monarchs, the Grays' attendance in D.C. immediately doubled. Crowds at Griffith Stadium averaged nine thousand to ten thousand against teams such as the Newark Eagles and the Birmingham Black Barons.[121]

Washington quickly overtook Pittsburgh as the Grays' "first" home city. The day before a June 28 Grays-Eagles Sunday doubleheader drew nine thousand fans at Griffith Stadium, the same two teams played a doubleheader at Forbes Field before only twelve hundred.[122] The Grays and Monarchs tried to replicate Griffith Stadium's magic formula July 21 in Pittsburgh by playing the first Negro League game under Forbes Field's new lighting system.[123] Paige's first appearance in Pittsburgh since 1936, a rematch between the Monarchs and Grays, and the first night game at Forbes Field netted only 11,500 fans. And yet, the *Pittsburgh Courier* called it "the largest crowd ever to attend a Negro ballgame in Pittsburgh."[124]

Attendance may have suffered in Pittsburgh, but, if anything, the level of drama during these Grays-Monarchs clashes only heightened. On July 21 at Forbes Field, Paige pitched all eleven innings, not wanting to leave the outcome in the hands of Hilton Smith. Paige did it all, knocking in the first two runs for the Monarchs (he always bragged about his mediocre hitting), striking out eight, and holding Gibson hitless.

It was during this July 21 Grays-Monarchs game at Forbes Field that Paige struck out Gibson after intentionally walking third baseman Howard Easterling so that Paige and Gibson could settle their rivalry before their old Pittsburgh fans.[125] Paige later called the moment "his greatest thrill."[126] Yet once again, the Grays defeated Paige and the Monarchs, 5–4, in eleven innings.[127]

The Grays proved two things during the Monarchs' return trip to Washington: (1) Washington was a better black baseball town than Pittsburgh, and (2) the Grays, to date, had the Monarchs' number. On August 13 at Griffith Stadium, the Grays defeated the Monarchs, 3–2, in twelve innings before 20,084 fans. The Monarchs continued to ignore the advice of Negro National League teams that the key to beating the Grays was a good left-handed pitcher. The best pitcher in black baseball was a right-hander, and he wanted revenge. Paige had pitched sixteen innings against the Grays with nothing to show for his efforts. This time he pitched all twelve innings. The result, however, was the same.[128]

Paige struck out twelve Grays and allowed only seven hits during those twelve innings. But with the Monarchs ahead 2–1 going into the bottom of the ninth, Paige couldn't hold the lead. Jerry Benjamin, after whiffing at two Paige fastballs, drove a change-up into center field for a single. Benjamin stole second and advanced to third on Howard Easterling's fly ball. Gibson stepped to the plate. Although he had not gotten a hit off Paige all season, the entire Monarchs infield deliberated whether Paige should pitch to the mighty slugger. That's how much they respected him as a hitter. Paige pitched to Gibson, who nearly ended the game with one swing, a 450-foot shot to left field, but foul. Gibson walked. Buck Leonard marked his return to the Grays from a broken hand with a clutch hit. Batting behind Gibson, Leonard singled to right field to score Benjamin and tie the game, 2–2. Leonard, who claimed years later never to have gotten a hit against Paige, had done just that to send the game into extra innings.[129]

The Grays won the game in the twelfth, once again thanks to the less-heralded section of their batting order. Vic Harris reached base on an infield hit and advanced to second on Chester Williams's groundout. Paige intentionally walked Ray Brown, who had relieved starter Roy Welmaker after eight innings. Dave Whatley then singled off Paige to score Harris and to give the Grays another victory over the Monarchs.[130]

During four games against the Monarchs in 1942 (including the preseason exhibition in New Orleans), the Grays had defeated the Monarchs four times—three times in extra innings, twice before more than twenty thousand fans at Griffith Stadium. "Every time I saw Satchel Paige, the Grays knocked him all over the place," *Afro* photographer Bill Scott recalled. "Beat his brains out! The only time I really saw him tame a baseball team was when Dizzy Dean brought some barnstormers here with Cecil Travis, who played for the Senators. I was out there! Satchel Paige even won, I think."[131]

Scott's memory may have been selective. The Grays never completely mastered Paige. But the image that stuck in the minds of most of Griffith Stadium's black baseball fans was of Paige, the hard-luck loser, and the Grays, the victors. After the Monarchs lost for the second time at Griffith Stadium, the Grays edged the Baltimore Elite Giants for the Grays' fifth Negro National League title in six years. The Monarchs also won their fifth Negro American League title in six years. The two teams met again in the 1942 Negro World Series—Paige's much-needed vehicle for revenge.

The World Series was more like a postseason barnstorming tour than an annual Fall Classic. It depended on the willingness of the two best teams in each league and on the availability of major league ballparks. It usually lasted more than seven games. Because few Negro League teams owned their own ballparks, the teams traversed the country playing a series of exhibition and actual World Series games in major and minor league ballparks.[132] Some of the games counted; some didn't. So when the Monarchs crow about their triumphs over the Grays in the 1942 World Series, it must be placed in the proper context.

The 1942 World Series reinforced that Griffith Stadium had become the Grays' most important venue, their home ballpark above all home parks, their principal moneymaker. Black Washington had become so enraptured with the Grays that, beginning with an August 7 game against the Baltimore Elite Giants at Bugle Field, the *Afro* sponsored live radio broadcasts of the Grays games on WWDC 1450.[133] The *Afro* also sponsored the radio broadcast of the second Grays-Monarchs clash.[134] Before Game 1 of the World Series, local businesses, from the Logan Hotel at Thirteenth Street and Logan Circle to the Pig N' Pit Bar B-Q on Fourteenth, sponsored a half-page advertisement in the *Afro* adorned with a large photo of Gibson batting and a headline that said, "Go Get 'Em, Grays."[135]

On September 8, twenty-five thousand fans braved rainy, humid weather for Game 1 of the World Series and the final Grays-Monarchs matchup of 1942 at Griffith Stadium. Paige retired the first ten Grays. With the game scoreless in the fourth inning, Bankhead and Easterling rapped back-to-back singles. Gibson, still hitless against Paige all season, came to the plate. He launched a fastball 420 feet to left-center field.[136] "By the sound of the crack, it was the usual Josh Gibson home run," O'Neil wrote. "I can still see the ball streaking across the dark blue sky."[137] O'Neil recognized the sound because he had heard it come from the bat of only one other man, Babe Ruth, whom O'Neil had seen play when the Monarchs' first baseman was just a boy. The first time O'Neil had heard that sound during batting practice at Griffith Stadium, he "ran down to the dugout in just my pants and my sweat shirt to see who was hitting that ball. And it was Josh Gibson. I thought, my land, that's a powerful man."[138] But on the night of September 8, O'Neil's eyes and ears fooled him. Griffith Stadium's left-center-field wall was more than 420 feet from home plate. Monarchs center fielder Willard Brown caught the ball on the warning track.

Gibson's sure home run that turned into a long out stunned the Grays into submission. From that point, besides a walk to Vic Harris, no Grays hitter reached base. The Monarchs poured on eight runs against Grays starter Roy Welmaker, whose teammates committed six errors behind him. Paige had departed with the Monarchs leading 1–0 after six innings; Jack Matchett finished off the Grays. With the Monarchs' 8–0 victory over the Grays, a 1–0 lead in the World Series, and another 0-for-3 day from Gibson, the 1942 Negro League World Series began and ended for the Grays that night at Griffith Stadium. After the game, Gibson sat in the locker room looking "forlorn and dejected," his pinstriped uniform partially unbuttoned, his pants rolled up to his knees, his stirrups pushed down to his ankles, and his hat in his hands.[139]

141

Paige's revenge and Gibson's humiliation was just beginning. The next game, in Pittsburgh, Paige humbled Gibson for eternity. With the Grays trailing 8–4, Paige struck out the mighty slugger with the bases loaded on three-straight pitches. This Paige-Gibson confrontation is probably the most memorable story among Negro

League lore, but it is also one of the most poorly documented. Although several players and historians contend that Paige intentionally walked two batters to load the bases and get to Gibson, the only apparent case of Paige intentionally walking a hitter to get to Gibson had taken place earlier that season at Forbes Field.[140] What we know for sure is that Paige struck out Gibson with the bases loaded, and the Monarchs defeated the Grays, 8–4. The most shocking statistic that night was the low turnout at Forbes Field: 5,219 fans. Although the *Afro* blamed two days of rain for the sparse crowd, Pittsburgh's inability to produce more than about five thousand fans for a Monarchs-Grays World Series game doomed Forbes Field as the Grays' primary home ballpark in 1943.

The Monarchs kept on winning World Series games. They won both games of a Yankee Stadium doubleheader before thirty thousand fans. Paige won the first game, 9–3 (Gibson finally got a hit, but not off Paige), and the Monarchs borrowed Birmingham Black Barons starter Gready "Lefty" McKinnis to win the seven-inning exhibition, 5–0.

Leading three games to none heading into Game 4 in Kansas City, the Monarchs purportedly allowed the ailing Grays to pick up some extra players from other teams (after the Grays had allowed them to use McKinnis). Borrowing Hall of Fame pitcher Leon Day and second baseman Len Pearson from the Newark Eagles and shortstop Buster Clarkson and outfielder Ed Stone from the Philadelphia Stars, the Grays defeated the Monarchs, 4–1, before ten thousand Kansas City fans. Not so fast, the Monarchs said. They protested the Grays' use of "ringers," and the game was thrown out.

After cold weather canceled a game in Chicago, the two teams finished the series September 29 at Philadelphia's Shibe Park. Paige didn't show up until the fourth inning after paying a speeding ticket in Lancaster, Pennsylvania. An exhausted Gibson had already removed himself from the game. With Paige pitching, the Monarchs came back from a 5–2 deficit to win 9–5. The Monarchs swept the Grays in four official World Series games (the others were merely exhibitions).

Several factors explain the Grays' downfall during the 1942 World Series. Leonard credited the Monarchs' deep pitching staff. Besides

Paige, the Monarchs relied on Hilton Smith (another Hall of Famer), Jack Matchett (who was particularly effective against the Grays during the World Series), Booker McDaniels, Jim LaMarque, and future major leaguer Connie Johnson. "They had the best pitching staff I ever saw," Leonard wrote. "They just mostly had ordinary players other than the pitchers."[141]

The Monarchs' most extraordinary pitcher, Paige, according to Paige's good friend Buck O'Neil, had gotten inside the heads of the Grays before the first World Series game at Griffith Stadium. Paige told Grays shortstop Chester Williams that Monarchs owner J. L. Wilkinson would be giving his players all the profits from the World Series. An incredulous Williams informed his Grays teammates, who knew that Posey wouldn't do the same for them. O'Neil wasn't implying that the Grays threw the 1942 Negro League World Series, but Paige had given them something extra to think about besides winning. "These guys, they were stirred up," O'Neil recalled. "They were only getting a percentage of the money. That upset them. We had more to play for than they had to play for." And, according to O'Neil, Wilkinson actually handed over all the proceeds to his players.[142]

After watching Game 2 in Pittsburgh, Grays public relations director John Clark concluded that the Monarchs played harder than the Grays during the 1942 World Series. "The Monarchs outplayed, outhustled and outgamed the Grays in every inning," Clark wrote Art Carter. "To my mind, the Grays showed a very indifferent spirit, in contrast to the Monarchs who played as if something was at stake."[143]

The most credible explanation is that the Grays were simply exhausted. They relied on a much older nucleus than the Monarchs did.[144] Leonard, Gibson, Vic Harris, Jud Wilson, Chester Williams, Jerry Benjamin, Ray Brown, and Sam Bankhead had been playing in the Negro Leagues since the mid-1930s. The Grays' merciless travel schedule had taken its toll. Injuries and defections mounted as the season wore on—with Bankhead breaking his arm before the first World Series game in New York, Partlow pitching with boils under his arm, infielder Jud Wilson injuring his heel before the World Series, outfielder Dave Whatley refusing to play because of a charley horse and then heading home because of a sore shoulder, infielders

143

Matthew Carlisle and Jelly Jackson leaving the team for lucrative defense jobs, and third baseman Howard Easterling heading home to Cincinnati on September 16 after being called for army service.[145]

The Grays' two best players, Leonard and Gibson, bore the brunt of the strain. Financially, they made out OK. Before the season had begun, they used the salaries offered to them by the Mexican League as negotiating leverage. Posey doubled Leonard's monthly salary (from five hundred to one thousand dollars) as well as Gibson's (from six hundred to twelve hundred dollars).[146] Although their salaries paled in comparison to those of Paige or major league stars, Leonard and Gibson were the two highest-paid position players in the Negro Leagues. Their problems were medical rather than financial.

Injuries slowed Leonard all season. A bad knee kept him out of the lineup for a few weeks in May, including the game against Dean's All-Stars. Ten days after he returned on June 18 against the Monarchs, he broke his left hand sliding into second base against the Newark Eagles. The hand injury kept him out of action for nearly two months.

Leonard's body broke down after years of enduring the Grays' cross-country travel schedule, bus rides from Pittsburgh to Washington and then back to Pittsburgh, and 150 to 200 games a year. He had labored for the Grays for a longer uninterrupted stretch than any other member of the team.[147] He was the Grays' captain, their iron man. His devotion to the Grays, however, finally caught up with him. For the first time since 1936, he missed the annual East-West All-Star Game. In early July, while Leonard was recuperating from his hand injury in Rocky Mount, Ric Roberts wrote: "Whatever Became Of—The batting eye of Buck Leonard who, in other years, was always a .400 hitter with a penchant for right-field home runs?"[148] Playing in only eight of fifteen games at Griffith Stadium that season, Leonard finished with a .217 average and two RBI.[149] His league numbers weren't much better: ten of twenty-one games, .233 average, and six RBI.[150]

These statistics fail to capture Leonard's season: the Griffith Stadium numbers exclude numerous games against white semipro teams, and the league numbers exclude games against both semipro teams and Negro American League teams such as the Monarchs. Neither figure conveys the importance of Leonard's game-tying, ninth-inning single off Paige August 13 at Griffith Stadium. But for the first time since Leonard's rookie season with the Grays, Posey left Leonard off his year-end All-American Team. In selecting Newark Eagles infielder Lennie Pearson over Monarchs first baseman Buck O'Neil as his All-Star first baseman, Posey wrote of Leonard: "We think Buck Leonard is the best Negro first baseman of all time, but Buck was out of almost 50 games in 1942."[151] In 1942, Leonard played like the 4-F he was.

Leonard's off-season employment in 1942 couldn't have been worse for a thirty-five-year-old ballplayer with a bad back and aching knees. The draft board forced him to return to work at the railroad station, loading and unloading boxcars for the Railway Express and Southern Express Company. He worked the night shift. The North Carolina winter was cold and wet, and the heavy lifting hurt his back. "That was hard work and I would rather have been playing baseball," he wrote, "but with us being in the war, things were different."[152]

As bad as things were for Leonard in 1942, things looked worse for Gibson. On the surface, everything appeared to be fine. In ten games at Griffith Stadium, he batted .297 with one home run and ten RBI.[153] And in nineteen league games, he fared slightly better: .311 (19 for 61) with a team-leading four home runs and sixteen RBI.[154] He had two hits and an RBI in the East-West Game, and he made Posey's All-American Team.[155]

Behind the numbers and the accolades, however, black baseball's most feared hitter suffered through a horrific season. In 1942, Gibson arrived at spring training in Raleigh, North Carolina, overweight— not a good sign for someone with knees bad enough to keep him out of the military.[156] His futility against Paige was a metaphor for his misfortune. He failed to get a hit off Paige all season.[157] After Paige intentionally walked Easterling to strike him out July 21 at Forbes Field, Gibson went into a tailspin. The nadir of Gibson's season was the second World Series game, when he struck out with the bases loaded against Paige. After the first World Series game at Griffith Sta-

145

dium, an *Afro* photographer captured the normally happy-go-lucky Gibson looking eerily sad.

Gibson showed signs of fatigue during the second half of the season. In August 1942, Posey answered Gibson's critics that the slugger had lost his home-run power of years past. Posey wrote that Gibson had injured himself sliding into a base, making it difficult for him to swing the bat or to reach low balls behind the plate. Against the advice of doctors and Grays management, Gibson insisted on playing through his injury. "We would like to see Josh taking his natural cut at the ball each time at bat or stay out of the game until he can do justice to his vocation," Posey wrote.[158] As the World Series indicated, however, Gibson's batting stroke never came around. The big catcher did not heed the advice of his doctors. During the final game in Philadelphia, he collapsed in the dugout and, after the third inning, mercifully ended his season.[159]

Gibson's body was the least of his problems compared with those inside his head. On New Year's Day in 1943, his whole world came crashing down. The newspapers reported that he had suffered a nervous breakdown. His sister, Anne Gibson Mahaffey, claimed that he suffered an alcohol-induced seizure and lapsed into a coma. She also claimed that doctors diagnosed a brain tumor but that he refused to allow them to operate. Medical records do not support the family's story.[160] After his ten-day stay at Pittsburgh's St. Francis Hospital, the black press continued to report that he had suffered a nervous breakdown.[161] Posey reported that Gibson was "ailing" during the 1942 season and failed to heed the advice of doctors to rest after the World Series. Gibson, according to Posey, had stopped by the Grays' Pittsburgh offices a few weeks later and appeared to be fully recovered.[162] For the rest of his life, however, Gibson battled his inner demons while continuing to perform at a high level on the field.

Despite Leonard's and Gibson's maladies, 1942 was an unmitigated success for the Grays. The Monarchs may have won the World Series, but Posey probably made more money than any other Negro League owner that year. "It was the best financial season ever enjoyed by Negro baseball as a whole," wrote Posey, adding that the Grays, Monarchs, and Clowns "profited most."[163] The source of Posey's windfall: Griffith Stadium.

In Griffith Stadium, Posey was sitting on a gold mine. Only Yankee Stadium—with a stadium capacity of seventy thousand and a larger overall black population in the New York area—drew more fans than the twenty-eight thousand–seat Griffith Stadium during the Negro League World Series. The Grays, however, negotiated directly with Griffith to use his ballpark, avoiding booking agents who forced Negro League teams to fork over a percentage of the profits to use major league ballparks, such as Yankee Stadium, Brooklyn's Ebbets Field, and Philadelphia's Shibe Park. Furthermore, as the home team at Griffith Stadium, the Grays received 70 percent of the profits (though slightly less when Paige pitched). Finally, no ballpark could top the attendance figures from the four games at Griffith Stadium involving the Grays and Paige—twenty-two thousand against Dean's All-Stars, twenty-eight thousand during the June 18 night game against the Monarchs, twenty thousand during the nighttime rematch with the Monarchs, and twenty-five thousand for Game 1 of the World Series. Although the Grays averaged only 6,125 fans during the six Negro National League games in Washington, attendance skyrocketed after Paige's initial appearance.[164]

With an assist from Paige, the Grays rivaled the Senators' popularity in Washington in 1942. During eleven home dates at Griffith Stadium during the 1942 season, the Grays drew 127,690 fans, an average of 11,608 fans a game.[165] By comparison, the Senators played sixty to seventy home games at Griffith Stadium and drew 403,493.[166] With a limited number of games and flexible scheduling in their favor, the Grays outdrew the Senators on many nights. The Grays won their third-straight NNL title while the Senators finished second to last in the American League for the third-straight season. The following year, the Grays found even more ways to put the Senators to shame.

Satchel Paige and the Monarchs drew the largest crowds for the Grays at Griffith Stadium, including the twenty-eight thousand who saw the Grays defeat the Monarchs, 2–1, on June 18, 1942, the first Negro League game under Griffith Stadium's new arc lights. (ART CARTER PAPERS, MOORLAND-SPINGARN RESEARCH CENTER, HOWARD UNIVERSITY)

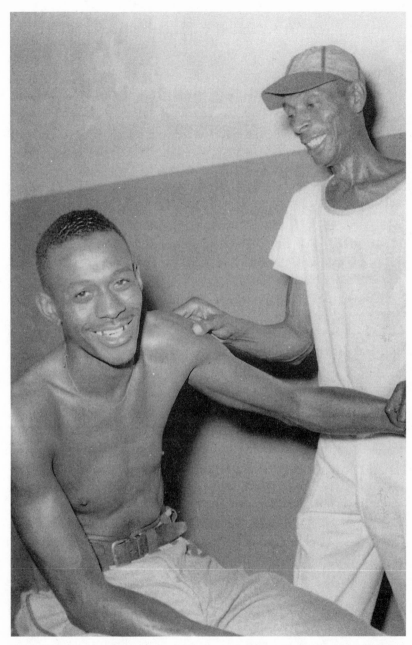

Satchel Paige gets a rubdown from his personal trainer, Frank "Jewbaby" Floyd. "I don't know why they called him 'Jewbaby,' because he was as black as I am," Buck O'Neil told a recent audience of World War II veterans in Washington. (AP/WORLDWIDE)

Buck Leonard reads the 1945 edition of *Negro Baseball* with his Grays teammate, pitcher Ernest "Spoon" Carter, pictured on the cover in his Grays uniform and a military uniform. The Grays lost fewer players during World War II than did other Negro League teams. (ART CARTER PAPERS, MOORLAND-SPINGARN RESEARCH CENTER, HOWARD UNIVERSITY)

Black fans take in a Grays game at Griffith Stadium. The Grays caught on in Washington in 1942, when Satchel Paige started coming to town and Art Carter took over promoting the team in D.C. (ART CARTER PAPERS, MOORLAND-SPINGARN RESEARCH CENTER, HOWARD UNIVERSITY)

Paige shows off one of his many windups at Griffith Stadium. Paige broke many barriers in the major leagues—he was the first black pitcher in the World Series with the Indians in 1948 and the oldest performer in major league history, pitching three innings of scoreless ball at age fifty-nine in 1965 with the Philadelphia Athletics. (ART CARTER PAPERS, MOORLAND-SPINGARN RESEARCH CENTER, HOWARD UNIVERSITY)

Josh Gibson hit more home runs (ten) over Griffith Stadium's left- and center-field walls than the entire American League (nine) in 1943. Gibson stands ready to hit in what has become a classic pose. (ART CARTER PAPERS, MOORLAND-SPINGARN RESEARCH CENTER, HOWARD UNIVERSITY)

SIX

JOSH THE BASHER

In 1943, Josh Gibson kept the Grays competitive compared to the Senators. He led the Grays to another NNL title, thrilled record crowds at Griffith Stadium, and usurped Paige's role as the top drawing card in Washington. Gibson possessed two distinct advantages over Paige as a gate attraction. First, as a position player, Gibson played every day. Second, he could do something that kept fans on the edge of their seats during his at-bats, brought them back to the ballpark, and gave them something to talk about on the street—he smashed titanic home runs.

Apocryphal stories about his home runs undermine the reality of Gibson's greatness. Several ballpark histories dubiously claim that he cleared the back wall of Griffith Stadium's left-field bleachers on two occasions (Mickey Mantle accomplished the feat in 1953 with his famous 565-foot home run off Chuck Stobbs). Nor has anyone ever proved that Gibson hit a ball out of Yankee Stadium, though in 1930 he was the first player to line one into the old left-field bullpen.[1] Robert Peterson's groundbreaking book *Only the Ball Was White* recites a ridiculous tall tale about Gibson's hitting a ball in Pittsburgh that was caught the next day for an out in Philadelphia.[2]

Gibson's Griffith Stadium home runs in 1943, however, are proof of his hitting prowess. He rebounded from his season of futility against Paige and his nervous breakdown with a season for the ages. The box scores and contemporary newspaper accounts confirm that he hit more home runs at Griffith Stadium than the entire Washington Senators team and more home runs over the left- and center-field walls than the entire American League.[3]

Keep in mind the daunting task of hitting a ball over the outfield walls at Griffith Stadium. Its faraway fences made it the toughest home-run park in the American League—405 feet down the left-field line, 421 to straightaway center, and 320 to right. The difficulty lay with the stadium's deep power alleys. Left-center field went from 383 feet to 409. Right-center field went from 378 to 457 (the deepest corner resulted from the right angle around five row houses and the Tree) to 420, backed by a thirty-foot-high wall with a forty-one-foot-high scoreboard in deep center.[4] For a straightaway hitter such as Gibson—who rarely pulled the ball and preferred to keep it in the center of the diamond—hitting a home run over the left- and center-field walls was like blasting a ball out of the Grand Canyon.[5]

Wartime travel restrictions gave Gibson more opportunities to hit home runs at Griffith Stadium than ever before. In 1943, the Office of Price Administration rationed gasoline and banned "pleasure driving." In March, Posey asked Joseph B. Eastland, the director of the Office of Defense Transportation, to allow Negro League teams to continue to use their buses. Posey received an assist from Griffith, who arranged and even agreed to attend the meeting with Eastland. The *Pittsburgh Courier* reported: "Griffith's participating in the meeting marks the first time in history that an owner of a major league team has ever injected himself officially into the operations of organized Negro baseball."[6] Although it is unclear whether Griffith actually participated, Eastland denied Posey's request.[7] The Grays leased their new bus to the government and traveled almost exclusively by rail.

154   Reliance on train travel forced Negro League teams to concentrate their games in railroad-accessible cities with major league ballparks—for the Grays, that ballpark was Griffith Stadium. John L. Clark, the team's Pittsburgh public relations arm, viewed Griffith Stadium as the Grays' primary advantage in 1943:

> The Grays get credit for stringing along with Griffith Stadium and made it pay last year. Washington Potomacs, Pittsburgh Crawfords

and Tom Wilson's Elite Giants tried Clark Griffith's ball yard and gave it up as a bad job. But the Grays made it pay off in big league figures last year for day and night games.[8]

For teams north, south, east, and west, Washington was one of the easiest cities to get to by train because Union Station was a major hub on the East Coast's rail line. From Washington, teams headed south to Norfolk (shifting into segregated cars in the nation's capital) or north to Philadelphia, Newark, and New York City. Few teams, however, veered off the main rail line to Pittsburgh. In 1943, the Grays' original home city was all but forgotten. "We drew a whole lot better [in Washington]," pitcher Edsall Walker recalled. "We didn't play too many games in Pittsburgh. . . . We might play in Pittsburgh maybe once a month."[9]

The Grays wore their uniforms with the Ws on their left sleeves more often in 1943 than at any other time in their history. That year, they played more than twice as many home dates in Washington (twenty-six) as in Pittsburgh (eleven), dwarfing their eleven appearances in the nation's capital in 1942. Negro League teams clamored to play in Washington, having heard about the twenty thousand–plus fans at the Grays' Griffith Stadium contests the previous season. In 1943, the Monarchs and Newark Eagles played there four times; the Baltimore Elite Giants, New York Cubans, Philadelphia Stars, and Birmingham Black Barons three times; the St. Louis Stars twice; and the Cleveland Buckeyes, Atlanta Black Crackers, New York Black Yankees, and the white semipro Brooklyn Bushwicks each made an appearance. "The club played to meager crowds of two thousand to three thousand for two seasons in Washington, the city they represent in the Negro National League," Carter wrote. "Then, like a bolt out of the sky, things began to click last season. Washington had become a boom-town under the strain of war-time government activity, and in its midst was the best-publicized and greatest club in colored baseball."[10]

Wartime travel restrictions provided the Grays with a captive audience. They prevented Washington's growing black middle class from escaping the city's brutal summer heat by heading off to Highland

155

Beach (the super-elite colony started by Frederick Douglass's grand-son on the Chesapeake Bay), Harpers Ferry, Saratoga, Martha's Vine-yard, or the Jersey Shore.[11] Washington's black war workers also thirsted for recreational outlets. *Crisis* magazine wrote: "Never before has there been such a demand for recreation and never before has there been so much money available for recreation. . . ."[12]

Black Washingtonians flush with money to spend flocked to Grays games at Griffith Stadium. They rode streetcars that ran along Florida Avenue and Seventh Street and stopped in front of the sta-dium. "During the war when the people couldn't get much gas, that's when our best crowds were," Leonard told John Holway. "People couldn't travel so they would have to stay in Washington on week-ends. After the war, our crowds started dwindling again."[13]

Midway through the 1943 season, after thirteen appearances at Griffith Stadium, the Grays crushed their single-season attendance record in Washington of 125,000 set in 1942.[14] Even by the most con-servative estimates based on incomplete box scores and declining attendance figures in late August and September, the Grays' remain-ing thirteen home dates at Griffith Stadium resulted in an additional 100,000 fans. All told, the Grays' twenty-six appearances in Wash-ington during the 1943 season attracted more than 225,000 people.[15] Sunday doubleheaders consistently drew ten thousand fans, and three of the Grays-Monarchs clashes fetched more than twenty thousand apiece. "We drew like mad," Walker recalled. "In the street, we asked people, 'Are you coming to the game tonight?' They'd say, 'No, we know who's gonna win.'"[16] The Grays won. People came. And not just because of Paige.

In front of record crowds, Gibson wrested center stage away from Paige by hitting a home run once every four games. The least of his accomplishments was outslugging the Senators. During the Grays' forty games at Griffith Stadium in 1943, Gibson hit ten (and arguably eleven, as explained later) home runs. The Senators, in seventy-six games and with nine hitters in their lineup, hit only nine.[17] Of the Senators' nine home runs, one was inside the park and five were over the closer right-field fence. Griffith's expansive ballpark forced him to build his team around speed, not power. The Senators' leading home-run hitter in 1943, Stan Spence, hit only two of his twelve homers in Washington.[18] Of the team's next leading home-run hitters, "Indian" Bob Johnson hit only two of his career-low seven home runs at Griffith Stadium, and Mickey Vernon managed only one.[19] As left-handed hitters, Spence and Vernon had the advantage of hitting to right field.[20] With the right-field fence listed as 328 feet from home plate (it was actually only 320 feet), Vernon and Spence merely poked the ball over the thirty-foot-high wall.

Gibson, by contrast, was a right-handed batter who smashed his homers to left and center. The Senators often heard about Gibson's exploits upon their return home. "When we came in from a road trip, some of the fellas in the clubhouse talked about the black teams that had played there the previous weekend," Vernon recalled. "They would talk about some ball Josh Gibson had hit high up in the bleachers."[21]

Gibson clouted more home runs over Griffith Stadium's left-field and center-field walls in 1943 than the entire American League. He launched ten home runs in forty games and roughly 160 at-bats. In seventy-six games and roughly 5,400 at-bats, two hundred–plus American Leaguers managed only nine over the same two fences. Of the twenty-three Griffith Stadium home runs by American Leaguers in 1943, four of them landed inside the park (a likely occurrence with a center-field corner extending to 457 feet) and ten of them over the 320-foot right-field fence.[22] That leaves only nine American League home runs over the left-field and center-field walls.

Gibson's success compared to the American League defies a single explanation. As a whole, American League home runs plummeted during the war years. American Leaguers hit nearly nine hundred home runs in 1940 but only about half as many during each of the 1943, 1944, and 1945 seasons.[23] Many players attributed the home-run drought to the quality of the ball. With rubber in short supply in 1943, Spalding replaced the ball's rubber core with balata, a substance from the milk of tropical trees used to make the cover of golf balls. The players complained that the balata baseballs didn't go anywhere.[24] The Senators ran out of the balata balls on May 2 and began using their old supply of rubber core balls from 1942. That same day Yankees outfielder Charlie Keller hit the first home run of the season at Griffith Stadium over the right-field fence.[25] Although league officials soon replaced the dead balata balls with a livelier version, home-run production did not pick up until the rest of the major leaguers returned from the war in 1946.

The Negro Leagues, however, also used a notoriously poor-quality ball, the Wilson W 150 CC. Grays pitcher Ray Brown and center fielder Jerry Benjamin endorsed the Wilson ball on the back page of the 1945 and 1946 *Negro Baseball* yearbooks.[26] In truth, Negro Leaguers hated the Wilson ball; they believed it "wasn't as lively as" Spalding's major league baseballs.[27] "They didn't go as far, they didn't last as long, [and] they didn't stay in uniform shape like the major league balls do," Leonard explained to John Holway.[28] The Negro Leagues used the Wilson ball because it was cheaper. Baseballs ranked among the biggest expenses during a typical game. The Grays bought between forty-eight and eighty-seven dollars worth of baseballs for a Griffith Stadium doubleheader.[29] Many teams reused old baseballs to save money. Newark Eagles owner Abe Manley once sent a note down to the dugout in the middle of a long at-bat by outfielder Fran Matthews, threatening to fine Matthews the cost of the ball if he fouled any additional pitches into the stands.[30]

Quality pitching and hitting factored more prominently than bad baseballs in comparing Gibson and his American League counterparts. Leonard was one of many Negro Leaguers who admitted that the Negro Leagues could not match the depth of pitching talent in the major leagues. Yet, during the war, the draft forced major league teams to send almost anyone out to the mound, including youngsters such as fifteen-year-old Joe Nuxhall, who played with the Cincinnati Reds in 1944. The draft also robbed the American League of its most prolific home-run hitters, with DiMaggio, Williams, and Greenberg serving their country in 1943. Negro League teams also suffered from a dearth of wartime pitching and hitting talent. When they came to Griffith Stadium, however, their ace pitchers faced Gibson and the Grays. Paige dueled with Gibson four times in Washington that year, and fellow Hall of Fame pitcher Leon Day of the Newark Eagles also squared off against Gibson. Comparing the quality of pitching, hitting, and baseballs was basically a wash.

A more important factor in explaining Gibson's success compared with the American League was his fundamentally sound swing. With a small stride, compact stroke, and enormous physique, Gibson never twisted up like a top after a strikeout, à la Ruth or Reggie Jackson. Gibson generated his power with his massive wrists. He loved curveballs. Occasionally, a pitcher could sneak a fastball by him. But more than a few pitchers who tried this tactic ended up seeing balls sailing over their heads and outfield fences. Griffith once said Gibson "hits a baseball for more distance with less effort than any player I ever saw."[31]

Signs of Gibson's offensive explosion began during the Grays' May 16 doubleheader sweep of the Baltimore Elite Giants. With Griffith and U.S. Senator James M. Mead of New York in attendance, Gibson was 2 for 3 in the first game and 3 for 4 in the second with four doubles overall (three of them in the second game).[32] Doubles and triples at Griffith Stadium, however, were standard fare.

Gibson's home-run barrage began May 23 in the second game of a doubleheader sweep over the Philadelphia Stars. In the sixth inning, Gibson clouted a 440-foot blast into the left-center-field stands (he also had homered the previous day at Philadelphia's Shibe Park).[33] The *Afro* headline blared, "Gibson's 440-Homer in Second Game Thrills 6,500 Fans." Harold Jackson was in his first year covering the Grays for the *Afro* (replacing Ric Roberts in January 1943) while doubling as the Grays' radio play-by-play man and public-address announcer. Having grown up going to Griffith Stadium, Jackson had seen dozens of games there. His *Afro* story described Gibson's home run as a "rare treat."[34]

Gibson made a liar out of Jackson by homering twice in the same game during the Grays' next Griffith Stadium appearance. Gibson slammed a 440-foot home run into the middle of the left-center-field bleachers during a 17–0 rout of the Elite Giants on May 31. In the seventh inning, he lined another home run 422 feet into center field. After Gibson's second home run, "the fans could hardly keep their seats," the *Washington Tribune* reported of the ten thousand on hand. "Money rained down on the slugging catcher from everywhere."[35]

Tigers first baseman Rudy York homered to left field off Senators pitcher Jim Mertz on June 3. Gibson 3, AL 1.[36]

York homered three days later to left field off Mertz. Gibson 3, AL 2.[37]

For an encore, Gibson walloped Griffith Stadium home runs numbers four and five in each game of a June 15 doubleheader with the New York Cubans. Both the *Afro* and the *Courier* described Gibson's bombs as 450-foot line drives.[38] They left the mighty slugger unfazed. "Josh hit two more homers and acted like he had done nothing outstanding," Harold Jackson wrote. "This was four homers in four games for the Grays' famous catcher."[39]

Senators outfielder Bob Johnson homered to center field off Philadelphia Athletics pitcher Jesse Flores on June 26. Gibson 5, AL 3.[40]

Gibson's sixth home run at Griffith Stadium won the second game of the Grays' July 4 doubleheader against the Newark Eagles. He set off his fireworks in the sixth, a 430-foot shot into the center-field bleachers with Leonard aboard to give the Grays a 6–5 victory.[41] Two days later, Gibson smashed the first pitch to him for number seven. The 420-foot line drive over the left-field fence led the Grays to an 11–3 victory over the white semipro Brooklyn Bushwicks.[42]

Johnson homered to left field off Boston Red Sox pitcher Yank Terry on July 15. Gibson 7, AL 4.[43]

York homered to left field off Senators pitcher Milo Candini on July 21. Gibson 7, AL 5.[44]

York homered to center field off Senators pitcher Dutch Leonard on July 22. Gibson 7, AL 6.[45]

160 *St. Louis Browns catcher Frankie Hayes homered to left field off Senators pitcher Ray Scarborough on August 1. Gibson 7, AL 7.*[46]

Senators second baseman Jerry Priddy homered to left field off St. Louis Browns pitcher Bob Muncrief on August 3. Gibson 7, AL 8.[47]

In the Grays' first game in nearly a month at Griffith Stadium, Gibson hit his eighth home run during an August 8 doubleheader with the Newark Eagles. In the first inning of the initial contest, Gibson nailed a 2–2 pitch from Eagles pitcher Len Hooker 430 feet into the center-field bleachers for a two-run homer.[48] In the second game, facing Leon Day, Gibson "blasted one of Day's pitches 480 feet out to the deep center field wall for a triple," according to Harold Jackson.[49] The deepest part of Griffith Stadium was 457 feet from home plate. The center-field wall plus the scoreboard was forty-one feet high. Either Jackson was exaggerating, or Gibson hit the ball fairly high up on the wall. Nonetheless, Gibson hit one of the nation's longest non–home runs.

Gibson's near home runs proved to be more exciting than the routine shots that landed in the stands. That's because he hit balls at Griffith Stadium where no one had hit them before. During the second game of an August 15 doubleheader against the New York Cubans, Gibson swatted a ball so far that it hit the number one figure on the clock above the right-center-field scoreboard. The right-center-field wall was well over four hundred feet from home plate. The scoreboard was forty-one feet high. The clock was above the scoreboard. The umpires, who halted play for about ten minutes to confer about the decision, ruled the blast a triple. Grays manager Candy Jim Taylor argued that it was a home run.[50] The umps blew the call. Major league baseball's 1943 "Official Playing Rules" for Griffith Stadium state: "If ball hits clock in right field, it is home run, as the clock is not in playing field."[51] Although technically the ball landed over the wall in right-center, it was closer to center field than right. Nonetheless, Gibson should have been credited with his ninth home run.

In late August and September, Gibson hammered additional home runs at Griffith Stadium that actually counted. Gibson registered his ninth official home run, a center-field shot, in the second game of an August 21 doubleheader with the Baltimore Elite Giants. The previous day in Pittsburgh, Gibson homered twice in a game against the Elites.[52] In the Grays' next game in Washington, the Black Yankees walked Gibson four-straight times until they found themselves with Gibson at the plate with the bases loaded. Gibson singled to right to score all three runs.[53]

Gibson's tenth home run, during a September 12 doubleheader against the Philadelphia Stars, came in dramatic fashion—the 420-

foot shot into the left-field bleachers broke an 11–11 tenth-inning tie and gave the Grays a 13–11 victory.[54] It was his final Griffith Stadium homer of the season—either his tenth or eleventh depending on your view.

The Grays finished with a 32–6 record at Griffith Stadium in 1943.[55] With Gibson, Leonard, and Cool Papa Bell on the same team, the 1943 Grays featured three future Hall of Famers. Posey placed four members of the Grays on his year-end All-American Team: Gibson, Leonard, third baseman Howard Easterling, and center fielder Jerry Benjamin. Offensively, the Grays pummeled the opposition. Right-hander John Wright (26–4) and left-hander Edsall Walker (18–5) emerged as the Grays' top two pitchers that season, with Ernest "Spoon" Carter and Ray Brown also carrying major portions of the load. "Look it, I would have paid to pitch for that team," recalled Walker, who rejoined the Grays in 1943 after a season of defense work and part-time duty with the Philadelphia Stars. "It was a cinch."[56]

The war forced the Grays to make personnel changes. Vic Harris (who had turned over the managerial reins to Candy Jim Taylor), infielder Matthew "Lick" Carlisle, and Brown preferred to hold onto lucrative, year-round defense jobs and play for the Grays on weekends. Pitcher Roy Partlow spent most of the season in the Mexican League. The Grays lost outfielder David Whatley and pitcher Roy Welmaker to the draft. To replace Whatley, the Grays signed the fastest man in the history of the Negro Leagues, 40-year-old James "Cool Papa" Bell. Bell led off, played left field, and proved he could still hit.

The players benefited from wartime travel restrictions. The Grays' owners no longer could shuttle them back and forth between Pittsburgh and Washington on the same day. The lack of constant travel was easier on older players, such as Leonard and Bell. It also gave them all time to enjoy Black Washington's sights and sounds. Leonard relished Howard Theater performances by comedian Dewey "Pigmeat" Markham. "If Pigmeat were on the stage, he didn't have to say anything," Lena Cox, Leonard's sister who lived in Washington, recalled. "Buck would just crack up if Pigmeat walked out there."[57]

Opposing teams looked forward to coming to Washington. "The Howard Theater was a must," O'Neil recalled. "We would come to Washington to see Redd Foxx and Moms Mabley. It was quite a time, really."[58] The Grays and the Monarchs played hard on the field but socialized together at night. The Monarchs depended on the Grays to fill them in about Black Washington's hot spots. "At night we would go to the same places," O'Neil recalled. "They would tell us, 'So-and-so's in town, let's go there.'"[59]

The best show in town in the summer of 1943 was Gibson versus Paige. Josh settled his score with Satchel several times that season. During the first game of a June 17 Griffith Stadium doubleheader, twenty thousand witnessed Gibson and the Grays pound Paige for seven runs in three innings. Gibson was 4 for 5 with two doubles and four RBI in the first contest, and 2 for 4 with two doubles in the second. Four days later at Forbes Field, Gibson homered off Paige to avenge the indignity of their previous meeting there—Gibson's three-pitch, bases-loaded strikeout.[60] Big Josh showed Satchel, not to mention the Grays' fans in Pittsburgh, who was king.

During the Monarchs' return to Griffith Stadium in mid-August, Monarchs manager Frank Duncan chose not to pitch Paige. With twenty-two thousand fans on hand, however, the Grays held up the game for fifteen minutes until Paige took the mound. Paige pitched five scoreless innings, Gibson mustered only one bad-hop base hit, and the Monarchs cruised to an 11–3 victory.[61] Of the annual East-West Game in Chicago, the *Washington Tribune*'s Lanier "Pee Wee" Covington wrote: "The only interest in the game for Washingtonians is the battle between the Grays' home run king, Josh Gibson, and the most publicized hurler in modern baseball, Leroy 'Satchel' Paige."[62]

Gibson bested Paige the remainder of that season. Gibson homered off Paige for the second time August 29 at Chicago's Wrigley Field. Paige's problem was that Wrigley Field's left-field wall was too close to home plate to contain Gibson's laserlike shots. In the first inning, Gibson poked a three-run homer 360 feet to left-center. Two innings later, he smacked a double off the same wall 368 feet away. At Griffith Stadium, those 360 and 368 shots would have been routine outs. In the fifth inning, Paige finally solved his problems with

Gibson (who finished the day 4 for 4) by walking him intentionally.[63] For Paige, walking other players to get to Gibson was a thing of the past. So were the Grays' troubles in the World Series. After capturing another Negro National League title, the Grays defeated the Birmingham Black Barons in the Negro League World Series four games to three. The World Series once again, however, turned into a farce, with Chicago American Giants catcher Ted "Double Duty" Radcliffe and other Negro American League players joining the Black Barons and meager crowds forcing the cancellation of the final exhibition game in New Orleans.[64]

Around this time, Gibson began receiving the national media attention traditionally reserved for Paige. In July 1942, *Sport* magazine glowingly profiled Gibson and dubbed him a "$200,000 catcher."[65] The following year, *Sport* featured the entire Grays team along with two pages of photographs, including a full-page close-up of Gibson in his catching gear. The magazine also included an image of Gibson surrounded by a group of admiring black children above a caption describing him as the "chocolate-skinned Babe Ruth."[66] In July 1943, *Time* magazine ran a one-page story on Gibson with a picture under the headline, "Josh the Basher." The article referred to Paige as "famed but fading."[67]

White Sox pitcher Eddie Smith homered to left-center field off Senators pitcher Bill LeFebvre on September 26. Gibson 10 (or 11), AL 9.[68]

The American League couldn't even catch up to Gibson after his season at Griffith Stadium had ended. He hit ten home runs to left and center (eleven including the right-center-field clock shot), compared with nine by American Leaguers over the same two walls, and nine by the Senators over any wall and inside the park. Carter, who first wrote about Gibson's dominance over the American League, dubbed Gibson "the uncrowned Home Run King of Baseball." Under the headline "Joltin' Josh Helps Grays hit the Jackpot," Carter posited that Gibson was the biggest reason for the Grays' new attendance record at Griffith Stadium. Carter went easy on the Old Fox's refusal to sign Gibson: "Clark Griffith, white haired owner of the Washington Senators, once called Gibson a $250,000 catcher and lamented the fact that his skin was black—an accident of birth that denies him the privilege of making the heavy 'sugar' paid major league players."[69] Griffith pumped up Gibson as a $250,000 ballplayer because Gibson made Griffith at least that much money at Griffith Stadium over the years. Grays' games had become so lucrative for Griffith by 1943 that he rescheduled one of the Senators' regular-season games so that the Grays could play a World Series game in his ballpark.[70]

Griffith attended almost every one of the Grays' home games. They piqued his curiosity because of the tremendous talent lurking in his ballpark when the Senators were out of town. Not everyone on the Grays was capable of playing in the major leagues. The play of Gibson and Leonard, however, raised Griffith's bushy eyebrows.

Sometime during the 1942 or 1943 season, Griffith's curiosity got the best of him. After one of the Grays' doubleheaders in his ballpark, he sent a message down to the locker room. Leonard and Gibson should report to Griffith's office immediately.

"Sam Lacey [sic] and Ric Roberts and a lot of the other fellows have been talking about getting you fellows on the Senators' team," Griffith told the two black superstars. "Well let me tell you something: If we get you boys, we're going to get the best ones. It's going to break up your league. Now what do you all think of that?"

"Well, we haven't given it much thought," they replied. "We'd be happy to play in the major leagues and believe that we could make the major leagues, but so far as clamoring for it, we'll let somebody else do that."

"Well, I just wanted to see how you fellows felt about it," Griffith said.

"Well if we were given the chance, we'd play all right, try to make it," they responded. "And I believe we could make it."[71]

Relaying the account of that meeting to John Holway, Leonard recalled:

I always thought the Senators might be the first to take a Negro, because Washington was about half Negro then. I figured if half the city boycotted the games, the other half would come. But Griffith was always looking for Cuban ballplayers. He had Joe Cambria down

165

there scouting for him. I guess he didn't have to pay them much money—but he wouldn't have had to pay us much either.[72]

The integration of professional baseball surfaced as a hot topic during the 1942 season. In March, a UCLA football star named Jackie Robinson and Nate Moreland, a former Baltimore Elite Giants and Mexican League pitcher, showed up at the Chicago White Sox's spring training facilities in Pasadena, California (Robinson and Moreland's hometown). The two players requested a tryout. The request was denied.[73]

A few months later, Brooklyn Dodgers manager Leo Durocher made national headlines by declaring that he would field black players if the owners and the commissioner would let him. Judge Landis, however, refused to play the fall guy. "There is no rule or understanding, 'subterranean' or otherwise, barring Negroes from participating in major league baseball," Landis declared in July 1942.[74] Larry MacPhail, then president of the Dodgers, responded that Landis's statement was "100 per cent hypocrisy" and that a tacit bar prevented blacks from playing in the majors.[75]

Durocher's comments and Landis's response ignited calls for integration in Washington. *Washington Times-Herald* columnist Vincent X. Flaherty, no racial liberal himself, tried to appeal to Griffith in language that the Old Fox could understand—dollars and cents. "Some day the colored star will make his way in either the National or American league. When? That's something else Judge Landis might answer," Flaherty wrote. "When it happens, you can look for greatly increased attendance figures from all fronts. Why not start it off by giving Josh Gibson the first try?"[76]

166   Griffith attempted to mollify the Senators' black fans while protecting his business interests in the Grays. "Colored people should develop their own big league baseball and challenge the best of the white major leagues," Griffith advised. "I am sure the latter would be willing to allow their best teams to meet such an accredited colored nine.

"Why take a few stars like Satchel Paige and Josh Gibson away and put them in with the whites and ruin organized colored baseball? No, build up your leagues for the benefit of all colored ball players instead of just a few."[77]

Grays manager Vic Harris echoed Griffith's prescription. "If they take our best boys," Harris said, "we will be but a hollow shell of what we are today. No, let us build up our own league and, as Clark Griffith said, we can then challenge the best white team in the majors and play them."[78] As the manager of the nation's best black baseball team in 1942, Harris was protecting his livelihood. Several of Harris's players, notably Jud Wilson, Ray Brown, Dave Whatley, and Jerry Benjamin, expressed skepticism that any progress would be made in the near future.[79] Gibson, however, remained optimistic: "Dozens of us would make the majors if given the opportunity to play under the same circumstances as whites."[80]

Paige's reaction to all of this talk about integration caused a firestorm. On the eve of black baseball's 1942 East-West Game, Paige told an Associated Press reporter in Albany, New York, that he would prefer to stay in the Negro Leagues rather than sacrifice his thirty-seven thousand dollar yearly salary. Paige refused to face "unharmonious other problems" playing in the majors. He said: "All the nice statements in the world from both sides aren't going to knock out Jim Crow."[81]

Paige publicly denied the story. Arriving at the East-West Game in the second inning, he entered the game in the seventh. Before taking the mound, he strode into the dugout and grabbed the public-address microphone. Players from both dugouts stood up and listened. Paige said he favored integration, but that it "might be a good idea to put a complete Negro team in the majors."[82] The speech took Paige off his game. He intentionally walked Gibson twice and allowed three earned runs as the East won 5–2 before 45,179 paying customers.[83] The black press leveled its criticism not at Paige's pitching performance but at his thoughts on integration.

Even in exile, Lacy tossed verbal grenades at Paige. As the assistant national editor for the *Chicago Defender*, Lacy lacked a sports column. So Lacy's closest friend among the white daily press corps, Bob Considine, turned over his entire *Washington Post* column to Lacy, who wrote:

Four years ago when I made what I guess you'd call an all-out effort to win a place in the majors for some truly great Negro players I told Clark Griffith that I didn't think Paige—though he was the best known—could last more than a few months in the big leagues. The reason: He's an "arm pitcher," not a "head pitcher." He's a remarkable physical specimen. His fast ball is as good today as it was ten years ago. He might still make a liar out of me, but I doubt it. . . .

Paige's proposal that a Colored team be admitted to one or both of the big leagues, as an entity, is foolish. There can be no compromise with prejudice. Unless Negro players are infiltrated, the same situation will exist. A separate club for Negroes is no more logical than a separate team for Italians, Irishmen, Germans, Poles, Lithuanians or Jews. I'm not convinced that just now is the time to accomplish our end.[84]

Although Lacy may have underestimated Paige's pitching talent, the sportswriter proved to be prescient about how integration would occur.

Lacy recognized that Paige's proposal mirrored Griffith's. At the end of his guest column in the *Post*, the erstwhile *Afro* sports columnist turned his vitriol on the Senators' owner: "Griff's advice to me [in December 1937] was to get our houses in order: strengthen our institutions, organize ourselves. He said that once these things were done that it 'would probably follow' that the majors would be forced to recognize us as a responsible minor league. . . . [N]o one asks the Norwegians, Cubans or French to organize themselves into formidable groups before being admitted to major competition."[85]

Lacy's attack on Griffith was a prelude of things to come. In 1942 and 1943, Washington's black press corps lacked a powerful voice such as Lacy's promoting integration. His guest column revealed seeds of radicalization in his thinking. He rejected an argument he had agreed with several years earlier—that black baseball should build up its own league. By 1942, he could no longer tolerate Griffith's hypocrisy.

Griffith's argument—"build up your own league"—was completely self-serving. His stale solution only padded his wallet. During the 1942 season, in which Griffith received 20 percent of the Grays' gate receipts on the 127,690 fans plus a fee for using his new lights, he probably made at least sixty thousand dollars. In 1943, given that the Grays' attendance at Griffith Stadium eclipsed 225,000, his take increased to one hundred thousand dollars. The revenue from Grays games kept Griffith from signing Gibson or Leonard. In making his primary concern his profits from black baseball, Griffith preferred that the Thunder Twins stayed in their own league. "Clark Griffith said our league wasn't organized," Leonard liked to say. "We were organized, but we weren't recognized."[86]

During the 1943 season, pressure on Griffith to integrate intensified as World War II accelerated the fight for racial equality in the nation's capital. Unlike the race riots in 1943 that exploded in Detroit, however, black Washingtonians mobilized for social change through nonviolent protest. In April 1943, a group of Howard University students led by spokeswoman Pauli Murray protested two whites-only restaurants, the Little Palace Lunch at Fourteenth and U Streets and Fish and Chips Restaurant in the 2400 block of Georgia Avenue. The students picketed for four days before the restaurants changed their policies. The protesters marched with banners that read: "Our boys and our brothers are fighting for you—why can't we eat here?"[87]

Perhaps the most tragic local symbol of the war was the death of Wilmeth Sidat-Singh. Syracuse's "Hindu" halfback whom Lacy had exposed in 1937 as an American-born black was a second lieutenant in the famous all-black flying force known as the Tuskegee Airmen. In May 1943, Sidat-Singh's plane caught fire during a routine flying mission and crashed into Lake Huron. Sidat-Singh drowned after ejecting from his plane.[88]

Amid wartime attention about segregation and discrimination, the black press exhorted black Washingtonians to abandon the Senators in favor of the Grays by appealing to their racial pride. In March 1943, Carter encouraged the *Afro*'s readers to boycott major league baseball over the integration issue. "If John Q. Fan says he wants to see colored players on the major league teams," Carter wrote, "and says it by word and deed, the stubborn owners would soon let down the bars."[89] Carter, mindful of his promotional position with the Grays, refrained from singling out Griffith for criticism.

The Grays played at Griffith Stadium so frequently in 1943 that people began associating the Grays with the Griffiths. Harold Jackson attempted to put the Griffith-owns-the-Grays rumors to rest in late May: "I think the Washington sports public can be assured that there is no truth to the story that the Grays are partially owned by Clark Griffith, or that he has a share in the Negro National League champions." Jackson identified Cum Posey and Sonnyman Jackson as the Grays' owners and See Posey as the team's business manager: "It is a pleasure to inform the fans of Washington that the Washington Homestead Grays are owned and operated by three colored gentlemen, who handle the affairs of the club the way a well organized business should be handled."[90] Basically, Carter and Jackson started a "buy black" campaign.

Aiding Carter and Jackson's efforts, Griffith showed a total disregard for the Senators' black fans by re-signing the Yankees' racist outfielder Jake Powell. The Senators needed another outfielder as they chased the Yankees for first place in the war-depleted American League. The Senators' second-place finish (thirteen and a half games behind the Yankees) in 1943 was their best since winning the AL pennant ten years earlier. Powell, who had been out of the majors since 1940, played for the Senators for the next three seasons. In 1948, he shot himself to death in a D.C. police station after being charged with passing bad checks.[91] Although Griffith was known for having a soft spot for his former ballplayers who were down on their luck, signing Powell in 1943 triggered the ire of the black press. "Local followers can answer this by staying away from the park, and letting it be known by mail their reason for doing so," Jackson wrote. "It is an insult in every meaning of the word."[92]

Despite Jackson's best efforts, the Senators' 1943 attendance increased by more than 170,000 to 574,694.[93] Griffith benefited from a competitive team, unlimited night games, and thousands of recreation-starved war workers. By comparison, more than 225,000 fans flocked to the Grays' twenty-six home dates at Griffith Stadium in 1943. The Grays sometimes attracted larger crowds than the Senators, but the Senators sometimes attracted larger crowds than the Grays. Either way, Griffith made money.

The Grays had at least one thing the Senators did not—"the uncrowned Home Run King of Baseball."[94] Gibson represented the best argument for integration. His home runs inspired black pride like a Joe Louis knockout punch or a Jesse Owens dash for Olympic glory. They symbolized black strength, black achievement, black superiority, and, in light of Gibson's mental breakdown after the 1942 season, black redemption.

Black Washington celebrated Gibson's magnificent 1943 season by making the Grays' September 6 game against the Philadelphia Stars "Josh Gibson Night." Although only six thousand people attended the rain-delayed affair and the Grays lost, 4–2, the slugging catcher had won Washington's affection. In between the sixth and seventh innings, with Gibson still wearing his shin guards and chest protector, a female Grays fan presented him with a floral wreath and an oversized, four-foot-tall baseball bat filled with money like a gigantic piggy bank and emblazoned with the moniker, "Josh the Basher." Posey, who rarely attended Grays games outside of Pittsburgh, presented him with two pieces of luggage.[95] Josh Gibson Night was much-deserved recognition for Gibson. In forty games at Griffith Stadium that season, he hit .503 (75 for 149) with twenty-one doubles, six triples, ten home runs, and fifty-nine RBI.[96] Although statistically his 1943 season appeared to be a miraculous recovery from his nervous breakdown and second-half slump in 1942, the fans never saw the depth of his suffering.

Gibson's homer-happy 1943 season masked a period of inner turmoil. Before spring training that year, he spent five weeks convalescing in Hot Springs, Arkansas.[97] During the season, however, he exacerbated his mental problems by abusing alcohol and possibly other drugs. Along with his best friend on the club, shortstop Sam Bankhead, he often violated team rules by drinking beer on the bus. Gibson, however, also took to drinking whiskey. His teammates even suspected that he smoked marijuana. In Washington, he dated a woman named Grace, the wife of an overseas serviceman, who may have turned him on to drugs.[98]

Under the influence of alcohol and possibly drugs, Gibson's behavior took an erratic turn. During an exhibition against the Birmingham Black Barons in Norfolk, Virginia, Gibson and five other players stayed at the home of Buck Leonard's wife's sister. Gibson had gotten so drunk that he began walking around the house naked. His alcoholic binges, according to Leonard, landed the Grays' slugger two fifteen-day stints at Washington's St. Elizabeth Hospital. Although Leonard insists that Gibson's stays in Washington's most famous mental hospital occurred in 1943, Gibson played in all forty games at Griffith Stadium that season. Indeed, the black press didn't report Gibson's Washington hospital stays until the following season. In 1943, Gibson's hitting didn't appear to have suffered. Alcohol abuse, however, affected his fielding. He struggled even harder to catch pop-ups. Leonard would race in from first base to catch them for him.[99]

Overshadowed by Gibson's home runs for much of 1943, Leonard rebounded from his disappointing 1942 campaign with another fantastic season. He played in all forty games at Griffith Stadium and finished second to Gibson in almost every major offensive category, hitting .326 with eleven doubles, six triples, two home runs, and thirty-eight RBI.[100] He also homered in the ninth inning of the 1943 East-West Game at Chicago's Comiskey Park before a record crowd of 51,723 fans.[101] Leonard's finest hour that season, however, came during that sparsely attended September 5 doubleheader against Paige and the Monarchs. Leonard rapped three hits against Paige, chasing him from the game in the fourth inning as the Grays coasted to an 8–1 victory.[102] In naming Leonard to his annual All-American Team, Posey wrote: "One of the greatest clutch hitters in Negro baseball, Leonard came back sensationally this year and was by far the best first sacker in the business."[103]

Buck was back. After the Grays' 1943 season, he joined a Negro League All-Star team headlined by Paige that played a series of exhibition games in California against a major league All-Star team led by Senators pitcher Bobo Newsom. Although Gibson did not play, perhaps because of his erratic behavior and mental problems, Leonard showed the major leaguers that he belonged. Leonard hit safely in seven of eight games and finished with a .333 average (9 for 27).[104]

For Leonard and Gibson, however, time was running out on their playing in the major leagues. They pulled off terrific seasons in 1943 because of experience and a lack of physical injuries. But they were playing on borrowed time. Only Lacy's crusade to integrate the major leagues could save them.

Josh Gibson looks skyward at Griffith Stadium. Gibson's major weakness defensively, particularly in his later years, was catching pop-ups. Some people, including Sam Lacy, believed that Gibson was only an average defensive catcher. (ROBERT H. MCNEILL)

Josh Gibson signs a baseball for Marva Louis, the wife of heavyweight champion Joe Louis, before the 1944 East-West All-Star Game in Chicago. (ART CARTER PAPERS, MOORLAND-SPINGARN RESEARCH CENTER, HOWARD UNIVERSITY)

A smiling Josh Gibson swings away at Griffith Stadium. When Gibson returned to the Grays in 1937, he "brought new life into everybody," according to Leonard. (ROBERT H. MCNEILL)

Jackie Robinson spent one unhappy season in the Negro Leagues with the Kansas City Monarchs in 1945, making two appearances at Griffith Stadium. In his second season with the Dodgers, Robinson wrote an article for *Ebony* magazine blasting the organization and conditions in the Negro Leagues.
(LIBRARY OF CONGRESS)

SEVEN

SAM'S CRUSADE

Sam Lacy returned to Washington, D.C., in 1944 with a completely different take on Griffith than he had in the past. After Lacy's groundbreaking interview with Griffith about integration in December 1937, Lacy and Griffith had seen eye-to-eye on a number of issues. Seven years later, however, Lacy viewed Griffith as public enemy number one.

Lacy's radicalization arose in part from his failures in Chicago. In 1942 and 1943, while on a self-imposed exile as the *Chicago Defender's* assistant national editor, Lacy lost his way. He lost his sports column—Frank "Fay" Young, the *Defender's* sports editor since 1907 and the dean of the black sporting press, refused to allow Lacy to write for the paper's sports section.[1] He lost proximity to his family and friends in Washington.[2] And he lost a pivotal public relations battle with the autocratic commissioner of major league baseball, Judge Landis.

Although as commissioner Landis had taken the moral high ground about gambling, he balked at any signs of racial progress. Landis forbade major league teams from playing exhibitions against their Negro League counterparts in the early 1920s, canceled the 1942 exhibition between Dizzy Dean and Satchel Paige's All-Stars in Indianapolis, and disingenuously declared that no rule barred blacks from playing in the majors. His best friends in baseball—Griffith, Philadelphia Athletics owner Connie Mack, and *Sporting News* publisher J. G. Taylor Spink—also happened to be some of the game's staunchest segregationists.

Landis revealed his antipathy toward integration in his dealings with Lacy. Shortly after arriving at the *Defender*, Lacy sent the Chicago-based commissioner a steady stream of letters about baseball's color barrier and repeatedly requested a meeting about the subject with the owners. On November 17, 1943, Judge Landis agreed to allow Lacy to bring a three-person delegation to address the owners at their annual meeting in early December.[3]

In agreeing to the meeting, Landis required Lacy to obtain the endorsement of an organization. Lacy suggested the Negro Newspaper Publishers' Association (NNPA).[4] The NNPA, however, failed to send a prompt letter to Landis. Nervous that Landis might change his mind without a swift endorsement, Lacy solicited letters of support from the Urban League, Congressman William L. Dawson of Chicago, the New York office of the NAACP, and the Associated Negro Press in Chicago. Lacy envisioned that the meeting would include speakers from these different camps, as well as an opportunity to address the owners himself.[5]

Instead, the NNPA elbowed Lacy aside. Three NNPA officers—John Sengstacke, general manager of the *Chicago Defender*; Ira F. Lewis, president of the *Pittsburgh Courier*; and Howard Murphy, business manager of the *Afro-American*—addressed the owners on the morning of December 3 in the second-floor conference room of New York's Roosevelt Hotel. Sengstacke, Lacy's boss at the *Defender* and the head of the NNPA, would not even allow Lacy to attend the meeting, much less speak to the owners.[6]

Lacy blamed Sengstacke and other publishers for hogging the podium and not marshaling the best arguments before the owners. A month after the event, Lacy wrote:

> It is only natural that the publishers, as businessmen, don't know the answers to a question which falls on the sports desk. Therefore, the arguments they used were of the flag-waving, puerile variety, far-removed from the pertinent issues and giving no sound solutions to

the problems which have prevented major league baseball's serious consideration of the plea.[7]

With Sengstacke in particular, Lacy felt a profound sense of betrayal.[8] Sengstacke represented Lacy's people, his profession, and his newspaper. As a result of the December 3 debacle, Lacy left the *Defender*.

Judge Landis also hijacked the December 3 meeting. First, the commissioner repeated his blather about there being no legal impediment to blacks playing in the major leagues. Second, he instructed the owners not to ask the delegation any questions. Finally, he invited a surprise speaker of his own: black actor/athlete Paul Robeson.

"I brought Paul here because you all know him," Landis told the owners. "You all know that he is a great man in public life, a great American."[9]

An All-America football player at Rutgers who had played on integrated professional football teams with the Akron Pros and Milwaukee Badgers during the early 1920s, a Columbia Law School graduate, and a stage star in London and on Broadway, Robeson was one of black America's greatest renaissance men. He appeared at the December 3 meeting sporting a beard fresh from his lead role in the Broadway production of *Othello*. For nearly twenty minutes, Robeson gave an impromptu performance about why the owners should hire black players based on examples from Robeson's own integrated life experiences. "They told me I would never be able to play Othello in America," Robeson said. "It has been my greatest success."[10] Neither Robeson's theatrics nor his facial hair put off the owners. In fact, they "broke into loud and sustained applause" after he had finished speaking.[11]

But Robeson's mere presence discredited the entire delegation. As Lacy wrote in the same article in which he chastised the black publishers:

179

While I have the utmost respect for Robeson, a fine artist, a great actor, and every bit a man, I feel he is definitely out of place in this campaign. The reason: Paul is generally regarded as having Com-

munistic leanings. And the major league club owners are almost
fanatical in their dislike for Communism. His presence on the occasion under discussion, and at the instance of Landis, reminds me of
a cartoon I once saw of a man extending his right hand in a gesture
of friendship while clenching a long knife in a left hand concealed
behind his back.

In other words, by this clever little maneuver, Landis told the
gullible colored folks, "Here's how I feel. This is your chance to put
it squarely up to the men who control the purse-strings of the game.
I'm with you, now go to it."

But on the other hand, he said to his owners, "Use your own judgment in this matter, but remember here's a Communistic influence
along with these people."[12]

Indeed, Griffith and Mack, according to the black press, had repeatedly described integration as "a Communistic plot to overthrow
baseball—to create confusion between the races and, finally, to overthrow the government."[13] The sports staff of the Communist *Daily
Worker* had been extremely active in the fight to integrate baseball.
After Robeson spoke, it didn't matter what the three publishers said.
The delegation was just a group of Communist agitators.

As instructed by Landis, after Robeson and the publishers had
finished speaking, none of the owners asked any questions. Branch
Rickey, president and general manager of the Brooklyn Dodgers,
remained silent during the entire presentation. A rabid anti-
Communist, Rickey scratched out several notes to himself, one of
which said: "Robeson a Communist?"[14]

"Well, I guess that's all gentlemen," Landis said as he sent Robeson and the black newspapermen on their way.[15] Then, without any
further discussion, the commissioner moved on to the next item on
the meeting's agenda.[16] After the meeting adjourned, Landis publicly
placed the onus of integration on the owners: "Each club is entitled
to employ Negroes to any and all extents it desires. The matter is one
solely for each club to decide without any restrictions whatsoever."[17]

Griffith reiterated his position on the front page of the *Baltimore
Afro-American*: "My opinion now is the same as it was then, and

that is that; colored players should have their own league and white players have theirs."[18]

The former "red-eyed radical," who as a player had jumped the National League and founded the American League, had turned into an "arch-conservative."[19] As an owner whose livelihood depended solely on his ball club, Griffith opposed all of the game's latest innovations: farm systems, night baseball (at least initially), and selling beer inside the park. He was not a virulent racist who, like his former manager Cap Anson, seemed to hate all black people and objected to their presence in the major leagues out of sheer prejudice. Griffith simply clung to all of baseball's traditions, and one of those traditions happened to be separate black and white professional leagues.

Those traditions included profiting from black baseball. Griffith wasn't about to give up his annual windfall from renting Griffith Stadium to the Grays in order to sign a black player. Indeed, during the next few years, he would sign almost anyone *but* a Negro, from racist Yankee outfielder Jake Powell to New York Sanitation Department worker Ed Boland to one-legged pitcher Bert Shepard.

Griffith's steadfast commitment to segregation after the December 3 owners meeting prompted a declaration of war from Lacy. He left the *Defender* and returned to Washington and the *Afro-American* newspapers.[20] With editions in Baltimore, Washington, Philadelphia, Richmond, and Newark, the Baltimore-based *Afro* was the nation's second-largest black newspaper. Its circulation ranked behind only that of the *Pittsburgh Courier* and ahead of those of the *Defender*, *Norfolk Journal and Guide*, and *Amsterdam News*.[21] These papers— known as the "Big Five"—achieved the status of national newspapers, reaching far beyond their own cities by appealing to many black communities that experienced common hardships and yearned for information about black colleges, churches, politicians, entertainers, and sports figures that white daily newspapers typically ignored.

The *Afro*, like many of the nation's largest black weeklies, was a family-owned, black-run operation. In 1892, John H. Murphy Sr., a whitewasher and Sunday school superintendent, purchased a church newspaper known as the *Afro-American* for two hundred dollars at an auction. Murphy, then fifty-two, had borrowed the money from his wife; his idea was to use the newspaper to unite the state of Maryland's Sunday schools. In 1907, he merged the *Afro-American* with another Sunday school paper, and for a time the paper became known as the *Afro-American Ledger*.[22] Murphy, who died in 1922, left the paper with a vision: "The *Afro-American* must become a biweekly, then a tri-weekly, and eventually, when advertising warrants, a daily."[23]

Murphy's son, Carl, came the closest to turning that vision into a reality. A small, quiet man who didn't drink, Dr. Carl—as the *Afro* staffers referred to him—began his career as a German scholar. He turned out to be a shrewd businessman, increasing the paper's circulation from 8,300 in 1917, to 38,377 in 1930, and to 79,352 in 1938.[24] Unlike the *Pittsburgh Courier* and the *Chicago Defender*, which thrived under their respective founding editors, Robert L. Vann and Robert S. Abbott, both of whom died in 1940, the *Afro* came of age under its second-generation boss.[25]

The *Afro*'s circulation, as well as the importance of the black press, skyrocketed during World War II. During the war, more than a million people read African-American newspapers each week.[26] The black press, like Negro League baseball, experienced rapid wartime expansion because of the migration, urbanization, and increased literacy of the post–World War I black population.[27] Indeed, the Big Five accounted for 40 percent of the total circulation of the black press, which rivaled the black church as one of the leading black-run industries in America.[28]

182

The *Afro* stood on the front lines in the fight against segregation and discrimination in the nation's capital. Carl Murphy made good on the newspaper's slogan—"Independent in all things, neutral in nothing"[29]—by injecting the paper into numerous controversies. The *Afro* financed the first lawsuit contesting the Southern Railroad's segregation of black passengers on all trains heading south beginning in Washington, D.C.[30] In 1939, Murphy also helped establish the Marian Anderson Citizen's Committee. And, in one of the paper's most memorable stories, the *Afro* dressed up three editors as African diplomats who received service at a whites-only downtown restaurant.

The *Afro* was not alone among black newspapers in using its position within the community to fight for racial justice. Gunnar Myrdal described the black press as "the greatest single power in the Negro race" and "a safety-valve of Negro protest."[31] In 1943, President Roosevelt and the Department of Justice withstood pressure to indict several black newspaper editors and to deny their allegedly seditious papers' newsprint.[32] The publishers reacted by lobbying the president through the newly formed NNPA.[33] The "safety valve" was a dangerous weapon.

Lacy returned to the *Afro* because Murphy gave him the freedom to carry on his crusade to integrate professional baseball. Murphy promised that Lacy would not be working for Murphy's daughter, doubled Lacy's salary, and appointed Lacy the *Afro's* sports editor. Lacy's good friend and the *Afro's* previous sports editor, Art Carter, had gone off to Italy and North Africa as one of seven *Afro* reporters serving as war correspondents.[34] Lacy didn't want to be perceived as stealing Carter's job. Murphy, who later made Carter editor of the Washington edition and eventually associate editor of the entire newspaper chain, promised Lacy, "We'll find a place for Mr. Carter."[35]

Lacy resumed doing what he did best—writing his "Looking 'Em Over" sports column. His first missive, on January 4, 1944, told the "real story—if it gets past the censors" of the December 3 owners meeting. He blasted Landis and the NNPA and set the record straight about the events leading up to the speeches by the NNPA and Robeson.

Lacy then turned the power of the black press on Griffith. He returned to the *Afro* with absolutely no tolerance for Griffith's "build up your own league" argument. World War II, Lacy's negative experiences at the *Defender*, and simply the passage of time had radicalized his position on Griffith's refusal to integrate the Senators.[36] In April 1939, Lacy had rejected the idea of a ballpark boycott because

183

Griffith "has done just about everything else that could be expected of him."[37] Five years later, Lacy's tune had changed. He lashed out at the Senators' owner in a February 1944 column:

> During those lean years, Uncle Clarkie could always look out there in the right field stands and find it generously filled with loyal colored fans. Well, many of those same loyal black rooters of the late 'teens and early twenties are puzzled by the Senators' steadfast refusal to consider use of qualified colored ball players on their roster.
>
> Many of those same fans will take this column and mail it to Uncle Clarkie, or write him a note of their own composition, reminding him that they, too, know how to play checkers, and that although he's just jumped them, they're giving him the chance for another move.[38]

Despite the references to "Uncle Clarkie" and the implicit threat of a Griffith Stadium boycott, Lacy still held out hope in early 1944 that Griffith would have a sudden change of heart.

What really burned Lacy about the Senators was their massive influx of Cubans. In 1944, Griffith brought eleven Cubans to his team's spring training facility on the University of Maryland campus, and he housed an additional six Cubans on a Williamsport, Pennsylvania, farm. The Senators' lineup in 1944 included third baseman Gil Torres, outfielder Roberto Ortiz, catcher Mike Guerra, as well as Venezuelan pitcher Alex Carrasquel.[39] Lacy's column, the first of many in the form of a letter to Carter or others serving overseas, commented:

> This year's roster includes men of the following nationalities: Irish, Dutch, Italian, French, (mixture) Polish, Czechoslovakian, Swedish, Lithuanian, Mexican, Cuban and Norwegian, among others. The Philadelphia Athletics have a full-blooded Indian.
>
> Can there be any doubt that it's simply a case of "anything but a—er—gentleman of African extraction?"

By the way, it's Clark Griffith and Connie Mack, you know, together with one or two other "old" heads, who stand in the way of baseball's acceptance of qualified colored players.[40]

Lacy exposed Joe Cambria's hunt for Latin players as focusing on light-skinned unknowns whom many Negro leaguers playing winter ball had never heard of while bypassing "can't-miss" darker-skinned prospects. "Word is that the Washington scout purposely overlooked them," Lacy wrote. "The reason: They're sundown brothers, brother."[41]

During the 1944 season, the Senators finished last. The team lost its budding star of a first baseman, Mickey Vernon, to military service. Several of the team's Cuban players had gone home in the middle of the season rather than face the prospect of being drafted.

Griffith was so desperate for talent that he signed Ed Boland, a thirty-six-year-old New York Sanitation Department worker. Boland, who had last appeared as an outfielder with the Philadelphia Athletics in 1935, most recently played at Griffith Stadium in 1943 with the white semipro Brooklyn Bushwicks. In that July game at Griffith Stadium, the Grays pounded Boland and the Bushwicks, 11–3. Gibson tripled and smacked a 420-foot homer to left field. Boland doubled and singled in four at-bats; he also committed an error.[42]

As during most Grays games, Griffith likely was on hand that day. But if Griffith was so desperate for a major league outfielder, why didn't he take a chance on the Grays' fleet-footed center fielder, Jerry Benjamin? If age wasn't the issue (as it clearly wasn't with the thirty-six-year-old Boland), why didn't Griffith try the Grays' legendary outfielder, James "Cool Papa" Bell? Although forty years old, Bell had a marvelous 1943 season and could still run as fast as Benjamin or anyone else in the Negro Leagues. Or, if Griffith wanted to get the most for his money, he could have signed the Grays' ace pitcher and outfielder, Ray Brown. Playing outfield against the Bushwicks that day, Brown knocked in three runs on three hits.[43] Benjamin, Bell, or Brown—not to mention Gibson and Leonard—could have helped the Senators out of the American League cellar. Boland, for his part,

185

appeared in only nineteen games for the Senators in 1944, his lone season with the team.

That year, Lacy turned up the heat on Griffith and the Washington Senators from every conceivable angle. Exposing the team's discriminatory hiring practices was just part of his strategy to integrate the game. If the campaign to integrate the major leagues could not be won in Washington, it would be won elsewhere by other black sportswriters.

Lacy's efforts were part of a national campaign led by the black sporting press. Black sportswriters endured many of the same hardships as the black ballplayers whom they covered every week. The sportswriters could not work at white daily newspapers, they stayed in second-rate accommodations while on the road, and they suffered racial slights while covering games at major league ballparks. Although black baseball has received belated recognition from books, documentaries, and magazine articles, the legacy of black sportswriters largely remains buried in libraries of old microfilm.[44] Lacy led a cadre of black writers who influenced the Washington market during the 1940s — Lacy, Carter, and Harold Jackson at the *Afro*; Joe Sewall and Lanier "Pee Wee" Covington at the *Washington Tribune*; and Wendell Smith and Ric Roberts of the *Pittsburgh Courier*.

Roberts, who left the *Afro* in 1943 and joined the *Courier* as the paper's Washington sports correspondent, displayed the widest array of talents. A former college football star at Clark University in Atlanta, Roberts drew terrific sports cartoons, wrote accounts of Grays games as well as any of his colleagues did, and possessed an encyclopedic knowledge of black baseball. Roberts ruled the regular backroom discussions at Beltrin Barker's Esso station at Eighth and Florida Avenue, just up the street from Griffith Stadium. "If Ric didn't know it, and Ric didn't say it, it wasn't right," photographer Robert McNeill recalled.[45]

Several black sportswriters lobbied hardest for the integration of baseball: Lacy, Joe Bostic of Harlem's *People's Voice*, Fay Young of the *Chicago Defender*, and Wendell Smith of the *Pittsburgh Courier*. Of

these men, only Smith could match Lacy's writing ability, his obsession with breaking down the color barrier, and his influence with
white major league owners. As sports columnists at the nation's two
largest black newspapers, Smith and Lacy sounded the loudest, most
consistent calls for change. Just as the *Courier* ranked ahead of the
Afro in terms of circulation, however, Smith maintained an edge
over Lacy.

There are two famous sportswriters named Smith—a white one
named Red, and a black one named Wendell. Wendell Smith was
simply the greatest black sportswriter of his generation. "He was a
better writer than I, I've always maintained that," Lacy recalled.[46]
"Wendell had that something extra," Lacy told author Jim Reisler.
"He was always thinking ahead and never quite satisfied with what he
had accomplished."[47] Smith had several advantages over Lacy: Smith
grew up in an integrated environment, he was a better athlete than
Lacy, and he graduated from college. Discrimination kept Smith
from becoming a professional ballplayer and drove his success as a
sportswriter.

Born and raised in Detroit as the son of Henry Ford's chef, Smith
grew up in an all-white neighborhood and was the only black student
at Southeastern High School. An all-city basketball and baseball star
at Southeastern, he won an athletic scholarship to West Virginia
State College and served as the team captain in both sports.[48]

Smith discovered baseball's double standard while still in high
school playing on an integrated American Legion baseball team.
After pitching his team to a 1–0 victory, he watched as a Detroit
Tigers scout signed his catcher, Mike Tresh, who went on to play in
the major leagues, as well as the opposing pitcher. "I wish I could sign
you, too, kid," Wish Egan, a famous Tigers scout, told Smith. "But I
can't." Smith, recounting the incident to sportswriter Jerome Holtzman in the early 1970s, said: "That broke me up. It was then that I
made the vow that I would dedicate myself and do something on
behalf of the Negro ballplayers. That was one of the reasons I
became a sportswriter."[49]

At West Virginia State, in addition to playing baseball and basketball, Smith served as sports editor of the school paper, the *Yellow*

187

Jacket, and as director of publicity for the school's athletic department. In the latter capacity, he contributed articles in the fall of 1936 to the *Pittsburgh Courier.*[50] On July 31, 1937, Smith met *Courier* editor Robert Vann in the office of sports editor Chester Washington Jr. Four days later, he wrote Vann asking for a job:

> I have had the pleasure of working with your very competent sports editor, Mr. Washington. Through his advice and coaching I have learned many essential things about the field of journalism.
>
> Although I have a little experience in this type of work, I realize that I have a great deal to learn. If given the opportunity I will work diligently to become a success.

The letter was signed, "J. Wendell Smith."[51]

Smith joined the *Pittsburgh Courier* as a cub reporter in the fall of 1937, nearly eleven years after Lacy had begun his career with the *Washington Tribune* and the same year as Lacy's first interview with Griffith. A year later, the *Courier* made Smith city editor and assistant sports editor, as well as giving him a sports column, "Smitty's Sport Spurts" (later known as "The Sports Beat"). In 1940, Smith replaced his mentor, Chester Washington, as the *Courier's* sports editor.[52]

Smith's big break resulted from a survey he conducted with white major leaguers during the 1939 season. Smith was not always welcome at the Pirates' Forbes Field because he was not a member of the Baseball Writers Association of America, so he interviewed many of the out-of-town major leaguers in the lobby of Pittsburgh's Schenley Hotel. He asked them how they would feel about having black players on their teams. Of the forty National League players and all eight managers interviewed, about 75 percent favored it, 20 percent were against it, and 5 percent had no opinion.[53] Boston Braves manager Casey Stengel, Brooklyn Dodgers manager Leo Durocher, Pittsburgh Pirates coach Honus Wagner, and Chicago Cubs pitcher Dizzy Dean were among those who favored integration. Durocher, who raved about the abilities of Paige and Gibson, said: "I certainly would use a Negro ball player if the bosses said it was all right."[54] New York

Giants manager Bill Terry opposed integration and declared: "I do not think that Negro players will ever be admitted in the majors."[55] The *Courier* ran team-by-team results of Smith's surveys in eight weekly installments, with the first few landing the young reporter on the front page.[56] "The paper was elated," Smith told Holtzman. "The managing editor was very enthusiastic. I got raises. It really got me on my way, got me going, helped me get my name in the sportswriting business."[57] Smith's series thrust him to the forefront of the black press's campaign to integrate baseball. It also put him in direct competition with Lacy.

The rivalry between Smith and Lacy was intense but friendly. Although they had met when Lacy refereed one of Smith's basketball games at West Virginia State, they became friends when they began covering the same events. Lacy recalled:

> Wendell and I were very close. It wasn't a deliberate thing where I would sneak off and try to get something on him, or he would sneak off and try to get something on me. If I came up on something, after I wrote it I shared it with Wendell. The same thing I'm sure was true with him. As a matter of fact, I know it was true of him.[58]

They shared a common love for the spotlight yet respected each other both personally and professionally. They often plotted strategy together about how to get black players into the majors.[59] Lacy supported many of Smith's endeavors. In 1944, for example, Lacy protested the Negro National League's decision to hire a white statistical agent (the Monroe Elias Agency that keeps the major league statistics) for five thousand dollars rather than accept Smith's bid.[60] Later that season, Lacy wrote: "The talk which has gone the rounds recently about my own efforts on behalf of colored baseball is waste in the wind compared to what should be said in favor of Smith."[61]

Though his attacks were less frequent given his home base in Pittsburgh, Smith proved equally adept at targeting Griffith for abuse. In February 1943, Smith questioned how major league baseball could support wartime morale by barring black players. He called Griffith "one of the typical big league 'morale builders'" and reacted

189

to Griffith's suggestion that blacks should build up their own league with outrage. "I wonder how much morale Mr. Griffith thinks he sold in Washington—or any place else, for that matter—when he made that epochal, un-American statement," Smith wrote. "Fundamentally that statement was in direct opposition to everything we're supposed to be fighting for."[62]

In their condemnation of Griffith, Lacy and Smith became comrades in arms. Smith joined Lacy in blasting Griffith's preference for Cuban players. In July 1944, several of Griffith's Cuban players returned home rather than stay in the United States and register for the draft. "We are glad to point out that Griffith is a victim of his own discriminatory practices," Smith wrote in a self-styled "editorial" stripped across the top of the Washington edition of the *Courier*'s sports section. "If he had selected one or two of the many available Negro players in this country—American citizens—his club might still have a chance to win the pennant. If, for instance, he had given Josh Gibson, Sammy Bankhead, Sammy Jethroe or any other Negro stars a chance, the Senators might still have a chance."[63]

A few months earlier, Smith unleashed his most vicious condemnation of Griffith's hiring of Latin players by emphasizing the embarrassment of fielding an all-white major league team in the capital of the free world and the home ballpark of the mighty Grays:

> Mr. Griffith's club is more than just another baseball team. It represents the capital of our great nation, from which the tentacles of democracy are supposed to spread and take hold in other sections of the country. His ballpark is situated in the heart of Washington's "black belt," just a stone's throw from Howard University, a citadel of Negro education. On all sides of Griffith stadium Negroes live and do business from day to day. Certainly, pursuing his baseball business in such a close proximity to Negroes, Mr. Griffith has heard their fervent pleas for justice—for a Negro player on his ball club. If Mr. Griffith had to go in the distant fields to find a competent Negro player it might be expecting too much of him. But he doesn't have to do that. The best Negro baseball team in the world,

190

loaded with players good enough to be with the Senators plays right in Mr. Griffith's ball yard.

When his team is away, Mr. Griffith rents his park to the Homestead Grays. All he would have to do would be to open the door of his office and call out for one of these players. They'd hear him and come a-running. They are, as a unit, the best Negro players in the United States, and there are some of us who truly believe they could wallop Mr. Griffith's Senators if given the opportunity.

Does M[r]. Griffith step out of his office and call for one of these great ballplayers? He does not! Does Mr. Griffith intentionally overlook good ballplayers? He does not! Has Mr. Griffith ever been accused of being a poor judge of ballplayers? He has not! Is Mr. Griffith in need of ballplayers? He sure in-the-hell is![64]

Clearly, Griffith wasn't going to catch a break from either Smith or Lacy as long as he refused to integrate his team.

Besides the black press, the group that played the most active role in the campaign for integration was the American Communist Party. When it came to issues of racial justice in America, the Communist Party exhibited a fairly good track record. In 1931, the Party's legal arm, the International Labor Defense (ILD), began representing the Scottsboro boys, nine young black men wrongly convicted by an all-white Alabama jury of raping two white women on a train. The ILD wrested control of the case away from the NAACP and during a period of nearly twenty years secured all nine defendants' freedom.[65]

The Party's efforts to integrate baseball emanated from its New York–based newspaper, the *Daily Worker*. In 1936, the *Daily Worker* hired Lester Rodney as sports editor and created a sports page reflecting the Communist Party's decision to highlight racial injustices in professional athletics. Rodney (and later Nat Low and Bill Mardo while Rodney served in the military) provided the *Daily Worker's* readers with extensive coverage of the Negro Leagues and aggressively pressured major league owners to hire black ballplayers.[66]

Griffith was one of the *Daily Worker's* principal targets. In September 1942, the "Daily Worker Committee to End Jim Crow in Baseball" ran a petition in the *Washington Afro-American* "[c]alling on GRIFFITH, owner of the Senators, to try out Negro players." The petition, signed by committee chairman Robert Paul, encouraged the *Afro's* readers to clip out the petition, sign it, and mail it to Griffith's home address.[67] No wonder Griffith thought the integration of baseball was a Communist plot. He probably received hundreds of petitions at his home. The petition ran on the eve of the Grays' 1942 World Series clash with the Monarchs and just above the half-page ad of local businesses showing their support for the Grays.

Griffith's part-time tenants knew firsthand about the *Daily Worker's* efforts. Buck Leonard recalled a *Daily Worker* reporter asking the Grays whether they belonged in the major leagues (they left the answer up to the writers), whether they would attend a major league tryout (yes, if the writers arranged it), whether they would sign a petition or make a formal statement in favor of integration (no), and whether they would demonstrate (no). "Any writing you want done, go ahead and do it," the players told the *Daily Worker*. "We're out here to play ball, we're not out here to demonstrate or anything like that."[68]

The day Paul Robeson addressed the owners in 1943, the *Daily Worker* recommended six players to the major leagues: Leonard, Gibson, and Bankhead of the Grays; New York Cubans pitcher Dave Barnhill; and pitcher Hilton Smith and shortstop Jesse Williams of the Kansas City Monarchs.[69] In 1941, the *Daily Worker* wired all sixteen major league owners about giving tryouts to black players. The following year, Pittsburgh Pirates owner William E. Benswanger agreed to try out four players selected by a *Pittsburgh Courier* poll: Gibson and Bankhead of the Grays, and shortstop Willie Wells and pitcher Leon Day of the Newark Eagles.[70] Benswanger also agreed to a 1941 tryout arranged by the *Daily Worker* for several players, including Baltimore Elite Giants and future Brooklyn Dodgers catcher Roy Campanella. None of the tryouts ever materialized because the weak-willed Benswanger reneged on his promises. The *Daily Worker's* efforts, however, did not go unnoticed.[71]

At least initially, the *Daily Worker's* biggest ally, according to sports editor Lester Rodney, was Wendell Smith. In August 1939, Smith wrote Rodney congratulating the *Daily Worker* on its own series of interviews with major leaguers about integration.[72] The *Courier* and the *Daily Worker* often exchanged Smith and Rodney's stories and ran them under their respective bylines.[73] But when the color ban eventually fell in 1947 and Smith allied himself with Dodgers president/general manager Branch Rickey, a committed anti-Communist, Smith disassociated himself from Rodney. Smith eventually wrote that the Communist Party "did more to delay the entrance of Negroes into organized baseball than any other factor."[74]

Although Smith initially viewed the *Daily Worker* as a helpful ally, Lacy always saw the Communists as retarding any chance for success. Lacy never wanted anything to do with Rodney or his Communist newspaper. "He said he didn't want to get tied up with the Reds," Rodney told writer Peter Duffy. "That's his privilege. I didn't knock him for that."[75] Lacy's anti-Communist stance may have stemmed from his bitterness over Robeson's involvement at the 1943 owners meeting or simply his recognition that "the major league club owners are almost fanatical in their dislike for Communism."[76] Lacy claimed that both he and Smith didn't want Robeson speaking at that 1943 meeting. "We wanted to be completely divorced from any communistic influence," Lacy told author David Falkner.[77]

During the early 1930s, several white sports columnists began calling for the integration of baseball, beginning with Westbrook Pegler, Jimmy Powers, and Heywood Broun.[78] Several others joined the brigade during the late 1930s and early 1940s. But as Smith pointed out to Jerome Holtzman, "the baseball writers, at that time, were very conservative."[79] Even the liberal white writers failed to champion the cause of the black ballplayer on a regular basis as black sportswriters such as Lacy and Smith did.

One white liberal writer rankled Lacy more than any other — legendary *Washington Post* sports columnist Shirley Povich. "If Red Smith was the all-time No. 1 sportswriter," the *Post's* former executive editor, Ben Bradlee, said, "Povich is 1-A."[80] Several decades before Bradlee and the Watergate scandal transformed the *Post* into a national newspaper, the *Post* was fourth in circulation among the city's five daily newspapers. Publisher Katharine Graham estimated that Povich's "This Morning" column "was responsible for one-third of our readership."[81]

The eighth of ten children, Povich grew up above his family's furniture store in the resort town of Bar Harbor, Maine. He spent his summers caddying for famous people, such as the then-owner of the *Washington Post*, Edward B. McLean. In 1924, McLean offered nineteen-year-old Povich a job as a copy boy at the *Post* for twelve dollars a week and as a weekend caddie at McLean's personal eighteen-hole golf course for another twenty dollars. McLean also paid for Povich's tuition to Georgetown Law School.[82] By 1926, the twenty-one-year-old Povich had been named the *Post*'s sports editor, a position he held on and off for the next fifty years.

From the outset, Povich stole Lacy's thunder on the integration issue. In April 1939, a little more than a year after Lacy's December 1937 conversation with Griffith, Povich wrote a column about a game between the Grays and the Newark Eagles at the Senators' spring training facility at Orlando's Tinker Field. Povich, who happened to be sitting with the Senators' Hall of Fame pitcher, Walter Johnson, described the scene:

> Curious Washington [Senators] players flocked to the game and went away with a deep respect for colored baseball. Walter Johnson sat in a box at the game, profoundly impressed with the talents of the colored players. "There," he said, "is a catcher that any big league club would like to buy for $200,000. His name is Gibson. They call him 'Hoot' Gibson, and he can do everything. He hits the ball a mile. And he catches so easy he might as well be in a rocking chair. Throws like a rifle. Bill Dickey isn't as good a catcher. Too bad this Gibson is a colored fellow."[83]

The comments from Johnson captured headlines in the black press.[84] The column cast Povich into the vanguard of white sportswriters promoting integration.[85] It also drew Lacy's ire.

194

Lacy attacked Povich's column about Gibson and the Grays. "I hate to remove what semblance of good faith there was from Shirley Povich's Friday morning column, but there were several inaccuracies reported. . . ." Lacy's column began.[86] Then, Lacy castigated Povich for not responding to Lacy's extensive polling of the white sporting press in his 1938 "Pro and Con" columns on integration in the *Washington Tribune*.[87]

Lacy pointed out several errors in Povich's column, including describing Paige as a left-hander who had retired at forty-four (he was right-handed, about thirty-three, and nursing a sore arm at the time). Moreover, Lacy took issue with Povich's opinions and judgment. "Povich fumbles the ball when he suggests that the Homestead Grays, operating as an entity, might finish at or near the top in a major league race," Lacy wrote. "He also seems somewhat careless in his truth in his inference that colored fans believe Satchel Paige and Josh Gibson [are] greater than any of their white counterparts."[88] Finally, Lacy admonished Povich about the behavior of his fellow white writers:

> If only Povich could persuade some of his brothers of the daily writing fraternity to wake up. If he could convince them, just once, that a game between two bona-fide colored teams (not the minstrel type) is something worth seeing. If he could only show them how foolish they look when they "write up" a game they haven't seen in their characteristic Amos-and-Andy vein, he would certainly do major league baseball — NOT the colored race — a service.[89]

Lacy's column held up Povich as a symbol for what was wrong with Washington's white daily press coverage of the Negro Leagues without explicitly lumping in Povich with the worst of the lot.

A few months later, Lacy revealed his personal contempt for Povich. In August 1939, Lacy wrote:

> Maybe, too, you didn't know that Shirley Povich, another local daily baseball writer, thinks that the colored player's best bet for a chance at the major league bankroll is to clown. Unless they find a way to make all their easy plays look spectacular, Povich told me recently,

the colored fellow will never have any real appeal; for they will just
be some more baseball players.

Remind me to remind Willie Wells and Josh Gibson and Buck
Leonard to learn how to stand on their eye-brows while performing
their chores next year.[90]

Lacy offered only these two paragraphs of observations about Povich,
without direct quotes or evidence from Povich's many sports
columns. At his column's outset, Lacy offered a disclaimer that the
summer heat had made him "punch-drunk, irrational."[91]

Even in his later years, Lacy harbored tremendous enmity toward
Povich. During an interview with Lacy at his northeast Washington
apartment, the mere mention of Povich's name caused Lacy to erupt.
Lacy simmered about one of Povich's stories from the 1940s that
quoted Lacy as saying that no Negro Leaguers were ready for the
majors. Lacy claimed that Povich had left off the last part of Lacy's
statement, that no Negro Leaguers were ready without at least a year
in the minors.[92] Lacy bristled that Povich had not called to check the
quotation. "I thought he did me a terrible injustice because at that
time I had established a pretty good reputation," Lacy recalled. "My
credibility had been accepted. That was a case where, in a sense, he
could have destroyed it."[93] Povich, however, was not the only person
to take that particular article by Lacy—an unusually harsh critique
of the Negro League's top players in the 1945 edition of *Negro Baseball*—out of context. New York Yankees president Larry MacPhail
also selectively quoted from Lacy's article to argue for separate
leagues.

Several hours after the interview with Lacy, he called to elaborate
on his problems with Povich. He railed about a 1991 article in the
Washington City Paper claiming that while Povich was the chairman of the Washington chapter of the Baseball Writers Association
of America (BBWAA) during the 1930s, he had admitted Lacy.[94] "The
[BBWAA] was closed to all blacks in the 1930s, and baseball itself was
all-white, so why would I need or want a baseball writer's credential?"
Lacy asked rhetorically. "I never held a baseball writer's membership
in the Washington chapter. I held it in the New York chapter and
later had it transferred to the Baltimore chapter."[95]

The BBWAA, whose credential served as a free pass into every major league ballpark, refused to admit black sportswriters because they worked for weekly newspapers and did not cover major league teams on a daily basis. After Lacy began covering Jackie Robinson, however, Joe King of the *New York Telegram* and Kenneth Smith of the *New York Mirror* nominated Lacy for membership in the New York chapter. In 1948, Lacy became the BBWAA's first black member.[96] He emphasized that his BBWAA membership was in no way attributable to the liberalism of Povich.

Povich, by contrast, never had any unkind words for Lacy. In the *City Paper*, Povich described Lacy as "aggressive, particularly when it came to black athletes."[97] Povich admitted that he did not read the black press's baseball coverage, but he recognized a few of the writers. "I know two or three, Sam Lacy and Wendell Smith. Those are the two that I recall most."[98] If there was a rivalry between Lacy and Povich, it was completely one-sided.

Lacy's animosity toward Povich could have stemmed from many sources. For starters, Lacy's skin color excluded him from working at a white daily newspaper, such as the *Washington Post*. Povich had a major hand in hiring the *Post* sports staff. Among Povich's hires during that era was another legendary Washington sports columnist, Morris "Mo" Siegel, whom Povich had met during the war. "In that era, the hiring was easy," Povich wrote. "No résumés, no personnel departments where you could cross-check with the past places he worked. You liked the cut of him, you gave him the job."[99]

Lacy's biggest pet peeve with Washington's white daily press was its dearth of black baseball coverage and the tone of what coverage there was. In contrast to other major cities, Washington's white daily press usually neglected the Grays. Sports columnists, such as the *Washington Star*'s Francis Stann and the *Washington Times-Herald*'s Vincent X. Flaherty, came out to Grays games at Griffith Stadium only to depict Paige as a minstrel performer. Povich, who was so busy covering the Senators that he never covered the Grays, candidly admitted that his paper did not report on the Grays on a regular basis. "When the Elite Giants came to town or something like that, but on a regular basis they weren't covered too well," Povich recalled. "We didn't figure they had great readership here."[100]

Although Lacy's beef with Povich could have festered from these sources as well as from petty jealousy over Povich's status as the top dog in town, it could not have been simply because Povich was white. Lacy was not a racist. Over the years, he befriended many white sportswriters.[101] Bob Considine, one of Povich's early protégés who wrote the foreword to Povich's autobiography, also endeared himself to Lacy. During a Senators game at Griffith Stadium, Considine once saw Lacy standing in the back of the press box and promptly found Lacy a seat. Before Considine's death he offered Lacy the services of his literary agent if Lacy wanted to write and publish an autobiography.[102] Another of Lacy's pals was the best sportswriter of them all, Red Smith. Lacy, who received the Red Smith Award from the Associated Press Sports Editors, recalled enjoyable encounters with Smith at the 1968 Summer Olympics in Mexico City, the 1972 Summer Olympics in Munich, and the 1975 Preakness Stakes in Baltimore. "Red Smith had no color hangups," Lacy wrote.[103] Later in Lacy's career, one of his close friends was longtime Baltimore sports columnist John Steadman.[104]

Ultimately, Lacy may have held Povich to a higher standard than Washington's other white columnists. Compared with Francis Stann of the *Star* and Vincent Flaherty of the *Times-Herald* (another Lacy friend), Povich was a bona fide liberal on racial issues. Lacy may have felt that Povich, as the most powerful liberal voice in Washington, didn't use it often enough on racial matters, particularly against Griffith.

Povich, however, poured his energies into exposing the racist attitudes of the keeper of the city's other major sports franchise, Washington Redskins owner George Preston Marshall. Marshall, who had moved the Redskins from Boston to Washington in 1937, was the last NFL owner to integrate his team in 1962. Two of Povich's most famous lines came in criticizing Marshall's racist hiring practices: "The Redskins' colors are burgundy, gold, and Caucasian," and "Jim Brown, born ineligible to play for the Redskins, integrated their end zone three times yesterday."[105] The Redskins integrated only after they moved out of Griffith Stadium. In March 1961, Stewart Udall, President Kennedy's secretary of the interior, threatened to prevent

Marshall from moving his team into the new D.C. Stadium (later known as RFK Stadium) unless Marshall integrated his team.[106] The following year, the Redskins drafted Syracuse's Ernie Davis and traded him to the Cleveland Browns for Hall of Fame running back–wide receiver Bobby Mitchell and rookie Leroy Jackson, two of four pioneering blacks on the 1962 Redskins. In 1969, Povich wrote: "It is no mere coincidence of history that the Redskins' last championship was in 1945, just one year before the recognition of the Negro in professional athletics."[107] Povich relentlessly hounded Marshall, so much so that Marshall litigated a two-hundred-dollar libel suit against Povich. Marshall lost. The two men didn't speak for years.[108]

As much as Povich despised Marshall, however, Povich delighted in talking with Griffith. The Old Fox charmed Povich just as he had charmed Franklin Delano Roosevelt and many other presidents before him. But Griffith needed Povich more than he needed Truman or Eisenhower. Povich outlasted the presidents whose favor Griffith courted every four years. Griffith used to call the *Post's* young sports editor during the 1920s and say, "Gimme a headline tomorrow morning, Walter Johnson's pitching."[109] In 1938, Povich wrote a thirty-three-part series about Griffith. Two years later, Povich and Bob Considine coauthored a two-part article on Griffith, subtitled "Baseball's Red-Eyed Radical and Archconservative," for the *Saturday Evening Post.*[110] Griffith didn't like the article, although it was overwhelmingly positive, because it mentioned a few of his bad trades. "Never mind the nice things you wrote about me," Griffith told Povich. "It's the bad things that count. You can't poison a man and then pump his stomach out and call yourself his friend."[111]

Marshall's boorishness and Griffith's impish charm may have blinded Povich, at least partially, to the Senators' owner's racial shortcomings. Although his 1961 *Sporting News* article described Griffith as having been "wrong" about baseball's color barrier, Povich wrote that after Jackie Robinson's success, "Griffith was completely won over." He also wrote that Griffith had failed to come up with a good Negro player, but that Griffith had made a dozen offers to Cleveland for Larry Doby, whom Griffith described as "the fellow who would do us more good than any other left-handed hitter in the league."[112]

Povich put a nice spin on Griffith's failure to sign a black player for seven years after Robinson played for the Dodgers. But it was the wrong spin.

Povich was wise to some of Griffith's motives regarding the Grays, but not all of them. Years later, Povich recalled:

> At the same time he was singing the praises of Josh Gibson, he was saying let's not interfere with the Negro Leagues. If we take too many ballplayers from them, they will break up the Negro Leagues and we shouldn't break them up. I think that was probably a cop-out: "Let them have their league and we'll have ours."[113]

Povich failed to understand that Griffith's pattern of praising Gibson, protecting the Negro Leagues, and refusing to integrate was a well-orchestrated financial strategy that kept the Senators afloat. Povich underestimated the revenue Griffith received from the Grays for renting Griffith Stadium. "He rented the ballpark to them, but he rented it cheaply to them," recalled Povich, unaware of the 20 percent for stadium rent plus light fees. "Actually he liked to go sit in the stands and watch the games himself. No, he possibly made some small profit but that was not a factor. The crowds were not that great to start with."[114]

Povich's ignorance about the Grays and misjudgment of Griffith's motives were understandable. During the 1940s, Povich did not have time to cover the Grays or to mount a regular campaign to integrate baseball. He wrote six columns a week while covering the Senators both home and away. The *Post* usually included a game story and a column from Povich in every paper. He didn't even have time to be the paper's sports editor, a position he relinquished four times over the years.[115] From November 1944 to the early summer of 1945, Povich took leave from the sports scene to serve as a war correspondent covering the Pacific theater.[116] And in Povich's defense, he never wavered from his uncompromising stance in favor of integration. During the 1940s, he was far more outspoken about the issue than Red Smith was, for example.[117] Black writers such as Wendell Smith admired Povich for his consistent pro-integration position.[118] Povich wrote a fifteen-part series on the integration of baseball titled "No More Shutouts" that the *Post* nominated for a Pulitzer Prize. Finally, Povich was not alone in preferring Griffith to Marshall. Many black fans boycotted Marshall's Redskins yet regularly followed Griffith's Senators. Lacy's father was one of them.

The most unfortunate aspect of Lacy's rift with Povich was that it severely damaged any chance of breaking baseball's color barrier in Washington, D.C. Povich was not only the most liberal white sports voice in Washington, he also was the most popular. In this pretelevision era of baseball, Povich ruled the local sports scene. Povich, moreover, had Griffith's ear; he had tremendous power over Griffith given the *Post's* coverage of the Senators. Publicly and privately, Povich could have exerted enormous pressure on Griffith to integrate.

In short, Lacy and Povich could have been allies in the campaign to integrate major league baseball. Lacy, to his discredit, allowed personal animosity to get in the way of his lifelong crusade. Lacy could have educated Povich about Griffith's relationship with the Grays and courted Povich's public support. Povich, who focused his energies on the more virulently racist owner in Marshall, was sympathetic to Lacy's cause, but Povich rarely used his pulpit to take Griffith to task. Unfortunately, this alliance was not meant to be. Instead, in 1945, Lacy and Wendell Smith kept the pressure on Griffith while searching for other allies.

The Kansas City Monarchs are the only team that rivaled the Grays in terms of its illustrious history in black baseball. The only difference is that they were owned by a white man, J. L. Wilkinson. The 1945 Monarchs are pictured here at Griffith Stadium, sans Paige, but with Jackie Robinson (kneeling third from left).
(ART CARTER PAPERS, MOORLAND-SPINGARN RESEARCH CENTER, HOWARD UNIVERSITY)

Sam Lacy sits at his desk at the *Afro*. He called the Jackie Robinson beat the "story of a lifetime." (National Baseball Hall of Fame Library)

The 1945 Kansas City Monarchs featured three future Hall of Famers: pitcher Hilton Smith (standing at left), Satchel Paige (fourth from left), and Jackie Robinson (kneeling at right). (Art Carter Papers, Moorland-Spingarn Research Center, Howard University)

Sam Lacy, Jackie Robinson, and the editor and publisher of the *Afro-American* newspapers, Dr. Carl Murphy, meet in 1947 at the *Afro*'s Baltimore offices. Robinson credited Lacy and other members of the black press with making his major league career possible. (NATIONAL BASEBALL HALL OF FAME LIBRARY)

EIGHT

POSEY'S POINTS

For the second consecutive year, the Grays held their annual pre-season banquet in Washington. Approximately one hundred guests, including black sportswriters from several Eastern cities, feasted on beer, fried chicken, hot rolls, tomato salad, and candied sweet potatoes.[1] Lacy, pinch hitting for his buddy and overseas war correspondent Art Carter, served as the master of ceremonies. Sitting three seats down from Grays owner Cum Posey, Lacy listened with a grim expression on his face as the head of the local Elks lodge "warned Negro sports writers not to be too zealous in their effort to get a few colored players in major league baseball without considering the possibility of tearing down the backbone of colored athletics—organized Negro baseball."[2]

The admonition may as well have come from Posey himself. Paul Robeson's speech at the 1943 major league owners' meeting had attracted national attention to the cause of integrating baseball and put Negro League owners, such as Posey, on the defensive. Dan Burley of the *Amsterdam News* reported that the barons of black baseball "right now are muttering, 'we gotta protect our investments,' meaning ball players they have under contract." An unidentified owner told Burley: "'We are built on segregation. If there was no segregation, we wouldn't have colored ball clubs; we wouldn't make money; and we'd all probably be out of business.'"[3]

Posey responded in his weekly *Pittsburgh Courier* column, "Posey's Points," by blasting Burley and his aggressive colleague at the *People's*

Voice, Joe Bostic. "For years we have conscientiously read the personal columns of Dan Burley and Joe Bostic," Posey wrote. "They have yet to write me one constructive article on Negro baseball." Posey bemoaned Burley and Bostic's refusal to run box scores and player averages in their respective newspapers. He also lauded his favorite sportswriters, Carter and Chester Washington of the *Pittsburgh Courier*, because they "seemed to follow the motto, 'If I cannot boost, I will not knock.'"[4] Lacy was much more of a knocker than a booster. Yet Posey wisely refrained from singling out Lacy for criticism.

If Lacy had a stealthy adversary in the campaign to integrate baseball, it was Posey. Since moving his team to Washington in 1940, the Grays' owner had formed a tacit alliance with Griffith. They shared a common goal of maximizing the Grays' profits at Griffith Stadium. That meant keeping other major league teams from stealing the Grays' players and maintaining a viable Negro National and Negro American League. While Posey praised major league magnates for allowing the Grays to use their ballparks, Griffith encouraged black baseball teams to build up their own leagues. Privately, both men opposed integration.

Of Lacy's three biggest adversaries—Landis, Griffith, and Posey—Posey was in the most precarious position. His primary aim was protecting his business. Yet Posey could not openly oppose integrated baseball and risk alienating his black fan base or his chief publicity arm, the black press. Just as Griffith needed headlines in the *Post* from Povich, Posey hankered for good publicity in the *Afro* from Lacy and in the *Courier* from Smith. Thus, Posey remained relatively silent while Lacy and Smith carried out their crusade.

While Lacy and Smith hammered Griffith for his discriminatory hiring habits, they exhorted Negro League owners to reform their business practices. In December 1943, Smith warned them that record profits would not last and integration was on the horizon. Smith and others contended that, in order to compete, black baseball needed a commissioner, regular scheduling, and uniform player contracts. "As they operate now, the Negro owners are in no position to bargain with major league teams for their players. The Negro owners will have to accept whatever they are offered," Smith wrote. "If the Negro leagues aren't organized, then a major league owner is in no way compelled to recognize the contracts and agreements which ordinarily apply to the trades and sales of ballplayers."[5]

Lacy argued that owners such as Posey depended too much on the availability of major league ballparks. According to Lacy, Ray Brown and Vic Harris of the Grays "took major exception to my saying that the ersatz ballplayers present a pathetic picture out there digging up the white folks' diamonds, etc."[6] Lacy redirected his criticism at the Grays' management, urging them to "get out of the 'dependable' class" by setting aside 5 percent of the net gate receipts "to underwrite the building of a LEAGUE PARK in each city where league baseball is played."[7] The following week, Lacy speculated as to when "Negro National and American League operators will tire of depending on the good graces of white major league owners for the continuance of our baseball?"[8]

The issue arose in Washington during the fall of 1944. Redskins owner George Preston Marshall banned local high school football teams and the all-black professional Washington Lions from playing their games at Griffith Stadium. Marshall, who rented the stadium from Griffith for $100,000 a season, could veto any perceived competition from playing there, just as Posey could thwart other Negro League teams from renting the ballpark. "The Grays corral thousands of dollars for the Griffith interests in the run of a season, and as a result, no Negro team can perform there without Mr. Posey's consent," Ric Roberts wrote. "Those who score Mr. Marshall claim, however, that Mr. Posey's option extends only to Negro outfits, and insist that Mr. Marshall be limited to the exclusion of white teams."[9] Harold Jackson suggested that the Grays build a stadium for Washington's black community. "I think the Grays should do it, but if not why can't some of our sportsmen or business men select a spot on the outskirts of town and do the job," Jackson wrote. "It would make a swell investment and would make way for new promotions."[10]

Posey was a shrewd businessman. He didn't build the Grays from a local steel mill team into the most successful franchise in the history of black baseball based on luck. He knew that building his own

207

ballpark would have been a financial disaster, based on the enormous capital outlay, limited real estate, and even more limited seating. Gus Greenlee floundered financially by building Greenlee Field, the Pittsburgh Crawfords' bandbox of a ballpark that was torn down at the end of 1938; the Baltimore Elite Giants never attained the financial success of the Grays playing at tiny Bugle Field. Posey knew that it was better to let other people build big ballparks, especially for an itinerant team such as the Grays with a regional as well as a national following.

Posey knew that publicly praising Benswanger and Griffith was good business. For several years, he had vigorously defended the Pirates' and Senators' owners as friends of the Grays, rather than portraying them as rapacious profiteers.[11] As early as 1942, Posey urged the black press to temper its criticism of major league officials. "The letters which are sent to Judge Landis and various club owners of major league clubs, despite the good intentions of the writers do not help the cause of Negro baseball and may cause the loss of some of the parks we now rent," Posey wrote. "That would set Negro baseball back 20 years."[12] A few years later, Lacy took offense at Posey's excuses for these segregationists: "If your administrators hold to the theory that they owe something to major league owners because the latter agree to make money for themselves by renting their parks, they're all wet."[13]

Posey mastered the art of renting major league ballparks by forging good working relationships with owners such as Griffith and Benswanger and circumventing white booking agents. For several years, Posey waged his own personal war against booking agents whose monopoly over major and minor league ballparks cost some black baseball teams as much as 40 percent of the profits.[14] He encouraged New York Cubans owner Alex Pompez to rent the Polo Grounds and Newark Eagles owner Effa Manley to rent Ebbets Field rather than go through a booking agent to rent Yankee Stadium. Eddie Gottlieb, a part owner of the Philadelphia Stars, promoted all of the black baseball games at Yankee Stadium and Philadelphia's Shibe Park for a percentage of the gate receipts.[15] Abe Saperstein, who owned the Harlem Globetrotters basketball team and retained partial stakes in the Indianapolis Clowns and Birmingham Black Barons, played a similar role in Chicago and Indianapolis. Posey organized a boycott of Saperstein's venues and visited several owners of Midwestern ballparks to dissuade them from submitting to Saperstein's business practices.[16] Saperstein basically controlled the Midwest, Gottlieb controlled part of New York and Philadelphia, and Posey controlled Pittsburgh and Washington. Posey, however, did not exploit his territory—he needed other Negro League teams to thrive to ensure the continued prosperity of the Grays.

Not owning his own ballpark was the least of Posey's problems heading into the 1944 season. Although the Grays had played to record crowds in Washington in 1943, train travel and other wartime expenses cut into Posey's profits.[17] In 1944, the Office of Defense Transportation allowed the Grays to use their bus for two thousand miles per month but also lifted the ban on pleasure driving—depriving the Grays of their captive audience in Washington.[18] In an article proclaiming black baseball a two million dollar enterprise, Ric Roberts wrote:

> Washington was, for example, an average 3,000-fan town until Paige's visits and good promotional work hiked it to well near a 10,000-fan average. The crowds leveled off in 1943 and began showing a slight over-all decline in 1944. This indicates the need of a new promotion series by the owners, and above all an elaborate public relations medium to "sell" Negro baseball to the public year 'round.[19]

During the Grays' fifteen home dates at Griffith Stadium in 1944, attendance dipped to seven thousand to eight thousand a game. The team drew fifteen thousand only twice that season, once for the home opener against the New York Black Yankees and once for a late June doubleheader against Paige and the Monarchs.[20]

As attendance fell, Posey's team was crumbling around him. Before the season, he was in such dire need for talent that he placed an application form in the *Pittsburgh Courier*.[21] Despite the discovery of a young pitcher and hard-hitting outfielder from Ohio named

David Hoskins, a combination of old age and the draft finally caught up with the Grays.

The pitching staff was particularly thin. Ace right-hander John Wright (26–4 in 1943) served stateside at Great Lakes (Illinois) Naval Base, and Ray Brown was reclassified 1-A.[22] Left-hander Roy Partlow had signed with the Philadelphia Stars, and left-hander Roy Welmaker wasn't discharged from military service until early August.[23] Only Brown, Ernest "Spoon" Carter, and Edsall Walker started the 1944 season with the team.

The draft also depleted the Grays' infield, with second baseman Matthew "Lick" Carlisle and third baseman Howard Easterling serving in the military.[24] The Grays called their good-field/no-hit shortstop of seasons past, Washington native Jelly Jackson, out of retirement to play second base. The departures of Carlisle and Easterling, however, put a strain on veteran infielders Sam Bankhead and particularly on Jud "Boojum" Wilson.

Over the years, Wilson had earned the much-deserved reputation as the Grays' best contact hitter (the only one who hit Paige regularly, according to pitcher Wilmer Fields) and meanest, most fiery player.[25] In late May, the stout, muscular Wilson was suspended three games and fined twenty-five dollars for tossing a bat at umpire (and former NNL player) Phil Cockrell.[26] Wilson's health problems curtailed the second half of his season, with veteran Rev Cannady or youngster Ray Battle often filling in for him at third base. Wilson suffered from epilepsy. Leonard recounted an afternoon game at Griffith Stadium during which the players discovered Wilson lying down at third base drawing little circles in the dirt with his finger. "Oh, wait a minute, look at Boojum," one of the players said.[27] The *Pittsburgh Courier* reported that Wilson was "seriously ill" and had to be removed from the Grays' 1944 Negro League World Series game at Griffith Stadium.[28] Wilson, who had grown up in the Foggy Bottom section of Washington, spent a September game against the Monarchs chatting with Harold Jackson in the dugout. "He isn't through, I'm sure," Jackson wrote, "but his best playing days are behind him."[29]

Most of all, the Grays desperately needed a backup catcher for Gibson (Robert "Rab Roy" Gaston was inadequate). Of all the Grays,

Gibson suffered the most during the 1944 season. Contrary to early reports in the *Afro*, he had not recovered from another off-season bout with his mysterious "illness," a combination of alcoholism and psychiatric problems that often landed him in mental hospitals.[30] He showed up drunk to several early games. Warned about "breaking training" during the team's Opening Day doubleheader in Washington, Gibson was "unfit for use" the next week during an exhibition game in Orange, New Jersey.[31] He was pulled from a game at Baltimore's Bugle Field for drinking, suspended from the team for two weeks by co-owner Sonnyman Jackson, and later arrested in Washington, D.C., for disorderly conduct. Gibson ended up in Washington's Gallinger Hospital for observation.[32] Harold Jackson made a public plea to the Grays' slugger to make amends: "Although his recent conduct has tossed him into disrepute with his bosses and caused his teammates to ostracize him, Josh must be fully aware that a turn in the right direction will put him back in the hearts of all and sundry."[33]

Gibson turned things around slightly during the second half of the season. In mid-June, he was hitting .295 (13 for 44) with no home runs and only six RBI.[34] A few weeks later, however, he raised his average to .357 (20 for 56), hit a home run, and doubled his RBI total to twelve.[35] In mid-July, Gibson hit two home runs and a triple against the New York Cubans before fourteen thousand fans at the horseshoe-shaped Polo Grounds—Gibson's favorite ballpark—where the left-field fence was only 280 feet from home plate backed by a 17-foot-high wall, child's play even for an inebriated, overweight Gibson.[36] A few days later, Gibson launched a ball into the upper deck of Shibe Park's center-field bleachers during a doubleheader against the Baltimore Elite Giants.[37] Although Gibson finished a respectable ninth in the Negro National League batting race with a .338 average (44 for 130), his drinking and weight problems made him a liability behind the plate.[38] Posey left the slugger off his annual All-American Team in favor of the Elite Giants' young catcher, Roy Campanella, who hit .350 (57 for 163). "We placed Campanella over Gibson because Gibson did not stay in shape to play regularly and even with Gibson in perfect shape, it is a close race between him and Campanella," Posey wrote.[39] The Grays' star first baseman, however, begged to differ. "I wouldn't say he was as good as Josh Gibson," Leonard said of Campanella. "He could only do one thing better than Gibson, and that was stay in shape."[40]

Leonard assumed Gibson's role as the team's principal offensive threat in 1944. In late April, he hit a three-run homer against the New York Black Yankees at Yankee Stadium.[41] During the second game of the Grays' home opener in Washington, Leonard and Gibson managed five doubles and a triple between them.[42] In early June, Leonard took over Gibson's cleanup spot in the batting order and never relinquished it. Leonard's seventh-inning home run off fellow North Carolinian Dave Barnhill broke a 0–0 tie in the first game of a Griffith Stadium doubleheader against the New York Cubans. At that point, Leonard sported a .394 average (13 for 33), a home run, and ten RBI.[43] His finest hour in 1944 came during the late June doubleheader against the Monarchs, when he registered six hits in eight at-bats, including two triples, and "was easily the hitting star of the afternoon."[44] The following week, in Newark, Leonard hit home runs in both games of a doubleheader against the Newark Eagles.[45] "The best hitter on that club—Buck Leonard," Monarchs catcher Othello "Chico" Renfroe told John Holway. "Yes, he was better than Josh Gibson, average-wise. I always get an argument on that, because a lot of people think Josh was a better hitter."[46]

Leonard stood out among the Grays as a class act. "Buck was a gentleman, and Buck played with a bunch of thugs, now I'm going to tell you," photographer Bill Scott recalled. "Boojum [Wilson] and that crowd, they were, but Buck was a gentleman, a really nice guy."[47] At the 1944 World Series, Wendell Smith described Leonard as the "best dressed ball player on the field."[48] It was no secret why Leonard roomed with Cool Papa Bell, the Grays' other leading hitter in 1944 and one of the best-dressed players off the field. Smart, quiet, and proud men, Leonard and Bell liked to get their beauty sleep. Before they went to bed, Bell talked Leonard into the habit of taking a few swigs of gin (mixed with lemon peels and two teaspoons of sugar) as a cure for arthritis.[49] These men weren't big drinkers; they were aging ballplayers trying to stall Father Time.

Leonard's hitting tailed off considerably at the end of the season. His .299 batting average was the lowest among the members of Posey's All-American Team. In December, discussing an aborted trade between the Grays and the Monarchs (center fielder Jerry Benjamin for shortstop Bonnie Serrell), the *Afro* reported that "Posey's willingness to consummate some kind of swap indicated that only Buck Leonard, first baseman, and Dave Hoskins, right fielder, were not on the block."[50] Although Hoskins may have been the Grays' best young prospect, thirty-seven-year-old Leonard was still the team's best player and black baseball's best first baseman. If any further evidence was needed, Leonard led the Grays with eight hits (including a home run) and a .500 batting average in the 1944 World Series.[51] He skipped the Grays' final two exhibition games because the draft board wanted him back in Rocky Mount unloading packages for the Railway Express Service.[52] There was no time for him to recover from an exhausting season.

Although Leonard, Bell, and pitcher Ray Brown helped the Grays gut out another NNL title in 1944, other teams questioned the validity of the championship. During the first half, the Newark Eagles protested a loss because the Grays used one of their former pitchers, Roy Partlow, who belonged to the Philadelphia Stars. The league ordered the Grays and the Eagles to replay the disputed game. In August, a home run by Gibson and sterling pitching by John Wright (on leave from his naval duties) sealed the Grays' victory and first-half title.[53] During the second half, the Philadelphia Stars protested because the Grays played the second game of a Labor Day doubleheader against the New York Cubans as an exhibition game, which could have cost the Grays the second-half title if it had been a league game and if the Grays had lost.[54] Nothing ever came of the Stars' protest. Lacy attributed the whole controversy to the league's uneven, haphazard scheduling. "The whole thing just doesn't make sense," he wrote. "That's why I stay out of that mess."[55]

Three leading black sportswriters—Lacy, Smith, and Frank Young—joined forces so that the 1944 World Series would not be marred by similar irregularities. At Smith's urging, they formed a World Series Arbitration Commission to resolve any disputes arising during the postseason series between the Grays and the Birmingham Black Barons.[56] The Grays won the series in five games after a bus accident seriously injured five Black Barons a week before the first game. The sportswriters allowed the Black Barons to add extra players to their roster. The significance of three sportswriters running the World Series was not lost on Posey.

As the owner of black baseball's best team located in one of its most profitable cities, Posey basically ran the entire Negro National League. Although nominally listed as the NNL secretary, he dominated the league's 1944 winter meetings. He secured the reelection of his choice for NNL president, Baltimore Elite Giants owner Tom Wilson; he prevented former Crawfords owner Gus Greenlee from entering a new team in the NNL despite rumors (which turned out to be true) of a rival black league; and he quashed attempts by NNL and NAL owners to hire a commissioner.[57] It was obvious why Posey was not in favor of having a commissioner: the de facto commissioner of black baseball was Cum Posey.

The threat of integration was Posey's biggest concern heading into the 1945 season, especially with the death of major league baseball's commissioner. Almost a year after sabotaging Lacy's meeting by inviting Paul Robeson, Judge Landis died of heart failure on November 25, 1944. He was seventy-eight. Per his request, his body was cremated, and there was no funeral.[58] Five days before his death, Landis received a birthday telegram from Clark Griffith on the occasion of Griffith's own seventy-fifth birthday celebration and Landis's seventy-eighth: "Judge, I feel sure that you are going to be okay soon and that you will be with all of us old fellows for a long time to come."[59] Landis, Griffith, and Connie Mack were golfing buddies.[60]

214   For years, Landis had served as Griffith and Mack's front man in keeping major league baseball all-white. Landis's insistence that no rule existed against black players in the majors masked their fears about integration's economic and social repercussions. Smith described the late commissioner as a "Gibraltar of Honesty" on all issues except integration. "Mr. Landis never set his teeth into the question of Negroes in the majors with the same zest that he did other problems which came under his jurisdiction," Smith wrote.

"Mr. Landis had 25 years to prove that he wanted to see Negroes in the majors. Yet, they buried him this week and we are still fighting for Negroes in the majors."[61]

The death of baseball's segregationist-in-chief sent the black press's campaign into overdrive. It decentralized major league baseball's governing body (leaving acting commissioner Leslie O'Connor and the American and National League presidents, William Harridge and Ford Frick, in a power struggle), and it provided a crucial opening for aggressive sportswriters, such as Lacy. Without Landis at the helm, neither Griffith nor Posey could keep Lacy and Smith at bay. It was open season on baseball's color barrier.

Lacy immediately took aim at Griffith. In January 1945, Lacy proposed a July 4 boycott of Griffith Stadium based on a report that Griffith had signed a Chinese prospect (though he was more likely Mexican), Miguel Hidalgo, along with thirty-five Cuban players scheduled to report to the Senators' spring training. Lacy, who dubbed his mass protest "lily-white baseball day," called on fans, stadium vendors, and cabdrivers to stay away from the ballpark on July 4:

> There are colored men or women in every major league city in the
> country, my dad among them, who have attended the home games
> of their local teams throughout the season for the past two decades.
> They could afford to miss one afternoon at the park in order to add
> their unspoken vote to the nation-wide protest.[62]

"Major league operators don't want us," Lacy concluded. "They should be able to do without us."[63] An enthusiastic *Afro* reader ("Brother, you've got something!") suggested turning Lily-White Day into a weeklong protest.[64] Lacy's proposed boycott, however, never came to pass.[65] The *Afro*, fearing a lawsuit from the major leagues, persuaded Lacy to moderate his public stance. "My publisher, who was a lawyer, told me to be careful," Lacy told author Peter Sheingold, "because I was stepping on very delicate grounds."[66]

Many black Washingtonians, including Sam Lacy's father, began boycotting Senators' games on their own. After signing a racist (Jake

Powell) in 1943 and a New York sanitation department worker (Ed Boland) in 1944, Griffith continued the trend in 1945 by signing a one-legged pitcher. Bert Shepard lost his right leg just below the knee when his plane was shot down over a German air base. After Shepard returned to the states a war hero, Griffith signed the left-handed pitcher and even put him into a major league game. Pitching against the Boston Red Sox with an artificial right leg, Shepard allowed three hits and one run in five and a third innings. Shepard's story was inspiring.[67] But, like his more well-known American League counterpart, the St. Louis Browns' one-armed outfielder Pete Gray, Shepard's presence on the Senators belittled the talented two-legged men on the Grays and alienated the Senators' black fans.

For Lacy's father, signing Shepard was the last straw. More than twenty years after Nick Altrock had spit in his face at the team's World Series parade, the seventy-seven-year-old Lacy decided not to attend Opening Day in 1945 for the first time since before the Senators had begun playing on the site of Griffith Stadium. Lacy's father wrote Griffith a letter explaining his reasons: he "found a one-legged man on [the] team and no colored given a tryout."[68]

The confrontational styles of two of Lacy's colleagues, Smith and Joe Bostic, convinced him that an *Afro*-sponsored boycott was not the best way to achieve his goals. On April 6, 1945, Bostic arrived unannounced at the Brooklyn Dodgers' Bear Mountain, New York, spring training site with two aging Negro Leaguers, Newark Eagles pitcher Terris McDuffie and the New York Cubans' fancy-fielding first baseman Dave "Showboat" Thomas. Bostic demanded a tryout for the two players. Enraged over being set up in what he regarded as a publicity stunt, Dodgers president–general manager Branch Rickey gave the two players a forty-five-minute workout and sent them away.[69]

Ten days later, Smith orchestrated a similar situation in Boston. Backed by city councilman Isadore Muchnick, Smith showed up April 14 and 15 at Fenway Park with three bona fide major league prospects: Philadelphia Stars second baseman Marvin Williams, Cleveland Buckeyes speedy outfielder Sam Jethroe, and a shortstop recently signed by the Monarchs named Jackie Robinson. After a two-day delay, the Red Sox worked out the impressive trio for about an hour and a half. Smith, who contacted the team ten days after the tryout, never heard from the Red Sox again.[70]

Lacy dismissed the idea of using similar tactics with Griffith and the Senators. "I don't think that you're going to get anywhere by taking two or three ballplayers and sending them in there and just crashing the gates, so to speak," Lacy said. "Right away, that's going to create some sort of resentment." Although a larger organization, such as the NAACP, may have been able to mobilize support for either an impromptu tryout or a massive boycott, as a sportswriter, Lacy did not want to jeopardize his credibility. "You see, you have to stay on an even keel, you have to think ahead," Lacy recalled. "You never promote things that may not work out."[71]

Instead of antagonizing major league baseball's powers-that-be, Lacy befriended them. During his efforts to secure a meeting with major league owners back in 1943, Lacy had found an important ally in Judge Landis's secretary and right-hand man, Leslie O'Connor. Serving as the acting commissioner since Landis's death, O'Connor played an instrumental role in facilitating Lacy's idea about forming a committee on integration. After Lacy addressed their April 24 meeting in Cleveland, the major league owners agreed to establish the committee with the dual purposes of discussing unspoken objections to integration and forging stronger relationships between the white and black leagues.

The committee initially included, among others, Lacy, Rickey for the National League, and New York Yankees president Larry MacPhail for the American League.[72] Although MacPhail had introduced night baseball, television, and air travel to the major leagues, he was among the most outspoken opponents of integration. MacPhail took up Griffith's build-up-your-league argument in part because of the Yankees' profitable stadium rentals. Lacy's committee rarely met because MacPhail "always had some excuse." Rickey told Lacy, "We'll just have to give up on him and let nature take its course."[73] At the time, Lacy didn't understand the full importance of Rickey's cryptic remark.

Wesley "Branch" Rickey talked like a preacher and ran his baseball team like a card shark.[74] He did not drink, refused to attend

217

Sunday games, yet often signed hard-drinking, foul-mouthed ballplayers who, like Rickey, hated to lose. A devout Methodist raised in rural Ohio, Rickey graduated from Ohio Wesleyan University and later from University of Michigan Law School. He was not much of a major league ballplayer, batting .238 in 120 games as a catcher and outfielder.

In 1907, Rickey slogged through his final major league season with the New York Highlanders, playing for a young manager named Clark Griffith. Coming to the Highlanders in a trade before the season, Rickey confessed to Griffith that he had a sore throwing arm. Griffith, however, was desperate for a catcher. One afternoon, Rickey established a major league record by allowing thirteen stolen bases in one game.[75] He batted .182 in fifty-two games with the Highlanders. In 1913, Rickey began a ten-year career as a field manager with the St. Louis Browns and St. Louis Cardinals.

Rickey found his calling as a major league executive—inventing baseball's farm system. He devised this training ground for future major leaguers by amassing players on Cardinal-owned or -affiliated minor league teams. At one point, the Cardinals had signed eight hundred players on fifty teams. These players were bound to the Cardinals under the reserve clause, barring emancipation by Judge Landis. The farm system method, which has since been adopted by every major league team, produced five National League pennants for the Cardinals in nine years from 1926 to 1934.

As the Brooklyn Dodgers' president and general manager beginning in 1942, Rickey saw integration as another way to a get a leg up on the competition and to enhance his reputation. He frequently couched his efforts on behalf of black players in high-sounding rhetoric that earned him the nickname "the Mahatma." He frequently told a story about Charlie Thomas, a black outfielder on the 1904 Ohio Wesleyan baseball team. Thomas had been denied lodging when the Rickey-coached team ventured to South Bend, Indiana, to play Notre Dame. Rickey had persuaded the hotel to allow Thomas to sleep on a cot in Rickey's room, where Rickey had found Thomas rubbing his hands and crying, "Black skin! Black skin! If only

I could make them white." Rickey claimed that the Charlie Thomas story haunted him and drove him to integrate baseball.[76]

As much as Rickey reveled in his moral stand, he desperately wanted the Dodgers to benefit from an untapped source of baseball talent. He was a visionary who viewed baseball scouting as a science. He was a notorious skinflint whom *New York Daily News* columnist Jimmy Powers nicknamed "El Cheapo." He was a master politician who knew how to work the media, other owners, and the public. And he was a pragmatist who understood that integration was more possible in racially sympathetic Brooklyn, where white sportswriters such as Powers had been lobbying for integration, than in southern towns like St. Louis and Washington.

Rickey single-handedly shifted the focus of Lacy and Smith's integration efforts from Washington to New York. After the tryout at Bear Mountain in the spring of 1945, he persuaded Dr. Dan Dodson, a New York University sociologist in charge of Mayor La Guardia's Committee on Unity, to establish the Mayor's Committee on Baseball to study the issue of admitting blacks into the professional game.[77] Rickey also began making overtures to black baseball through Gus Greenlee's newly established United States League (USL), a rival black organization formed in 1945. In May, Rickey pledged his full support to the league, raked in profits by renting out Ebbets Field, and eventually assumed ownership of a USL franchise, the Brooklyn Brown Dodgers.[78] Although the six-team league folded after the 1946 season, the Brown Dodgers gave Rickey the perfect vehicle through which to scout black talent.

Rickey's involvement with the USL also began a season-long war of words with his former manager on the 1907 New York Highlanders. Griffith charged Rickey with "trying to dictate the affairs of colored baseball" and attacked the Dodgers president–general manager for meddling with Posey's domain:

> Mr. Rickey is attempting to destroy two well organized leagues which have been in existence for some time and in which colored people of this country have faith and confidence.

219

> This is not the age of dictators, and when one man sets himself up to foster the new organization which only has in mind the thought of destroying the existing two colored leagues, then I think the time has arrived when a halt should be called.[79]

Griffith cared as much about protecting his profits from renting his ballpark to the Grays as about protecting the Negro Leagues. Rickey, when pressed for a response by Sam Lacy, retorted: "Whenever some one does anything to interfere with his making of a dollar, that fellow gets all upset. I won't even bother to answer him."[80]

A few weeks later, Smith elaborated on Rickey's criticism of Griffith. Having begun working behind-the-scenes with Rickey, Smith attacked Griffith for signing dozens of foreign players from Cuba and Mexico but not a single American-born black. "All he has to do is look out the window of his office at Griffith Stadium on any day the Homestead Grays are playing there and see plenty of players good enough to play with the Senators," Smith wrote.[81] Smith also seized on Rickey's point about Griffith's obsession with losing the profits from his stadium rentals:

> Clark Griffith's defense of the present Negro leagues is not motivated by anything but his own selfish interests. He makes money by renting his park to the Homestead Grays. He doesn't want any one fooling around with that profitable mellon [sic]. He'll do anything he can to help perpetuate the present setup in Negro baseball because it's to his advantage. . . .
>
> Although he makes his money in the shadow of the Capitol of the United States, Griffith is in no way democratic on this issue of Negroes in the majors. Therefore, anything he advocates in Negro baseball must be looked upon with suspicion. He is no friend. No one who helps perpetuate segregation and discrimination is a friend of the Negro.[82]

Smith failed to mention Griffith's silent ally.

Posey chose his words carefully after Rickey's USL announcement. He avoided antagonizing the Grays' black fans in Washington by expressing his criticism through the mouths of Rickey's fellow major league magnates. Several major league owners were "giving him hell!" Posey told Sam Lacy. "William Benswanger called me on the phone and said it was bad stuff, and Clark Griffith thinks he's crazy."[83]

While Griffith publicly denounced Rickey, Posey launched a guerilla attack on the integration campaign. In June 1945, Lacy sent a letter to the Negro National League and the Negro American League presidents imploring them to send a representative to the major league committee meetings. The NNL and NAL owners declined because of a "faction . . . reputedly led by Cum Posey."[84] Although one of the committee's goals was to improve relations between the black and white leagues, Posey and other Negro League owners objected that "Lacy should not be permitted to 'run our business' and that 'our representatives would be outnumbered in any controversial voting.'"[85]

Posey's distaste for Lacy's diplomatic efforts also extended to Bostic and Smith's confrontational approaches. Many members of the black press criticized the two impromptu major league tryouts. Bostic brought two players, Thomas and McDuffie, both past their primes, to the Dodgers camp; Smith showed up in Boston with Robinson, Jethroe, and Williams, younger but relatively unproven players. People wondered, according to the *Defender*'s Fay Young, "why players like Buck Leonard, Washington Grays first sacker, or some others weren't chosen."[86] An *Amsterdam News* writer made a more specific suggestion:

> Why not contact some of the ball players on the Grays and get them up here for tryouts. Or even get them into Griffith Stadium, where they could show themselves off as the classy ball players they are. By the way, Clark Griffith, owner and president of the Senators, has been hiring Cuban ball players for some years now—why not try him as the man to give the Negro a break in the big game. I shouldn't doubt it in one instant, that the President would get great satisfaction in tossing out the first ball to start the first game of the season in Griffith Stadium to an American team having Americans of all creeds and races on the field. It would show true Americanism on the part of the "National Pastime."[87]

221

On April 12, 1945, two days before the weekly *Amsterdam News* came out, Griffith's good friend, Franklin Delano Roosevelt, died. Roosevelt's death destroyed any national publicity value from the two major league tryouts.

A major obstacle to integration, aside from Griffith's opposition, was Posey. In April 1945, Posey denied Smith's request to bring Gibson to the Red Sox tryout. "They wouldn't let Josh go because he was their ace drawing card," Smith told Jerome Holtzman.[88] Posey also rejected Smith's request to bring the Grays' young outfielder, Dave Hoskins.[89] In a short article in the *Pittsburgh Courier,* Posey described the two major league tryouts as a "travesty" and "the most humiliating experience Negro baseball has yet suffered from white organized baseball."[90] Citing the lack of running and throwing drills during the workouts, Posey said marginal white prospects would have received more complete evaluations. The Grays' boss concluded:

> You can bet your ears that no owner in white organized baseball will ever get a chance to low-rate and criticize a player of the Homestead Grays as long as this writer is part owner of the club, unless that particular member of organized baseball requests an option on the player's services, written on the club's stationery. Then we will be certain that he will get a tryout as same as all other players get.[91]

Although many people criticized the two tryouts, nothing short of incorporating the Grays into the major leagues would have completely satisfied Posey.

What Posey desired most during the 1945 season was for the Grays to continue to perform well on the field. In April 1945, Roger Treat, a liberal white writer with the *Washington Daily News,* wrote that "the Homestead Grays would beat the Washington Senators six days a week and twice on Sunday."[92] That may have been true in 1942 or 1943, but not in 1945. With the exception of Vic Harris replacing Candy Jim Taylor as the team's manager, Posey failed to upgrade the Grays' aging roster from 1944. The team's three top pitchers in 1945 remained veteran right-hander Ray Brown, left-hander Roy Welmaker, and right-hander John Wright, when he could get leave from the Great Lakes (Illinois) Naval Base. Third baseman Jud Wilson and shortstop Sam Bankhead continued to wear down, creating a huge hole on the left side. And Leonard and Gibson, though still two of the league's best hitters, weren't getting any younger.

The Grays won both halves of the Negro National League title, their sixth straight and eighth in the previous nine years, but, according to Lacy, they "'backed' into this year's title because the rest of the teams either couldn't or refused to take advantage of one of the flimsiest clubs to wear Homestead uniforms in all of a decade."[93] The Grays' home opener at Griffith Stadium was indicative of their season. They barely swept a doubleheader (4–2 and 2–1) against the lowly New York Black Yankees, who were missing half of their team because of car trouble, and had lost to the same club, 5–4, the previous day in Pittsburgh.[94] Art Carter wrote that though the Grays dominated at Griffith Stadium, they hadn't won a league game at Pittsburgh's Forbes Field over the previous two seasons.[95] The team was simply getting old.

The Grays lost the Negro League World Series to the young Cleveland Buckeyes (led by future major league outfielder Sam Jethroe) in four-straight games. Buckeyes player-manager Quincy Trouppe regarded the World Series as a grand upset.[96] Lacy, however, saw it coming. A week before the World Series, he brutally picked apart the Grays' NNL season:

> Their only redeeming features, as I see it, were (1) Jerry Benjamin's steadiness at center field (and let me add here that I think Benjamin has turned up to be the best outfielder in baseball); (2) Roy Welmaker's spectacular pitching; (3) Johnny Wright's dependability (even when pitching under the name of Leftwich, Leftwell, et al); (4) Gibson's terrific hitting at opportune times; and (5) the grit that is legendary with the Grays, making so true the adage that "one mistake against them means your soul is lost."[97]

That grit came from Posey—a grit he instilled in his longtime players, such as Leonard, Harris, Brown, and Bankhead, but a grit that

223

could carry the Grays only so far. The Buckeyes' sweep of the Grays signified the end of the Grays' dominance over black baseball.

The Grays also lost their hold on Washington. Although the team's 1945 home opener against the Black Yankees attracted thirteen thousand fans, the Grays averaged about five thousand a home game.[98] In August, thousands of black Washingtonians crowded into U Street to celebrate the official end of World War II.[99] Maybe it was the impending end to the war, maybe it was all the talk about integration, but large numbers of black Washingtonians rarely flocked to Griffith Stadium in 1945 to see the Grays.

One exception was the Grays' June 24 doubleheader sweep of the Kansas City Monarchs—between eighteen thousand and twenty thousand people came out to see the Monarchs' new shortstop, Jackie Robinson.[100] As a former UCLA football star, Robinson, not Paige, received top billing when the Monarchs came to Washington. The *Afro*'s pregame story featured a larger picture of Robinson, a smaller picture of Paige, and a headline that said: "Jackie Robinson to Make D.C. Bow with Monarchs."[101] Paige apparently resented the publicity heaped on Robinson, forcing the Monarchs to ask local newspapers to return a group photograph of the two players.[102]

Robinson played according to his scouting report—as an exciting base runner and a good hitter, but with an arm too weak for shortstop. He had seven consecutive hits (including two doubles), tying Dave "Showboat" Thomas's Negro League record for consecutive hits at Griffith Stadium. In the first game, however, Robinson threw wildly to home plate with the bases loaded, allowing two runs to score that broke the game open.[103] Although Robinson may not have been the best black player in 1945, his lone Negro League season, he certainly was in the top ten. Veteran black players such as Leonard never contemplated that Robinson was headed for the majors. "We just thought he was a big ol' college boy coming into the league," Leonard wrote. "He was running and ripping and we just said, 'Well, soon as he gets tired, he's going to calm down just like the rest of us.'"[104]

After Robinson's only other visit to Griffith Stadium in August 1945 as part of a four-team doubleheader, the *Afro*'s Harold Jackson came away notably impressed. "I feel pretty sure that sports writers, players, and fans who have seen him in action can hardly disagree that Jackie Robinson, shortstop of the Kansas City Monarchs, is the rookie of the year," Jackson wrote, citing Robinson's .349 batting average and daring baserunning, "if not the most outstanding player on the diamond for 1945, in colored baseball."[105] Jackson also asked Robinson about playing in the majors. "I hope like most of the fellows in our leagues that we may be playing on one of the major league teams one day," Robinson said. "But since the war's ended, I can't help feeling that it is going to be a lot tougher now, to crash the big show."[106]

Rickey had been trailing Robinson for several months. Shortly after Rickey pledged his support for the United States League, Smith told Rickey about Robinson's impressive tryout with the Boston Red Sox. Smith also informed Rickey about Robinson's educational and athletic background in California: the brother of an Olympic sprinter, a standout football player at UCLA, and a former army lieutenant. Rickey was so intrigued that during the summer of 1945 he sent Dodgers scout Clyde Sukeforth (as well as several others) to follow Robinson around the country and to evaluate the player Rickey referred to on the telephone with Smith as the "Young Man from the West."[107]

While Smith and Rickey privately conferred about Robinson, Lacy publicly agreed that Robinson was the right player to break baseball's color barrier. Lacy wrote a controversial article, "Will Our Boys Make Big League Grade?" in the 1945 edition of *Negro Baseball* evaluating all the potential black major leaguers with the undue harshness that Lacy brought to his weekly coverage of the Grays. In fact, the article was so critical that New York Yankees president Larry MacPhail took it out of context before Mayor La Guardia's committee to support his arguments against integration.[108] MacPhail quoted Lacy as follows:

225

> I am reluctant to say that we haven't a single man in the ranks of colored baseball who could step into a major league uniform and disport himself after the fashion of a big leaguer. . . . There are those

among our league who might possibly excel in the manner of hitting or fielding or base-running. But for the most part, the fellows who could hold their own in more than one of these phases of the game, are few and far between—perhaps nil.[109]

MacPhail, however, left out the intervening paragraph in which Lacy characterized many black players as "'potential' big leaguers" and said that with the same opportunities for development as white players they could succeed among postwar major league talent. Despite labeling many black players "potentials," Lacy refused to tout any one player as a bona fide major league star.[110]

Lacy favored the players Smith had brought to the Red Sox tryout, particularly Robinson. "I liked Jackie Robinson for more reasons than one," Lacy wrote in the magazine that came out in late July/early August 1945:

> Having played football with an otherwise all-white team at UCLA, the Kansas City shortstop would be well versed in diplomacy. He would have neither the inferiority complex we must avoid nor the cocky bull-dozing attitude we likewise should abandon. All his life has been spent in an interracial setting, a fact that is bound to be a distinct help as a trailblazer.[111]

Lacy's prescient comments forecast the racial abuse Robinson would endure over the next few seasons. Lacy named other "potentials," including former Grays third baseman Howard Easterling, current Grays outfielder Dave Hoskins, Baltimore Elite Giants second baseman Sammy Hughes, and Newark Eagles infielder Larry Doby.[112] As one of the first writers to make a hard play for Robinson, however, Lacy earned the admiration of his colleagues in the black press, such as Ric Roberts, who believed that Lacy's article "got the ball rolling toward cracking the color line."[113]

A somewhat surprising name high on Lacy's list of "potentials" was the Grays' troubled catcher. Josh Gibson once again butted heads with Grays management in 1945 by "going on another of his escapades"—some combination of being drunk, overweight, and psychologically unstable that usually landed him in a mental institution. Gibson was "at various times suspended, fined, and destined for trade to one of the lowlier teams in the Negro National League as penalty for breaking training and other demeanor not exactly keeping with the standards of a $1,000 per month ball player."[114] Posey even left Gibson off the East's team for the 1945 East-West All-Star Game in Chicago, leading Smith to write that Gibson "probably has seen his last season with the Homestead Grays."[115]

Lacy, of all people, rushed to Gibson's defense. "I take the floor at this time as attorney for the defense in the case of 'The People vs. Josh Gibson,'" Lacy wrote. Lacy's defense of Gibson was an unusual one—the Grays expected too much of him. Lacy wrote:

> I have never considered him the cream of the crop among colored catchers and have never been able to understand the high rating given him as such. . . . In recent months, Josh has shown himself to be nothing more or less than I've always called him: namely a hell-firing batsman but just an ordinary backstopper.[116]

Lacy pointed out that the ineffectiveness of Rab Roy Gaston forced Gibson to catch every Negro National League game, magnifying Gibson's defensive liabilities. In late July, Gibson's two passed balls in a game at Baltimore's Bugle Field contributed to the Grays' 5–4, tenth-inning loss to the Elite Giants.[117]

Gibson still reigned supreme as a hitter, though. His home-run output at Griffith Stadium dropped from his 1943 levels, but he still finished with at least four home runs there.[118] By comparison, the Senators, who rebounded from their last-place finish in 1944 to finish second, hit only one home run at Griffith Stadium during the entire 1945 season.[119] By season's end, Gibson had captured the Negro National League batting championship with a .393 average.[120] Gibson belonged on Lacy's list of potential major leaguers for his hitting alone.

Given Gibson's lack of mental stability, however, he was totally incapable of playing in the majors. That winter, playing for the Santurce Crabbers in Puerto Rico, he once again suffered a nervous

227

breakdown and landed in a mental hospital. He escaped from the hospital, and the Puerto Rican police discovered him in the mountains naked and without the ring and watch he usually wore.[121] Although Gibson returned to his Puerto Rican team for a time, the police again found him drunk, naked, and wandering the streets of downtown San Juan claiming to be "on 'his way to the ballpark.'"[122] The team eventually sent him home. Gibson wouldn't be making the grade anytime soon.

Leonard was further down on Lacy's list of potential major leaguers than Gibson was. The Grays' first baseman anchored his team's cleanup spot for almost the entire 1945 season, and deservedly so. In late July, Leonard earned another starting berth in the East-West Game and was leading the Negro National League with a .396 (40-for-101) batting average.[123] Although Leonard finished third in the NNL batting race with a .375 (48-for-128) average, he wore down during the second half and sat out the last month of the season with another broken hand before returning for the World Series.[124] About Leonard's major league prospects, Lacy wrote:

> Leonard is definitely of big league calibre. But the venerable Buck has become much too brittle of late to expect any great deeds. There is some doubt in my mind, therefore, as to whether or not he would be equal to the demands of a daily program such as is required of major league performers.[125]

Leonard lacked Gibson's defensive deficiencies, never drank too much or suffered from mental problems, and, when healthy, proved to be the second-most feared hitter in the league.

228

Contrary to Lacy's scouting report, Leonard seemed to have a better shot than Gibson at playing in the majors. That winter, playing on a team of black All-Stars with Jackie Robinson in Caracas, Venezuela, Leonard hit two home runs, including one off the Senators' Venezuelan-born pitcher, Alex Carrasquel.[126] The only difference between Leonard and Carrasquel: Carrasquel was lighter-skinned and spoke a foreign language. Robinson, although privately expressing doubts about his own ability to make the majors, raved to Wendell Smith about Leonard's home-run hitting.[127]

One player whom Lacy completely wrote off as a potential major leaguer was Paige. "Satchel soon learned that he could make more money as a showman than he could ever hope to draw as a brilliant flinger," Lacy wrote. Lacy believed that the thirty-nine-year-old Paige was too old and "could not hope for more than two years of successful throwing in the big time."[128] Lacy, like so many people, underestimated Paige.

Paige seemed to know, however, that he would not be the first black major leaguer. During the 1945 season, Paige reiterated to both Lacy and Smith that the best way to integrate would be to admit two black teams to the major leagues. Paige blasted Negro League owners for holding back the campaign. "All they want to do is sit in their own little pond and be the great big fish," Paige told Lacy. "They don't have sense enough to see they could pool their resources and fight along with you newspaper guys to put two teams in organized baseball and still go on doing their own league business just the same." Paige also criticized the black press for promoting only one or two players for the majors. "You harp on, 'give them a chance, give them a chance,' without thinking how tough it's gonna be for a colored ball player to come out of the club house and have all the white guys calling him 'n****r' and 'b***k so-and-so,' etc." Then Lacy asked Paige if he ever heard such epithets pitching against white teams. "No," Paige replied, "but then I was only one man and, besides, I was better than any of them. They couldn't call me anything but 'Mr. Paige.'"[129]

Paige intuited that the only way older players such as Gibson, Leonard, and himself would be the first ones in the major leagues was as part of an All-Star team. "What is wrong with Booker McDaniels, Kansas City pitcher, Buck Leonard and Josh Gibson of the Homestead Grays, and Bonnie Serrell of Kansas City?" Paige wrote Smith. "Too old? Listen there are a lot of big leaguers now playing that are over thirty years of age. The men I have named, and plenty of other Negro players, are just as good and better than a lot of the big leaguers the same age."[130]

Paige's vision of a team of Negro League veterans breaking the color barrier never came to pass. Years later, however, major league owner Bill Veeck claimed that he had tried to pull off just such a move by buying the last-place Philadelphia Phillies before the 1943 season and turning them into a first-place team by stocking them with Paige, Gibson, Leonard, and other Negro League All-Stars. According to his autobiography, Veeck's mistake was revealing his plan to Judge Landis, who, along with National League president Ford Frick, engineered the sale of the Phillies to lumber mogul William Cox.[131] This story, although seemingly plausible given Veeck's liberal hiring of black players as the owner of the Cleveland Indians and St. Louis Browns, has been exposed by several baseball historians as a myth.[132]

"Baseball's Great Experiment," as historian Jules Tygiel referred to it, began as an individual affair. In late August, after a historic meeting between the two men at the team's Brooklyn offices, Rickey signed Robinson to play in the Dodgers organization. Although Smith revealed in the *Pittsburgh Courier* that the meeting had occurred, Rickey shrouded the details in secrecy.[133] Rickey officially signed Robinson to a professional contract with the Montreal Royals, the Dodgers' Triple-A farm club, on October 23. "I know that my position was obtained only through the constant pressure of my people and their press," Robinson told the *Afro*, alluding to the work of Lacy and Smith. "It's a press victory, you might say."[134]

October 23 was Lacy's birthday. He authored two of his most memorable paragraphs in one of his first columns about Rickey's signing of Robinson:

> Baseball, in its time, has possessed its full share of men from every other racial strain except Robinson's. It has given employment to known epileptics, kleptomaniacs and a generous scattering of saints and sinners.
>
> A man who is totally lacking in character has often turned up to be a star in baseball. A man whose skin is white or red or yellow has been acceptable. But a man whose character may be of the highest or whose ability may be Ruthian has been barred completely from sport because he is colored.[135]

Lacy believed that Rickey had found the right man in Robinson, in terms of both character and ability.

The announcement sent shock waves through black baseball. Leonard, having played with Robinson that winter in Venezuela and against him during the 1945 season, said, "we did not think too much of Robinson. . . . He was a hustler but other than that he wasn't a top shortstop. We said, 'We don't see how he can make it.'"[136] In hindsight, Leonard observed that Robinson's college-educated background made him the right person for the job.[137] Paige, although publicly supportive of Robinson ("he's the greatest colored player I've ever seen"[138]), was crushed about not being the first player chosen. "Signing Robinson like they did still hurt me deep down," Paige recalled.[139] Gibson was off in Puerto Rico losing his mind. And Negro League owners faced the prospect of losing their best young ballplayers without a cent of compensation.

Rickey stole Robinson from the Monarchs because he knew he could get away with it. "Branch Rickey raped us," outspoken Newark Eagles owner Effa Manley told author William Marshall years later. "We were in no position to protest, and he knew it. Rickey had us over a barrel."[140] Rickey signed Robinson without even bothering to ask the Monarchs for permission, much less to negotiate a settlement. Initially, Thomas Baird, a white co-owner of the Monarchs along with J. L. Wilkinson, protested the Dodgers' signing of Robinson and threatened to appeal to the new major league commissioner, Albert "Happy" Chandler. Baird, however, later claimed that he had been misquoted.[141] A white owner of a black team could not be perceived as standing in the way of integrating major league baseball. The Monarchs' owners publicly expressed support for Robinson, as did Negro American League president J. B. Martin. The rest of the Negro League owners seethed in silence — at least initially.

Responding to the charges of theft like the skilled lawyer he was, Rickey publicly derided the Negro Leagues as a "booking agent's paradise" with uneven schedules, team owners serving as league presidents, and nonexistent contracts. He dared the Monarchs to produce a contract with Robinson's signature on it. Then he personally attacked the Negro League owners, alluding to many of their occupations as numbers operators. "I do not regard either of the Negro baseball organizations as leagues, and will not until they clean

231

house," Rickey told Wendell Smith. "They have the semblance of a racket and operate for the best interests of certain individuals."[142]

One of those individuals, the Old Fox, stood up for the silent Negro League owners. Griffith, who had predicted that integration would not occur until the Negro Leagues improved their organization, voiced the strongest initial protest among major league magnates. Suddenly, black baseball no longer needed any building up. "The only question that occurs to me is whether organized ball has the right to sign a player from the Negro league," Griffith said. "That is a well established league and organized baseball shouldn't take their players. The Negro league is entitled to full recognition as a full-fledged baseball organization."[143] Major league teams "can't act like outlaws in taking their stars," Griffith said in comments that made headlines in some of the nation's largest newspapers.[144]

Griffith's stand exposed him to attack over his financial relationship with the Grays. Rickey immediately picked up on this theme:

> Don't let Mr. Griffith fool you. He's not interested in Negro baseball other than from the standpoint of financial gain. He's afraid he won't make the big hunk of money next year that he got this year from the Homestead Grays. Griffith's thinking more about his pocketbook than he is about the right and wrong in the thing.[145]

Lacy agreed with Rickey about Griffith's motives: "his interest in 'protecting' our sport lies primarily in his ability to remember that he pulls down approximately $55,000 a year in rentals to the Homestead Grays."[146] Lacy, however, grossly underestimated Griffith's yearly profits off the Grays.

232   Griffith made more money from black baseball than almost every other major league team made from black baseball. In 1943, Griffith's profits from the Grays totaled at least $100,000.[147] By comparison, the Yankees rented out Yankee Stadium and their minor league parks in Newark, Kansas City, and Norfolk to Negro League teams for a yearly profit of $100,000. It is not surprising, therefore, that Griffith and MacPhail led the opposition to integration. "Club owners in the major leagues are reluctant to give up revenues amounting to hun-

dreds of thousands of dollars every year," according to the initial draft of a secret major league steering committee report issued on August 27, 1946, part of which was submitted to a 1951 congressional committee. "They naturally want the Negro leagues to continue."[148]

The difference between the Yankees and the Senators was that Griffith's profits from the Grays represented the difference between finishing the season in the red or in the black. "Clark Griffith used to say, 'If I could draw 350,000 people, I can make money.' He made money 25 consecutive years there," his nephew Calvin recalled. "The money that he made, though, was $1,000, $2,000, or $3,000, sometimes $10,000 or $15,000."[149] The Senators' financial statement from 1960, the Griffith family's last season in Washington, indicates that the team made $5,565.06 in net profits that year and $7,393.93 from stadium rentals.[150] Although it had been ten years since the Grays contributed $50,000 to $100,000 per year to play at the ballpark, stadium rentals still meant the difference between a profit and a loss. "They were our bread and butter," Calvin Griffith said of the Senators' black fans. "The Homestead Grays . . . brought in money all summer—14 games or so. You're not gonna knock anybody that kept you alive."[151] During the war, the stadium rentals from the Grays equaled, if not surpassed, the $100,000 yearly fee the Griffiths received from the Redskins. Griffith's defense of the Grays represented a defense of his financial survival. Smith told Jerome Holtzman: "In Washington, it was said that the Negro teams, by renting Griffith Stadium, were saving the Senators from bankruptcy."[152]

Griffith and the other major league owners disagreed that their lost stadium rentals could be recouped by integrating their teams and increasing black attendance. According to the secret major league report, which was probably authored by MacPhail, "[a] situation might be presented, if Negroes participated in major league games, in which the preponderance of Negro attendance in parks such as the Yankee Stadium, the Polo Grounds and Comiskey Park could conceivably threaten the value of Major League franchises owned by these Clubs."[153] Increased black attendance from integration was a definite possibility in Washington, where many blacks loved baseball and lived near Griffith Stadium. The report, alluding to twenty-eight

233

thousand fans who saw the Grays-Monarchs night game in 1942, mentioned that "[a] Negro league game established an all-time attendance record at Griffith Stadium in Washington."[154] For financial reasons, as well as fear of change, Griffith preferred the status quo.

In defending the Grays, Griffith also drew attention to his history of signing dark-skinned foreign players. Passing off Cuban outfielder Bobby Estalella and Venezuelan pitcher Alex Carrasquel as white players came back to haunt Clark Griffith during his condemnation of Rickey, who charged Griffith with "initiating the practice of bringing 'Negroes' into baseball."[155] Red Smith, who had recently switched papers from the *Philadelphia Record* to the *New York Herald Tribune*, quipped: "Rickey responded that hiring Negroes was nothing new to Clark Griffith. This seemed to imply that there was a Senegambian somewhere in the Cuban batpile where Senatorial timber is seasoned."[156] At least one member of Washington's white press corps defended Griffith. Frank (Buck) O'Neill of the *Washington Times Herald* suggested that by referring to Griffith's Cuban players as black, Rickey should be sued for libel.[157]

Lacy responded with a pointed editorial titled, "Just Clark, That's All," in which he dismissed the argument about protecting the Negro Leagues as "typical Griffithian double-talk" and his hiring of Cubans as downright hypocrisy. "You can place into your hat all the Cubans Griffith actually 'bought' from the Cuban league, and still leave room for your head," Lacy wrote. "His conscience doesn't begin until ONE player is sought from a colored league."[158]

Griffith withstood these brutal attacks and helped the heretofore silent Negro League owners, led by Posey, craft a course of action. In an eight-paragraph letter to the new commissioner, Happy Chandler, the owners made their case. "We are not protesting the signing of Negro Players by white organized baseball," the letter said. "We are glad to see our players get the opportunity to play in white Organized Baseball. We are protesting the way it is done."[159]

The letter, which was dated November 9 and signed by the Negro National and Negro American League presidents, Thomas Wilson and J. B. Martin, as well as by Posey, had Posey's fingerprints all over it. It detailed Rickey's recent pursuit of John Wright, the Grays' ace right-handed pitcher. It also emphasized the validity of Negro League player contracts, citing a 1941 order from the Court of Common Pleas of Allegheny County (Pennsylvania) awarding the Grays ten thousand dollars when Gibson had jumped his contract in order to play in Mexico. Finally, it asked Chandler to intervene on black baseball's behalf: "We feel that the clubs of Organized Negro baseball who have gone to so much expense to develop players and establish teams and leagues should be appraoched [sic], and deals made between clubs involved, even though Negro Organized Baseball is not a part of White Organized Baseball. That is the only way in which we can be assured that Negro Organized Baseball *can* continue to operate."[160]

Griffith stood firmly behind Posey's efforts to save black baseball. Griffith urged Chandler to "protect the rights" of Negro League teams with regard to their players. After receiving an advance copy of Posey's letter, Griffith wrote the Grays' owner an optimistic reply. Griffith told Posey that "*custom* makes *law* and that both the Negro National and American Leagues are under this custom entitled to every consideration and fair dealing from Organized Baseball."[161]

Griffith used his letter to Posey to answer Rickey's criticism. "Mr. Rickey publicly denounced Negro Baseball as *racket*," Griffith wrote. "This assertion you can prove not to be true." Griffith argued that the Negro Leagues always have respected the rules and contracts of "Organized Baseball," and they have built up a "splendid reputation" among "colored people all over this country as well as the decent white people." In response to Rickey's assertion that the Monarchs had no written contract with Robinson, Griffith emphasized that oral agreements between black teams and their players constitute enforceable contracts. Finally, Griffith offered Posey words of encouragement. "Mr. Posey, anything that is worth while is worth fighting for, so you folks should leave not a stone unturned to protect the existence of your two established Negro Leagues. Don't let anybody tear it down. . . . It is my belief that the Commissioner will give you relief."[162]

The baseball commissioner, however, was no longer Judge Landis, Griffith's buddy; it was Albert B. "Happy" Chandler. A former gov-

235

ernor and U.S. senator from Kentucky, Chandler was a former college and semipro baseball player and a lawyer. In the Senate, Chandler had opposed a work-or-fight bill threatening to shut down baseball during World War II. The bill had been introduced by a Kentucky congressman embittered about the cancellation of the Kentucky Derby, but not baseball, during the war.[163] A surprise choice for commissioner, Chandler seemed like a natural foe of integration—he had been recommended for the job by MacPhail, and he was an elected official from a segregated state.[164] Yet when Chandler took office as baseball's second commissioner in late May 1945, he expressed tepid support for integration. "If it's discrimination you are afraid of, you have nothing to fear from me," Chandler told the *Pittsburgh Courier's* Ric Roberts.[165] The difference between Landis and Chandler was that Chandler meant it.[166]

In January 1946, Chandler met with Negro National and Negro American League presidents Thomas Wilson and J. B. Martin. During the meeting, the two men informed Chandler that black baseball had adopted the major leagues' bylaws and its standard player contract (including the reserve clause).[167] They implored Chandler to force major league teams to honor the Negro Leagues' player contracts.[168] Chandler's message was clear—he told them to "get their house in order."[169] He said the Negro Leagues could not be integrated into the white minor league system until all black teams had their own ballparks. This was an impossible requirement. Nor did Chandler promise to intervene in black baseball's disputes with major league owners.[170] Chandler turned out to be Rickey's ace in the hole.[171]

Lacy and Smith had been warning black baseball to get its house in order for several years—to hire a commissioner, adopt uniform player contracts, reduce their reliance on major league ballparks, and play more regular league schedules. Lacy expressed "little sympathy" for the black owners. In a lengthy story about the owners' refusal to send a representative to the major league committee on integration in June, Lacy wrote that the owners had "turned a deaf ear to the *AFRO* appeal" and that appealing to Chandler to block the signing of the league's best players "is just a lot of slush."[172] Smith also criticized their appeal to Chandler and commented on the public's negative reaction. "The fact that Clark Griffith of the Washington Senators instructed them how to do it and what to say to Chandler hasn't hit so well with the public, either," Smith wrote, comparing Griffith to two arch-segregationist Mississippi congressmen. "Where Negro ball players are concerned, Griffith is about as liberal as [Sen. Theodore] Bilbo and [Rep. John] Rankin. . . ."[173]

Borrowing Smith's column in early February 1946, Posey made some of his final points. The Grays' owner blamed Eddie Gottlieb for charging promotional fees to use Philadelphia's Shibe Park and Yankee Stadium. He blamed Negro National League president Thomas Wilson for not standing up to Gottlieb and Negro American League president J. B. Martin. He blamed Martin for dominating the East-West Game, permitting Abe Saperstein to promote the event, and allowing Martin's family to own stakes in two Negro American League teams, the Memphis Red Sox and the Chicago American Giants. From Posey's perspective, the future of Negro League baseball was bleak and the chance of success with Chandler and other white officials was nonexistent.[174]

Posey called for change: regular league schedules, shifting the East-West Game from Chicago to an East Coast city, ending multi-team ownership, and hiring a commissioner. "If there are no changes made, then there is no reason to appeal to white Organized Baseball for help," he wrote. "The baseball public is more interested in seeing Negro baseball properly operated than they are in having white organized baseball clubs pay for players secured from Negro Organized Baseball clubs."[175]

Unfortunately for Posey, his calls for change came too late. Shortly after Chandler rejected the Negro League owners' appeal, Rickey stole one of Posey's players, right-handed pitcher John Wright. Wright's background could not have been more different from Jackie Robinson's: Wright was not college-educated, he was a southerner who still lived in his hometown of New Orleans, and he had spent nearly ten years in the Negro Leagues. Wright led the Grays' pitching staff with a 26–4 record in 1943 and pitched for the Grays in 1944 and 1945 when he could get away from the Great Lakes Naval Base.

During his military service, Wright sometimes pitched for the Grays under the name of Leftwich (either because he couldn't get an official leave or to thwart the protests of Negro League officials). He competed against several major league teams with the integrated Floyd Bennett Naval Air Base team in New York; he also finished with a 16–4 record pitching for the all-black Great Lakes Navy team in Illinois.[176]

Rickey had been wooing Wright for several months. In December 1945, Wright denied having signed a minor league contract with the Dodgers and pledged his loyalty to Posey and the Grays.[177] Along with outfielder Dave Hoskins, the twenty-nine-year-old Wright was one of the Grays' best young players. More than just a roommate and traveling companion for Robinson on the Montreal Royals, as some have suggested, Wright was a legitimate prospect.[178]

Lacy broke the news to Posey that the Dodgers had signed Wright. Although Posey was "in a rage," the brunt of his displeasure was aimed at Wright. Posey explained how he had increased Wright's salary to $150 a month in the middle of Wright's stellar 1943 season and also paid Wright $250 a month "the whole time he was in the Navy." In the wake of this desertion by one of his ballplayers, Posey failed to hide his sense of betrayal. "Why, he told me a week ago that he wasn't going to leave us because we had been too good to him," Posey said. "If Wright's done that, I don't know what to think of him.'"[179]

A notoriously sore loser, Posey wouldn't let it go. He called Wright a "dirty so-and-so." Then he began picking apart Wright's weaknesses, including his inability to field bunts or to hold runners on base. "Oh, he'll have a tough ride, Sam, take it from me," Posey said.[180] Posey turned out to be right. Of Rickey's initial four recruits— Robinson and Wright at Triple-A Montreal and Roy Campanella (Baltimore Elite Giants) and Don Newcombe (Newark Eagles) at Class-B Nashua—only Wright did not become a star. According to Rickey and Robinson, Wright could not handle the pressure of being a racial pioneer.[181] The Dodgers demoted Wright after a month to Three Rivers in the Class-C Canadian-American League. They replaced him with left-handed pitcher Roy Partlow, whose stay in

Montreal also proved to be short-lived. Partlow, however, thrived with Wright at Three Rivers.[182] The Grays' erstwhile hero on the June 18, 1942, night during the 2–1 come-from-behind victory over the Monarchs, Partlow had been pitching with the Philadelphia Stars. Rickey paid one thousand dollars for Partlow because the Stars produced a written contract and because Partlow was a midseason acquisition.[183] It marked the only time Rickey ever paid a Negro League team for a player's services.

When Rickey signed Wright, Posey publicly expressed confidence that Chandler would stop Rickey's raids on the Negro Leagues. "I'm sure Commissioner Chandler isn't going to let Branch Rickey get away with this," Posey told Lacy. "I took the matter up with him [Chandler] personally just this month.'"[184] Privately, however, Posey knew better. "Do you realize we have not made one single change for the better since Negro baseball was called a 'racket?'" Posey wrote Effa Manley.[185] Posey's personal appeals, his conferences with Griffith, and his anger about Wright all amounted to nothing. Chandler allowed Rickey to raid the Negro Leagues with impunity. "It was like coming into a man's store and taking the commodities right off his shelf without paying a dime," Posey told Ric Roberts. "You don't know how much it cost me to build this team. I've been struggling with this damn thing since 1913. I guess I won't live to fight anymore.'"[186]

About two months later, on March 28, 1946, Cum Posey died. He was fifty-four. Posey, who had been battling a lung infection for the previous year, spent his final three weeks at Pittsburgh's Mercy Hospital. From his hospital bed, the day after the doctors collapsed one of his lungs, Posey called the *Pittsburgh Sun-Telegraph*'s Harry Keck to thank him for a column about how the "Dodgers stole our pitcher, Johnny Wright, for their Montreal club. That column did me a lot of good." The day before he died, Posey left the hospital to be driven around Homestead; he wanted one last glimpse at his old hometown.[187]

Posey was revered by people of all races in his community. He had been serving on the Homestead school board since 1931. On April 1, Homestead closed its schools in his honor. During halftime of a 1949

239

high school football game, the people of Homestead dedicated the Cumberland W. Posey Memorial Field House."[188]

In his later years, Posey rarely traveled with the Grays; he kept his distance while his older brother, Seward ("See"), served as the traveling secretary. Nothing, however, escaped Posey's attention, and many of his observations found their way into his weekly newspaper column.

Posey wielded his *Courier* column, "Posey's Points," with a sanctimoniousness and self-righteousness that rubbed many people the wrong way. According to *Pittsburgh Courier* president Ira Lewis, Posey "prided himself on never being a good loser because, as he said, 'Good losers are seldom winners.'"[189] He never admitted to losing an argument, and he often alienated the black press. In June 1943, Smith wrote that "Posey's holier-than-thou attitude is typical. His record in Negro Organized Baseball is far from impressive. I am sure that anyone who has had the pleasure of doing business with Cumberland in baseball will agree with me. He's quite a fellow that Cumberland Posey . . . so he says!"[190]

It was hard to argue with the Grays' success. Posey claimed to have made money every year from 1912 to 1929. He had survived battles with Rube Foster in the 1920s, Gus Greenlee in the 1930s, and white booking agents in the 1940s. His team had won eight of the previous nine Negro National League titles. Certainly no black team made more money than the Grays during World War II. Posey single-handedly turned Griffith Stadium into a baseball gold mine, succeeding in Washington after many other black teams had failed.

Posey, like all great businessmen, constantly adapted to change. He put his star players on salary in the early 1920s to prevent other teams from stealing them away. He eventually joined the Negro National League, yet maintained his team's status as an independent outfit because the Grays could make more money barnstorming. He started his own league after Foster's folded, yet had enough sense to join Greenlee's revived Negro National League. He found a numbers man, Rufus "Sonnyman" Jackson, to bankroll the Grays to prevent Greenlee from stealing his players. He recognized that the Grays could not survive financially by playing their home games at Pittsburgh's Forbes Field, so he developed a larger home base in Washington. The only thing Posey could not adapt to was integration, a concept antithetical to the Grays' long-term financial success.

Not many people associated with black baseball loved Posey, but ultimately they respected him. Fay Young, the *Chicago Defender's* sports editor since 1907, had witnessed Posey's rise and fall and frequently disagreed with Posey over the years. "It is a sad state of affairs when both friends and enemies wait until the man dies before they will admit his true worth," Young wrote. "Posey and we disagreed many times. He always said we were for the Negro American League and the West. Sometimes, he'd hop on us through his column but never with any spleen—simply a difference of opinion. Then he'd meet us and we would shake hands. His only excuse would be, 'Well, that's the way I thought it at the time,' and laughingly would add, 'You know there ain't no way for me to rub the doggone thing out.'"[191]

Smith, also more charitable after Posey's death, described him as "the John McGraw of Negro baseball. . . . He gave no quarter and asked no quarter. His ballclub—the Homestead Grays—came first. That's probably why he was able to build the greatest organization in Negro baseball history." Smith subtly acknowledged his prior differences with Posey: "Posey's life was dedicated to the team he made, the Homestead Grays. Some may charge that his tactics were crude and his aims selfish. Some may say he crushed the weak as well as the strong on his way to the top of the ladder. But no matter what his critics say, they cannot deny he was the smartest man in Negro baseball and certainly the most successful."[192]

Lacy, who fought for integration in the face of Posey's quiet opposition, characterized Posey as "one of those cussing, fighting, rootin' tootin' hombres who cared little about what he did to you and less about whether you liked it."[193] Posey lost the battle over the color barrier. Fortunately for him, he did not live to see just how big a loss it turned out to be.

A fellow loser in the integration fight, Griffith, sent flowers to Posey's funeral. Later that year, Griffith was inducted into the Baseball Hall of Fame after more than a half century as a major league pitcher, manager, and owner. Posey, who still has not been elected

241

to the Hall of Fame, passed into obscurity along with his three decades of accomplishments.

There was a distinct difference between Griffith and Posey's opposition to integration. Griffith could have recouped his lost stadium rentals from the Grays by signing the best black players and increasing his black fan base. Posey, however, was simply protecting the Grays the only way he could—by resisting integration and insisting on compensation from major league teams for his best players. The Grays represented much more than a financial investment for Posey. They were his legacy.

Leonard and most of his teammates did not attend Posey's funeral. The Grays had just left for spring training in Jacksonville, Florida. The city of Jacksonville voted to cancel a March 23 spring training game between the Montreal Royals and the Jersey Giants rather than allow Robinson and Wright to play there.[194] Instead, the two players attended the Grays' game on the other side of town.[195] The sight of Robinson and Wright in the stands and the Grays on the field signified the last time the champions of black baseball occupied center stage.

The Negro National League owners gather at a league meeting. The Grays are represented by Rufus "Sonnyman" Jackson (standing at left), Art Carter (standing second from left), and Cum Posey (seated back row, second from right). (ART CARTER PAPERS, MOORLAND-SPINGARN RESEARCH CENTER, HOWARD UNIVERSITY)

Clark Griffith (left) and Philadelphia Athletics owner Connie Mack (center) were two
of the biggest opponents of integration, which they characterized as a Communist plot
to ruin baseball. Cleveland Indians owner Bill Veeck (right) was one of integration's
biggest proponents. Veeck brought Larry Doby to the Indians in the middle of the 1947
season, the same year Jackie Robinson broke in with the Dodgers, and added Satchel
Paige the following year. Paige also played on the Veeck-owned St. Louis Browns and
Triple-A Miami Marlins. (AP/WORLDWIDE)

Sam Lacy fought for integrated hotel accommodations for black major leaguers at spring training facilities in Florida and Arizona. At spring training during the 1950s in Arizona, Lacy (back left) is seated with Giants and Indians players, including Monte Irvin (back right), Larry Doby (seated third from left), and Willie Mays (front right). (NATIONAL BASEBALL HALL OF FAME LIBRARY)

Josh Gibson, looking forlorn and leaning on a bat for support, posed for only a few photographers at the 1946 East-West Game in Chicago. This may be the last photograph taken of Gibson before he died in January 1947. (NATIONAL BASEBALL HALL OF FAME LIBRARY)

NINE

THE GRAYS FADE TO BLACK

The Grays turned a profit for the last time during the 1946 season despite Posey's death and stiff competition. The postwar boom injected new life into white professional baseball. Black fans largely focused their energies on whether Jackie Robinson would make good with the Montreal Royals. White fans flocked to major league games in record numbers as attendance skyrocketed from 10.8 million in 1945 to 18.5 million in 1946.[1] In Washington, the Senators drew more than a million fans for the only time in the team's history.[2] The Nats, as headline writers referred to the team known as the Senators or Nationals, managed a respectable fourth-place finish, and their first baseman, Mickey Vernon, captured the American League batting title. Along with established stars Joe DiMaggio and Ted Williams, Vernon returned to the majors that season from military service.

The postwar boom also benefited black teams whose best players returned home. The Newark Eagles cruised to their first Negro National League and Negro League World Series titles because of the return of future major league sluggers Monte Irvin and Larry Doby and pitchers Leon Day and Max Manning. The Monarchs, who fell to the Eagles in the World Series, regained the services of first baseman Buck O'Neil, center fielder Willard "Home Run" Brown, and right fielder Ted Strong.

The Grays could not compete with the Eagles or Monarchs. Nothing could rejuvenate Posey's decrepit team, not even the return of

pitcher Wilmer Fields (who emerged as the staff ace) and third baseman Howard Easterling or the addition of young second baseman
Luis Marquez and forty-three-year-old backup catcher–pitcher Ted
"Double Duty" Radcliffe. In 1946, the Grays depended on an aging
lineup of Josh Gibson, Buck Leonard, Cool Papa Bell, shortstop Sam
Bankhead, and center fielder Jerry Benjamin. The pitching staff suffered from the losses of ace John Wright to Rickey's Dodger farm
teams, lefty Roy Welmaker to Venezuela, and stalwart Ray Brown to
an arm injury and then to Mexico.[3] For the first time in ten years, the
Grays failed to earn at least a share of the Negro National League
title. They didn't even come close, finishing third (18–15) in the first
half and fourth (9–13) in the second half after a late five-game winning streak kept them out of the cellar.[4]

In one of his few columns about the Grays in 1946, Lacy seemed
to delight in the demise of the once-mighty franchise as it languished
in last place. The Grays' veterans, according to Lacy, attributed
their poor showing to too many grueling bus trips. Lacy concluded
that the Grays won so many Negro National League titles during the
war because they "were stronger in 4-F and overage material than
the rest of the clubs."[5] The Grays' championship run, according to
Lacy, depended on "pitching magic, terrific batting power or just
plain thievery." He argued that Posey's strong-arm tactics turned
league games into exhibitions and exhibitions into league games to
boost the Grays in the standings. "Usually, that ended it," Lacy wrote.
"If it didn't, the Poseys simply went to league meetings, threw their
weight around a little bit, and came out with the blessings of the
organization."[6]

Certainly, the 1946 Grays missed Posey's fighting spirit, his eye for
talent, his influence in the NNL offices, and his manipulation of the
team's league schedule. With Posey in charge, the Grays might have
been able to eke out at least a share of the 1946 title. Posey's motives
were not pernicious; he just wasn't above bending the rules if it
enabled his team to win. Over the previous decade, the Grays had
consistently fielded black baseball's strongest team. They deserved
their reputation as champions. Unlike his colleagues Fay Young and

Wendell Smith, however, Lacy wrote uncharitably about Posey after his death.

While Lacy tore the Grays down, Art Carter built them back up. In 1946, Carter not only resumed his old job as the Grays' Washington promoter but also was named the Negro National League's public relations director. He also returned to the *Afro*, where he shifted from chronicling the lives of black troops overseas to covering black professional baseball at home.

The Grays made money for the last time in 1946 largely because of Carter's promotional genius. He showered the Grays with publicity in the pages of the *Afro*, running previews, box scores, and summaries of recently played contests. He expanded his free pass list, which originally had included about sixty people, to more than five hundred.[7] He arranged three- or four-team Sunday doubleheaders that diluted the Grays' share of the profits but increased attendance to as many as fifteen thousand fans.

Carter also cultivated a new Griffith Stadium attraction in the Indianapolis Clowns. In the past, Posey had refused to schedule the Clowns in Washington because of his feud with their owner, Abe Saperstein, and because many fans found their minstrel-type show degrading. The Clowns featured between-innings gags performed by a midget named Spec Bebop and a tall, lanky mascot known as King Tut, who performed with an oversized glove and a swallow-tailed coat. Globetrotters star Goose Tatum doubled as the Clowns' first baseman. Before games, Tatum and the other players performed a famous "shadow ball" routine in which they took infield practice without a ball. The Clowns also played serious baseball, but it was the other stuff that brought out the fans.

Carter orchestrated one last league-wide windfall at Griffith's ball yard—the 1946 All-Star Classic. It represented one of Posey's last wishes to move the East-West Game from Chicago to an East Coast city like Washington. Promoted by Carter, hosted by the Grays, and sponsored by Negro National League officials, the All-Star Classic proved that black baseball could still thrive in the nation's capital.[8] Played on the night of August 15, three days before the East-West

Game, the All-Star Classic received begrudging support from the Midwestern-based Negro American League and featured the same players headed for Chicago.[9] The East team included Leonard and Gibson from the Grays, and Doby, Irvin, and Day from the Newark Eagles. The West team included Sam Jethroe of the Cleveland Buckeyes and pitcher Dan Bankhead (Sam's younger brother) of the Memphis Red Sox. The *Courier* hyped the game for several weeks, predicting a record crowd of thirty thousand fans.[10] Carter and Wendell Smith estimated a slightly more conservative twenty-five thousand people.[11] Amid all this advance publicity, the West All-Stars mounted a successful pregame strike and delayed the start of the game for fifteen minutes until the promoters raised their take from fifty dollars to one hundred dollars a player.[12]

Although it didn't live up to the black press's lofty predictions, the All-Star Classic attracted a respectable 15,009 paying customers, grossed more than thirty thousand dollars, and netted more than seventeen thousand dollars. Griffith received $6,337.50 for stadium rental plus $1,179.06 for ballpark expenses. Each league took home $6,753.01, presumably divided among its respective teams. For their troubles, Carter and his Pittsburgh counterpart, John Clark, split eight hundred dollars.[13]

The success of the All-Star Classic was remarkable considering the rival attractions. About two weeks earlier, Robinson and the Montreal Royals traveled to one of their southernmost destinations for a four-game series against the Triple-A Baltimore Orioles. While enduring endless racial taunts from segregated Baltimore's white fans, Robinson basked in the adoration of his black admirers. Black Washingtonians headed to Baltimore's Municipal Stadium by the busload, contributing to attendance of eighteen thousand on Friday, twenty-one thousand on Saturday, and about twenty-eight thousand for a Sunday doubleheader.[14]

Two weekends later at the All-Star Classic, fifteen thousand people deigned to watch two black All-Star squads compete at Griffith Stadium as the East team defeated the West team, 6–3.[15] The *Afro* and the *Courier* estimated the crowd at more than sixteen thousand, and it seemed like more.[16] Lacy wrote:

Griffith Stadium in Washington, D.C. is said to hold 32,000 people for baseball. A crowd which looked suspiciously like 23,000 saw the all-star game there Thursday night. The turnstile report was slightly more than 16,000. Where they could have put another 16,000 people in the ball park Thursday is something for the late Houdini to determine.[17]

The attendance paled in comparison to the 45,474 fans who attended the more-established East-West All-Star Game in Chicago three days later. Nonetheless, the All-Star Classic represented black baseball's last hurrah in Washington. For Carter, it was the final display of his promotional talents. For the fifteen thousand in attendance, it was an early farewell to a dying industry. For the ballplayers, it was a way to show people that they belonged in the major leagues.

The All-Star Classic served as a showcase for future major leaguers such as Larry Doby (Cleveland Indians) and Monte Irvin (New York Giants), as well as Quincy Trouppe (Indians), Sam Jethroe (Boston Braves), and Dan Bankhead (Brooklyn Dodgers). Major league scouts on hand included Clyde Sukeforth, the man who evaluated Robinson for the Dodgers.[18] Grays batboy Billy Coward remembered the extra effort the ballplayers displayed on the field and the look of anticipation in their eyes as they sat in the dugout:

> You could sense the enthusiasm of the ballplayers really wanting to put out. They were shifting gears. They were really motivated because any of them could be brought up to the major leagues. See, this I remember, that it was just like some new found blood or something, the enthusiasm that was generated by someone breaking the color ban for the most part.[19]

No one wanted to break major league baseball's color barrier more than Gibson, who put on his Grays jersey with a W on the sleeve for one of the final times that night. Three days later, at the East-West Game in Chicago, photographer Ernest Withers captured Gibson looking frail, withdrawn, and downright sad. "There were fifty-one photographers on the field," Withers said, "but Gibson would only

251

pose for a few of us."[20] Gibson's blank stare was similar to the one the *Afro* had captured after Game 1 of the 1942 Negro League World Series, shortly before his first nervous breakdown. The man who once used his six-foot, one-inch, 215-pound frame to slam balls over Griffith Stadium's faraway fences leaned on a bat for support, just as his white counterpart Babe Ruth did two years later in his farewell speech at Yankee Stadium. Gibson made no speeches at Griffith Stadium or Comiskey Park. He just withered away.

Overweight, nursing bad knees, and burdened with mental and substance abuse problems during the 1946 season, Gibson had no realistic chance of playing in the majors. The Grays signed Double Duty Radcliffe in part because of doubts over whether Gibson would even begin the season with the team.[21] Gibson played the entire year and capped off his career with a .331 batting average (third highest on the team) and a team-high twelve home runs and fifty-one RBI in forty-eight league games.[22] After a two-year home-run drought, Gibson's power stroke returned during his final campaign. His weight, however, ballooned to 230 pounds; his aching knees prevented him from crouching behind the plate; and his fondness for alcohol—and possibly other drugs—eroded his mind. After the season, Gibson did not play winter ball for the first time in many years and instead returned home to Pittsburgh.

On January 21, 1947, Carter received a telegram at his home from Grays owner Rufus Jackson: Gibson had passed away the previous day. He was thirty-six.[23] Wracked by hypertension, extreme weight loss (his weight crashed to 180 pounds), and alcoholism, Gibson died of a stroke.[24] His sister, contrary to his doctors and autopsy reports, claimed that her brother had been suffering from a brain tumor.[25] Others erroneously posited that his disappointment over not being chosen for the majors caused Gibson to die of a broken heart.[26] Leonard labeled the broken-heart theory hogwash.[27] Neither Gibson nor Leonard, who served as a pallbearer at Gibson's funeral, had been considered top-flight major league prospects since the early 1940s. Gibson was not a martyr, according to biographer William Brashler; he was a victim of segregation and discrimination that robbed many people of the opportunity to see him play.[28] In many ways, Gibson's death symbolized the death of the Negro Leagues. The big kid whom Cum Posey had plucked off the Pittsburgh sandlots in 1930 was black baseball's most feared home-run hitter, its Moses who never lived to see the Promised Land.[29]

For Lacy, Robinson developed into the story of a lifetime. Robinson integrated the minor leagues in 1946 with the Triple-A Montreal Royals and the major leagues in 1947 with the Brooklyn Dodgers. As soon as Robinson officially signed a contract with Montreal, Lacy switched his beat to full-time coverage of Robinson. In the spring of 1946, Lacy and Smith traveled to the Dodgers' spring training camp in Florida. Lacy, Smith, *Courier* photographer Billy Rowe (who doubled as their driver), John Wright, and Robinson all lived together. For the next few seasons, Lacy and Smith served as Robinson's chroniclers, confidants, and travel companions. By staying in the same segregated hotels and sometimes in the same rooms as the first wave of black major leaguers, they got the inside scoop.

Lacy also experienced a few of Robinson's racial obstacles firsthand. Before one of the Royals' spring training games in Sanford, Florida, local officials denied Robinson and Lacy entrance to the stadium; they sneaked in through a loose plank in the outfield wall. A year later, while making their way North, the Dodgers stopped in Macon, Georgia. Lacy and Robinson, while staying in a rooming house in the black community, awoke to a cross burning on the front lawn.[30]

Some racial incidents Lacy endured on his own, most of them because of a lack of access to the press box. At the 1946 Little World Series between the Triple-A International League and the American Association champions, he covered Robinson and the Royals from the far corner of the right-field stands near a sign that said, "The Black Press." These slights often occurred during Southern spring training stops. Refused entry to a press box in New Orleans, he decided to take in the game from the roof. Several New York sportswriters—Dick Young of the *Daily News*, Gus Steiger of the *Mirror*, Bill Roeder of the *World Telegram*, and Roscoe McGowan of the

Times—joined him up there. They said they wanted to work on their tans. In Beaumont, Texas, the Dodgers arranged for Lacy to cover the game from the team's dugout. The white players treated him with respect, and one of the black players usually lent him a team jacket during the cool Texas nights. Driving Dan Bankhead's black Lincoln Continental on the way to the Senators' spring training site in Orlando one year, Lacy was stopped by the police. The police wouldn't let him go until they called the Senators' traveling secretary, former *Washington Star* reporter Burton Hawkins, who vouched for him.[31] For years, Lacy wrote about the second-class hotel accommodations afforded black players during spring training. For Lacy, the issue was personal.

Lacy's problems did not end in the South or during spring training. At a Dodgers game in Cincinnati, Tom Swope, the head of the local chapter of the Baseball Writers Association of America (BBWAA), denied him access to the press box. The Reds provided him with his own private box near the playing field. Even after he received his BBWAA credential from the New York chapter in 1948, he still experienced ugly incidents, such as the time a Yankee Stadium attendant denied him entrance to a 1952 Yankees-Dodgers World Series game. "Why can't he come in?" Milton Richman of United Press International asked. "He's got the same card that I have." Lacy and Richman walked in together without further incident.[32]

During those first few seasons, however, Robinson became closer to Lacy's friendly competitor, Smith. By the end of October 1945, Smith had been exchanging letters with both Rickey and Robinson.[33] Rickey put Smith on the Dodgers' payroll at fifty dollars a week (matching Smith's salary at the *Courier*), as a scout for black talent and as Robinson's official traveling companion.[34] Smith's sunnier disposition, his position at the largest black newspaper, his college education, and his unparalleled writing talent may have endeared him to Robinson. Smith wrote Robinson's first autobiography, *Jackie Robinson: My Own Story*, which was published in 1948.[35] Another Robinson autobiography, *I Never Had It Made*, cowritten with Alfred Duckett and published in 1972, credited Smith with getting things started with the 1945 Red Sox tryout and his recommendations to

Rickey: "I will be forever indebted to Wendell because, without his even knowing it, his recommendation was in the end partly responsible for my career."[36]

At some point, Smith and Robinson had a falling out. Robinson biographer Arnold Rampersad suggested that the seeds of discontent began with the bad financial deal surrounding Robinson's first autobiography.[37] Perhaps the two men drifted apart after Smith himself crossed over to the white *Chicago American*, leading to a successful career in Chicago as a weekly columnist for the *Sun-Times* and as a television broadcaster. By the time Robinson endorsed Richard Nixon for president in 1960, the rift was complete. *Pittsburgh Courier* executive editor P. L. Prattis, who wrote a column excoriating Robinson for his endorsement of Nixon, received several nasty letters from the former Dodgers infielder.[38] Smith sided with Prattis, complimenting him on the column and criticizing the tone of Robinson's letters.[39] "It is very typical and very insulting," Smith wrote Prattis. "I am not surprised, however. I am sure you have never received a letter from him thanking you for a story praising him. In fact, I do not know of any writer who has."[40]

Although critical of Robinson at several points during his playing career, Lacy maintained a warm relationship with Robinson and his family. He wrote about Robinson showing up overweight to spring training in 1948 and about a feud between Robinson and Campanella in 1950. Each time Robinson, who was sensitive about criticism (particularly from his allies in the black press), got angry with Lacy. Each time, however, Robinson got over it. Robinson inscribed a copy of his autobiography *I Never Had It Made* as follows: "To Sam with thanks and appreciation for helping make our career possible. I'll always be appreciative, Jackie Robinson."[41] In her later years, Jackie's wife, Rachel, spoke fondly of Lacy. And Lacy often wrote glowingly about her.[42] Lacy loved and admired Robinson; he admired Robinson's courage, his outspokenness, and his character. Lacy wanted his son, Tim, to grow up to be like Robinson—not like Robinson the ballplayer, but like Robinson the man.[43]

Robinson's outspokenness sometimes hurt those who had made it possible for him to succeed. In 1949 Robinson testified against sus-

255

pected Communist Paul Robeson before the House Un-American Activities Committee (HUAC). On April 20, 1949, Robeson told a Paris audience: "It is unthinkable that American Negroes would go to war on behalf of those who have oppressed us for generations against the Soviet Union which in one generation has raised our people to full human dignity."[44] Robinson, encouraged by Rickey to accept the invitation to testify, told a packed hearing room: "I know that I've got too much invested for my wife and child and myself in the future of this country, and I and other Americans of many races and faiths have too much invested in our country's welfare, for any of us to throw it away because of a siren song sung in bass."[45] Six years earlier, Robeson had pleaded with the major league owners to make Robinson's career possible. Although much has been written about the Robinson-Robeson relationship, Robinson's HUAC testimony foreshadowed the way Nixon and others would use Robinson as a political pawn.[46] Near the end of his life, Robinson admitted that he had "grown wiser and closer to painful truths about America's destructiveness" and therefore had "an increased respect for Paul Robeson."[47]

A year before testifying against Robeson, Robinson blasted the Negro Leagues on behalf of Branch Rickey. Having grown up in an integrated environment in Southern California and having played on integrated athletic teams, Robinson hated playing in the Negro Leagues. He despised the second-class accommodations, run-down buses, and grueling travel schedule. Furthermore, the teetotaling, soon-to-be-married, and college-educated Robinson could not relate to many of his hard-drinking, womanizing, and uneducated fellow ballplayers. As a recently discharged army lieutenant, he signed with the Monarchs because he desperately needed money. "For me," Robinson recalled years later, "it was a pretty miserable way to make a buck."[48]

In 1948, a year after making it to the majors with the Dodgers, Robinson wrote an article for *Ebony* magazine titled "What's Wrong with Negro Baseball."[49] Echoing Rickey's justifications for stealing black players from their respective Negro League teams, Robinson criticized black baseball's lack of written contracts, "low salaries,"

256

"sloppy umpiring," "uncomfortable buses," "hotels . . . of the cheapest kind," and "questionable business connections of many of the team owners." Robinson concluded that the Negro Leagues needed a "housecleaning from top to bottom."[50] Robinson's article alienated many Negro Leaguers who had publicly supported him and privately tutored him. It was a slap in the face to the proud men on his former team, the Monarchs, and on their Eastern rivals, the Grays. Newark Eagles owner Effa Manley, in an article of her own a few months later, rebutted Robinson's negative characterization of black baseball.[51] In disrespecting the Negro Leagues in 1948 and testifying against Robeson in 1949, Robinson betrayed many of those who had come before him.

Buck Leonard soldiered on with the Grays. The team lost or got rid of its aging players such as Gibson (who died before the 1947 season), Jud Wilson (who retired after the 1945 season), Cool Papa Bell and Double Duty Radcliffe (both released after the 1946 season), Ray Brown (Mexico), Howard Easterling (Mexico, New York Cubans), and Jerry Benjamin (traded after the 1947 season to the Cubans for Tom Parker). Besides manager Vic Harris, who rarely if ever still played, only Leonard and shortstop Sam Bankhead survived the purges.

A team in transition in 1947, the Grays began taking on the character of their young players. By 1948, the Grays' strength lay in their trio of young outfielders: Luis Marquez, a converted infielder; Luscious "Luke" Easter, a six-foot, four-and-a-half-inch, 240-pound slugger with a weakness for curveballs but massive home-run power; and Bob Thurman, who pitched some but mostly played outfield. The pitching staff relied heavily on Wilmer Fields and John Wright, the latter returning to the Grays in 1947 after floundering in the Dodgers' minor league system. Wright and pitcher Frank "Groundhog" Thompson jumped the Grays at midseason in 1948 to play in Mexico.[52]

Leonard found himself with so little in common with these younger players that after Cool Papa Bell left, Leonard roomed with

257

Johnny Maynor, the team's bus driver.[53] Some of the younger Grays represented the types of guys Leonard had not wanted his younger brother, Charlie, exposed to back in the 1930s. During the team's long bus rides, they passed the time by gambling and playing cards (no singing quartets like in the old days). On one occasion, the diminutive Thompson accused the enormous Easter of cheating. Just over five feet tall, walleyed, with a harelip, Thompson pulled a knife on Easter. "'If you try to hit me, I'll cut you down to my size,'" Thurman recalled Thompson as saying. "Groundhog made a believer out of Easter."[54]

The Grays' fortunes still depended on their crossword-puzzle-completing, teetotaling team captain. Leonard missed more than a month with a fractured hand in 1947, and he did not play in the East-West Game in Chicago.[55] Although he hit over .400 and finished second on the team in batting behind Marquez, the Grays finished back in the pack in the 1947 Negro National League title race. The reason, according to Harris: "We didn't have Leonard."[56]

The Grays' grand old man filled so many roles. First and foremost, Leonard represented the team's institutional memory as the Grays player with the longest uninterrupted tenure. Sam Bankhead had joined the Grays in 1939 after several seasons with the Pittsburgh Crawfords and spent the 1940 and 1941 seasons in Mexico. Harris had begun his career with the Grays in 1925, though he had jumped to the Crawfords in 1934, held down a defense job in 1943, and stopped playing regularly after 1945. Leonard was not a vocal, inspirational leader like Bankhead; he was not an openly mean, fiery player like Harris; but he exhibited a quiet competence that his teammates admired. "I copied after certain traits of some of them ballplayers," Wilmer Fields recalled, "and one of them was Buck Leonard. He was determined, he couldn't stand losing."[57]

Over the years, Leonard also earned the trust of the Grays' management. In the team's final few seasons, See Posey forced him to serve as the team's traveling secretary/road business manager. Leonard assumed this role on long road trips that the elder Posey could not make, not on the Grays' big Sunday doubleheader dates in New York, Pittsburgh, or Washington. He loathed the responsibility of carrying hundreds of dollars in cash in his pants pocket, doling out meal money to his teammates, and keeping track of which players had asked for advances on their salaries. He even carried the money with him on the field, hiding it in his hip pocket tied in a handkerchief. Sometimes See Posey had to give the money to the bus driver because Posey knew that Leonard would refuse it. The aging first baseman just wanted to play ball.[58]

In 1948, Leonard's salary derived from a hefty percentage of each game's gate receipts. The financial arrangement benefited Leonard, especially since the Negro National League decided in 1948 to cap each team's salary at six thousand dollars a month (or roughly three hundred dollars a player).[59] Playing for a percentage enabled him to circumvent the salary cap and made 1948 the biggest payday of his career. Playing for the Grays in the summer and in Cuba during the winter, he made ten thousand dollars.[60] As long as the Grays drew reasonably well, he made more money than he ever could on a monthly salary. For example, during an August 8 Griffith Stadium Sunday doubleheader between the Grays and the New York Black Yankees, the Grays earned $1,145.09, the Black Yankees $286.27, and Leonard $343.50.[61] Leonard deserved his new salary arrangement— he had played for the Grays longer than anyone else, he had earned the trust of management, and, most important, he still proved himself to be the team's best player, hands down.

Leonard won the 1948 Negro National League batting title and returned the Grays to their former glory. He led off the season with two home runs in the team's opener before twelve thousand fans in Newark, pacing the Grays to a 5–4 victory over the Eagles. During the Grays' next game, May 11 in Baltimore, the Grays trailed 2–0 entering the ninth inning but won, 3–2, on his run-scoring single. In mid-May, Leonard led the team with a .467 average; the Grays won six of their first eight league games and jumped atop of the NNL standings.[62]

Leonard's hot hitting and the Grays' winning ways continued. In June, he hit home runs in successive at-bats against the New York Cubans at the Polo Grounds, bringing his season home-run total to seven.[63] During a July 14 night game against the Indianapolis Clowns benefiting Mary McLeod Bethune's National Council of Negro Women, he drove in five runs with a homer over the right-field wall and a triple to deep center to lead the Grays to a 13–4 victory.[64] At midseason, he earned a starting spot in the 1948 East-West Games in Chicago. In August, the *Pittsburgh Courier* ran a photograph of Leonard with his hands at his hips above the headline: "Going Strong."[65] He finished second in the league in home runs (ten), one behind teammate Easter.[66] Leonard hit over .400 for much of the 1948 season and bested Lester Lockett of the Elite Giants and Easter for the NNL batting title.[67]

In 1948, Leonard led the Grays to their final Negro National League championship. The Baltimore Elite Giants nipped the Grays for the first-half title, and the Grays won the second half. During the playoffs at Baltimore's Bugle Field, the Grays won the first two games. In the third, the Grays appeared to break a 4–4 tie in the top of the ninth inning. After considerable stalling by the Elite Giants, however, the local umpire declared the game a tie because of an 11:15 P.M. curfew. After the Elite Giants won the next game, they refused to play the remainder of the disputed game. The NNL president declared the Grays league champions.[68]

The Grays once again defeated the Birmingham Black Barons in the Negro League World Series, four games to one. The Barons featured a seventeen-year-old center fielder named Willie Mays. Testing the youngster's arm, the forty-one-year-old Leonard tried to advance from first to third on a single to center. "I said to myself, 'That young boy's out there and he ain't going to throw true to third base,'" Leonard wrote. "'I'm going on to third base.'" Mays threw him out.[69] The Grays' World Series victory capped a fitting end to the history of the Negro National League, which folded after the 1948 season and merged into a ten-team Negro American League.

During the last day of the regular season, at a September 4 three-team doubleheader featuring the Monarchs and the Clowns, the Griffith Stadium faithful recognized Leonard's accomplishments by holding "Buck Leonard Day." A committee led by Dr. Claude Carmichael—a local physician and longtime black baseball enthusiast—sought contributions from Grays fans to buy Leonard a tele-

260

vision. The *Afro* predicted a turnout of ten thousand, the largest crowd of the season. Local merchants promised to donate a radio and a suit of clothes.[70]

The ceremony, emceed by Harold Jackson in between the doubleheader, didn't live up to its billing. The committee, lacking enough money for a television, presented Leonard with about two hundred dollars cash. The local merchants, instead of a radio and a new suit, presented him with a "two-unit leather traveling set" and a "swanky sports shirt." Just like on Josh Gibson Day, only six thousand fans showed up for Buck's tribute.[71]

Leonard, who had four hits in seven at-bats and was 3 for 3 in the second game against the Monarchs, thought the Grays held the celebration to nudge him into retirement. He received a book containing testimonials from New York Cubans owner Alex Pompez; NNL secretary Curtis Leak; Chester Washington and Ric Roberts of the *Pittsburgh Courier*; and Lacy, Carter, Al Sweeney, and Fred Leigh of the *Afro-American*. Then Leonard took the microphone and put the retirement talk to rest: "I want to thank all the fans of Washington for this testimonial, and I want to say that I believe I can give you two or three more years of service."[72]

That Buck Leonard Day and a doubleheader featuring the Grays, Monarchs, and Clowns attracted only six thousand people spoke volumes. Nobody really cared about Leonard's batting title or the Grays' World Series triumph. The Grays' largest crowds of the season at Griffith Stadium included eighty-five hundred on July 14 against the Indianapolis Clowns, seven thousand at a preseason exhibition against the New York Black Yankees, and six thousand at Buck Leonard Day. By the end of the season, the Grays' attendance dwindled to an average of fewer than three thousand. "The Grays' box-office troubles aren't just confined to Washington," Sweeney wrote in July 1948. "In fact, all in all, the local club is averaging better attendance figures than any other member of the loop with the exception of Baltimore."[73]

The Grays no longer played in the shadow of the Senators; they played in the shadow of the inaugural class of black major leaguers. In April 1950, black Washingtonians boarded chartered buses at

Fourth and K Streets, Southwest, to Baltimore to see a preseason exhibition between Robinson's Dodgers and the Triple-A Baltimore Orioles. The game drew nineteen thousand.[74] Dr. William McNeill took more drastic measures by buying the family's first television, which began regularly showing major league baseball games in 1949. Instead of ending his office hours early to attend Senators games, the prominent Howard University obstetrician/gynecologist spent his afternoons in his favorite chair in his living room watching Robinson on television. "I came in the room, he would ask us to get him a drink of water or something like that," his son, black photographer Robert McNeill, recalled. "And he would say, 'I never thought it would happen. In my whole life, I never thought it would happen.' And you could see tears."[75]

Because the Dodgers played in the National League, Robinson didn't kill the Grays' attendance in Washington; Larry Doby, Satchel Paige, and other black players in the American League did. In July 1947, Cleveland Indians owner Bill Veeck bought Doby's contract for fifteen thousand dollars from the Newark Eagles and immediately promoted him to the major leagues. That same season, the St. Louis Browns negotiated a five thousand dollar option with the Monarchs for Willard "Home Run" Brown and Hank Thompson. Brown and Thompson brought massive crowds to Griffith Stadium in 1947, but St. Louis released the two players after a month.[76] The Indians' "experiment" with Doby and other black players continued. The following year, in July 1948, Veeck signed forty-two-year-old Paige.

The only Negro League legend who succeeded in crossing over to the major leagues, Paige displayed the same flair, showmanship, and skill that he always had. His self-deprecating antics, his tardiness for the team's scheduled rail departures, and his selfish disregard for the team's curfew on the road alienated Paige from his young roommate, the quiet and introverted Doby. "I didn't like it when guys laughed at Satch's stories," Doby told his biographer, Joseph Thomas Moore, "because I knew they were also laughing at Satch himself as a black man."[77] Robinson, who kept in frequent contact with Doby in 1947 despite playing in the other league, despised his former Monarchs teammate for the poor image Paige set as one of the first black major leaguers.[78]

Doby and Robinson saw only Paige the minstrel performer; they didn't see how, in his own way, Paige broke barriers. He refused to take a salary cut to play in the major leagues, forcing Veeck to pay him a full season's salary in 1948 for only three months of work. The *Sporting News* and others viewed Veeck's signing of Paige as a publicity stunt that degraded the game. Veeck, however, insisted that the Indians needed a reliever and spot starter for the stretch run. With Paige starting and relieving and Doby starting in the outfield, the Indians won the 1948 World Series. Paige, who finished with a 6–1 record and 2.48 ERA in 1948, was the first black pitcher in World Series history.

Paige knew that he could still pitch and that he could still draw enormous crowds. On July 18 and 19, he made two scoreless relief appearances against the Senators at Griffith Stadium.[79] In one of his first starts, on August 3, Paige defeated the Senators, 4–3, before seventy-two thousand Cleveland fans. Paige's starts brought record crowds to countless American League ballparks—seventy-eight thousand in Cleveland and more than fifty-one thousand in Chicago.[80] And of course, there was Griffith Stadium.

With the Indians locked in a tight pennant race on August 30, Paige dominated the Senators in a 10–1 complete-game victory at Griffith Stadium before a capacity crowd of 28,058. Griffith turned away an additional five thousand eager fans. Paige allowed only seven hits, and he induced Senators outfielder Bud Stewart to swing and miss at a blooper pitch. "I don't think I shall ever forget that night, . . ." the *Afro's* Al Sweeney wrote, describing the California-born Stewart as a "red-necked outfielder from way down yonder." "Stewart was so angry about it all that after popping up the next pitch, he deliberately cut across the diamond near the pitcher's mound to express his dissatisfaction to Paige."[81]

Doby also brought black Washingtonians to the ballpark with his own electrifying moments. On May 8, 1948, he stepped to the plate with two on in the eighth and launched what sportswriters described

263

as "the second longest ball ever hit at Griffith Stadium." The ball, which traveled an estimated 450 feet, hit a loudspeaker atop the stadium's thirty-foot-high center-field wall and caromed back into play. Doby raced around the bases for an inside-the-park home run. Only Babe Ruth's 460-foot blast in 1922 into the Tree beyond Griffith Stadium's center-field wall registered as a longer clout.[82] The *Pittsburgh Courier's* Chester Washington, citing a recent national magazine article, dubiously claimed that Gibson smashed a 485-foot shot into the back rows of the left-field bleachers that outdid both of them.[83] The *Afro* argued that Doby's "feat equaled that accomplished by Babe Ruth in 1922 and five years later by the late Josh Gibson."[84] Gibson never played at Griffith Stadium in 1927, and the contemporary accounts of his home runs in 1943 never mentioned his reaching the back wall of the left-field bleachers. Nonetheless, Doby secured himself a place in the annals of great Griffith Stadium home runs.

A year later, Doby outdid both himself and the Babe. Before the largest crowd of the season on a Wednesday night in late May 1949, Doby blasted a five hundred–foot shot off Sid Hudson over Griffith Stadium's forty-one-foot-high right-center-field scoreboard, over an alleyway, off the roof of a row house, and onto U Street in LeDroit Park. The blow was longer than Ruth's 1922 center-field shot into the Tree. Ric Roberts charted the path of Doby's blow in a *Pittsburgh Courier* cartoon, comparing it to other famous Griffith Stadium clouts and declaring that it traveled a major league–record five hundred feet.[85] Lacy wrote: "A throng of 28,573 goggle-eyed fans gasped as Sir Larry's fourth frame clout cleared the wall at the Chesterfield advertisement and plunked down on the roof of a house on distant U St."[86]

264

Griffith declared Doby's May 1949 blast the longest ball in the history of his ballpark (until Mickey Mantle's 565-foot shot in 1953). The Old Fox told Lacy:

> If my memory holds up, I don't believe Ruth ever hit a ball longer than that one. He really gave it a ride. I didn't give Doby credit for that one here last year when he hit into the amplifiers in dead cen-

ter. The newspapers raved about it, but I didn't think it deserved the praise it got.

There was a stiff wind that night and it helped the ball considerably. That one tonight, though, was legitimate.[87]

Griffith confirmed that Doby's homer traveled nearly five hundred feet: "It is 395 feet to the base of the fence where the ball cleared, and the fence itself is 20 feet high. With the carry, I would say it was better than 480 feet. I couldn't be too sure of that, naturally. But my guess would be pretty darned close to 500 feet."[88]

With Doby's emergence as a star, Griffith began lavishing praise on the Indians outfielder the same way he used to do with Gibson. He also encouraged Veeck to start Paige in Washington. "As much as Clark Griffith might disapprove of me in Cleveland," Veeck wrote in his autobiography *Veeck as in Wreck*, "he would also call and plead with me to pitch Satchel Paige in a night game at Griffith Stadium."[89]

The pressure mounted on Griffith to integrate his own team. During Doby's first Griffith Stadium appearance in 1947, a group known as the "American Youth for Democracy" picketed the ballpark to protest Griffith's refusal to hire black players.[90] In response to Griffith's complaints about a lack of talent at the Senators' 1948 spring training camp, the *Afro* wrote an open letter to Griffith urging him to try the "wealth of good material" in the Negro Leagues. The letter, titled "Griffs Could Use Colored Players" and most likely written by Lacy, declared: "It is a travesty on democracy that the major league team representing the nation's capital should continue to display discrimination by its steadfast refusal to give colored players an opportunity." The letter concluded: "It would be better that you relinquish control of the Nats to some one with a more liberal attitude than to inflict the shame on the nation's capital that the lily-white Nats represent."[91]

In July 1949, the Senators held a four-day baseball school and tryout camp in Alexandria, Virginia. Two days after several black players showed up, the Senators closed the camp. "Everybody got a chance, but the players were so far from being good league prospects, we just canceled the school," Senators farm director Ossie Bluege said. In the past, the Senators had complied with Virginia's segregation laws by holding separate schools there.[92] Even if the Senators had opened a tryout camp to black players, they had no place to put them. With most of their minor league teams in Southern locations such as Charlotte, Chattanooga, and Orlando, the Senators could not have placed a black prospect in its meager excuse for a farm system. The integration of Southern minor leagues did not begin until 1951 and persisted well into the 1960s.[93] The curse of Jim Crow continued for the Senators, who finished last in the American League in 1949 with their worst won-loss record (50–104) in forty years.

Shortly after the Indians' Larry Doby and Luke Easter (formerly of the Grays) drew 24,228 fans at Griffith Stadium in late July 1950, the *Afro* tried to shame Griffith into integrating. "The crazy-quilt pattern of racial prejudice is well illustrated at Griffith Stadium," the article asserted. It reviewed Griffith's racially conscious seating practices: his old pattern of seating the black fans in the right-field pavilion versus his current habit of seating early black arrivals in the grandstand directly behind home plate and latecomers "scattered throughout the stands." Then the article compared Griffith's steadfast refusal to hire black players with his hiring of Cubans that mired his team in fifth place. Finally, it addressed the economic illogic behind Griffith's discrimination: "He is unalterably opposed to colored players in the big leagues, except that he has never hesitated to take his share of the gate receipts made larger by the presence of Doby and Easter in the Indians lineup."[94] In July 1950, however, Griffith's refusal to integrate the Senators placed him among the overwhelming majority of American League teams, of which only the Indians fielded black players. Integration remained almost entirely a National League phenomenon.

Griffith's prediction to Leonard and Gibson about integration destroying the Negro Leagues came true. The Grays could not compete at the box office with Paige and Doby playing eleven games a season against the Senators at Griffith Stadium. Furthermore, the Grays' rebuilding efforts of 1947 and 1948 did not help the team's

dwindling attendance figures because major league teams kept plucking away the Grays' top talent.

Affiliating themselves with the minor leagues represented the
Negro Leagues' last best chance for financial survival. At the suggestion of Yankees president Larry MacPhail, the Negro Leagues
improved their scheduling, adopted bylaws and uniform player contracts, and filed an official application to join the white minor league
system. George M. Trautman, president of the National Association
of Professional Baseball Leagues, denied the application because the
black teams would have infringed on the "territorial rights" of exist-
ing minor league teams and most Negro League teams played in
ballparks owned by other minor league affiliates.[95]

Instead, the Negro Leagues served as the unofficial training
ground for future major league stars, such as Hank Aaron (Indi-
anapolis Clowns), Ernie Banks (Kansas City Monarchs), and Willie
Mays (Birmingham Black Barons). Although the Monarchs and
Clowns prepared more players for the majors in part because the two
teams hung around longer, the Grays contributed their share of
future major leaguers, including Luis Marquez (Boston Braves), Luke
Easter (Cleveland Indians), Bob Thurman (Cincinnati Reds via the
Kansas City Monarchs), Dave Hoskins (Indians via the Louisville
Buckeyes), Dave Pope (Indians), and Bob Trice (Philadelphia Athletics).[96] Roy Welmaker, the former Grays pitcher who had been
pitching in Venezuela, walked into the Indians' spring training camp
in 1949 and received a Triple-A contract.[97] At least one of the Grays'
other top players, pitcher-outfielder Wilmer Fields, turned down a
Triple-A contract with the Yankees because Fields felt more comfortable and made more money in black baseball, Latin America, and
Canada.[98] Not everyone, however, chose to be left behind.

The absence of young outfielders Marquez, Easter, and Thurman
from the Grays' 1949 roster and the competition from the Cleveland
Indians at Griffith Stadium put the future of the Grays in jeopardy.[99]
Furthermore, Grays president and longtime financial backer Rufus
"Sonnyman" Jackson wanted out. When the Negro National League
folded and merged into a ten-team Negro American League in

267

December 1948, Jackson refused to allow the Grays to join the new NAL because of the exorbitant travel costs of a widely scattered league. The Grays lost a total of forty-five thousand dollars in 1947 and 1948.[100] Jackson, already in ill health, couldn't afford to lose any more money. "The Grays enjoyed highly profitable seasons in Washington during the war period, but within the last two seasons attendance had declined steadily," the *Afro* reported. "During the past year, the club attracted an average of only 2,000 per game although it won the league championship and the World Series."[101]

See Posey sought to carry on his late brother's ball club. "Sonny has not told me finally that he is quitting. As soon as I get something definite I will write you," See Posey wrote Art Carter on December 17, 1948. "In no way are we turning Griffith Stadium loose."[102] With the Grays refusing to join the new NAL, Posey correctly feared that other NAL teams would try to encroach on the Grays' home grounds. About a month after Posey's first letter, Baltimore Elite Giants president Vernon Green wrote Carter inquiring about Griffith Stadium. "Have you heard from S. H. Posey lately?" Green wrote in a letter dated January 22, 1949. "Our league members have decided not to play the Grays in Washington. If this is true I would like to play some open dates in Washington if you could arrange for me to play there."[103]

Posey, however, already had beaten the Elite Giants and the rest of the NAL to the punch. Three days before Green's letter, Posey inquired with Senators ticket manager John Morrissey about two open dates in early May. Posey promised "to get things straightened out" with the NAL and to meet with Carter in Washington. "Sonny is not well," Posey confided to Carter. "I think I can manage if I can get a little money to start us out."[104] In early March 1949, Jackson died at the age of forty-eight after an operation for a brain tumor.[105] Cum Posey's widow, Ethel, technically co-owned the team along with Jackson's widow, Helen; See Posey, however, maintained full control of the team's daily operations.[106]

Unable to arrange an associate membership in the new NAL in 1949, the Grays joined the eight-team Negro American Association (NAA), a black minor league circuit based in Virginia and North

268

Carolina.[107] Vic Harris, after nearly twenty-five years with the Grays organization, left the club to serve as a coach with the Baltimore Elite Giants. Sam Bankhead, the Grays' respected shortstop-outfielder, became the new field manager. Leonard, already saddled with the job as the team's part-time traveling secretary, wanted no part of managing.

Cum Posey would have rolled over in his grave if he had seen his once-mighty Grays toiling in a two-bit black sandlot circuit. Perhaps the only player the new arrangement benefited was the forty-two-year-old Leonard. With teams in Norfolk (Virginia), Durham, Raleigh, Charlotte, Greensboro, and Winston-Salem, the new league allowed Leonard to play closer to his Rocky Mount, North Carolina, home.

The new league also brought Buck physically closer to his younger brother, Charlie. As the head of the state unemployment board for the black residents of Kinston, North Carolina, Charlie had ascended to a position of power and influence. Buck had discovered this several years earlier when the Grays played an exhibition game in Kinston that he and Gibson had decided to sit out. Charlie pleaded with them at least to put on their uniforms and make an appearance. When they refused, Charlie vowed that the Grays would not play in North Carolina ever again. And they didn't, at least not until 1949.[108]

Playing in the Negro American Association, the Grays suffered through a financially disastrous 1949 season. Negro American League teams refused (at least initially) to play the Grays at Griffith Stadium, so the Grays filled their home dates by playing American Association teams, such as the Charlotte-Asheville Blues, the Greensboro Red Wings, the Raleigh Tigers, and the Norfolk–Newport News Royals. Down South, things looked even worse. "At home, the situation has been fair, with average crowds of 2,800," the *Afro* reported, "but in Virginia and North Carolina where the club plays its league rivals when not at Griffith Stadium the pickup has been terribly low."[109]

The Grays pieced together a fairly decent team. In addition to Leonard and Wilmer Fields, the Grays reacquired lefty Roy Partlow from the Philadelphia Stars.[110] Partlow, who fared only slightly better than John Wright in the Dodgers' farm system, held down the mound duties with Fields. In mid-September, the Grays boasted a 104–22 record, though mostly against inferior competition.[111] During the second half of the 1949 season, a few NAL teams relented and agreed to play the Grays. The Grays finished with a 6–2 record against NAL teams. In July, they defeated the New York Cubans, 8–1, at the Polo Grounds. The Cubans featured former Grays Wright and Howard Easterling, both of whom returned from playing in South America. The Grays also defeated the Indianapolis Clowns in four of five games during a Midwestern barnstorming swing, and the Grays split games with the Baltimore Elite Giants.[112]

The Grays, however, ran into some bad luck in booking NAL teams at Griffith Stadium. Rain canceled home dates against the Cubans and one involving the Clowns and the Stars.[113] Finally, in a late September Sunday doubleheader, the Grays defeated the Stars, 5–1, and tied the second game, 3–3. Only twelve hundred saw the Grays' lone NAL contest at Griffith Stadium that season.[114]

The Grays gave it one last shot in 1950, their eleventh season in Washington. The NAL, perhaps needing the Grays as much as the Grays needed the league, agreed to make them an associate member. The Grays still belonged to the second-tier Negro American Association, but they had more freedom to book NAL opponents at Griffith Stadium. The Grays scheduled home games against the Clowns on April 23 and 26, the Baltimore Elite Giants on May 18, and the New York Black Yankee Travelers on May 21. The crowds never returned in 1950 as Robinson played exhibitions in Baltimore and Doby and Easter came to Washington with the Indians. In 1949 and 1950, the Grays lost thirty thousand dollars. See Posey died the following year.[115]

270   Fittingly, the Grays' final game at Griffith Stadium turned out to be a Sunday doubleheader in September 1950 against Satchel Paige. Paige pitched for the Philadelphia Stars in between major league stints with Veeck's Indians and St. Louis Browns. Always an entrepreneur, Paige negotiated a 15 percent share of the gate receipts— only about five hundred dollars a game but often more than each team earned.[116] In 1950, not even Paige could bring fans out to black

baseball games. Of the Grays' crowds after integration, Leonard said: "We couldn't draw flies."[117]

The Grays bade farewell to Paige and Griffith Stadium in style. They sacked Satchel for two runs during his three innings of work, romping to a 7–1 victory. Ray Brown, the team's longtime ace who had not pitched for the Grays since 1945, returned from Canada to face Paige. Josh Gibson Jr., playing third base for the Grays, vowed, "I'll hit Satch, just like my dad did."[118] Paige responded by hitting the nineteen-year-old Gibson, who never amounted to much as a ballplayer yet was 2 for 3 that day with a triple. The Grays also walloped the Stars in the second game, 12–2. The attendance figures must have been unspeakably low because they evaded the attention of the black press.[119]

The Grays, who finished the 1950 season with a 100–26 record, ended the history of the franchise with a 7–2 victory over the Parkersburg Stars in Parkersburg, West Virginia.[120] Immediately after the season, the Grays embarked on a barnstorming tour led by Dodgers pitcher Dan Bankhead through Alabama and Mississippi. Leonard, who negotiated a salary of twenty-five dollars a game, left the tour just before the money ran out.[121] The decision to dissolve the Grays, according to the team's first baseman, rested with the players. "The team met and decided that they didn't want to play anymore. And that included me because I didn't see any future for the team," Leonard wrote. "I felt like they couldn't continue. So they decided not to try to operate anymore."[122]

The only member of the Grays to play all eleven seasons in Washington, Leonard gave the Griffith Stadium fans exactly what he had promised them in 1948—two more good seasons. He gave the Mexican League an additional five. The only thing he would not give the game was his baby brother, Charlie. On October 10, 1952, thirty-nine-year-old Charlie Leonard died at his home in Kinston, North Carolina, of stomach cancer.[123] Buck could not get back in time from Mexico to attend the funeral.

From 1940 to 1950, Buck Leonard gave the black community of Washington, D.C., relief from feelings of inferiority. He gave them happiness. He gave them disappointment. He gave them love. He gave them identity. The migrant poor, the middle and working classes, the light-skinned elite—they rallied around the Grays. As Ronald K. Crockett, who grew up watching the Grays at Griffith Stadium, told journalist Daniel Cattau:

> We still don't realize what an important part of the community the Grays were. Josh was people. Buck was people. They didn't act like big shots or big stars. They were just down-to-earth, regular fellas. We still don't realize what a good thing we had.[124]

Black Washington sacrificed the Grays for the larger cause of integration and opportunity that left Leonard and many others behind.

The 1944 Grays pose on the top step of the Griffith Stadium dugout, including Josh Gibson (fifth from right), Buck Leonard (fourth from right), Dave Hoskins (third from right), Jerry Benjamin (second from right), and James "Cool Papa" Bell (far right). (ROBERT H. McNEILL)

A strong, proud man and Gibson's closest friend on the team, Sam Bankhead played shortstop and center field for the Grays. Bankhead, a Pittsburgh native who was shot and killed in 1976, is thought by some to be the inspiration for the main character in August Wilson's Pulitzer Prize–winning play, *Fences*. (ROBERT H. MCNEILL)

Buck Leonard stands with two unidentified Grays fans at Griffith Stadium, probably at "Buck Leonard Day" in 1948. Leonard, who thought the Grays were trying to nudge him into retirement, promised the fans two more good seasons, and he made good on that promise. (SMITHSONIAN MUSEUM)

Seward "See" Posey (center) and Rufus "Sonnyman" Jackson (right) took over ownership of the Grays after Cum Posey's death before the 1946 season. They are taking in a game at Griffith Stadium. (ROBERT H. MCNEILL)

The 1946 Grays stand in front of Griffith Stadium's thirty-foot-high right-field wall. The sign says it was 328 feet from home plate, but it was actually 320. Josh Gibson (standing third from left), Buck Leonard (kneeling third from left), and Ted "Double Duty" Radcliffe (kneeling far left) are pictured. (ART CARTER PAPERS, MOORLAND-SPINGARN RESEARCH CENTER, HOWARD UNIVERSITY)

Wendell Smith (standing at left) and Sam Lacy (standing second from right) attend the Hall of Fame induction of Satchel Paige (standing center) in 1971. Smith and Lacy were part of the committee that helped make Paige the first Negro Leaguer elected. Future Hall of Famers Judy Johnson (standing second from left) and Monte Irvin (standing right) and Hall of Famer Roy Campanella (seated right) are also present. (NATIONAL BASEBALL HALL OF FAME LIBRARY)

EPILOGUE

After the Grays

In March 1949, Clark Griffith informed Sam Lacy that the Senators intended to scout black players. "Yes, I've been convinced we may have overlooked an opportunity here and there to strengthen the Senators," Griffith announced during an exclusive interview with Lacy at Orlando's Angevelt Hotel. "And you can say I'm definitely interested in signing a good young colored player."[1]

It had been nearly a dozen years since Griffith predicted to Lacy that "the time was not far off" for black players in the major leagues.[2] Griffith's latest revelation landed on the *Afro*'s front page below the headline: "Senators Search for Tan Players." Griffith instructed scout Joe Engel to find " 'the right kind of boy' in the talent-rich North Carolina area." According to Griffith, the Senators' first black player had to be not only good enough to avoid the team's Southern-based minor league system but also young enough to make the investment worthwhile.[3]

The Old Fox rejected the idea of signing a veteran member of the Grays to boost his team's ticket sales. The seventy-nine-year-old Griffith told Lacy:

I've opposed this thing from the beginning because I've been opposed to exploitation.

They had a rumor out there that we were interested in Buck Leonard, the Homestead Gray's [sic] first baseman.

Now what in the world would we do with Leonard? A fine ball player in his day, but so were a lot of other fellows.

Why Buck's as old as I am.[4]

Lacy credited Griffith for his sincerity. Unlike other owners, such as the Yankees' Larry MacPhail, Pirates' William Benswanger, or Cubs' Phil Wrigley, Griffith had never made empty promises or given the local black fans false hope. "From the very beginning of the campaign for integration, Griffith refrained from expressing a willingness to employ colored players," Lacy wrote. "The aged Washington boss has steadfastly refused to say he was even interested in the experiment."[5]

Although Lacy acknowledged that "Washington's first tan American Leaguer may be a long way off" and "in fact may never become a reality," he saw "a shining ray of hope in Griffith's new attitude. . . . Now things look brighter."[6] Lacy wrote that his father, who had died the previous spring, "would have loved this day." In 1947, the elder Lacy had stopped going to Senators games altogether because of Griffith's opposition to integration.[7] Despite the Old Fox's "change of heart" in March 1949, the first black player on the Senators was indeed more than five years off.

Things were changing all around Griffith's ballpark. In November 1948, a committee published a ninety-one-page report titled "Segregation in Washington." Its author was Kenesaw M. Landis II, the nephew of the late baseball commissioner and former Griffith ally. "In the Nation's Capital," the report concluded, "we must mean what we say, and give people of all races and colors an equal chance to life, liberty, and the pursuit of happiness."[8]

During the summer of 1949, ninety-year-old Mary Church Terrell formed a committee that sought enforcement of the "lost" laws of 1872–73 prohibiting discrimination in the city's public accommodations. The committee picketed downtown restaurants that refused to serve blacks, including Thompson's Restaurant at 725 Fourteenth Street, N.W. Two other establishments, Kresge's Seventh Street vari-

ety store and the lunch counter at Murphy's Dime Store, relented—
Thompson's would not. In 1953, after four years of protests and court
battles, the United States Supreme Court upheld the city's nineteenth-century antidiscrimination laws and ordered Thompson's and
all other area establishments to serve blacks.[9] "Insist on the enforcement of the law," Terrell said, "for these laws can be lost again."[10]

Howard University law dean Charles Hamilton Houston led black
Washington's quest for justice in the courts. Five years before the end
of Terrell's public accommodations battle, he had argued a Supreme
Court case about restrictive housing covenants on behalf of Washington's black home buyers. In a group of cases collectively known
as *Shelley v. Kraemer*, the high court ruled that judicial enforcement
of restrictive covenants constituted state action that violated the
Fourteenth Amendment's equal protection clause.[11] Although Washington's white residents could draw up all the restrictive covenants
they wanted, they couldn't get the courts to enforce them.[12]

Houston, who died in April 1950, didn't live to see the ultimate
fruit of his labor on May 17, 1954—the Supreme Court's landmark
Brown v. Board of Education decision outlawing segregation in the
public schools.[13] The Court ruled in *Bolling v. Sharpe* that Washington's segregated schools violated Fifth Amendment liberties under
the due process clause.[14] In *Brown*, Chief Justice Earl Warren wrote
for a unanimous Court that racial separation among schoolchildren
"generates a feeling of inferiority as to their status in the community
that may affect their hearts and minds in a way unlikely ever to be
undone."[15]

After the *Brown* and *Bolling* decisions, Griffith's Senators represented a conspicuous pillar of segregation in the nation's capital. In
celebration of his fifty-year association with the American League in
1952, the Old Fox told his life story to good friend and fellow segregationist J. G. Taylor Spink of *The Sporting News*. At one point in the
interview, Griffith suddenly turned confessional. "I had been wrong
because I had assumed the mental attitude of the Old Guard, with
its worship of the ancient fetishes of the game," Griffith said. "In
assuming a more tolerant position, I helped myself in the long run."[16]
He was referring to night baseball, not integration.

281

Since his team's last World Series appearance in 1933, Griffith resisted many changes to major league baseball—night games, farm systems, and integration. The opposite of Posey and the Grays, Griffith refused to adapt. "They were trying to be a corner grocery store in a supermarket world," Shirley Povich told Jon Kerr. "They got behind the times in minor league development and in payrolls. . . . Mr. [Clark] Griffith used to be a gambler. But in later times when the pot got too big, he shied off. Maybe he didn't think he had the resources."[17]

The image of the Senators as a mom-and-pop operation, however, obscured the enormous profits Griffith reaped in owning Washington's major league team. "He's a rich man," Ed Fitzgerald wrote in 1954, "one of the few to become rich in the game to which he has devoted his life."[18] In taking over as Washington's new field manager in 1912, Griffith had mortgaged his Montana ranch to purchase a 10 percent interest in the team for $27,500. Seven years later, Griffith obtained majority ownership with help from Philadelphia grain dealer William Richardson for an additional hundred thousand dollars. At the time of his death in 1955, the franchise's estimated value was four million dollars.[19] Griffith's heirs eventually sold the team for nine times that amount.

The minimal profits at the end of each season masked the hefty salaries Griffith doled out to his family members. Griffiths working for the team included his nephew and heir apparent, Calvin; his niece (and adopted daughter), Thelma; his niece, Mildred; and his nephews, Billy, Jimmy, and Sherry Robertson—the latter had a ten-year playing career with the Senators and the Philadelphia Athletics. Historian Harold Seymour wrote: "It is also, of course, possible for a club's books to show little or no profit while an owner and even his relatives make a comfortable living out of salaries and expenses, as in the case of the Griffith family when it was running the Washington American League club."[20]

In his later years, Calvin repeatedly claimed that his Uncle Clark refused to integrate the Senators at the insistence of the Grays. Calvin told Jon Kerr:

There were two brothers that owned the [Homestead] Grays. And they were talking to Mr. Griffith about one of these days they wanted to challenge the Major Leagues for the championship. And that's the only reason Mr. Griffith didn't sign some of 'em. But Branch Rickey went out and broke it all up by signing Jackie Robinson. If he hadn't signed Jackie Robinson there could have been in the years to come, a challenge of the black to white.[21]

A few years later, a public television producer from Washington asked Calvin why the Senators did not sign Gibson or Leonard. "I said Mr. Griffith already had black ballplayers on there, but he couldn't publicize it," Calvin recalled, referring to the team's Cuban players. "Then I went on and told her about [how] the Posey brothers and the other ballclubs wanted to get good enough to play the white teams. The black boys play the white boys. Not many people know that."[22]

Griffith's opposition to integration was rooted in both prejudice and greed. Griffith believed he could make more money renting his stadium to black baseball teams than he could by increasing attendance from signing black players. Before 1945, he encouraged black baseball to build up its own leagues, helped owners such as Posey promote their businesses, and lavished praise on star players such as Paige, Gibson, and Leonard. After 1945, he defended the Negro Leagues as an economic entity and blasted Rickey for raiding black teams without compensating them. Griffith wanted the Negro Leagues to survive because he wanted to keep profiting off them. "He wouldn't think of taking black ballplayers from the Grays," the *Courier's* Ric Roberts told John Holway. "I don't call that prejudice. He just had a yen for making money."[23]

Lacy, though less charitable than Roberts, looked back on Griffith's racial policies with the same caution that marked Lacy's integration campaign. He refused to call Griffith a racist, but he said Griffith "acted the part of a racist." Lacy explained:

That's the reason I say to you, it's kind of hard for me to get into his mind. But I will say his actions, see again, you can't say that a man is racist. You can't say that a man is racist, you can say that he acted the part of a racist. There's quite a difference. That's the reason I dismiss Clark Griffith's attitude.[24]

Griffith opposed integration at least in part based on underlying social concerns. His resistance to change, his position with Connie Mack as the leaders of baseball's traditionalist old guard, and his Southern clientele in Washington made his stance about more than just dollars and cents. During the late 1940s and early 1950s, Griffith's economic rationale no longer made sense. By that time, the Grays drew meager crowds at Griffith Stadium and then disbanded. Meanwhile, Griffith saw firsthand how Paige and Doby brought out the city's black fans en masse. By finding a few black players of his own, Griffith could have cultivated sellout crowds every night.

During his July 1952 *Sporting News* interview, Griffith addressed his failure to integrate the Senators:

> To those who persist in speaking of me harshly on the Negro players issue, let me say that I would welcome the addition of players like Robinson, Campanella, Harry Simpson, Don Newcombe, Larry Doby, and Orestes [Minnie] Minoso to the Washington roster.
>
> I stand ready, eager, to place Negro players on our Washington club. But they must rate the jobs on the basis of ability, and not merely because they happen to be Negroes.
>
> I will not sign a Negro for the Washington club merely to satisfy subversive persons. I would welcome a Negro on the Senators if he rated the distinction, if he belonged among major league players.
>
> The Washington club has a large Negro clientele. It represents some of the best citizenship of the District of Columbia. I would be only too glad to give that clientele a chance to root for a player of their own race.[25]

Sportswriter A. S. "Doc" Young questioned the sincerity of Griffith's *Sporting News* comments because "while his Senators fell on their faces like so many Stoopnagles, playing in his park were the Homestead Grays and greats such as Josh Gibson and Buck Leonard. But, Griffith wanted none of them."[26]

In April 1953, Cleveland Indians general manager Hank Greenberg proposed trading Doby to the Senators for their young outfielder Jackie Jensen. But when Greenberg suggested the Doby-Jensen swap, the Old Fox "told Hank I did not want to talk trade."[27] After the 1953 season, Griffith traded Jensen to the Red Sox for two white players, pitcher Mickey McDermott and outfielder Tom Umphlett. Griffith, citing four dark-skinned Cuban prospects in his minor league system, defended his record on race:

> Insinuations that the Washington club really is opposed to playing Negroes on its team are lies.
>
> If I could find another Doby or Minoso, I would make a place on the Senators for him. But nobody is going to stampede me into signing Negro players merely for the sake of satisfying certain pressure groups.
>
> The Washington club would benefit financially from Negro representation in the field.[28]

In September 1954, four months after the *Brown* and *Bolling* decisions, Griffith finally integrated his team but in his own perverse way. In 1953 and 1954, seven teams promoted black players to the majors (the Boston Red Sox integrated last, in 1959). Griffith chose Carlos Paula, a twenty-six-year-old Cuban-born outfielder who spent parts of three seasons with the Senators. Unlike Griffith's former Cuban players who passed as white, there was no mistaking that Paula was black. Officially, Paula broke the Senators' color barrier on September 6, 1954, before 4,865 fans and hardly any media attention.[29] He did not help the Senators on the field or at the box office.

The way Griffith integrated the Senators affronted the city's black fans. "I think most of them recognized the fact that he was simply putting a token in there," Lacy recalled. "Neither Carlos Paula nor Angel Scull [another dark-skinned Cuban prospect] was a legitimate major-league ballplayer. But it was a case where he brought them in because they were black, and there was no mistake about whether they were Negro or not."[30] Seven years after Robinson made his major league debut, Griffith still could not find an American-born black man to play on his team. "Mr. Griffith would give Washington fans dark players from other lands," the *Pittsburgh Courier* wrote, "but never an American Negro!"[31]

Griffith kept a sign on his desk: "For long life: Sleep plenty, eat moderately, and keep your conscience clear."[32] His conscience did not bother him—about his segregationist stance, his "Old Fox" reputation as a pitcher who had scuffed the ball with his sharpened spikes, and "placing bets" or "holding stakes" for Abe Attell, one of the principal gamblers in the Black Sox scandal.[33] Griffith simply forgot about his misdeeds. "In later years, an interesting pattern began unfolding in Griffith," Povich wrote. "He started speaking from Sunday school pulpits, literally, and a new high moral sense overtook this man who used to boast about playing poker with the best of them in a Reno gambling saloon."[34]

Griffith was civic-minded. During World War I, he established the Clark Griffith Bat and Ball Fund for overseas troops. He never sold beer in his ballpark (though he plastered its outfield walls with beer and cigarette advertisements). On Sunday afternoons, he regularly admitted hordes of schoolchildren, black and white, for free. He often made his ballpark available to the black community that surrounded it, turning Griffith Stadium into the neighborhood's "outdoor theater."[35] He loyally supported his employees, from ticket takers and ushers to batboys and ballplayers. People who knew Griffith loved him, from eight U.S. presidents such as FDR to sports columnists such as Povich. At age eighty-five, Griffith died on October 27, 1955, of complications from a stomach hemorrhage. Given his long life, he undoubtedly passed away with a clear conscience despite his record on integration.

The day after Griffith's death, the *Washington Post* published a Povich column headlined: "Griffith Always Played It Hard Until Final Out." Although he addressed Griffith's reluctance to integrate in subsequent articles, Povich initially ignored Griffith's record on race. Instead, the bard of Washington sportswriters reviewed Griffith's fifty-year career as a player, manager, and owner; he regaled readers with Griffith anecdotes; and he expressed admiration for the man everyone called Griff. Povich concluded: "To me he was both philosopher and friend."[36]

The *Washington Afro-American* viewed Griffith's death in less sentimental terms. In a twelve-paragraph editorial titled "No Tears for Griffith," the *Afro* wrote:

> We wish we could shed a tear for Clark Griffith, the 85-year-old president of the Washington Senators, who was buried Monday.
>
> Mr. Griffith was revered by many students of the game as one who had done more than anyone, past and present, for organized baseball. . . .
>
> But Clark Griffith's contributions to baseball were accompanied by no desire to include us in it.

In fact, the paper simply ignored Paula's September call-up a year before Griffith's death: "Mr. Griffith never was convinced that colored Americans were good enough to play on the Washington Senators. . . . To this day there has never been a colored player in a Washington Senator uniform." The editorial concluded with an admonition: "We hope that his son, Calvin, will be enough in tune with the tempo of the times to reverse the undemocratic and outmoded policy of his father."[37]

With Calvin at the helm, however, public relations quickly deteriorated. Calvin possessed his uncle's keen eye for baseball talent, but he lacked the old man's polish in dealing with people. Calvin tried everything from moving in Griffith Stadium's faraway fences for the team's young home-run hitters—such as Roy Sievers, Jim Lemon, and Harmon Killebrew—to selling beer. But he proved incapable of turning around his uncle's floundering franchise or dealing with the changes outside his ballpark.

During the 1950s, Washington officially became a majority black major city.[38] As integration began to affect Washington's schools,

287

department stores, and restaurants, whites fled to the suburbs in Maryland and Virginia. The city as well as the immediate vicinity around the ballpark had become increasingly black and poor.

Calvin publicly vowed to stay the course. In a bylined *Washington Post* article on January 15, 1958, he wrote:

> I have lived in Washington, D.C. for about 35 years. I attended school here and established many roots here. The city has been good to my family and me. This is my home. I intend that it shall remain my home for the rest of my life.
>
> As long as I have any say in the matter, and I expect that I shall for a long, long time, the Washington Senators will stay here, too. Next year. The year after. Forever.[39]

Privately, however, he begged the owners at their annual meeting to allow him to relocate because "the trend in Washington is getting to be all colored."[40] Three years after promising to keep the Senators in Washington "forever," Calvin moved the team to Minnesota. In their final season in Washington in 1960, Griffith's Senators drew 743,404 fans, their highest single-season attendance total since 1949 and sixth highest in team history.[41] The following season, however, the team became known as the Minnesota Twins; Washington received an American League expansion franchise also known as the Senators.

The 1961 season was the new Senators' last at Griffith Stadium. President Kennedy threw out the first ball on Opening Day. The last game in the old ball yard, a September 21 loss to the Twins (of all teams), drew a season-low 1,498.[42] Across the street from the ballpark at Elder Michaux's Church of God, the organ played a fitting requiem: "Auld Lang Syne."[43]

After the Senators moved to D.C. (and later RFK) Stadium, Griffith Stadium was torn down in 1965. In 1963, Howard University, rumored to be part owner of the ballpark but merely with first option to buy it, persuaded the federal government to purchase Griffith Stadium for $1.5 million plus $250,000 for demolition.[44] Two years later, Howard began building a $19 million hospital that still stands on the site. Howard University president James Nabrit Jr. supervised the project.[45] The man who had argued *Bolling v. Sharpe* before the Supreme Court regularly attended Senators and Redskins games at Griffith Stadium. He had been there the afternoon the Japanese bombed Pearl Harbor. Yet Nabrit steeled himself for change. "You can't just be thinking of the good times you had here. I miss all those experiences, but I feel about this as I feel about all other progress," he said. "This wasn't adequate for baseball and football in a city the size of Washington, it had to go."[46]

Major league baseball, however, did not fare well in Washington. The new Senators played eleven seasons in Washington before becoming the Texas Rangers. Part of the reason for the Senators' failures arose from their American League competition just up the road in Baltimore; in 1954, Clark Griffith and the other owners had permitted the St. Louis Browns to become the Baltimore Orioles. Another factor was his family's refusal to sign black players. If either Clark or his nephew Calvin had reached out to the city's black community—both in words and in deed—the original Senators might still be playing in Washington.

Up in Minnesota, the Twins enjoyed an initial run of success. Behind several young Cuban players, such as Tony Oliva and Zoilo Versalles, and home-run hitter Harmon Killebrew, the Twins captured the American League pennant in 1965 and division titles in 1969 and 1970. Calvin's keen eye for baseball talent never failed him—he scouted and signed Hall of Famers Rod Carew and Kirby Puckett. His big mouth, racial insensitivity, and penuriousness, however, eventually ruined him.

During a September 1978 speech at the Lions Club in Waseca, Minnesota, Calvin revealed the real reason he had moved his ball club to Minnesota. He said: "It was when I found out you only had 15,000 black people here. Black people don't go to ball games, but they'll fill up a rassling ring and put up such a chant it'll scare you to death. It's unbelievable. We came here because you've got good, hardworking white people here."[47] He also commented that his best player at the time, Carew, was "a damn fool" for signing a three-year, $170,000 contract.[48] A *Minneapolis Star Tribune* reporter happened to be sitting in the audience. After reading Griffith's comments in the local paper, Carew responded: "The days of Kunta Kinte are over" and "I refuse to be a slave on his plantation and play for a bigot."[49] Carew forced a trade to the California Angels in 1979. Calvin's reputation in Minnesota never recovered.

After Calvin's comments in Waseca, his sister confirmed the family's racially conscious reason for leaving Washington. "The problem that we had run into in Washington was that our ballpark was in a very black district, and people were afraid of getting their tires cut up all the time and things like that, not that whites don't do the same thing, I don't mean that," Thelma Haynes, Calvin's sister and co-owner of the team, told Jon Kerr. "But it was hard to control and we didn't have parking facilities like here [Minnesota]."[50]

The Griffiths finally left baseball in 1984. Calvin could not stomach free agency, particularly the thought of giving multimillion dollar, multiyear guaranteed contracts to unproven players. Unable to adapt to the changes in baseball, much like his Uncle Clark thirty years earlier, he sold the Twins to Carl Pohlad for what today seems like a bargain-basement price, thirty-six million dollars. Three years later, with players largely signed by Calvin, the Twins won the World Series.

Calvin left baseball a rich man, with houses in Florida and Montana, but a lonely man. Baseball cost him his marriage (his first wife left him in 1974); and it severely damaged his relationship with his son, Clark II, a Dartmouth-educated lawyer who didn't speak to Calvin for years. During a two-day visit with Calvin at his Florida apartment in 1996, Calvin exhibited the same combination of garrulousness, old-world charm, and ignorance that he had in the past. He admired a framed pen-and-ink drawing of Griffith Stadium and pointed out his Uncle Clark's box. He talked about Ken Burns's *Baseball* documentary ("I think they catered too much to the blacks"). Then he received a phone call from his son, Clark II. The two men had patched up their differences. Clark II wanted some advice. "Of course, my son is trying to buy the goddamn Twins," Calvin said, matter-of-factly. "I think he's nuts."[51]

The Griffiths never got back into baseball. Calvin lived out his days in Florida and Montana. Like his Uncle Clark, Calvin lived a long time because he kept his conscience clear. "Regrets?" Calvin said. "I don't have any regrets. I don't know why I should. I have no idea."[52] On October 20, 1999, he died at age eighty-seven of heart ailments and a kidney infection in Melbourne, Florida, and was buried next to his Uncle Clark at Fort Lincoln Cemetery near Washington, D.C.

The Griffith family's racial attitudes destroyed a bond between Washington's black community and the Senators and alienated a future generation of the city's black baseball fans. The Griffiths are partly to blame for why Washington, D.C., has not experienced major league baseball for more than thirty years. Sadly, that is the Griffith family's legacy in the nation's capital. At a recent symposium about Griffith Stadium at Howard University Hospital, former Mayor Walter Washington issued a challenge to Clark Griffith II: "Mr. Griffith, you should take the lead in bringing baseball back to town."[53] When major league baseball returns to Washington, it will be in spite of, not because of, the Griffiths.

Buck Leonard lived every Southern migrant's dream of returning home a hero and a success.[54] Although technically he never left Rocky Mount, he spent every summer traveling with the Grays and eight winters playing in Puerto Rico, Cuba, or some other Latin American locale. From 1951 to 1955, he played in the Mexican League. He spent his first three summers with Torreón and two with Durango, as well as two winters with Obregón and one with Xalapa.[55] The Mexican League played only three games a week, enabling him to play until he was forty-eight. They called Leonard, one of the league's few home-run threats, "Durango's Babe Ruth."[56]

Word reached the States in the early 1950s that Leonard could still hit. During the winter of 1951, he finally got the call from Bill Veeck that for so many years never came from Griffith. In 1951, Veeck assumed control of the St. Louis Browns, and he wanted Leonard to play on his team. Leonard declined. Winfield Welch, the former manager of the Birmingham Black Barons, called on Veeck's behalf to inform Leonard that they would send him money in advance.

Leonard told them not to send it. Maybe if they had approached him shortly after Robinson broke in with the Dodgers in 1947, when Leonard was only thirty-nine years old, he would have gone. Four years later, however, Leonard knew it was too late. "I told him [Veeck] I was too old to play major-league baseball," he wrote. "I was almost forty-five years old. My legs were gone and I knew I couldn't play ball every day. I didn't even want to try it."[57]

Veeck also approached Leonard's former roommate, Cool Papa Bell, about playing for the Browns. Bell, almost forty-eight, gave Veeck the same negative response. Bell told John Holway:

> People told me I should have tried for the job just for the money, but I couldn't do it just for a paycheck. I never had any money, so I never worried about it. I just didn't want the fans to boo me, and if I had played at that age they sure would have. Sometimes pride is more important than money.[58]

From 1951 to 1953, Satchel Paige pitched three seasons for the Browns and several more for the Triple-A Miami Marlins. In 1965, at the age of fifty-nine, Paige miraculously threw three shutout innings for the Kansas City Athletics. The performance made him the oldest player in major league history. Paige would do anything to make a buck. Leonard and Bell, however, didn't want to embarrass themselves in the major leagues; they wanted to be remembered as Negro League stars, not as shells of their former selves.

In 1953, Leonard made a brief minor league appearance with the Portsmouth Merrimacs in the Class-B Piedmont League. With about a month left in the season, the owner of the Merrimacs asked Leonard to help the team win the pennant. During that stretch, Leonard hit .333.[59] Twenty years after leaving Rocky Mount to play for the all-black Daughtry's Black Revels, Leonard finished his American professional baseball career on an integrated team in the same city. Both Leonard and professional baseball had come a long way.

Leonard returned to Rocky Mount for good in 1955 having passed on his major league dreams but with his head high. He worked for a year with a cigar company, ten years as a truant officer, and two

292

more as a playground attendant for the public school system. In 1959, he received his real estate license after obtaining his high school equivalency degree. He built up his real estate business and from 1962 to 1975 served as the vice president of the local minor league team, the Rocky Mount Leafs, of the Class-A Carolina League.[60]

Leonard had only two regrets: not pursuing his education and not having any children.[61] "I wish I had had some children," he said. "They might have grown up to be ballplayers."[62] Although childless during twenty-seven years of marriage, Buck and Sarah lived a happy life together. She was his partner, companion, and best friend. On February 15, 1966, Sarah died of a heart attack. "That was the hardest thing in my life I ever had to deal with," Leonard wrote. "It was the worst time of my life." Two years later, his mother, whom he called Miss Emma until the day she died, passed away.[63]

In a sense, Leonard had raised three children: his brothers, Herman and Charlie, and his youngest sister, Lena. Leonard recognized Charlie's academic gifts and made sure that Charlie would not get sidetracked by playing black baseball. After Charlie died in 1951, all three of his children graduated from college and became engineers.[64] Leonard's sister, Lena, moved to Washington, D.C. Her daughter graduated from Bennett College and then worked as a chemist at the National Cancer Institute at the National Institutes of Health.[65] The Leonards ascended into the middle class, in large part because of the sacrifices that Leonard made for his younger brothers and sister. The entire family viewed Leonard as a father figure.

Leonard's crowning achievement was his 1972 induction into the Baseball Hall of Fame with his deceased Grays teammate Josh Gibson. Six years earlier, Ted Williams had used his Hall of Fame speech to lobby for the inclusion of Negro Leaguers such as Paige and Gibson. "I hope that some day Satchel Paige and Josh Gibson will be voted into the Hall of Fame as symbols of the great Negro players who are not here only because they weren't given a chance," Williams said.[66] In 1971, the Hall of Fame made Paige its first Negro League inductee. Originally, the Hall of Fame planned to put the Negro Leaguers into a separate wing. After considerable uproar in the media, then–baseball commissioner Bowie Kuhn persuaded the

Hall not to segregate men who had endured years of second-class treatment. Paige walked through the Hall's front door. Leonard and Gibson immediately followed him.

At his August 7, 1972, induction ceremony in Cooperstown, Leonard told the crowd:

> Sometimes we baseball players think our greatest thrill comes from something we do on the baseball field. But my greatest thrill did not come from a home run that I hit nor a catch that I made or stealing a base. I ought not to have said that maybe. But, anyway, my greatest thrill came from what somebody did for me. And that was select me for the Baseball Hall of Fame.[67]

The Hall of Fame changed Leonard's life. Even before his induction, he had developed into an eloquent spokesman about the Negro Leagues; his stories about Gibson and the Grays made up a vital component in the early histories of black baseball. After his Hall of Fame induction, autograph requests flooded his mailbox. He answered every one. Interviewers arrived from all over the country at his house on Atlantic Avenue about a mile off Interstate 64 on the Edgecombe County side of Rocky Mount. He invited them into his small wood-paneled office, surrounded by photographs and memorabilia from his playing days, and regaled them with stories about Gibson, Cum Posey, the Grays, and Griffith Stadium.

In 1986, Leonard suffered a stroke that paralyzed his right side, slurred his speech, and robbed him of his short-term memory. Shortly thereafter, he married his second wife, Lugenia, a member of his church who helped him adapt to his new lifestyle. He continued his role as the Negro Leagues' torch bearer. He learned how to sign autographs with his left hand. He still gave interviews in his photograph-covered room. He remembered details of his life from forty years earlier; he just couldn't expound on subjects as expansively as he had before. He appeared at Negro League reunions. The stroke may have deprived him of a starring role in Ken Burns's *Baseball* documentary (a role filled by former Kansas City Monarchs first baseman Buck O'Neil). It may have forced him to use a walker and eventually a

294

wheelchair, but it did not keep him from enjoying the autumn of his years. He loved being Buck Leonard, Hall of Fame baseball player.

On Thanksgiving Day in 1997, Leonard passed away at age ninety. Two days later, the *New York Times* ran a picture of him in his photograph-covered office above the following caption: "Negro-League Star Dies: Buck Leonard, 90, teamed with Josh Gibson and was compared to Lou Gehrig, but his color kept him from the majors." The picture and the caption ran on the *Times*'s front page.[68] Not bad for a twenty-five-year-old railroad worker who had started playing professionally because he had been laid off during the Depression and needed a way to feed his family. Leonard played hard, lived clean, and stood out as the best black first baseman of his era. After his Hall of Fame induction, he wrote: "I found out that there are folks who will have a little more respect for you if they feel you live a clean, decent life."[69]

On December 2, 1997, mourners packed Rocky Mount's St. James Baptist Church, Leonard's place of worship for more than seventy years, and honored his life and career. "Buck's song was not sung for a long time, until they put him in the Hall," Buck O'Neil said. "I'll cry tonight. But not because of Buck's passing. I'll cry for the people who didn't get to see him and know of his great things. He was one of the greatest who ever lived."[70]

In his own lyrical way, O'Neil rejected the description most often associated with Leonard—"The Black Lou Gehrig." Although Leonard treasured the comparison to the Yankees first baseman, it obscured the uniqueness of Leonard's struggles and accomplishments. "I'm sure there's a great ball club in Heaven," O'Neil said. "Saint Peter probably asked God, 'What about Lou Gehrig at first base?' But God said, 'Lou Gehrig's on the other team.'"[71] Leonard was a success story of the great black migration, a Negro League star, and a gentleman. Anyone lucky enough to have seen him play at Griffith Stadium would have recognized his greatness.

Well into his midnineties, Lacy would arise at 3:00 A.M., drive from his northeast Washington apartment to the *Afro*'s Baltimore offices, climb three flights of stairs, and tackle the day's sports news. Three times a week, Lacy worked from 4:00 A.M. to noon as the paper's sports editor and wrote out his weekly column in longhand. An automobile accident and arthritis had made it too painful for Lacy to type his columns. Nothing, however, could keep him from writing them. Lacy was the iron man of the black press.

Lacy's experiences growing up in segregated Washington and his failure to make it as a player in the Negro Leagues drove his campaign to integrate professional baseball. Shortly after Robinson's major league debut in 1947, Negro League teams such as the Baltimore Elite Giants blamed Lacy for the demise of their two million dollar industry. Lacy recalled the Elite Giants' criticism:

> There was no animosity or anything like that. The Elite Giants felt that I had deserted them by advocating integration. I was asked about it at one point. They wanted to know whether or not I realize, as Clark Griffith said, that I was going to destroy the black leagues if my intentions were successful.
>
> My answer was always that the black leagues were an institution, of course, and nobody likes to attack an institution. But at the same time they were a symbol of the dark ages when it was contended and maintained that [the Negro Leagues were] separate but equal. In this case it was separate but unequal, of course. While I didn't like to attack an institution, I certainly didn't want to support or stand by idly and see a symbol for frustration.[72]

The blame, however, did not rest with Lacy. The impact of integration could not be controlled, and it affected all aspects of life in black Washington.

Integration changed Lacy's world. The black elite moved out of neighborhoods near U Street and Howard University, eschewing communities such as Logan Circle and LeDroit Park for upper Sixteenth Street enclaves known as the Gold and Platinum Coasts. The black middle class also left the city for outlying suburbs, transforming Prince George's County, Maryland, into the wealthiest majority black county in America. In 1968, the riots after the death of Martin

Luther King Jr. destroyed many of the businesses on U Street. Although Washington remained one of the nation's wealthier majority black cities, the city's demographics had changed.[73] Dunbar High School became a poor neighborhood school where only 30 percent of its students went on to college in 1976, compared with 80 percent during the pre–World War II era.[74] Although still one of the finest historically black colleges, Howard University is no longer considered the center of the black intellectual universe.

The black press, in fighting for integration in baseball and other aspects of life, contributed to its own undoing. World War II marked the economic apex of black businesses like the Negro Leagues and the black press. "The Negro press," Gunnar Myrdal wrote, "is bound to become even stronger as Negroes are increasingly educated and culturally assimilated but not given entrance to the white world."[75] Once white media organizations opened their newsrooms to black reporters and began covering issues in the black community, black Washingtonians forgot about the *Afro-American*. With a combined circulation close to 230,000 during the war, the *Afro* put out a Baltimore edition and a national edition that by 1969 reached about seventy thousand people.[76] In 1992, the *Afro* celebrated its one hundredth anniversary with a paid circulation between fifteen thousand and thirty thousand.[77] The Murphy family still runs the Baltimore-based newspaper.

Lacy spent a lifetime at the *Afro*, working there for more than fifty-eight years after returning from the *Chicago Defender* in January 1944. Over the years, he turned down numerous offers from white daily newspapers. "The *Afro* gave me the opportunity to pursue the Jackie Robinson story, my landmark story, which newspapers from the *Portland Oregonian* to the *Dallas Morning News* to the *Boston Globe* would not have allowed me to put three years into developing," Lacy recalled. "I couldn't turn my back on the *Afro*, no matter what kind of offer."[78] With the *Afro*, Lacy covered six Olympics, numerous World Series, and Robinson's Hall of Fame induction. He mentored many young black sportswriters, including *New York Times* columnist William Rhoden, and inspired countless others. He wrote his "From A to Z" column almost every week and for a time even doubled as a television sports commentator for WBAL-TV in Baltimore. Lacy's second wife, Barbara, died in 1969. He never remarried and still wears his wedding ring.

Lacy outlasted all his colleagues in the sporting press. Wendell Smith crossed over to the white *Chicago American*, worked as a television commentator at WGN, and eventually wrote a weekly column for the *Chicago Sun-Times*. He died at age fifty-eight of cancer on November 26, 1972, just over a month after Robinson's death. Harold Jackson, the former *Afro* sportswriter and radio personality, left Washington to become one of the kings of New York black radio. He survived the payola scandal accusing disc jockeys of receiving kickbacks during the 1950s, bought WBLS-FM along with former Manhattan Borough Chief Percy Sutton, and today still spins an eclectic mix of tunes on his weekly show, "Sunday Morning Classics." Ric Roberts left the *Courier* and from 1970 to 1976 served as Howard University's sports information director before his death. Art Carter spent his final years as the editor of the *Afro's* Washington edition until he died of cancer at age seventy-six. Lacy even outlasted Povich, who delighted Washingtonians with his sports columns until 1998, when he died of heart failure at age ninety-two.[79]

In his later years, Lacy turned into somewhat of a curmudgeon. He zealously guarded his time and his privacy and quickly grew tired of doing interviews about his life. He always, however, entertained the questions of students and volunteered his time to charities. His son and best friend, Tim, who is in his sixties, also wrote a sports column for the *Afro*. Lacy's friends refer to him as "Coach Lacy."

Although the Negro Leagues began receiving national recognition in the early 1970s, it took longer for people to acknowledge the work of Lacy and his black colleagues. In 1993, Smith gained posthumous admission to the Baseball Hall of Fame's writers' wing. Lacy applauded Smith's selection. During the fiftieth anniversary of Robinson's first season with the Dodgers, the spotlight turned to Lacy. Soon, he began receiving numerous accolades and awards.

In 1997, the Hall of Fame made Lacy the first inductee who had spent his entire career with a black newspaper. Although he stumbled on his way to the podium that day, Lacy accepted the J. G. Taylor Spink Award, named for the segregationist owner of *The Sporting News*, with honor and class. With a nod to Ted Williams's 1966 call for the inclusion of Negro Leaguers in the Hall of Fame, Lacy said: "For my part, I hope that my presence here today will serve to gain public recognition for the quality of the black press. . . ."[80]

Lacy spent nearly half of his brief induction speech thanking an unlikely source: Miss Caroline Calloway, his algebra teacher at Armstrong High School. Lacy told a story about his impending failing grade in Miss Calloway's algebra class. After conferring with one of his athletic coaches, Miss Calloway agreed to give him a passing grade as long as he agreed not to take her geometry course the next semester. Lacy concluded: "'Thank you, Miss Calloway, wherever you are,' for without you, instead of standing on the threshold of this edifice of triumph, I might still be a 94-year-old sophomore in a Washington, D.C., high school."[81]

During the last years of his life, Lacy's old U Street neighborhood regained some of its glory. People started referring to it as the "New U." The Lincoln Theater reopened in 1994 after a beautiful remodeling. The True Reformers Building, where Duke Ellington played some of his first gigs, underwent a massive renovation in 2000.[82] Bohemian Caverns, an upscale jazz club, reopened its doors in 2001 at Eleventh and U. A host of trendy bars and clubs now line U and Fourteenth Streets.[83] The opening of the Metro's green line has increased foot traffic in the area. There is even talk of salvaging the crumbling, boarded-up Howard Theater, which sits on Seventh and T Streets near where Griffith Stadium once stood.[84]

The transformation of U Street, however, is not without its drawbacks. As young whites flood into the neighborhood from nearby Dupont Circle and Adams Morgan, real estate developers have been snatching up old brick homes, renovating them, and reselling them for as much as seven figures. Housing and rental prices have soared.[85] U Street is not in any danger of losing its African-American presence anytime soon, but the so-called gentrification has the potential to rob the neighborhood of its roots. The entire area, loosely referred to as Shaw, has been named a historic district.

Conspicuously absent is a landmark, plaque, or some other recognition of the legacy of the Grays. Washington, D.C., is the city of monuments. Every week the city seems to designate another spot as a historic landmark or to unveil another memorial. The names Buck Leonard and Sam Lacy do not mean anything to most of the neighborhood's current residents. Given the city's obsession with monuments and the need to preserve U Street's African-American roots, it would be fitting to honor both Leonard and Lacy with statues outside Howard University Hospital, where the ballpark once stood and the Grays once played. Their presence in stone—Lacy at his typewriter and Leonard at first base—would serve as constant reminders that sports can play a positive role in an evolving society. That way, children heading up and across the street to the Banneker Recreation Center will know that a great black baseball team once played there.

In 1997, Sam Lacy was the first sportswriter who had spent his career in the black press to be elected to the writers' wing of the Baseball Hall of Fame.
(NATIONAL BASEBALL HALL OF FAME LIBRARY)

Buck Leonard stands with Commissioner Bowie Kuhn at Leonard's 1972 Hall of Fame induction. Josh Gibson was posthumously inducted along with Leonard.
(NATIONAL BASEBALL HALL OF FAME LIBRARY)

NOTES

INTRODUCTION

1. Robert W. Creamer, *Babe: The Legend Comes to Life* (New York: Simon and Schuster, 1974), 185. The controversy about Babe Ruth's ethnic origins has recently resurfaced after filmmaker Spike Lee raised the issue in a column in *Gotham* magazine. See Daniel Okrent, "A Background Check: Was Babe Ruth Black? More Important, Should We Care?" *Sports Illustrated*, 7 May 2001, 27; Clarence Page, "Could It Be True That Babe Was Black?; Moviemaker's Column Revives Rumors About Ruth," *Chicago Tribune*, 13 May 2001, C-19.

CHAPTER 1

1. Sam Lacy, taped interview by author, Washington, D.C., 15 July 1992.
2. Lawrence S. Ritter, *Lost Ballparks: A Celebration of Baseball's Legendary Fields* (New York: Viking Studio Books, 1992), 190 (citing a May 4, 1944, Associated Press blurb that the Browns and Cardinals "have discontinued their policy of restricting Negroes to the bleachers and the pavilion at Sportsman's Park. Negroes may now purchase seats in the grandstand"). As at Griffith Stadium, most blacks at Sportsman's Park sat in the right-field pavilion. See id.; Philip J. Lowry, *Green Cathedrals: The Ultimate Celebration of All 271 Major League and Negro League Ballparks Past and Present*, rev. ed. (Reading, Mass.: Addison-Wesley, 1992), 231 ("Black fans were restricted to the right-field pavilion seats during the era of segregation").
3. In her monograph on Black Washington, historian Constance McLaughlin Green wrote:

   > Except for the haunts of boot leggers and other elements of the underworld, by 1923 the only places in Washington where racial segregation did not obtain were on the trolleys and buses, at Griffith Stadium, and in reading rooms of the public library and the Library of Congress. When one of the "Senators" knocked out a home run, white and black rooters in the stadium bleachers delightedly slapped each other on the back and together discussed the team's prospects. Although no Negro player was allowed on the team, when Washington won the pennant in 1925, the colored *Daily American* wrote: "Long live King Baseball, the only monarch who recognizes no color line."

Constance McLaughlin Green, *The Secret City: A History of Race Relations in the Nation's Capital* (Princeton, N.J.: Princeton University Press, 1967), 201–2. Other historians, such as Washington native Rayford W. Logan, have written that Griffith Stadium wasn't segregated. Rayford W. Logan, "Growing Up in Washington: A Lucky Generation," *Records of the Columbia History Society of Washington, D.C.*, vol. 48 (1971–1972), ed. Francis Coleman Rosenberger (University of Virginia Press, 1973), 506.

4. Bill Gilbert, taped interview by author, 9 July 1992, Potomac, Md., and telephone interview, 3 June 1992.

5. Calvin Griffith, taped interview by author, Indiatlantic, Fla., 10–11 February 1995. The reason for separate seating, according to Calvin Griffith, was partly economic and partly social. "[They] came to Mr. Griffith and asked him if he would build them a section where they could go and not be disturbed by anybody," Calvin said. "They built a place in right field called the pavilion. And that was strictly for the black people and the cost of that was either fifty cents or seventy-five cents, either one of the two. It was cheaper." See also Jon Kerr, *Calvin: Baseball's Last Dinosaur* (Dubuque, Iowa: Wm. C. Brown Publishers, 1990), 137.

6. Lacy interview, 15 July 1992. In his recently published autobiography, Lacy described the right-field stands at Griffith Stadium as the "Jim Crow pavilion." Sam Lacy with Moses J. Newson, *Fighting for Fairness: The Life Story of Hall of Fame Sportswriter Sam Lacy* (Centreville, Md.: Tidewater Publishers, 1998), 25.

7. Southern congressmen who had seized control of the D.C. government legally segregated the schools from 1878 to 1954. Green, *The Secret City*, 116; Alvin E. White, "Washington Is (Not) a Jimcrow Town," *Our World* 9:1 (January 1954), 23.

8. In the mid-1930s, a park official put up signs segregating the Rock Creek Park picnic area. The signs were removed, but segregation persisted through "the deft use of picnic permits." Victor R. Daly, "Washington's Minority Problem," *Crisis* 46:6 (June 1939), 170. The same was true on streetcars, which ran along Seventh Street and stopped at Griffith Stadium. Signs that said "This car reserved exclusively for colored people" hung from the streetcars in 1862, but Congress legally integrated all streetcars three years later. William Tindall, "Beginning of Street Railways in the Nation's Capital," *Records of the Columbia Historical Society* 21 (1928), 76–77. See also Green, *The Secret City*, 66–67 (placing the date of the Congressional ordinance at 1862). The 1862 ordinance may have applied to one streetcar company, but there were several competing streetcar companies at that time. The ordinance wasn't extended to all companies until 1865, according to Tindall. For the history of D.C. streetcars, see LeRoy O. King, *100 Years of Capital Traction: The Story of Streetcars in the Nation's Capital* (Dallas: Taylor Publishing, 1972); John W. Boettijer, "Street Railways in the District of Columbia" (master's thesis, George Washington University, 1963). The all-white bus and streetcar operators continued to discriminate by driving "non-stop express buses through thickly populated Negro Districts." Daly, "Washington's Minority Problem," 170.

9. These laws fined businesses one hundred dollars and revoked their licenses for one year for refusing to serve "any well-behaved and respectable person, in the same room and at the same prices, as other well-behaved and respectable persons are served." Letitia Brown and Elsie M. Lewis, *Washington in the New Era, 1870–1970* (Washington, D.C.: Smithsonian Institution, 1972), 4.

10. C. Vann Woodward, *The Strange Career of Jim Crow*, 3d rev. ed. (New York: Oxford University Press, 1974), 102.

11. John Clagett Proctor, "Early Base Ball Games in the Capital," *Washington Evening Star: The Sunday Star Magazine*, 1 October 1933, pt. 7, 6–7; Douglas E. Evelyn and Paul Dickson, *On This Spot: Pinpointing the Past in Washington, D.C.* (Washington, D.C.: Farragut Publishing, 1992), 238–39.

12. Griffith Stadium Scorecard and Program, 1957; Gordon M. Thomas, "Griffith Stadium: 30th Anniversary of the Finale," (September 1991; unpublished article on file with author).

13. "Griffith Stadium was, putting it uncharitably, a dump," sportswriter Dick Heller wrote. "But it was our dump." Dick Heller, "Griffith Stadium Was Ugly, Charming and Uniquely D.C.," *Washington Times*, 24 September 2001, C13.

14. "Play Ball April 12," *Washington Post*, 18 March 1911, 1; "New Stand April 12," *Washington Evening Star*, 18 March 1911, 1.

15. The grandstand was far from complete. "Much of the concrete [was] still clad in wooden forms. All of the seats were uncovered, and no box seats had been installed except for the presidential party." Bill Shannon and George Kalinsky, *The Ballparks* (New York: Hawthorn Books, 1975), 235.

16. "Ready for 'Fans'" *Washington Sunday Star*, 9 April 1911, pt. 1, 3.

17. Scorecard and program, 1957.

18. "The enlarged park, when completed, will be known as the Clark Griffith Stadium." Denman Thompson, "Big Stadium Here to Handle 50,000 Ready by Autumn," *Washington Evening Star*, 21 August 1923, 1. The concrete bleachers enlarged the park's seating capacity to between twenty-eight thousand and thirty-two thousand. Griffith periodically vowed to enlarge the stadium's seating capacity beyond thirty thousand but never made good on the promise. Id.; Kirk Miller, "Owner of Nats Plans to Enlarge Baseball Park by 12,000 Seats," *Washington Times*, 24 December 1938, 16; Burton Hawkins, "Plant to Seat 40,000 Baseball, 44,000 Grid Crowds, Nats Plan," *Washington Evening Star*, 5 July 1946, A-10.

19. William B. Mead and Paul Dickson, *Baseball: The President's Game* (New York: Walker Publishing Company, 1997), 24–25. Presidents Nixon and Ford threw out the first ball for Opening Days of the expansion Senators of the 1970s at RFK Stadium.

20. Ken Denlinger, "There Used to Be a Tree, and a Ballpark, and a Team," *Washington Post*, 10 July 1985, B1.

21. David Von Sothen, *The Last Out* (1964), documentary.

22. In 1927, a sociologist listed fourteen pool halls between the 1200 and 2000 blocks of Seventh Street/Georgia Avenue. William H. Jones, *Recreation and Amusement Among Negroes in Washington, D.C.* (Washington, D.C.: Howard University Press, 1927; reprint Westport, Conn.: Negro University Press, 1970) 136–38. The 1924 city directory lists five pool halls in the 2000 block of Georgia Avenue. 1924 City Directory, 1680. By the 1930s, the storefront churches with names such as New Rising Mt. Zion Baptist Church (1527 Seventh Street), Bible-Way Church of Christ (1541 Seventh Street), and House of Prayer Church (1719-21 Seventh Street) lined Seventh Street. 1935 City Directory, 2577.

23. Sandra Fitzpatrick and Maria R. Goodwin. *The Guide to Black Washington* (New York: Hippocrene Books, 1990), 152; Henry Whitehead, *Remembering U Street: There Was a Time* (private publication on file with author).

24. Mark Gauvreau Judge, "A Washington Landmark; In a City of Monuments, No Room for the Howard?" *Washington Post*, 25 April 1999, B3; Christine Montgomery, "Next Act in the Wings; New Effort to Save Historic Howard Theatre Would Make It Part of Black Cultural District," *Washington Times*, 22 April 1999, C8.

25. David Ritz, *Divided Soul: The Life of Marvin Gaye* (New York: De Capo Press, 1985), 31.

26. Mark Tucker, *Ellington: The Early Years* (Urbana, Ill.: University of Illinois Press, 1991), 26.

27. Edward Kennedy Ellington, *Music Is My Mistress* (New York: De Capo Press, 1973), 23.

28. Langston Hughes, "Our Wonderful Society: Washington," *Opportunity* (August 1927), 227. Upon the publication of his first major collection of poetry, *The Weary Blues*, Hughes gave a reading at a Washington playhouse at 1814 N Street, NW. On that day in 1926, Hughes had tried unsuccessfully to hire "a Seventh Street bluesman, funky and unfettered, to howl during the intermission." Arnold Rampersad, *The Life of Langston Hughes*, vol. 1 (New York: Oxford University Press, 1986), 123.

29. Jean Toomer, *Cane* (New York: Liveright, 1923, 1975), 39.

30. See Juan Williams, "14th & U: When Being There Meant Being Somebody," *Washington Post Magazine*, 23 February 1988, 23; Whitehead, *Remembering U Street*; Linda Wheeler, "A Building of the People: On U. Street Blacks Created a Powerful Symbol," *Washington Post*, 18 January 1999, A1.

31. "In Washington there are more colored people who are well educated and well to do than in any other city in the world," Mary Church Terrell wrote in 1904. Mary Church Terrell, "Society Among the Colored People of Washington," *Voice of the Negro*, vol. 1, 1904 (New York: Negro University Press, 1969), 151. Willard B. Gatewood, *Aristocrats of Color: The Black Elite, 1880–1920* (Bloomington, Ind.: Indiana University Press, 1990), 39.

32. Gatewood, *Aristocrats of Color*, 39.

33. E. Franklin Frazier, *Black Bourgeoisie* (New York: The Free Press, 1957), 235.

34. Ibid., 197. See also E. Franklin Frazier, *Negro in the United States*, rev. ed. (New York: The Macmillan Company, 1957), 287–89; E. Franklin Frazier, "The Negro Middle Class and Desegregation," *Social Problems* 4:4 (April 1957), 295 (critiquing the problems of the "black middle class").

   According to John Hope Franklin, a former colleague of Frazier's at Howard, Frazier based his best-known book, *Black Bourgeoisie*, on his wife's late-night poker games. "He was talking about his wife, by the way," Franklin recalled. "I don't think she understood that he was writing about her." John Hope Franklin, taped interview by author, Durham, N.C., 21 April 1994. In *Black Bourgeoisie*, Frazier described the members of black elite who reveled in poker games and playing the numbers as "worshipers of the God of chance." Frazier, *Black Bourgeoisie*, 210–11.

35. The date and place of Lacy's birth are shrouded in some mystery. His autobiography says he was born on October 23, 1903, in Mystic, Connecticut, that his family moved back to Washington in 1905, and that neither Lacy nor his family ever returned to Connecticut. Lacy, *Fighting for Fairness*, 14. Yet the 1900 census lists Lacy's family as living with his grandfather in Washington. The 1900 census taker recorded Lacy's grandfather as Henry Lacy, but this is clearly Lacy's family. Lacy's father, mother, two sisters, and older brother are all listed. Bureau of the Census,

Twelfth Census of the United States: 1900 — Population, District of Columbia, vol. 5, E.D. 58, sheet 13a, lines 6–12; 1900 Index, District of Columbia, L200, at roll 22.

There is no record of the Lacy family ever living in Connecticut or of Lacy having been born there. The town of Mystic, Connecticut, has a substantial history of Native Americans living there, and Old Mystic is home to The Indian and Colonial Research Center. Mystic is located in two townships — Groton and Stoningham. The town clerk of Groton could not find a birth certificate for a Samuel Harold Lacy (or Lacey) born on October 23, 1903. Furthermore, the town clerk of Stoningham found no record of a Lacey or Lacy born there between 1902 and 1907. Joan Cohn, President, The Indian and Colonial Research Center, Old Mystic, Connecticut, letter to author, 28 June 1999. The lack of a Connecticut birth certificate does not prove that Lacy wasn't born there. At that time, not all births were recorded, particularly African-American or Native-American births. However, there are no other indicia that the Lacy family ever lived in Connecticut between 1900 and 1905, either in the census, at the Center in Black Roots in Southeastern Connecticut, 1650–1900, or in "Tapestry — A Living History of Black Families in Southeastern Connecticut." Id.

The 1910, 1920, and 1930 census all indicate that Lacy was born in Washington in 1905. Bureau of the Census, *Thirteenth Census of the United States: 1910 — Population*, District of Columbia, E.D. 153, sheet 4a, line 40 (listing Lacy as five years old and born in Washington, D.C.); Bureau of the Census, *Fourteenth Census of the United States: 1920 — Population*, District of Columbia, vol. 13, E.D. 192, sheet 9b, line 83 (listing Lacy as fifteen years old and born in Washington, D.C.); Bureau of the Census, *Fifteenth Census of the United States: 1930 — Population*, District of Columbia, roll 300, E.D. 287, sheet 5a, line 17 (listing Lacy as twenty-five years old and born in Washington, D.C.). This is confirmed by the 1920 Census Index, District of Columbia, L200. No birth record, however, has been found in Washington, D.C., either. The Washington, D.C., archives did not have a birth certificate for Sam Lacy on October 23, 1903, October 23, 1905, or on any surrounding dates.

Although no birth records have been found, Lacy probably was born in 1905 in Washington. Lacy graduated from high school in 1924, not 1922 as his autobiography claims. Lacy's 1924 graduation date is confirmed by his high school yearbook. "The Reflector: Class of 1924 — Armstrong Technical High School," 83, The Charles Sumner School Museum and Archives, Washington, D.C.; but cf. Lacy, *Fighting for Fairness*, 24 (listing his graduation as 1922).

For information about Lacy's grandfather, see Lacy, *Fighting for Fairness*, 15; Ron Fimrite, "Sam Lacy: Black Crusader," *Sports Illustrated* (29 October 1990), 90. Most members of the black elite could point to a member of their family as a "first" something in the white world. Lacy's sisters, Evelyn Hunton and Rosina Howe, were public school teachers, coveted and respected positions within the middle-class black community. See Lacy, *Fighting for Fairness*, 14; 1930 Census, roll 300, E.D. 287, sheet 5a, lines 27, 29.

36. The uncertainty over Lacy's year and place of birth stems from another family legend. Fifty years into his life, Lacy learned from one of his sisters (who had learned from one of her mother's sisters) that their mother, Rose, was "a Shinnecock Indian, of the Mohawk nation." Lacy, *Fighting for Fairness*, 14–15. The 1920 and 1930 censuses say Rosa B. Lacy was born in Washington and that her parents were born in

Maryland. 1920 Census, District of Columbia, vol. 13, E.D. 192, sheet 9b, line 79; 1930 Census, District of Columbia, roll 300, E.D. 287, sheet 5a, line 26. The 1920 Index also lists Rose Lacy as having been born in the District of Columbia, as do the 1900 and 1910 Censuses. None of this data contradicts the family story that Lacy's mother was a Shinnecock Indian. In his autobiography, Lacy recalled his mother sheltering him from a heavy thunderstorm during his grandfather's funeral in July 1910: "She had slick black hair and the water was running off her head and seemed to be going right down her corset and into her shoes. That impressed me; I realized the strength of my mother. Later I came to realize she was the dominant figure in my upbringing." Lacy, *Fighting for Fairness*, 14–15.

The 1910 Census lists Lacy's mother and all of her children as "Mu," which stands for mulatto. Lacy's father is listed as "B" for black. 1910 Census, District of Columbia, E.D. 153, sheet 4a, lines 37–42. The validity of these racial classifications often depended on the diligence and perception of the family's census taker. The Lacys' census taker in 1920 listed the entire family as "B" for black, while other nearby families on Lacy's block were listed as "Mu" for Mulatto. 1920 Census, District of Columbia, vol. 13, E.D. 192, sheet 9b, lines 78–83. The 1900 Census merely lists everyone in the Lacys' neighborhood as "B" for black. 1900 Census, District of Columbia, vol. 5, E.D 58, sheet 13, lines 6–12. The 1930 Census classified all blacks, including Lacy's mother, as "neg" for Negro. She was not listed as "In" for Indian. 1930 Census, District of Columbia, roll 300, E.D. 287, sheet 5a, line 17.

37. Lacy, *Fighting for Fairness*, 15.
38. The 1900 Census lists Lacy's father, who was thirty at the time, as a government clerk. 1900 Census, District of Columbia, vol. 5, E.D. 58, sheet 13, line 39. The 1910 Census lists Lacy's father's "trade or profession" as a lawyer, the "nature of his business" as a notary public. 1910 Census, District of Columbia, E.D. 153, sheet 4a, line 37. The 1920 Census simply lists Lacy's father as a "notary public" who works in his "own office." 1920 Census, District of Columbia, vol. 13, E.D. 192, sheet 9b, line 78. The 1930 Census also lists him as a "notary public." 1930 Census, roll 300, E.D. 287, sheet 5a, line 25. The District of Columbia City Directories from 1910 and 1911 list Lacy's father as a notary, and the 1910 City Directory lists an office address at 609 F Street, NW. 1910 City Directory for the District of Columbia, 828; 1911 City Directory for the District of Columbia, 890. A *Sports Illustrated* profile described Lacy's father as "a researcher in a law office, a rare position of responsibility for a black man in the early part of this century." Fimrite, "Black Crusader," 90. Lacy's biography is silent about his father's occupation, other than to say his father supported the family and had a penchant for reading and saving newspapers. Lacy, *Fighting for Fairness*, 15.

39. When Lacy was born in 1905, his family lived with Lacy's grandfather at 1625 Tenth Street. Lacy's father, who was in his early thirties in 1900, worked as a government clerk. 1900 Census, District of Columbia, vol. 5, E.D 58, sheet 13a, line 7. In 1900, Tenth Street consisted of middle- and working-class blacks. The Lacys' neighbors included a hotel bellman, a railroad waiter, a government messenger, government laborers, a schoolteacher, a police officer, a barber, a waiter, and a cook. Id. at lines 1–50.

Shortly thereafter, Lacy's father rented a house a block away from his grandfather's house at 1730 Tenth Street, between R and S streets. A historical survey of the neighborhood indicates that from 1900 to 1910, Lacy's Tenth Street block changed from a mostly white area to mostly mulatto. Cultural Resources Survey 1991–1992.

The Lacys' neighbors included a Navy Department messenger, a hotel waiter, a laborer/contractor, a hod carrier, a music teacher in the public schools, a clerk in the government printing office, a charwoman at the Treasury Department, a driver, a building contractor, and an engineer. 1910 Census, District of Columbia, E.D. 153, sheets 4a, 4b, 5a, lines 6–100, 1–31.

The 1911 City Directory lists the family as having moved again, to 1910 Thirteenth Street. 1911 District of Columbia City Directory, 890. Between 1910 and 1920, Thirteenth Street also changed from white to black and mulatto. Cultural Resources Survey 1991–1992. Lacy's immediate neighbors included a government laborer, a street laborer, and a hotel cook. 1920 Census, District of Columbia, vol. 13, E.D. 192, sheet 9b, lines 67–100.

Lacy's family also took in several boarders. The 1920 census says that two brothers from Kentucky, Philip and Wallace Brooks, ages twenty-two and twenty, respectively, lived with the family as "roomers." The census also lists Rachel Bell, a forty-nine-year-old public schoolteacher, as a "sister-in-law" living with the family. Bell, indeed, may have been Lacy's mother's sister because Lacy's mother is named Rosa B. Lacy. Bell's parents, however, are listed as having been born in Washington, D.C., whereas Rosa's were born in Maryland. 1920 Census, District of Columbia, vol. 13, E.D. 192, sheet 9b, lines 78–87. This discrepancy can be explained in two ways: (1) an error by the census taker, or, more likely, (2) the sister-in-law label was a pretense for taking in a female boarder. Lacy's parents were not averse to disguising unmarried females living in their home as relatives. Lacy's autobiography recounts several stories about Aunt Susie, another boarder whom his parents referred to as their aunt "simply to allay any curiosity we might have." Lacy, *Fighting for Fairness*, 18.

Lacy's father moved two more times during the mid-1920s and 1930s. Id. at 19. The 1924 city directory lists Sam's father's address as 1719 Fifteenth Street, NW. 1924 District of Columbia City Directory, 902. The 1930 census says that the elder Lacy owned a fifteen thousand dollar house at 1222 Kenyon Street, NW, a mostly black neighborhood with a few Russian and European immigrant families. 1930 Census, roll 300, E.D. 287, sheet 5a, line 25. Lacy's sister and brother-in-law lived next door at 1223 Kenyon. See id. at lines 28–31. Lacy and his wife, Alberta, lived several doors down at 1216 Kenyon. See id. at lines 17–18; 1931 District of Columbia City Directory, 931. Lacy's father stayed at his house on Kenyon Street. See 1935 District of Columbia City Directory, 1175.

40. Lacy, *Fighting for Fairness*, 19. The 1920 census lists Rosa B. Lacy as a "hairdresser" who worked at her "own shop." 1920 Census, District of Columbia, vol. 13, E.D. 192, sheet 9b, line 79. The 1930 census, however, does not list an occupation for Lacy's mother. 1930 Census, roll 300, E.D. 287, sheet 5a, line 26.

41. Sam Lacy, "The 'Y' a Mine That Yielded Many Goals," *Baltimore Afro-American*, 25 February 1995, A8; Lacy, *Fighting for Fairness*, 15–16; Linda Wheeler, "Preserving a Century of Service in Shaw; History YMCA Finds New Community Role," *Washington Post*, 24 September 1998, J1.

42. Lacy interview, 15 July 1992; Lacy, *Fighting for Fairness*, 20–21.

43. Ellington's addresses included 1803, 1805, and 1816 Thirteenth Street (between T and S), and 1206 and 1212 T Street (between Twelfth and Thirteenth). Whitehead, *Remembering U Street*, 2; Raymond M. Lane, "Jazzed on Duke," *Washington Times*, 18 May 2000, M4; M. Dion Thompson, "The Duke of U Street," *Baltimore Sun*, 29 April 1999, 1E.

44. Tucker, *Ellington,* 17–20, 24–27.

45. One of the school's first principals was Richard Greener, the first black graduate of Harvard. Another of the school's early principals was Robert Terrell, a graduate of Harvard and then Howard University Law School. Mary Church Terrell, "History of the High School for Negroes in Washington," *The Journal of Negro History* 2:3 (July 1917), 256. Dunbar's teachers arrived armed with undergraduate degrees from Harvard, Yale, Amherst, Dartmouth, Radcliffe, and Oberlin. Id., 261; Dr. Robert C. Weaver, taped interview by author, New York, N.Y., 30 July 1992.

46. During the 1943–44 school year, the average annual salary of principals, supervisors, and teachers in the District of Columbia school system was equal for blacks and whites: $2,610. Although its funding of the school systems, based on per pupil allocations, was vastly unequal, the District of Columbia was apparently one of only three segregated school systems with equal teachers' salaries. Report of the President's Committee on Civil Rights, *To Secure These Rights* (Washington, D.C.: GPO, 1947), 64. It had been that way for decades. Jervis Anderson, "A Very Special Monument," *The New Yorker,* 20 March 1978, 107. Robert Weaver said that Dunbar paid its teachers higher salaries than Howard University paid its professors. He recalled: "I had teachers from Amherst, teachers from Yale, teachers from Dartmouth, they were Phi Beta Kappa men, too, teachers from Harvard, and teachers from Radcliffe." Weaver interview.

    As Jervis Anderson's *New Yorker* article on Dunbar High School pointed out, if educated blacks did not have law or medical degrees, they could aspire to be "postal clerks, low-level government workers, soldiers, Pullman porters, manual laborers . . . teaching was the most distinguished career open to them." Anderson, "A Very Special Monument," 107.

47. Lacy, *Fighting for Fairness,* 16.

48. Anderson, "A Very Special Monument," 97–98.

49. Anderson quoted a 1975 letter to the editor in the *Washington Post*: "The pride that Dunbar alumni rightfully have in the academic achievements of their school should be substantially tempered by sadness—the criteria for a guaranteed comfortable and successful student sojourn at Dunbar were, in order of importance (1) parents in professional jobs, (2) a minimum of melanin in the skin, and (3) a fairly high scholastic average, not necessarily deserved." Anderson, "A Very Special Monument," 103. Constance McLaughlin Green wrote: "Negro school administrators and teachers believed their first obligation was to the most able of the colored school population." Green, *The Secret City,* 245.

    Although describing the students' socioeconomic backgrounds as "lower middle class" in light of their fathers' occupations as "clerks and messengers," Mary Gibson Hundley conceded that the "community was the most fortunate colored group in the country." Mary Gibson Hundley, *The Dunbar Story (1870–1955)* (New York: Vantage Press, 1965), 31.

50. Anderson, "A Very Special Monument," 107–8. Dr. Clark, of course, harbored his own biases. He was a lifelong integrationist who sought to minimize the achievements of a segregated school system. Dr. Clark's controversial doll test constituted part of a sociological study that the Supreme Court cited in overruling the constitutionality of segregated schools. *Brown v. Board of Education,* 347 US 483, 495 n. 11 (1954).

51. Lacy, *Fighting for Fairness*, 18. Houston later served as the principal at Armstrong, running into trouble with the New Negro Alliance when he crossed one of its picket lines. See infra Chapter 3, text accompanying note 26.
52. Lacy, *Fighting for Fairness*, 16.
53. Although four high schools eventually served Washington's black students, Armstrong was Dunbar's lone rival when Lacy switched schools. Opened in 1902 on P Street between First and Third Streets, NW, the Armstrong Manual Training School actually had begun in 1894–1895 as a "noncollege preparatory technical course." Lillian G. Dabney, "The History of Schools for Negroes in the District of Columbia 1807–1947" (Ph.D. diss., Catholic University of America, 1949), 139–40. Eventually, it would become known as Armstrong Technical High School. Two other black high schools opened during this period: Cardozo (for business education, in 1928) and Phelps (vocational). Id., 141–42.
54. For a discussion of the philosophical differences between DuBois and Washington regarding higher education, see David Levering Lewis, *W. E. B. DuBois: Biography of a Race (1868–1919)* (New York: Henry Holt, 1993), 165, 206, 261–62; David Levering Lewis, *W. E. B. DuBois: The Fight for Equality and the American Century* (New York: Henry Holt, 2000), 2, 76.
55. Lacy interview, 15 July 1992.
56. Lacy, *Fighting for Fairness*, 19; Lacy interview, 15 July 1992.
57. The 1924 Armstrong yearbook says that Lacy played on the basketball and baseball teams from 1922 to 1924 and on the football team in 1923 and 1924. "The Reflector—Class of 1924, Armstrong Technical High School," 83. The class history, however, omits Lacy's name as one of the leaders on those teams: "Frederick Ellis, Harry Turner, Francis Honesty, Chester Anderson, Norman McCoy, Vantile Harris, and Preston Allen began to forge to the front because of their athletic prowess. These young men have played a part in many of the athletic achievements of Armstrong, but more about them and their records will be found in other pages of this book." Id., 62. The omission of Lacy is perhaps because the yearbook discusses Armstrong's success only in football and perhaps because Lacy was a transfer student. Lacy is pictured on Armstrong's football team and basketball team, but oddly not on the baseball team. See id., 119, 133, 137.

    Lacy's basketball coach taught him zone defense and fast-break offense. Armstrong lost in the black high school national championship to Chicago's Wendell Phillips High School. Lacy, *Fighting for Fairness*, 19–20. In 1923, Lacy's junior season, the *Washington Tribune* noted that "Lacey" was one of five "subs" in Armstrong's 23–16 victory over Dunbar. *Washington Tribune*, 10 March 1923, 4.
58. Lacy, *Fighting for Fairness*, 19.
59. Kelly Miller, "Howard: The National Negro University," in *The New Negro: An Interpretation*, ed. Alain Locke (New York: Albert and Charles Boni, 1925), 312.

    Founded by whites (Congregationalist ministers started it as a theological seminary in 1866), named after one of its white founders (General Oliver O. Howard, the head of the Freedmen's Bureau), and led by whites until the third decade of the twentieth century (it did not have a black president until 1926), Howard handed out its first diplomas to four daughters of its all-white faculty. In 1867, Congress officially chartered Howard University and provided annual federal funding to advance "the education of youth in the liberal arts and sciences." The school's purpose was to foster biracial education. Under the financial auspices of the Freedmen's Bureau, however, Howard evolved into a free person of color's ticket to self-advancement. Rayford W. Logan, *Howard University: The First Hundred Years, 1867–1967* (New York: New York University Press, 1969), 12–14; "Howard University: It Is America's Center of Negro Learning," *Life* 2:21 (18 November 1946), 100.

60. Professor Logan's authoritative history of Howard credits Johnson's predecessor, President Durkee, with changing Howard's mission by repeatedly referring to it as "an institution of higher learning for Negroes" and by increasing the number of black faculty members. Logan, *Howard University*, 244. Technically, Johnson was not Howard's first black president. In 1873, John Mercer Langston was named acting president. Howard's trustees, however, passed over Langston for the presidency in favor of a white candidate. Henry F. Pringle and Katherine Pringle, "America's Leading Negro University," *Saturday Evening Post*, 221:34 (19 February 1949), 97; Fitzpatrick and Goodwin, *Guide to Black Washington*, 133.

61. Howard's dream team chafed under Johnson's leadership. Johnson gave his faculty unlimited academic freedom to speak, write, and teach about any subject, "within reason, because President Johnson was one of the most fearless critics of American democracy in modern times." Their academic freedom came at a price. Howard historian Rayford W. Logan, in his book about the university, wrote: "There is, however, one view about him on which friends, adversaries, and neutrals tend to agree—that he possessed a 'messianic complex.' In certain 'messianic moments' he would tell the late E. Franklin Frazier the kind of sociology to write or the late Abram Harris the kind economics to study." Logan, *Howard University*, 249.

While faculty members tolerated Johnson's "messianic moments," they simmered about their "limited voice in running the University." Id., 251. Johnson stifled faculty criticism of his administration. "You were forbidden to write a member of the Board of Trustees, and if you did you had to take it into the president's office for him to mail," John Hope Franklin recalled. "You know, that kind of plantation conduct we didn't like." John Hope Franklin interview, 21 April 1994. By the end of his tenure at Howard, Johnson had alienated most of his academic superstars.

"It was the pinnacle for any black scholar," recalled Franklin, a member of Howard's history department from 1947 to 1956. "You can look at it another way and say that it was a dead end because that was as far as you could go. There was never any thought on the part of a black scholar that you could go beyond Howard University." Id.

62. In an era when Northern graduate and professional schools limited their black enrollment, Howard's medical, law, dental, pharmacy, engineering, and architecture schools offered the black elite an entree into the professional world. Howard's medical school was one of only two among traditionally black colleges, with Freedmen's Hospital (located between the University and Griffith Stadium) serving as the medical school's teaching hospital. Howard's law school offered the country's first course on civil rights and prepared Thurgood Marshall and a generation of black lawyers to contest the constitutionality of segregation. As of 1946, "half of all the Negro physicians, surgeons, and dentists and 80 percent of all the Negro lawyers in the U.S. [were] Howard graduates." Pringle and Pringle, "America's Leading Negro University," 36; Logan, *Howard University*, 18–20, 23.

63. The 1926 city directory lists Samuel H. Lacy as a student living at his father's house at 1719 Fifteenth, NW. 1926 District of Columbia City Directory, 919.

64. Asked why he did not graduate from Dunbar, Lacy told me: "Because I wasn't interested in medicine or law. I came up at the same time as Bill Hastie, Montague Cobb, and Charlie Drew. They were in my age level; they went to Dunbar." Lacy interview, 15 July 1992.

65. The 1924 city directory lists Erskine Lacy as an elevator operator. The 1935 city directory lists Erskine Lacy as a skilled laborer at the government printing office. Lacy's autobiography recounted the story about Erskine's quitting his job to hustle pool. Lacy, *Fighting for Fairness*, 14.

66. Ibid., 17.

67. Louis R. Lautier, "Sports Chatter," *Washington Tribune*, 12 September 1925, 4.

68. Henry Whitehead, telephone interview by author, 19 January 1995.

69. "When Dunbar won there would always be a fight because they thought it was rigged. Armstrong guys would figure they were playing favorites," recalled Robert McNeill, a major on Dunbar's team. "If you were on a winning company and you were a Dunbar student, you didn't put on the ribbon that you won. You got home as quietly and unobtrusively as you possibly could." Robert McNeill, taped interview with author, Washington, D.C., 17 August 1993.

70. Green, *The Secret City*, 208.

71. Ibid., 239.

72. *Washington Afro-American*, 23 September 1944, 15.

73. Frank Rasky, "Harlem's Religious Zealots," *Tomorrow* (November 1949), 12.

74. In 1920, Washington's black population (109,966) was slightly ahead of that of Chicago (109,458) and Baltimore (108,322) and third behind New York (152,467) and Philadelphia (134,229). Bureau of the Census, *Negroes in the United States 1920–1932* (Washington, D.C.: GPO, 1935), tbl. 10, p. 55.

75. H. Scott, "Sports Chatter," *Washington Tribune*, 12 April 1924, 4.

76. McNeill interview, 17 August 1993.

77. Sam Lacy, "Looking 'Em Over," *Washington Tribune*, 13 July 1933, 12.

78. Griffith interview, 10–11 February 1995.

79. In his autobiography, Lacy quotes an old column saying that Altrock threw a wet towel in his father's face. Lacy, *Fighting for Fairness*, 25. For years, Lacy refused to divulge the identity of the Senators player, but he distinctly recalled the man spitting in his father's face. Ron Fimrite, "Sam Lacy: Black Crusader," *Sports Illustrated* (29 October 1990), 94. Lacy relayed the incident to John Steadman as a man spitting in his father's face. John Steadman, "Lacy Has Spent Life Furthering Minorities, but Race He's Helped Most Is Human One," *Baltimore Evening Sun*, 16 November 1992, 4C. Lacy later told Steadman it was Altrock. For more on Altrock's career as the first clown prince of baseball, see Jim Blenko, "Nick Altrock," *The National Pastime: A Review of Baseball History* no. 18 (Cleveland: SABR, 1998), 73–77.

In his autobiography, Lacy claimed that his father stopped going to games after the Altrock incident in the 1924 World Series. Lacy, *Fighting for Fairness*, 25. Lacy's father actually stopped attending Senators games after Griffith signed Bert Shepard, a one-legged pitcher, in 1945. See infra Chapter 7.

80. Lacy, *Fighting for Fairness*, 25.

81. Jones, *Recreation and Amusement*, 30.

82. Neil Lanctot has a terrific discussion of this issue. Neil Lanctot, *Fair Dealing and Clean Playing: The Hilldale Club and the Development of Black Professional Baseball, 1910–1932* (Jefferson, N.C.: McFarland, 1994), 183.

83. H. Scott, "Sports Chatter," *Washington Tribune*, 28 July 1923, 4.

84. H. Scott, "Sports Chatter," *Washington Tribune*, 12 April 1924, 4.

85. The Pilots made a brief comeback in 1934.

86. Lacy interview, 15 July 1992.

87. Art Carter, "From the Bench," *Washington Tribune*, 17 July 1937, 12.

88. *Washington Afro-American*, 5 February 1938, 18.

89. Dick Powell, taped interview by author, Baltimore, Md., 24 August 1992.

90. Donn Rogosin, *Invisible Men: Life in Baseball's Negro Leagues* (New York: Atheneum, 1988), 93.

91. McNeill interview, 17 August 1993.

92. "Ben Taylor Plans to Enter His Team in N.N.L. in 1940," *Washington Tribune*, 29 July 1939, 13; Russell Awkard, taped interview by author, Silver Spring, Md., 26 August 1993.

93. H. Scott, "Sports Chatter," *Washington Tribune*, 12 April 1924, 4.

94. Ibid.

95. Leonard interview, 20 July 1992. Ruth actually had two doubles in that first game, one to right in the first inning and one off the left-field wall in the sixth. *Washington Daily News*, 5 July 1924, 1. Buck Leonard with James A. Riley, *Buck Leonard: The Black Lou Gehrig* (New York: Carroll and Graf, 1995), 7.

96. Gehrig played in only thirteen games in 1923 and in ten games in 1924, coming to bat only twelve times in his second major league season. Gehrig's famous consecutive-games streak of 2,130 did not begin until June 1925.

97. The first reference to Leonard's first major league baseball game appears in an article published three years before Leonard suffered a debilitating stroke in 1986 that affected his ability to speak and his memory. Barry Jacobs, "Buck Leonard," *Baseball America*, 1 June 1983, 5. More was learned about that game in Leonard's recently published autobiography based on interviews conducted before the stroke. Leonard, *The Black Lou Gehrig*, 7 (calling it "the thrill of my life until that time"). In his autobiography, Leonard incorrectly states that the game took place on the Fourth of July. Indeed, a doubleheader with the Yankees occurred that day, a Friday. However, in a poststroke interview with the author, Leonard specifically recalled his first game as a matchup between Herb Pennock and Walter Johnson. Buck Leonard, taped interview by author, Rocky Mount, N.C., 20 July 1992. According to numerous newspaper accounts, the only Pennock-Johnson matchup of the 1924, 1925, or 1926 seasons occurred July 5, 1924. Leonard also recalled sitting in right field. Leonard interview, 20 July 1992.

98. Lena Cox, taped interview by author, Chillum, Md., 29 August 1992.

99. His great grandfather, Thomas Leonard, was born in 1824 in the Cedar Rock Township of Franklin County, North Carolina. After the Civil War, Thomas Leonard continued to work on the farms of one of the surrounding white landowners in Franklin County. He had married another slave, Manerva, and they had nine children: William, Henry, Maxine, Margaret, Lucy, Sallie, Davy, Mary, and Spencer.

Bureau of the Census, *Ninth Census of the United States: 1870—Population*, North Carolina, Franklin County, Cedar Rock Township, sheet 19, lines 24–33; Marriage Register 1901–1917, Nash County, Spencer Leonard to Sallie Knight, June 12, 1909, Nashville, North Carolina (on file with author). Leonard's autobiography mistakenly refers to his grandfather "Spence," who lived about twenty-four miles from Rocky Mount in Castalia, a town in western Nash County near the Franklin County line. Leonard, *The Black Lou Gehrig*, 3. Although Spencer was the youngest child of Thomas and Manerva Leonard, he was Leonard's great-uncle, not his grandfather. Lena Cox interview, 21 April 1995; Buck Leonard interview, 27 April 1995.

Unable to read or write, Thomas Leonard probably was owned by a white farmer named Frederick Leonard (or one of Frederick's nearby white relatives) and worked on the cotton and tobacco farms that thrived in this section of Eastern North Carolina. After Thomas's death during the 1870s, Manerva supported her youngest children by working in the fields. Bureau of the Census, *Tenth Census of the United States: 1880—Population*, North Carolina, Franklin County, Cedar Rock Township, roll 963, vol. 8, E.D. 91, sheet 9, lines 11–13; 1880 Soundex, North Carolina, L563, roll 44. Thomas Leonard was deceased not only by the 1880 census but also by the October 1879 marriage of his son Henry.

Leonard's grandfather, Henry Leonard, was the second oldest of Thomas and Manerva Leonard's children. Born in 1857, Henry Leonard eventually moved to Nash County, which is one county east of Franklin County and encompasses the west side of Rocky Mount. On October 6, 1879, Henry Leonard married Ida Harrison, the daughter of Wesley and Sarah Harrison of Nash County. Marriages Register 1862–1900, Nash County, Henry Leonard to Ida Harrison, October 6, 1879, Nashville, North Carolina (on file with author). Also unable to read or write, Henry and Ida Leonard lived and worked on a farm on the Nash County side of Rocky Mount. Bureau of the Census, *Tenth Census of the United States: 1880—Population*, North Carolina, Nash County, Rocky Mount Township, vol. 15, E.D. 170, sheet 17a, lines 26–30. They had two children, James and John.

Leonard's father, John Leonard, was born on July 23, 1882, in Nash County. In 1902, John married Emma Sessoms. Marriage Licenses, Edgecombe County, 1901–03, reel 153, John Leonard to Emma Sessoms, June 22, 1902, Tarboro, North Carolina. The second oldest of Lena and Daniel Sessoms's four children, Emma Sessoms came from one of Rocky Mount's most prominent black families. She received her education from a private school in Norfolk, Virginia. In 1885, her mother, Lena Sessoms, was one of the founding members of the St. James Baptist Church. Lena Cox interview, 21 April 1995; St. James Baptist Church, Centennial Edition: 1885–1985, 12; Lisa Angel, "The Appointment of a Black Postmaster, Rocky Mount, North Carolina, 1897–98" (senior honors essay, University of North Carolina, 1990), 51 (recognizing the Sessoms family as members of the black elite).

Tracing Leonard's roots back to a specific white family is an inexact science. Black families were not included by name in the census until 1870. The 1850 and 1860 Slave Schedules list slaves only under their respective owners according to age, sex, and skin color. Rounding out the picture are the wills and estates from Franklin County, North Carolina, located at the North Carolina State Archives in Raleigh.

In 1870, Leonard's great-grandparents, Thomas and Manerva Leonard, were forty-six and forty years old, respectively. 1870 Census. See supra. By 1880, Thomas had died and Manerva was listed as forty-five years old. 1880 Census. See supra. Exactly how old Thomas and Manerva were remains somewhat of a mystery. In 1850, Thomas would have been about twenty-six years old and Manerva between twenty and twenty-five.

Frederick Leonard is the white farmer who probably owned Thomas and Manerva. An eighty-three-year-old farmer in 1850, Frederick Leonard owned more slaves than any other Leonard in Franklin County. Bureau of the Census, *Seventh Census of the United States—Population*, 1850 North Carolina Free Schedules, Franklin Country, roll 630, unofficial page 766, line 5; id., 1850 North Carolina Slave Schedules, Franklin County, roll 652, unofficial page 649, col. 1, line 42, col. 2, line 1.

In 1850, the slave schedule for Franklin County lists Frederick Leonard as owning a thirty-year-old female slave and a twenty-nine-year-old male slave. 1850 Slave Schedule. Frederick's neighboring white relative, Bennett H. Leonard, owned a twenty-five-year-old male mulatto slave. Id., at roll 652, unofficial page 653, col. 1, lines 11–12. Frederick's son, Frederick Jr., owned a twenty-year-old female slave as well as her two infant children. Id., roll 652, unofficial page 609, col. 2, lines 23–25. Any of these slaves could have been Thomas and Manerva Leonard.

Frederick Leonard died in 1856. His will somewhat clarifies the picture. An inventory of his estate includes a slave with a name that looks like Manerva and a slave named Tom whose name is crossed out. Franklin County Wills and Estates, Box 039.508.46, Folder Frederick Leonard 1856, North Carolina State Archives, Raleigh, North Carolina. An "Account of Sale of Negroes" belonging to Frederick's estate describes the sale of a "woman Manerv [unclear] and children" for $1,230.00 to Dr. E. Lawrneo [unclear]. Id., Folder Frederick Leonard 1816. No other antebellum wills and estates from Franklin County's white families named Leonard include slaves with names Manerva, Tom, or Thomas.

In 1860, the Franklin County Slave Schedule lists no male slaves in their early to middle thirties belonging to someone named Leonard. Frederick Leonard, presumably Frederick Sr.'s son, owned a thirty-four-year-old female slave. Bureau of the Census, *Eighth Census of the United States*, 1860 North Carolina Slave Schedules, Franklin County, roll 922, page 5, col. 2, line 2. Bennett Leonard also owned a thirty-five-year-old female slave. Id., roll 922, page 7, col. 2, line 28. According to Frederick Leonard's will, however, Manerva Leonard had been sold in 1856.

It remains unclear which white farmer named Leonard in Franklin County, North Carolina, owned Thomas and Manerva. Frederick Leonard probably owned them at some point because slaves named Tom (crossed out) and Manerva (different spelling) appeared in his will and estate. Frederick owned more slaves, about two dozen, than any other white Leonard in Franklin County. He also seems to have given many slaves to his children even before his death. Thus, Frederick Leonard or one of his children most likely owned Buck Leonard's great-grandparents, Thomas and Manerva Leonard.

100. Leonard, *The Black Lou Gehrig*, 6–7; John Holway, *Voices from the Great Black Baseball Leagues* (New York: Da Capo Press, 1975; rev. ed, 1990), 254; Lena Cox interview, 29 August 1992.

Leonard's two older sisters died young. In 1937, his oldest sister, Fannie, died of carbon monoxide poisoning while house-sitting. Lena Cox interview, 21 April 1995. In March 1922, Leonard's other older sister, Willie B., died of tuberculosis while away at college. Id.; North Carolina Death Certificates, Willie B. Leonard, 20 March 1922, vol. 681, p. 323, S. 123.131, North Carolina State Archives, Raleigh, North Carolina. The death certificate said Willie died of "pulmonary tuberculosis" on March 20, 1922, at 9:30 A.M. She was eighteen years, six months, and twenty-nine days old and listed as a "student."

101. George A. Kennedy, "A Brief History of the Atlantic Coast Line R.R." (1991) in Atlantic Coast Line Railroad Records, No. 4572, Southern Historical Collection, Wilson Library, University of North Carolina, Chapel Hill, North Carolina; Angel, "The Appointment of a Black Postmaster, Rocky Mount, North Carolina," 4.

102. Cox interviews, 29 August 1992 and 21 April 1995; Leonard, *The Black Lou Gehrig*, 3.

103. In 1910, John and Emma Leonard borrowed $625 plus interest to purchase a 48 1/3-by-150-foot tract of land. Deed of Trust, John and Emma Leonard to J. P. Bunn, Trustee, 19 May 1910, book 182, page 184, Nash County Registry, Nashville, North Carolina. They built a four-room, wood-frame house (along with a bathroom and a front and back porch) in the 500 block of Raleigh Road. During the next six years, John paid off the loan in full. Id. The 1930 census lists the house as owned by Emma and worth about one thousand dollars. Bureau of the Census, *Fifteenth Census of the United States: 1930—Population*, North Carolina, Nash County, Rocky Mount Township, vol. 78, E.D. 33, sheet 9a, line 34.

104. Leonard, *The Black Lou Gehrig*, 7–8. The 1930 census lists Leonard as a "laborer" at the "rail road shop." 1930 Census, vol. 78, E.D. 33, sheet 9a, line 35.

105. Cox interview, 5 August 1992. 1930 census, however, says that the Leonard family did not own a radio. 1930 Census, vol. 78, E.D. 33, sheet 9a, line 34. The census taker may have been mistaken (none of the families on the block owned radios), or Leonard may have purchased the radio after 1930.

106. Leonard, *The Black Lou Gehrig*, 4–5.

107. Cox interview, 5 August 1992.

108. Herman was two years younger than Leonard, and Charlie was five years younger than Leonard. In his autobiography, Leonard wrote that he got his nickname from Charlie. Leonard, *The Black Lou Gehrig*, 4. Lena, however, said it was from Herman. Cox interview, 29 August 1992. The general story is confirmed by an article in the Rocky Mount newspaper. *Rocky Mount Sunday Telegram*, 9 July 1972, 2D.

109. The 1920 and 1930 censuses list Emma's occupation as "laundry." *Bureau of the Census, Fourteenth Census of the United States: 1920—Population*, North Carolina, Nash County, Rocky Mount Township, vol. 61, E.D. 86, sheet 22a, line 12; *1930 Census*, vol. 78, E.D. 33, sheet 9a, line 34. It was common in those days, before the washing machine replaced the washboard, for black women in Rocky Mount to do the laundry of white families to make extra money. Cox interview, 21 April 1995.

Emma Leonard was well educated (see supra note 99) and active in her community. During the 1940s, she served as treasurer and finance chair of the NAACP's Rocky Mount chapter. NAACP Papers, Moorland-Spingarn Research Center, Manuscript Division, Howard University, Washington, D.C., box 78-53, folder 1236; C. D. Leonard, taped interview with author, Oxon Hill, Md., 26 December 1994.

110. Cox interview, 5 August 1992.

111. Leonard, *The Black Lou Gehrig*, 11–12.

112. Rob Ruck, *Sandlot Seasons: Sport in Black Pittsburgh* (Urbana, Ill.: University of Illinois Press, 1993), 39–46.

113. Leonard, *The Black Lou Gehrig*, 12.

114. Buck Leonard interview, 20 July 1992; Leonard, *The Black Lou Gehrig*, 12–13.

115. Cox interview, 21 April 1995; C. D. Leonard interview, 26 December 1994. Before entering college, Charlie worked as bootblack at a local barbershop. *1930 Census*, vol. 36, E.D. 33, sheet 9a, line 37.

116. *The Brick Bugle* (Bricks, N.C.), February 1931, vol II, no. 5; C. D. Leonard interview, 26 December 1994.

117. Leonard, *The Black Lou Gehrig*, 13–14.

118. Years later, Leonard confessed that he did not believe Charlie's ankle was broken. Buck Leonard interview, 12 October 1992. Lena Cox vividly remembered this incident but claimed that Leonard was playing for Norfolk and Charlie was playing for Wilson. Cox interview, 5 August 1992. Lena recalled the game as being in the late 1920s because she left Rocky Mount in 1932. Cox interview, 29 August 1992. Leonard, however, did not begin playing for Portsmouth (which is right next to Norfolk) until April 1933. Buck (Portsmouth) and Charlie (Rocky Mount) clashed on opposing teams in 1933, but Charlie did not break his ankle that season.

119. "Rocky Mount Elks in Training," *Norfolk Journal and Guide*, 18 April 1931, 12.

120. Leonard, *The Black Lou Gehrig*, 17.

121. *Washington Tribune*, 23 June 1923, 5; id., 7 July 1923, 5; id., 11 August 1923, 4. Lacy also pitched in relief in the Buffaloes' 12–1 loss to the Piedmonts. Id., 18 August 1923, 4. In his autobiography, Lacy recalled his first sandlot experience as being with another D.C. team, the Teddy Bears. Lacy said he didn't like the "drinking, womanizing and other carousing that was going on" and he switched to the LeDroit Tigers. Lacy, *Fighting for Fairness*, 25–26. The *Washington Tribune*, however, indicates that Lacy played for the Buffalo A.C. before playing for the Tigers.

122. *Washington Tribune*, 1 September 1923, 4.

123. "Mantyne Harris Pitches Brilliant Games as Tigers Lose to Lincolns," *Washington Tribune*, 12 August 1922, 4.

124. A year after proclaiming themselves the 1922 city sandlot champions, the LeDroit Tigers applied for membership in one of the top two black professional leagues, the Eastern Colored League. "LeDroit Tigers Claim Championship," *Washington Tribune*, 30 September 1922, 4; Lanctot, *Fair Dealing*, 98–99. The Tigers' application was denied, but the team continued to send players to the black professional ranks. *Washington Tribune*, 16 June 1923, 5; id., 23 June 1923, 5.

125. *Washington Tribune*, 1 September 1923, 4.

126. Ibid., 22 September 1923, 4.

127. Lacy wrote: "My own baseball career ran simultaneously with high school, college, and my writing career, starting, as I've indicated, at Dunbar and Armstrong high schools and continuing on into the years when I was writing for the *Washington Tribune* and the *Afro-American*." Lacy, *Fighting for Fairness*, 25. Tom Callahan said Lacy wrote for a nickel an inch. Tom Callahan, "For 70 Years, Restlessness, Curios-

ity Drove Sam Lacy to Chronicle History," *Washington Post*, 21 June 1991, D3. Peter Sheingold, however, said it was twenty-five cents an inch. Peter M. Sheingold, "In Black and White: Sam Lacy's Campaign to Integrate Baseball" (undergraduate thesis, Hampshire College, 1992), 23.

128. Lacy, *Fighting for Fairness*, 23.

129. *Washington Tribune*, 5 July 1924, 4. Id., 2 August 1924, 4. Lacy lost again the following week. Id., 9 August 1924, 4.

130. Black baseball's finest players of that era, including John Henry Lloyd, Dick Lundy, and Oliver Marcelle, played for the Bacharachs. In 1926 and 1927, the Bacharachs captured the Eastern Colored League championship before falling to the Negro National League's Chicago American Giants in black baseball's World Series. Robert Peterson, *Only the Ball Was White* (New York: Oxford University Press, 1970; rev. ed., 1992), 67–68; Lanctot, *Fair Dealing*, 40, 140, 245 n. 17; Dick Clark and Larry Lester, eds., *The Negro Leagues Book* (Cleveland: SABR, 1994), 25–26; Rogosin, *Invisible Men*, 28; John B. Holway, *Blackball Stars: Negro League Pioneers* (Westport, Conn.: Meckler, 1988), 32, 136.

Two years after forming in 1916, the Bacharach Giants folded. In 1919, several black New Yorkers revived the team as the New York Bacharach Giants. The original Atlantic City Bacharachs re-formed in 1922 and merged with the New York Bacharachs the following year. Lanctot, *Fair Dealing*, 75, 96; Neil Lanctot, E-mail, 22 November 2000 (on file with author). After the Bacharachs joined the ECL in 1923, they folded again in 1929 before being revived two years later in Philadelphia.

131. Steve Katz, "Sam Lacy Traveled Rough Road with Black Athletes," *Baltimore Sun*, 17 August 1980, C5; Patrick Ercolano, "He Went to Bat for Blacks," *Baltimore Sun Magazine*, 6 April 1986, 15; Eunetta Boone, "The Write Stuff," *Baltimore Evening Sun*, 18 August 1989, C1; Mark G. Judge, "Writing the Good Fight," *Washington City Paper*, 17 May 1991, 29; Sheingold, "In Black and White," 23.

At least two interviewers, about ten years apart, wrote that Lacy played for both the Bacharachs and the Baltimore Black Sox. *Baltimore Sun*, 17 August 1980, C5; *Washington City Paper*, 17 May 1991, 29. These interviewers may have confused the Baltimore Black Sox with another sandlot team that Lacy played for during the 1920s, the Washington Black Sox.

Three of the best profiles of Lacy do not mention that he played for the Bacharachs. Fimrite, "Black Crusader," 90 ("He also played semipro ball in the all-black leagues in and around Washington, often against such stars of the Negro leagues as Oscar Charleston, Biz Mackey, John Henry Lloyd, and Martin Dihigo"); Callahan, "For 70 Years," D3 ("A middle infielder with a middle infielder's quick intellect [but unfortunately, a bat as light as balsa], Sam knocked about semi-pro ball on the periphery of the Negro leagues in and around Washington"); Jim Reisler, *Black Writers/Black Baseball* (Jefferson, N.C.: McFarland, 1994), 11 ("Later, he played semi-pro baseball in and around Washington, competing against some of the stars of the Negro league ball like Martin Dihigo and John Henry Lloyd"). Although both Callahan and Reisler may have relied on Fimrite's profile, the cautiousness of these three writers reinforces that Lacy may not have played with the Bacharachs.

132. Lacy interview, 15 July 1992. Lacy told at least one other interviewer the same thing. *Washington City Paper*, 17 May 1991, 29.

133. *Washington Tribune*, 16 June 1923, 5.
134. "Ready to Start '23 Home Campaign in Atlantic City," *Atlantic City Daily Press*, 30 May 1923, in Black Baseball Notebook, Heston Collection, Atlantic City Free Public Library.
135. Although Lacy implied to several reporters that he was a Howard graduate, he has attempted to correct the error both in the newspaper and in his autobiography. "To please my mother, I went to Howard University for a year," Lacy wrote. "After that, it was back to concentrating on the sports world." Lacy, *Fighting for Fairness*, 24. See also "Prime Time: To Right the Record," *Baltimore Afro-American*, 27 June 1998 and 3 July 1998, A12 ("I *did not* receive a degree [of any kind] from Howard University.") (emphasis in original).
136. Lacy, *Fighting for Fairness*, 23.
137. Ibid., 25.
138. Lacy wrote:

    > With these [sandlot] teams, as well as with the Bachrach [sic] Giants, I got to play against professional teams such as the Hilldales [sic], New York Cubans, Philadelphia Stars, Baltimore Black Sox, the Cuban Giants out of Havana, and the House of David.
    > . . . Among the professionals I played *against* were Dick Lundy, Pop Lloyd, Nip Winters, Stringbean Williams, Dick Seay, Pat [sic] Lloyd, John Henry Lloyd, Scrip Lee, and Jim West.

    Ibid. (emphasis added). This passage also mentions three variations of John Henry Lloyd's name.
139. Ibid., 25.
140. Lloyd played for the Bacharachs in 1922, joined the Hilldale Club in 1923, and then returned to the Bacharachs from 1924 to 1926. Lanctot, *Fair Dealing*, 102–3; Clark and Lester, eds., *The Negro Leagues Book*, 48, 86, 88. In 1925, Lloyd also managed the Bacharachs. Although a shortstop for most of his career, Lloyd made room for fellow shortstop Dick Lundy in 1924 and 1925 by playing second base. Lanctot, *Fair Dealing*, 134; Clark and Lester, eds., *The Negro Leagues Book*, 86, 89; Holway, *Blackball Stars*, 45. Lacy described Lloyd as a second baseman.

     The forty-one-year-old Lloyd would have been substantially older than the nineteen-year-old Lacy, also consistent with Lacy's description of the team. The man affectionately known as Pop, however, was not a drinker, womanizer, or carouser. Pop Lloyd never even swore (his expletives included "Dad Burn!" or "Dad Gum It!" or "Gosh bob it!"). Lanctot, *Fair Dealing*, 134; Holway, *Blackball Stars*, 45. Lacy may have been right about the low moral character of many of his Bacharach teammates, but Pop Lloyd's only fault would have been preventing Lacy from playing second base.

     In revealing his all-time black baseball team for author Jim Reisler, Lacy included Lloyd as well as three other members of the 1925 Bacharachs: shortstop Dick Lundy, third baseman Oliver Marcelle, and pitcher Andrew "Stringbean" Williams. Jim Reisler, letter to author, 20 June 1996 (on file with author).
141. One of the few columns Lacy wrote about his professional baseball experiences involved a breezy day in Connecticut, presumably in 1929, when Lacy's curveball wouldn't curve and his fastball, never particularly swift, wasn't fast. Sam Lacy, "Looking 'Em Over," *Washington Afro-American*, 13 July 1940, 23.

142. "Cyclone Williams Due to Wear Uniform of Bees," *Atlantic City Daily Press*, 11 April 1925, 17; "Marcell [sic] Comes Back to Bees in Big Trade," id., 9 May 1925, 18; "Marcell [sic] Voted Off B-Giants," id., 16 June 1925, 20; "Bees Purchase New Players," id., 29 June 1925, 16; "B-Giants Play Melrose Today," id., 1 July 1925, 18; "Bees to Visit Camden Today," id., 18 July 1925, 25; "Bacharach Giants Conquer Bloomer Girls in Comedy," id., 4 September 1925, 20; "B-Giants End Season Here," id., 18 September 1925, 19; "Bees to Close 1925 Season," id., 26 September 1925, 12; "Bacharach Giants Close Season; Lose to Cubans," id., 1 October 1925, 11; "Giants Trade Star Players," *Atlantic City Sunday Press*, 21 June 1925, 10-N.

143. In 1926, Lacy allowed seven runs and six walks before the Tigers hit for him in the ninth. *Washington Tribune*, 23 April 1926, 6. Of Lacy's 1927 relief appearance, the *Tribune* wrote:

    "Three local hurlers, Smith, Lacy and Bland were unable to stem the attack of the invaders."

    Id., 26 August 1927, 5.

144. *Washington Tribune*, 10 September 1926, 6.

145. The 1926 Washington, D.C., city directory lists Samuel H. Lacy as a student living at his father's house at 1719 Fifteenth, NW. 1926 District of Columbia City Directory, 919.

146. *Washington Tribune*, 22 October 1926, 6.

147. *Washington Tribune*, 3 December 1926, 6.

148. Lacy, *Fighting for Fairness*, 24.

149. Ibid., 27. Their marriage is not recorded in the extensive marriage records of the District of Columbia. Lacy may have been married in nearby Maryland, which was known for its shorter waiting period. Sam and Alberta were twenty-three and twenty-one, respectively, when they married. *1930 Census*, roll 300, E.D. 287, sheet 5a, lines 17-18. The 1930 census lists Alberta as a "waitress" at a "tea room." Id., line 18. The 1932 city directory lists her as a "waiter." 1932 District of Columbia City Directory, 951. The next two city directories list her as a "water girl" at Woodward and Lothrop, a local department store. 1933 City Directory, 937; 1934 City Directory, 943.

150. *Washington Tribune*, 9 September 1927, 5.

151. *Washington Tribune*, 5 July 1929, 5. Lacy's autobiography mentions that while he was working as a hotel waiter, an all-white team from Connecticut invited him to pitch for them and billed him as an Algonquin Indian. Lacy, *Fighting for Fairness*, 20.

152. Lacy could have played for the Bacharachs during this period. He was absent from the *Atlantic City Daily Press* box scores and coverage of the 1929 Bacharachs. See, e.g., "Bees to Take on Cuban Nine," *Atlantic City Daily Press*, 1 June 1929, 20; "Bees, Grays Clash Today," id., 26 June 1929, 12; "B-Giants Split Twin Bill with Grays; 4–5, 11–2," id., 28 June 1929, 16.

    In his interview with me, Lacy claimed to have played for the Bacharachs in the early 1930s—1930 through 1932. Although the Bacharachs had folded after the 1929 season, ballpark owner Harry Passon reorganized them in 1931 as a Philadelphia-based outfit. *Philadelphia Tribune*, 18 June 1931, 10. John Henry Lloyd, at the age of forty-seven, joined the Bacharachs as a first baseman/manager at the beginning of 1931 and returned only as a first baseman in 1932. A sketchy Bacharachs' box score from April 1931 lists "Lloyd" at first base and "Payne" at shortstop. Id., 23 April 1931, 11. This is consistent with Lacy's recollection of Lloyd and Payne as his Bacharach teammates. At the start of the 1932 season, a review of the Bacharachs' roster in the *Philadelphia Tribune*, a black weekly newspaper, included Lloyd at first base as well as a "Howard Lacey, of Newport News, Va., shortstop." Id., 14 April 1932, 11.

Several factors weigh against Sam Lacy's having played with the Philly-based Bacharachs during the early 1930s. First, the chances of Lacy beginning his professional career with the Bacharachs at age twenty-six in 1931 would have been extremely slim. The new Bacharachs played the same high-caliber professional baseball as the old Atlantic City–based outfit. The Bacharachs' players from 1931 and 1932 included future Hall of Famers Lloyd and Norman "Turkey" Stearnes (briefly) as well as Negro League stalwarts such as manager/outfielder Otto Briggs, pitcher Jesse "Nip" Winters, and third baseman Obie Lackey. Id., 18 June 1931, 10; id., 14 April 1932, 11. This was a top-flight black baseball team, not a weak semipro club—the jump from the D.C. sandlots would have been enormous. Second, the 1930 census and city directories from 1931 and 1932 list Lacy first as a reporter for the *Washington Tribune* and then as a mail carrier for the U.S. post office. He could not have retained these jobs while taking the summers off to play for the Bacharachs, especially during the depths of the Great Depression. Third, Lacy repeatedly claimed to have played for the Atlantic City Bacharach Giants, not for the Philadelphia-based version. If he ever played for the Bacharachs, which is doubtful, he would have played for them when they played in Atlantic City and shortly after his 1924 season with the LeDroit Tigers.

153. Lacy, *Fighting for Fairness*, 27.
154. The 1930 census lists him as a "reporter" for a "newspaper." *1930 Census*, roll 300, E.D. 287, sheet 5a, line 17. Although no occupation is listed for him in the 1929 and 1930 local city directories, the 1931 city directory lists him as a "reporter" for the "Washington Tribune Publishing Co." 1931 District of Columbia City Directory, 976. The 1932 city directory, however, lists him as postal carrier. 1932 District of Columbia City Directory, 951.
155. 1932 District of Columbia City Directory, 951; 1933 District of Columbia City Directory, 937. He played for the Post Office baseball team and even made the *Tribune's* 1933 All-Star Department Baseball Team as a right fielder. *Washington Tribune*, 14 September 1933, 12; id., 7 September 1933, 12. In 1933 and 1934, Lacy pitched for the Deanwood Athletic Club as well as serving as the player-manager for a local sandlot team known as the Hillsdale Athletic Club. Id., 14 June 1934, 12; id., 21 June 1934, 12; *Washington Afro-American*, 15 September 1934, 21. The Hillsdale A.C. should not be confused with the Philadelphia-based Hilldale Club, one of the best black professional teams from 1910 to 1932. Lanctot, *Fair Dealing*, 2. In 1935, he played for a sandlot team called the Forty Elks. *Washington Tribune*, 3 August 1935, 12.
156. *Washington Tribune*, 27 June 1933, 12.
157. Social economist Gunnar Myrdal observed: "In railroad service, there were once a few Negro engineers, and Negroes long held a practical monopoly as firemen. But during the last generation [the 1930s] they have been gradually displaced even from those 'Negro Jobs.'" Gunnar Myrdal, *An American Dilemma: The Negro Problem and Modern Democracy* (New York: Harper and Brothers, 1944), 282.

158. Leonard, *The Black Lou Gehrig*, 7–8.

159. Ibid., 8–9, 12.

160. Ibid., 17–18.

161. Contrary to many accounts of his early career, Leonard never played for a team called the Portsmouth Firefighters. See, e.g., Clark and Lester, eds., *The Negro Leagues Book*, 46. Before the start of the 1933 season, an ownership dispute had forced Abram Daughtry to change the name from the Firefighters to Daughtry's Black Revels. Leonard, *The Black Lou Gehrig*, 17–18.

162. Daughtry had signed several North Carolinians, including Leonard, pitcher Harry Sledge, and future Newark Eagles catcher Leon Ruffin. "Blacks Revels Face Black Sox in 2-Game Series; Portsmouth Elks to Play Monday, Also Sewanees," *Norfolk Journal and Guide*, 15 April 1933, 12.

163. "Le Droit Tigers Win Two Games," ibid., 10 June 1933, 12, 15; E. B. Rea, "From the Press Box," ibid., 10 June 1933, 14.

164. Ibid.; E. B. Rea, "Rookie Southpaw Whiffs 11 Black Sox Batters As Mates Lend Good Support," *Norfolk Journal and Guide*, 22 April 1933, 12.

165. Leonard, *The Black Lou Gehrig*, 95.

166. "Leonard suffered his first strikeout of the year in local territory when Ellis called the third strike on him," the *Journal and Guide* reported after nearly a month of play. "Rookie Hurler Is 'Big Shot' In Sunday Victory," *Norfolk Journal and Guide*, 13 May 1933, 12.

167. Leonard, *The Black Lou Gehrig*, 18.

168. Cox interview, 5 August 1992.

169. "Rocky Mt. Blanks Black Revels, 8–0," *Norfolk Journal and Guide*, 20 May 1933, 13.

170. E. B. Rea, "'Buck' Leonard Shines At Bat in 9–0 Victory," ibid., 20 May 1933, 12.

171. The *Norfolk Journal and Guide* described the slow-footed first baseman as the "former Rocky Mount flash." Navy Armstrong, "Slade Performs Brilliantly for Portsmouth Nine," ibid., 17 June 1933, 12.

172. Buck Leonard interview, 27 April 1995.

173. "Stars Divide with Swans," *Norfolk Journal and Guide*, 1 July 1933, 12.

174. *Washington Tribune*, 24 February 1923, 4; Paul Debono, *The Indianapolis ABCs: History of a Premier Team in the Negro Leagues* (Jefferson, N.C.: McFarland, 1997), 32, 95–96, 154–55.

175. Evidently, Abram Daughtry had relinquished control of the Black Revels. Shortly after Leonard had left Portsmouth, the team became known as Gilliam's Black Revels. *Norfolk Journal and Guide*, 8 July 1933, 12.

176. "Half-Pint Allen Limits Sox to 3 Scratches," ibid., 1 July 1933, 12. The next day, Allen and the Stars defeated future Hall of Fame third baseman Ray Dandridge's Albemarle All Stars, 4–0, and then lost, 2–1. In the first game, Dandridge knocked out three hits against the Stars. Dandridge, however, did not join Buck and Charlie on the Ben Taylor's team. "Ben Taylor's Crew Wins and Loses," id., 1 July 1933, 12. Later that season, Taylor's brother, "Candy Jim," while managing the Detroit Stars, bribed Dandridge's father twenty-five dollars to persuade his son to leave Richmond. Dandridge signed with the Detroit Stars for sixty dollars a month, better than Leonard's deal with the Baltimore Stars but equal to Leonard's salary with the Black Revels. James A. Riley, *Dandy, Day and the Devil* (Cocoa, Fla.: James A. Riley, 1987), 22–24.

177. "Ben Liked Them So He Took Two," *Norfolk Journal and Guide*, 1 July 1933, 12.
178. "Ben Taylor Heads New Baltimore Ball Club," *Washington Afro-American*, 4 March 1933, 17. Leonard, *The Black Lou Gehrig*, 19–20; Holway, *Voices*, 254–55.
179. Leonard, *The Black Lou Gehrig*, 21-22; Holway, *Voices*, 255-56.
180. In a late July doubleheader against the Kennett Square (Pa.) sandlot club, Leonard batted cleanup and played first base. He finished 1 for 2 in each game and made an error in the first one. "Taylor's Stars Win Twin Bill," *Washington Afro-American*, 29 July 1933, 21.
181. Leonard, *The Black Lou Gehrig*, 20–21; Holway, *Voices*, 255.
182. Theo Baron, "Balto. Stars Lose 2 Games to Dixie Nine," *Washington Afro-American*, 5 August 1933, 21.
183. Leonard, *The Black Lou Gehrig*, 21–22. Leonard, however, told John Holway that the team had been playing so poorly that it couldn't get any bookings. Holway, *Voices*, 255–56.
184. Leonard, *The Black Lou Gehrig*, 23.
185. Leonard consistently recalled sending Charlie home to get him to junior college. Leonard, *The Black Lou Gehrig*, 23; Holway, *Voices*, 256. Charlie, however, would have already finished at Brick by the summer of 1933 and headed for Talladega, where he attended school at least through 1935.
186. Leonard, *The Black Lou Gehrig*, 25.
187. Lanctot, *Fair Dealing and Clean Playing*, 188 (quoting sportswriter W. Rollo Wilson describing the Brooklyn Royal Giants in 1928 as "an old soldiers' home, a port for foundering hulks which have walloped through the seven seas on baseball"); Ruck, *Sandlot Seasons*, 118 (describing Strong). During the 1930s, the Royal Giants largely played against semipro teams in the New York area. "Royal Giants Face Bronx Carltons," *New York Amsterdam News*, 23 August 1933, 8; "A's Split with Royal Giants," id., 27 September 1933, 8.
188. Leonard, *The Black Lou Gehrig*, 25–28.
189. Ibid., 30; Cox interview, 5 August 1992.
190. "Cum Posey's Pointed Paragraphs," *Pittsburgh Courier*, 6 April 1934, sec. 2, p. 3.
191. Leonard, *The Black Lou Gehrig*, 33-34; Holway, *Voices*, 257.

CHAPTER 2

1. David W. Zang, *Fleet Walker's Divided Heart: The Life of Baseball's First Black Major Leaguer* (Lincoln, Nebr.: University of Nebraska Press, 1995), 47. For Zang's wonderful account of Walker's two years with Toledo, see id., 35–45.
2. Jerry Malloy, "Introduction: Sol White and the Origins of Major League Baseball," in *Sol White's History of Colored Base Ball: With Other Documents on the Early Black Game, 1886–1936*, by Sol White (Lincoln, Nebr.: University of Nebraska Press, 1995), xviii. For a concise history of black baseball, see Jules Tygiel, "Black Ball," in *Total Baseball: The Official Encyclopedia of Major League Baseball*, eds. John Thorn et al. (New York: Total Sports, 1999), 493–509.
3. Rayford W. Logan, *The Negro in American Life and Thought: The Nadir, 1877–1901* (New York: Dial Press, 1954). See also Malloy, "Introduction," in White, *Sol White's Base Ball*, xviii (initially placing the rise of black baseball in the historical context of "the Nadir").

4. Based on an 1887 account in *New York Age*, black baseball historian Jerry Malloy refuted the traditional history that the Cuban Giants originated as hotel waiters who also happened to play baseball. Tygiel, "Black Ball," in *Total Baseball*, eds. Thorn et al., 495; Peterson, *Only the Ball Was White*, 35; White, *Sol White's History of Colored Base Ball*, 8–10. In describing the formation of the Cuban Giants through the merger of the three black sandlot teams, Malloy contended that "any duties the players performed [at the hotel] as waiters, bellhops, porters, and the like were incidental to their primary obligation, which was to entertain the hotel's guests." Malloy, "Introduction," in White, *Sol White's Base Ball*, ix; id., 134–35. Malloy is probably correct given that the *New York Age* article came out two years after the formation of the Cuban Giants; White's original guide was not originally published until 1906.
5. Peterson, *Only the Ball Was White*, 63–70.
6. Lanctot, *Fair Dealing*, 93–102.
7. For another excellent explanation of the development of the Negro Leagues, see Bill James, *The New Bill James Historical Baseball Abstract* (New York: The Free Press, 2001), 166–70.
8. Margaret Byington, *Homestead: The Households of a Mill Town* (New York: Russell Sage Foundation, 1910), 14.
9. Ruck, *Sandlot Seasons*, 11; Curtis Miner and Paul Roberts, "Engineering an Industrial Diaspora: Homestead, 1941," *Pittsburgh History*, 72:1 (Winter 1989), 8.
10. Ruck, *Sandlot Seasons*, 128; Holway, *Blackball Stars*, 302.
11. Ruck, *Sandlot Seasons*, 131.
12. "Press," *The Bulletin Index*, 14 January 1943, 5; David Hepburn, "The Pittsburgh Courier Goes to Bed," *Pittsburgh Courier* (undated story) in Percival Leroy Prattis Papers, Howard University, Manuscript Division, Moorland-Spingarn Research Center, box 144-24, folders 12, 14.
13. Holway, *Blackball Stars*, 302.
14. W. Rollo Wilson, "Down the Long, Long Trail with Cum," *Pittsburgh Courier*, 20 January 1934, sec. 2, p. 4.
15. Ibid.; "In Memoriam: Cumberland Willis Posey," *Negro Baseball Yearbook* (Washington, D.C.: 1946), 3; Harry Keck, "Late Cum Posey Was Heart of Grays," *Pittsburgh Sun-Telegraph*, 26 March 1946, 26; Ruck, *Sandlot Seasons*, 124–27; Holway, *Blackball Stars*, 301–3.
16. Merlisa Lawrence, "Blazing a Trail from the Bluff: Duquesne Gave Black Athletes Push Up Ladder of Success," *Pittsburgh Press*, 7 April 1991, C3.
17. Charley Walker, a part owner of the Grays beginning in 1923, died in 1940. Cum Posey, "Posey's Points," *Pittsburgh Courier*, 12 October 1940, 17. Ruck, *Sandlot Seasons*, 130–31; Holway, *Blackball Stars*, 304.
18. Clark and Lester, eds., *The Negro Leagues Book*, 40; Robert Charles Cottrell, *The Best Pitcher in Baseball: The Life of Rube Foster, Negro League Giant* (New York: New York University Press, 2001), 19. Cottrell said newspapers began referring to Foster as "Rube" during the 1905 season. Id.
19. Peterson, *Only the Ball Was White*, 103. See also Holway, *Blackball Stars*, 8 (describing Foster as "Christy Mathewson, John McGraw, Connie Mack, Al Spalding, and Kenesaw Mountain Landis—great pitcher, manager, owner, league organizer, czar—all rolled into one"); Cottrell, *The Best Pitcher in Baseball*, 184–90.

20. Peterson, *Only the Ball Was White*, 131.
21. Ruck, *Sandlot Seasons*, 131.
22. Holway, *Voices*, 224, 264.
23. Sam Lacy, "Looking 'Em Over," *Washington Afro-American*, 24 August 1940, 23.
24. This story first appeared in Robert Peterson's groundbreaking book on black base-
    ball, promulgated by Grays third baseman Judy Johnson, who claimed to have been
    the Grays' manager in 1929 who "discovered" Gibson by calling him out of the
    grandstand when Smokey Joe Williams was pitching against the Monarchs. Peter-
    son, *Only the Ball Was White*, 162–66. The Grays' longtime outfielder and man-
    ager, Vic Harris, discredited Johnson's claim about discovering Gibson. Harris
    pointed out that Johnson was not the team's manager (it was still Cum Posey). Har-
    ris wrote: "In 1930 when Josh was gotten from the Pittsburgh playground Judy was
    captain part of that season." Letter from Vic Harris to Art Carter, 8 March 1971, box
    1, folder 5, Art Carter Papers, Manuscript Division, Moorland-Spingarn Research
    Center, Howard University. Historian John Holway cast additional doubt on John-
    son's story by claiming to have found the box score from Gibson's reputed first game
    against the Monarchs, which was in 1930 and showed the Grays' pitcher as Lefty
    Williams. John Holway, *Josh and Satch* (Westport, Conn.: Meckler, 1991), 23.

    William Brashler, Gibson's first biographer, argued that the story was only "par-
    tially true." Gibson's first game was not July 25 against the Monarchs, and he was
    not called out of the stands. Brashler said that catcher Buck Ewing hurt his finger
    against the Dormont club; the Grays temporarily inserted Vic Harris behind the
    plate; and Gibson, playing across town at Ammon Field for the Crawford Colored
    Giants, arrived via taxi in time to take over the catching duties. According to one
    of Posey's own columns, Posey had "contacted Gibson and told him to be ready at
    any time." William Brashler, *Josh Gibson: A Life in the Negro Leagues* (New York:
    Harper and Row, 1978), 22–24.

    Gibson biographer Mark Ribowsky wrote that Gibson was in Ingomar, Penn-
    sylvania, playing for the Crawfords the night that Ewing hurt his finger, but that
    Gibson debuted for the Grays later that weekend against the Monarchs. Ribowsky,
    however, confirmed through box scores and oral interviews with Harold Tinker
    that Gibson came out of the grandstand and that he replaced Ewing midgame.
    Mark Ribowsky, *The Power and the Darkness: The Life of Josh Gibson in the Shad-
    ows of the Game* (New York: Simon and Schuster, 1996), 41–43.

    Wherever the truth lies, Gibson began his Negro League career with the Grays
    in July 1930. The eighteen-year-old Gibson initially took over the catching duties
    from the injured Ewing and eventually earned the role as the Grays' primary back-
    stop and chief batting threat.
25. W. Rollo Wilson, "Grays Win Eastern World Series," *Pittsburgh Courier*, 6 Octo-
    ber 1930, sec. 2, p. 5.
26. "Homestead Grays Win Title As Champions of the East in 10 Games with Lin-
    colns," *New York Age*, 4 October 1930, 6. A third account, contradicting the other
    two eyewitness accounts and Gibson himself (see infra text note 28), claimed that
    "Gibson drove the ball into the center field bleachers on the first bounce for a
    home run. . . ." "That Last Game Saturday," *New York Amsterdam News*, 1 Octo-
    ber 1930, 12.

326

27. W. Rollo Wilson, "They Could Make the Big Leagues," *The Crisis: A Record of the Darker Races* 41:10 (October 1934), 305.

28. "Posey's Points," *Pittsburgh Courier*, 2 April 1938, 17.

29. Ibid.

30. Negro League historian John Holway interviewed three eyewitnesses from that 1930 contest: Judy Johnson and Jake Stephens of the Grays and Bill Yancey of the Lincoln Giants. Based on these accounts, Holway concluded that Gibson hit the ball nearly 500 feet into the distant left-field bullpen. Holway, *Josh and Satch*, 31–34; John B. Holway, *The Complete Book of the Negro Leagues: The Other Half of Baseball History* (Fern Park, Fla.: Hastings House Publishers, 2001), 268–69. See also Brashler, *Josh Gibson*, 29–30 (discussing the Yankee Stadium homer).

31. W. Rollo Wilson, "Grays Win Eastern World Series," *Pittsburgh Courier*, 6 October 1930, sec. 2, p. 5.

32. "Posey's Points," *Pittsburgh Courier*, 2 April 1938, 17.

33. "Cum Posey's Pointed Paragraphs," 7 March 1936, sec. 2, p. 4.

34. "In Memoriam: Cumberland Willis Posey," *Negro Baseball Yearbook* (Washington, D.C.: 1946), 3; Harry Keck, "Late Cum Posey Was Heart of Grays," *Pittsburgh Sun-Telegraph*, 26 March 1946, 26.

35. Lanctot, *Fair Dealing*, 215–17.

36. Peterson, *Only the Ball Was White*, 92.

37. For the best profile of Gus Greenlee, see Ruck, *Sandlot Seasons*, 137–69. See also James Bankes, *The Pittsburgh Crawfords: The Lives and Times of Black Baseball's Most Exciting Team* (Dubuque, Iowa: Wm. C. Brown Publisher, 1991), 91–99.

38. In 1932, Posey rejected Greenlee's entry into the East-West League because Greenlee refused Posey's terms: a five-year contract with the league and installing Posey's brother, Seward ("See"), as the team's manager. Ruck, *Sandlot Seasons*, 155. Perhaps Posey's harsh terms reflected his bitterness over losing many of his players.

39. W. Rollo Wilson, "Sports Shots: Press Box & Ringside," *Pittsburgh Courier*, 17 September 1932, sec. 2, p. 4.

40. Larry Lester, *Black Baseball's National Showcase: The East-West All-Star Game, 1933–1953* (Lincoln, Nebr.: University of Nebraska Press, 2001), 1–7.

41. Greenlee's NNL initially included the Grays, but he kicked them out at midseason for raiding players. The Grays claimed to have left the new NNL during the 1933 season because independent baseball was more profitable than contributing 5 percent of all gross profits to the league. Cum Posey, "Independent Ball Only Hope for Survival," *Pittsburgh Courier*, 8 July 1933, sec. 2, p. 4. League officials contended that the Grays stole two players, third baseman Jimmy Binder and outfielder John "Big Boy" Williams, from the Detroit Stars, and that they canceled league games without proper notice. John L. Clark, "Baseball's Future Lies in Organization," *Pittsburgh Courier*, 22 July 1933, sec. 2, p. 5.

42. Peterson, *Only the Ball Was White*, 93.

43. Although Jackson helped Posey meet the team's payroll at the end of the 1933 season, Posey formally announced Jackson as the team's co-owner at the beginning of 1934. Charles Walker was listed as the Grays' president, Posey as secretary, and Jackson as treasurer. "Cum Posey's Pointed Paragraphs," *Pittsburgh Courier*, 28 April 1934, sec. 2, p. 5; Ruck, *Sandlot Seasons*, 171.

44. "Posey's Pointed Paragraphs," *Pittsburgh Courier*, 26 May 1934, sec. 2, p. 5; "League Sec'y Scores Posey for Tactics," *Pittsburgh Courier*, 2 June 1934, sec. 2, p. 7.
45. Leonard, *The Black Lou Gehrig*, 35.
46. Ibid.
47. Peterson, *Only the Ball Was White*, 14; Holway, *Voices*, 257–58; Leonard, *The Black Lou Gehrig*, 34–35.
48. Leonard, *The Black Lou Gehrig*, 36–37.
49. Leonard's "Joe Scott" story is true. In the third week of April, Posey touted "Scott, a left-handed first baseman from Indianapolis" as the team's starter. "Grays in Drills at Wheeling Ball Park," *Pittsburgh Courier*, 21 April 1934, sec. 2, p. 5. In the following week's paper, Posey promoted Leonard for the job. "Cum Posey's Pointed Paragraphs," *Pittsburgh Courier*, 28 April 1934, sec. 2, p. 5.
50. "Grays Gain Edge Over Philly on Eastern Trip," *Pittsburgh Courier*, 2 June 1934, sec. 2, p. 6.
51. W. Rollo Wilson, "Sport Shots," *Pittsburgh Courier*, 9 June 1934, sec. 2, p. 4.
52. Chester Washington, "Grays Win Second Holiday Tilt, 4–3," *Pittsburgh Courier*, 7 July 1934, 1; William G. Nunn, "Noted Speed-Ball Ace of Craw Fans 17 As Grays Are Beaten, 4–0," *Pittsburgh Courier*, 7 July 1934, 1.
53. "Baltimore to Battle Grays; Ft. Wayne Mixed Club Coming," *Pittsburgh Courier*, 28 July 1934, sec. 2, p. 5.; Chester L. Washington, "'Smoky Joe' Fans First Batter; Ft. Wayne Loses," *Pittsburgh Courier*, 11 August 1934, sec. 2, p. 5.
54. Leonard, *The Black Lou Gehrig*, 38.
55. "Cum Posey's Pointed Paragraphs," *Pittsburgh Courier*, 3 November 1934, sec. 2, p. 4.
56. W. Rollo Wilson, "Sport Shots," *Pittsburgh Courier*, 15 September 1934, sec. 2, p. 4.
57. Wilson, "They Could Make the Big Leagues," 305.
58. "There is a totally different class of colored people, who run houses of ill fame and gambling on Sixth Avenue; a 'sporty' element which is more in evidence and creates for the race an unpleasant notoriety," Margaret Byington wrote of Homestead in 1910. "These people frequently appear in police courts and form a lower element in the town's life." Byington, *Homestead*, 14; Miner and Roberts, "Engineering an Industrial Diaspora," 9, n. 9.
59. "Cum Posey's Pointed Paragraphs," *Pittsburgh Courier*, 28 April 1934, sec. 2, p. 5; "The Grays' Travel-Log," *Pittsburgh Courier*, 2 June 1934, sec. 2, p. 6 (displaying a photograph of the bus); Leonard, *The Black Lou Gehrig*, 126.
60. Leonard, *The Black Lou Gehrig*, 70.
61. Holway, *Voices*, 258.
62. "Lundy to Work Out at Hot Springs," *Pittsburgh Courier*, 6 April 1935, sec. 2, p. 4. The Newark Dodgers and the Grays played each other in Wilson. Cum Posey, "Binder Injured, New Catching 'Find' Unearthed at Grays' Camp," *Pittsburgh Courier*, 13 April 1935, sec. 2, p. 4.
63. Chester Washington, "Sez Ches'," *Pittsburgh Courier*, 26 January 1935, sec. 2, p. 5.
64. William G. Nunn, "Mule Suttles 'Steals' East-West Classic Again," *Pittsburgh Courier*, 17 August 1935, sec. 2, p. 5; Leonard, *The Black Lou Gehrig*, 63.
65. Leonard, *The Black Lou Gehrig*, 64–66; Holway, *The Complete Book of Baseball's Negro Leagues*, 331; "Four Reds Pitchers Fail to Halt Foes," *Pittsburgh Courier*, 7 March 1936, sec. 2, p. 5; "Brown's 3-Base Hit Defeats Leaguers," 14 March 1936, sec.

2, p. 4; "Buck Back From Porto [sic] Rico, Atlanta-Bound," *Pittsburgh Courier*, 28 March 1936, sec. 2, p. 5. In the only box score of those games published in the *Pittsburgh Courier*, Leonard was 0 for 2. "Brown's 3-Base Hit Defeats Leaguers," 14 March 1936, sec. 2, p. 4. Fellow Grays outfielder Vic Harris and pitcher/outfielder Ray Brown played with Leonard on that team.

66. "Posey's Points," *Pittsburgh Courier*, 1 August 1936, sec. 2, p. 5.

67. "Cum Posey's Pointed Paragraphs," *Pittsburgh Courier*, 16 November 1935, sec. 2, p. 5; Cum Posey, "Satchell, Matlock and Leonard Make Posey's All-American Team," *Pittsburgh Courier*, 17 October 1936, sec. 2, p. 6.

68. "'Young Buck' Named Best in the 'Tarheel' State," *Pittsburgh Courier*, 21 September 1935, sec. 2, p. 4.

69. C. D. Leonard interview.

70. Charlie Leonard is not listed in any of the major reference books as having played for the Newark Dodgers, who were purchased by Abe and Effa Manley in 1936 and combined with the Brooklyn Eagles in order to form the Newark Eagles. "Cum Posey's Pointed Paragraphs," and "Black Yankees Bid for Berth in Ass'n Tabled," *Pittsburgh Courier*, 1 February 1936, sec. 2, p. 4; See Clark and Lester, eds., *The Negro Leagues Book*, 115, 117, 119; James A. Riley, *The Biographical Encyclopedia of the Negro Baseball Leagues* (New York: Carroll and Graf, 1994); Peterson, *Only the Ball Was White*. Seldom-used players such as Sam Lacy or Charlie Leonard often did not make the active rosters.

Lena Cox specifically recalled Charlie playing for Newark at Griffith Stadium in the mid-1930s. Lena Cox interview, 5 August 1992. Leonard confirmed her account. Buck Leonard interview, 12 October 1992.

The Newark Dodgers likely took an interest in Charlie while training in Rocky Mount in the spring of 1935. "Lundy to Work Out at Hot Springs," *Pittsburgh Courier*, 6 April 1935, sec. 2, p. 4. The Dodgers as well as the rest of the NNL did not play at Griffith Stadium until the Elite Giants moved their home base to Washington in 1936. Given that Charlie was still at Talladega during the 1935–36 school year and the *Pittsburgh Courier* article at the end of 1935 still referred to Charlie as Wilson's manager, he could not have played for Newark before 1936; 1936 also makes sense because that season the Grays played Newark a week before Newark played the Elite Giants at Griffith Stadium.

This entire incident, however, could have occurred in 1937. The Grays played the Newark Eagles on May 15, 16, and 20; Newark did not play at Washington until June 5, 6, and 7. "National League Revised Schedule," *Pittsburgh Courier*, 8 May 1937, 16. Although either season is possible, Charlie probably played for Newark in 1936 because: (1) many Dodger players who had trained in Rocky Mount in 1935 were still on the team in 1936; (2) the games between Newark, the Washington Elite Giants, and the Grays were only a week apart that season; (3) Charlie more likely played in the Negro Leagues in July and August, when school was definitely out of session, than in early June; and (4) Tex Burnett, Leonard's old teammate, managed the Eagles only in 1936.

71. "Newark Wins 2 of 3 from Elites," *Pittsburgh Courier*, 8 August 1936, sec. 2, p. 4.

72. Lena Cox interview, 5 August 1992.

73. Newark faced the Grays on July 25 and 26, a full six days before the Denver Post tournament began on August 1. "League Data," *Pittsburgh Courier*, 1 August 1936,

sec. 2, p. 5. Thus, before leaving for Denver, Leonard had plenty of time to instruct the Dodgers, a struggling Negro League franchise, to release Charlie. Cum Posey, "Posey's Points," *Pittsburgh Courier*, 24 July 1937, 16.

74. Lena Cox interview, 5 August 1992; C. D. Leonard interview.
75. Lena Cox interview, 5 August 1992.
76. Leonard, *The Black Lou Gehrig*, 23.
77. Buck Leonard interview, 12 October 1992.
78. Lena Cox interview, 5 August 1992.
79. "Grays Get Josh Gibson in Big Deal, Pay $2500," *Pittsburgh Courier*, 27 March 1937, 16. The Grays also received Hall of Fame third baseman Judy Johnson in the deal, but Johnson never reported to the team.
80. Leonard, *The Black Lou Gehrig*, 80; see also Holway, *Voices*, 258.
81. Leonard, *The Black Lou Gehrig*, 80.
82. Wendell Smith, "The Sports Beat," *Pittsburgh Courier*, 27 July 1946, 16.
83. For a terrific article analyzing Gibson's hitting and fielding ability, see John Schulian, "Laughing on the Outside," *Sports Illustrated*, 26 June 2000, 90.
84. "Gibson Gets 2 Homers as Grays Beat Miami, 10–7," *Pittsburgh Courier*, 10 April 1937, 17.
85. "Leonard Leads NNA Batters with .500 Average," *Pittsburgh Courier*, 10 July 1937, 17. These figures represented league games only, not including the team's many barnstorming games.
86. Cum Posey, "Posey's Points," *Pittsburgh Courier*, 31 July 1937, 16.
87. Wendell Smith, "'Smitty's' Sports Spurts," *Pittsburgh Courier*, 23 July 1938, 16. Historian John Holway, who has meticulously attempted to reconstruct Negro League statistics, lists Leonard as finishing the 1937 season with a .356 batting average and ten home runs. Holway, *Complete Book of the Negro Leagues*, 343–44. Holway included only games against teams of "'major league' caliber," excluding games against many white semipro teams. Id., 10. The discrepancy between the two figures further demonstrates the danger of relying solely on statistics to determine a Negro League player's worth. See also Clark and Lester, eds., *The Negro Leagues Book*, 8 (discussing the inherent problems with Negro League statistics).
88. "Grays Leonard Tops NNL Hitters," *Pittsburgh Courier*, 2 July 1938, 16.
89. Wendell Smith, "'Smitty's' Sports Spurts," *Pittsburgh Courier*, 23 July 1938, 16.
90. Ibid.
91. Marriage Licenses 1935–1939, Edgecombe County, Register of Deeds, Tarboro, North Carolina, reel 162, p. 2533.
92. Sarah's parents, according to her December 1937 marriage license with Leonard, are listed as Washington and Cora Lee Wroten, both deceased. Ibid. Leonard's autobiography mistakenly refers to Sarah's hometown as "Jalisbury," which he described as being "about 150 miles from here over on the coast." Leonard, *The Black Lou Gehrig*, 91. The 1900 census lists Washington and Cora Lee Wroten as living in Currituck County, on the northeast coast of North Carolina. Jarvisburg is the only coastal city in Currituck County that resembles "Jalisbury." Born in North Carolina in July 1865, Washington Wroten was a literate farmer who owned his own house. Bureau of the Census, *Twelfth Census of the United States—Population*, North Carolina, Currituck County, Poplar Branch Township, roll 1191, vol. 20, E.D. 36, sheet 6, lines 51–55; 1900 *Index—North Carolina*, W635, roll 166. Nei-

ther Washington nor Cora Wroten are listed in the 1910, 1920, or 1930 census index for North Carolina, nor in the main records for Currituck County.

93. Lena Cox interview, 21 April 1995.
94. Ibid., 5 August 1992.
95. C. D. Leonard interview.
96. Leonard, *The Black Lou Gehrig*, 92.
97. Ibid., 79.
98. John L. Clark, "Grays, Craws to Act on Gibson," *Pittsburgh Courier*, 20 March 1937, 16 ("With all of his ability, he has not developed that 'it' which pulls the cash customers through the turnstiles although he has been publicized as much as Satchel Paige"). Clark was the Crawfords' public relations director.
99. John L. Clark, "The Rise and Fall of Greenlee Field," *Pittsburgh Courier*, 10 December 1938, 17.
100. Leonard claimed that the Grays played between 200 and 210 games a year before he played winter ball in Cuba and Puerto Rico. See Holway, *Voices*, 258.
101. "Team Press Releases," box 2, folder 7, Art Carter Papers.
102. Powell interview, 24 August 1992.
103. Leon Day, taped interview by author, Baltimore, Md., 24 August 1992.
104. Wendell Smith, " 'Smitty's' Sports Spurts," *Pittsburgh Courier*, 11 June 1938, 17.
105. Cum Posey, "Posey's Points," *Pittsburgh Courier*, 10 December 1938, 17. For more on Greenlee Field, see John L. Clark, "The Rise and Fall of Greenlee Field," *Pittsburgh Courier*, 10 December 1938, 17; Ruck, *Sandlot Seasons*, 156–57, 163.
106. Lester, *Black Baseball's National Showcase*, 13.
107. Pittsburgh gained fewer than 8,000 black residents from 1930 (54,983) to 1940 (62,216). Bureau of the Census, *Sixteenth Census of the United States: 1940 — Population* (Washington, D.C.: GPO, 1943), vol. II, pt. 6, tbl. C-35, p. 218. Washington, by contrast, gained more than 50,000 from 1930 (132,068) to 1940 (187,266). Id., vol. II, pt. 1, tbl. 2, p. 956.
108. *Pittsburgh Courier*, 8 July 1939, 17.
109. Ibid. Several weeks later, the *Washington Tribune* reported the rumors. Joe Sewall, "As Athletes Pass," *Washington Tribune*, 22 July 1939, 12.
110. Wendell Smith, "Time Out!" *Pittsburgh Courier*, 29 July 1939, 15.

CHAPTER 3

1. Robert W. Creamer, *Baseball in '41: A Celebration of the "Best Baseball Season Ever" — In the Year America Went to War* (New York: Viking, 1991), 45–46.
2. Morris A. Bealle, *The Washington Senators: An 87-Year History of the World's Oldest Baseball Club and Most Incurable Fandom* (Washington, D.C.: Columbia Publishing Co., 1947), 164.
3. Clark Griffith, as told to J. G. Taylor Spink, "Clark Griffith's 50 Golden Years in the American League: Sale of Son-in-Law Cronin 'Nats' Financial Salvation," *The Sporting News*, 30 July 1952, 12. In his latest historical baseball abstract, Bill James wrote: "The team fell into a 25-year malaise after they sold Joe Cronin in 1934." James, *The New Bill James Historical Baseball Abstract*, 148. Although James correctly observed that the Senators were a good team during Griffith's first twenty years, selling Cronin was not the problem. It was merely symptomatic of the Sen-

ators' inability to compete against teams able to invest in elaborate farm systems, and later on, willingness to sign black players.

Griffith contended that he received $250,000 in the Cronin trade, whereas other sources place the figure at $225,000. Either way, the move indicated that Griffith was strapped for cash.

4. Robert L. Tiemann and Peter Palmer, "Major League Attendance," in *Total Baseball*, eds. Thorn et al., 106–07; Joseph L. Reichler, ed., *The Ronald Encyclopedia of Baseball* (New York: Ronald Press Co., 1962), 240–41.

5. Sam Lacy, "Looking 'Em Over with the Tribune," *Washington Tribune*, 3 August 1935, 12.

6. Ibid.

7. Lacy, *Fighting for Fairness*, 31.

8. *Washington Tribune*, 31 August 1933, 12.

9. *Washington Tribune*, 22 September 1934, 12; Lacy, *Fighting for Fairness*, 31–32.

10. *Washington Tribune*, 23 March 1935, 12.

11. *Washington Tribune*, 17 August 1935, 12.

12. *Washington Tribune*, 19 October 1935, 12; Lacy, *Fighting for Fairness*, 31–32.

13. James Roland Coates Jr., "Gentlemen's Agreement: The 1937 Maryland-Syracuse Football Controversy" (master's thesis, University of Maryland, 1982), ii–iii. For an excellent article on Sidat-Singh, see Luke Cyphers, "Lost Hero: Sidat-Singh a Two-Sport Star, Harlem Renaissance Man," *New York Daily News*, 25 February 2001, 82, and 30 March 2001.

14. *Washington Tribune*, 30 October 1937, 1.

15. Ibid.

16. Coates, "Gentlemen's Agreement," 62–64.

17. *Washington Tribune*, 30 October 1937, 1.

18. Ibid.

19. Ibid., 12.

20. Ibid.

21. Richard Kluger, *Simple Justice: The History of* Brown v. Board of Education *and Black America's Struggle for Equality* (New York: Alfred A. Knopf, 1976), 186–94; Juan Williams, *Thurgood Marshall: American Revolutionary* (New York: Times Books, 1998), 75–79. Williams exploded the myth that Marshall had been rejected by the University of Maryland Law School; indeed, Marshall admitted to both Kluger and Williams that Marshall never even applied to Maryland. Williams, *Thurgood Marshall*, 52–53 and n. 1. In addition to Kluger's excellent recitation of the *Murray* case, see the NAACP Collection, Library of Congress, Washington, D.C.; Mark Tushnet, *The NAACP's Legal Strategy Against Segregated Education, 1925–1950* (Chapel Hill, N.C.: University of North Carolina Press, 1987).

22. *Murray v. Maryland*, 182 A. 590 (1936), 169 Md. 478 (1937).

23. The list of founders included Allison Davis, William Hastie, Belford Lawson, Frank Thorne, Clyde McDuffie, and Howard Fitzhugh. "Theory of the Alliance," Eugene C. Davidson Collection, Moorland-Spingarn Research Center, Manuscript Division, Howard University, Washington, D.C., box 91-1, folder 14, p. 5.

24. "Theory of the Alliance," Eugene C. Davidson Collection, box 91-1, folder 14, p. 4.

25. Ibid., 5–6; Green, *The Secret City*, 229–30.

26. Letter from G. David Houston to Eugene Davidson, 16 July 1938, Eugene C. Davidson Collection, box 91-1, folder 23.

27. Dr. Harold O. Lewis, taped interview by author, Washington, D.C., 19 August 1992.

28. Brown and Lewis, *Washington in the New Era*, 33.
29. Bob Considine and Shirley Povich, "Old Fox: Baseball's Red-Eyed Radical and Archconservative Clark Griffith," *Saturday Evening Post*, 13 April 1940, 127.
30. Ed Fitzgerald, "Clark Griffith: The Old Fox," *Sport* 16:5 (May 1954), 45, 77.
31. Ibid., 45, 70; Considine and Povich, "Old Fox," 127; Clark Griffith, as told to J. G. Taylor Spink, "Clark Griffith's 50 Golden Years," 11; Frederick G. Lieb, "Griffith Canny as Hill Star, Pilot, Owner," *The Sporting News*, 2 November 1955, 11.
32. Considine and Povich, "Old Fox," 129.
33. Anson's autobiography referred to Chicago's 1880s mascot as a "little coon," "darkey," and "no account nigger." Adrian C. Anson, *A Ballplayer's Career* (Chicago: Era, 1900), 148–50.
34. Stovey sat out the game and reportedly "complained of sickness." Peterson, *Only the Ball Was White*, 29; Zang, *Fleet Walker's Divided Heart*, 54–55. In 1883, Anson refused to play against Walker, and the Toledo manager inserted the injured Walker into the game. Peterson, *Only the Ball Was White*, 29; Zang, *Fleet Walker's Divided Heart*, 38–39. Although an 1884 contest between the two teams was canceled, Anson apparently received future assurances from Toledo that neither Walker nor any other black player would take the field against Anson's team. Zang, *Fleet Walker's Divided Heart*, 42–43. In 1888, Anson again refused to play an exhibition game against Walker, who was playing for Syracuse. Id., 59.
35. Malloy, "Introduction," in *Sol White's Colored Base Ball*, by Sol White, xx–xxi; Peterson, *Only the Ball Was White*, 30. Anson, according to early black baseball historian Sol White, kept both Walker and his former Newark batterymate Stovey from being signed by the New York Giants or any other National League team. Zang, *Fleet Walker's Divided Heart*, 55; White, *Sol White's Colored Base Ball*, 76.
36. Fitzgerald, "Clark Griffith," 73.
37. Shirley Povich, *All These Mornings* (New Jersey: Prentice-Hall, 1969), 130–31; Charles C. Alexander, *John McGraw* (New York: Penguin Books, 1988), 75–76. For a terrific comparison of the lives and careers of Griffith, Comiskey, and McGraw, see Jules Tygiel, *Past Time: Baseball as History* (New York: Oxford University Press, 2000), 35–63.
38. Clark Griffith, as told to J. G. Taylor Spink, "Griff, as Reds' Pilot, Inked Marsans as His First Cuban," *The Sporting News*, 30 July 1952, 12.
39. Harold Seymour, *Baseball: The Golden Age* (New York: Oxford University Press, 1989), 85; Peter Bjarkman, "Cuban Blacks in the Majors Before Jackie Robinson." *The National Pastime* no. 12 (Cleveland: SABR, 1992), 60.
40. Lieb, "Griffith Canny as Hill Star, Pilot, Owner," 14.
41. Guy Waterman, "The Upstart Senators of 1912–1915," *The National Pastime* no. 13 (Cleveland: SABR, 1993), 24–27.
42. Al Costello, "Griff's Adopted Son Cal Trained to Take Over," *The Sporting News*, 13 August 1952, 11.
43. Gary Smith, "A Lingering Vestige of Yesterday," *Sports Illustrated*, 4 April 1983, 107.
44. Lieb, "Griffith Canny as Hill Star, Pilot, Owner," 14. For the two best books on the Senators, see Bealle, *The Washington Senators*, and Shirley Povich, *The Washington Senators: An Informal History* (New York: G. P. Putnam's Sons, 1954).
45. In 1913, Griffith signed Cuban outfielders Jacinto "Jack" Calvo and Balmadero "Merito" Acosta. In 1920, he signed Acosta's brother, Jose, catcher/first baseman Ricardo Torres, and Calvo (again).
46. Powell interview, 24 August 1992.

47. For example, Cambria bought the Albany club for $7,500, sold off $60,000 worth of players, and then sold the team for $65,000 to the Giants. Warren Bornscheur, "Ivory Hunter Unique," *Baltimore Morning Sun*, 2 March 1941, sec. 1, p. 2.

48. Bill James, *The Bill James Historical Baseball Abstract* (New York: Villard Books, 1986), 134–139; Ron Fimrite, "His Own Biggest Fan," *Sports Illustrated*, 19 July 1993, 79.

49. J. G. Taylor Spink, *Judge Landis and 25 Years of Baseball* (New York: Thomas Y. Crowell Company, 1947), 232–40; David Pietrusza, *Judge and Jury: The Life and Times of Judge Kenesaw Mountain Landis* (South Bend, Ind.: Diamond Communications, 1998), 361–70.

50. Bornscheur, "Ivory Hunter Unique," sec. 1, p. 2.

51. Shirley Povich, taped interview by author, Washington, D.C., 12 January 1993. Historian Bill James recounts a run-in Cambria had with minor league officials in 1937 that forced the Class-D Salisbury (Maryland) team to forfeit (unjustly according to James) twenty-six games. There were several Cubans on that team, including future Senators catcher Mike Guerra. James, *The New Bill James Historical Baseball Abstract*, 162–65.

52. Roberto González Echevarría, *The Pride of Havana: A History of Cuban Baseball* (New York: Oxford University Press, 1999), 270; Bornscheur, "Ivory Hunter Unique," sec. 1, p. 2. Echevarría, *The Pride of Havana*, 269–270.

53. Burton Hawkins, telephone interview with author, Arlington, Tex., 25 July 1993.

54. Povich interview.

55. Rogosin, *Invisible Men*, 159.

56. Calvin Griffith interview.

57. Robert Heuer, "Look What They've Done to My Game!" *Americas*, 1 May 1995, 36; Robert Heuer, "Give Hispanics Some Spots in Baseball's Management Lineup," *Houston Chronicle*, 5 March 1989, 5H.

58. Echevarría, *The Pride of Havana*, 264.

59. Ibid., 265.

60. James, *The New Bill James Historical Baseball Abstract*, 195.

61. Povich interview.

62. Povich, *The Washington Senators*, 208.

63. Echevarría, *The Pride of Havana*, 45, 253, 255 (classifying both Estalella and de la Cruz as nonwhite major leaguers); Fred Lieb, *Baseball As I Have Known It* (New York: Coward, McCann & Geoghegan, 1977), 260 (claiming to have met Bithorn's black first cousin); Bjarkman, "Cuban Blacks," 61–62 (making the case for both Bithorn and de la Cruz).

    In 1936, Bithorn pitched for the Brooklyn Eagles team that Leonard played on in Puerto Rico against the Cincinnati Reds. "Brown's 3-Base Hit Defeats Leaguers," *Pittsburgh Courier*, 14 March 1936, sec. 2, p. 4. Bithorn was obviously dark-skinned enough to pitch for a black team in Puerto Rico in 1936 but light-skinned enough to pitch for the Cubs in the early 1940s.

64. Kerr, *Calvin*, 138.

65. Echevarría, *The Pride of Havana*, 270; Bob Considine, "Ivory from Cuba: Our Underprivileged Baseball Players," *Colliers*, 3 August 1940, 19, 24. Other "Cuban and South American players" on the Senators had "been subjected to all sorts of

abuses," including beanings from opposing pitchers, discrimination in hotel accommodations, and players on their own team refusing to eat or room with them. Eddie Gant, "I Cover the Eastern Front," *Chicago Defender*, 25 July 1942, 21. Since the first decade of the twentieth century, major league teams hurled racial taunts at Native American and Cuban players. Seymour, *Baseball: The Golden Age*, 84.

66. Art Carter, "From the Bench," *Washington Afro-American*, 26 March 1938, 22.
67. "Dark-Skinned Cubans Face Color Phobia in Big Leagues," *Washington Tribune*, 15 April 1939, 13.
68. Bealle, *The Washington Senators*, 173.
69. Ibid.; Povich, *The Washington Senators*, 218–19.
70. "Cuban Ball Players on Washington Senators Snubbed by Own Team Mates," *Pittsburgh Courier*, 8 June 1940, 16 (running the *Washington Daily News* story written by Bob Ruark picked up by the wire services on June 6, 1940).
71. Ibid.
72. Connie Small, "Baseball's Improbable Imports," *Saturday Evening Post*, 225:5 (2 August 1952), 90. Estalella won out, playing seventy-eight games at third base in 1942, his final season with the Senators and Harris's last in his second of three stints managing the team.
73. Heuer, "Look What They've Done to My Game!" 36.
74. Calvin Griffith interview.
75. Povich, *The Washington Senators*, 189.
76. Spink, *Judge Landis and 25 Years of Baseball*, 219–25; Pietrusza, *Judge and Jury*, 375–77.
77. Kerr, *Calvin*, 138.
78. Sam Lacy, "Looking 'Em Over with the Tribune," *Washington Tribune*, 25 December 1937, 12.
79. Sheingold, "In Black and White," 29. Other papers took notice. See, e.g., Art Carter, "From the Bench," *Washington Afro-American*, 29 January 1938, 18; Cum Posey, "Posey's Points," *Pittsburgh Courier*, 22 January 1938, 16.
80. Sam Lacy, "Looking 'Em Over with the Tribune," *Washington Tribune*, 25 December 1937, 12.
81. Ibid.
82. Ibid.
83. Ibid.
84. Calvin Griffith interview. Griffith's interracial World Series theory was widely reported in the black press. See infra Chapter 6 text accompanying notes 77–78. For example, in August 1942, Fay Young of the *Chicago Defender* wrote:

> Clark Griffith of the Washington Senators advises, and does so rightfully, "build up your own league" but still clings to the jim crow attitude of most of the owners. He believes that since Negro baseball has been attracting so much attention that, if properly supervised, the Negro leagues can pay larger salaries and develop stars to such an extent that "someday top teams (meaning Negro) could play our clubs for the world championship and thus have a chance to really prove their calibre."

Fay Young, "Through the Years," *Chicago Defender*, 1 August 1942, 19.
85. Trezzvant W. Anderson, "Washington Senators Owner Sees Bright Future for Negro Baseball," *Pittsburgh Courier*, 3 September 1932, sec. 2, p. 5.

335

86. Cum Posey, "Posey's Points," *Pittsburgh Courier*, 22 January 1938, 16.

87. Anderson, "Washington Senators Owner Sees Bright Future for Negro Baseball," *Pittsburgh Courier*, 3 September 1932, sec. 2, p. 5.

88. "Pro and Con on the Negro in Organized Baseball," *Washington Tribune*, 25 January 1938, 13; id., 5 March 1938, 13; id., 19 March 1938, 13; id., 26 March 1938, 12; id., 2 April 1938, 13; id., 11 June 1938, 13; id., 23 July 1938, 13.

    Blacks had played professional football with whites during the 1920s, though no blacks played in the National Football League from 1933 to World War II. During the 1930s and 1940s, however, blacks and whites played football together on major college teams.

89. Reed Rennie, "Jake Powell Suspended," *Washington Post*, 31 July 1938, sec. 2, p. 1; "Fans Would Bar Powell for Life," *Washington Afro-American*, 6 August 1938, 22. For more on the Jake Powell incident and reaction of the press, see Richard Crepeau, "The Jake Powell Incident and the Press: A Study in Black and White," *Baseball History* (Westport, Conn.: Meckler, Summer 1986), 32; Chris Lamb, "L'Affaire Jake Powell: The Minority Press Goes to Bat Against Segregated Baseball," *Journalism and Mass Communication Quarterly* 76:1 (Spring 1999), 21–34; Lester, *Black Baseball's National Showcase*, 107–09.

90. Shirley Povich, "This Morning with Shirley Povich," *Washington Post*, 1 August 1938, 13.

91. Povich wrote of Ruth's final at-bat as a Yankee:

> Away it went, taking the long route to deep center field, where Jake Powell gathered it in.
>
>   With that, Ruth doffed his cap, waved a farewell to his admirers, and dashed to the dressing room. It was finis.

Shirley L. Povich, "12,000 Pay Tribute to Babe Ruth in Final Game of 22-Year Career," *Washington Post*, 1 October 1934, 15. Povich concluded his game story as follows: "But the ballgame had been only an anticlimax. Unlike Hamlet, the Babe, not the play, was the thing." Id., 17.

92. Povich, *The Washington Senators*, 177.

93. That same year, as a member of the Yankees, Powell had tried to run over Senators first baseman Joe Kuhel. For a recitation of Powell's scrapes, see Shirley Povich, "This Morning with Shirley Povich," *Washington Post*, 5 November 1948, 19; "Jake Powell, Bad Boy of Big Leagues, Kills Self," *The Sporting News*, 10 November 1948, 22; "Ready for Fight or Frolic," *The Sporting News*, 17 November 1948, 11.

94. Sam Lacy, "Looking 'Em Over with the Tribune," *Washington Tribune*, 13 June 1933, 12.

95. "Fans Don't Want to See Powell in Washington," *Washington Afro-American*, 6 August 1938, 22.

96. Shirley Povich, "Red Ruffing, Gomez Yield 6 Hits Each," *Washington Post*, 17 August 1938, sec. 2, p. 18.

97. Vincent X. Flaherty, "Bottles Rain on Powell as Yankees Win Twice," *Washington Herald*, 17 August 1938, 15.

98. Shirley Povich, "This Morning with Shirley Povich," *Washington Post*, 17 August 1938, sec. 2, p. 18.

99. Vincent X. Flaherty, "Griffith to Curb Bottle Throwing with Paper Cups," *Washington Herald*, 17 August 1938, 17.

100. Wendell Smith, "'Smitty's' Sports Spurts," *Pittsburgh Courier*, 6 May 1939, 14.
101. Logan, *Howard University*, 382.
102. When Anderson died at the age of 96 in 1993, the D.A.R. reasserted that no color line had existed and that Constitution Hall had been reserved. Abigail Van Buren, "Dear Abby: Setting the Record Straight on DAR's 'Racism'" *Chicago Tribune*, 7 February 1994, C-9; Ellen Goodman, "Sorry About That," *Boston Globe*, 26 December 1993, 23.
103. Michael Kernan, "The Object at Hand; Marian Anderson's Mink Coat," *Smithsonian*, 24:3 (June 1993), 14; "Jim Crow Concert Hall," *Time*, 6 March 1939, 33–34.
104. *New York Times*, 7 June 1993, A16. Anderson eventually performed at Constitution Hall in 1943 to raise money for United China Relief. D.A.R. agreed not to segregate seating, but it balked at agreeing not to ban Anderson in the future. "Marian Anderson at Last Sings in D.A.R.'s Hall," *Life*, 25 January 1943, 102. D.A.R.'s ban on black artists continued until 1952. Kernan, "The Object at Hand," 14.
105. "Citizens Protest Marian Anderson Bar," *Washington Tribune*, 18 February 1939, 1; Marian Anderson–D.A.R. Controversy Collection, Moorland-Spingarn Research Center, Howard University, Manuscripts Division, Washington, D.C.
106. Ibid., box 2, folders 45, 47.
107. "Schools Bar Marian Anderson," *Washington Tribune*, 18 February 1939, 1.
108. "'Strings' on Action, However, May Cause Rejection of Hall," *Pittsburgh Courier*, 11 March 1939, 1.
109. Marian Anderson–D.A.R. Controversy Collection, box 2, folder 45.
110. Mrs. Roosevelt, however, played no actual role in securing Anderson's eventual venue. Although she subsequently organized a White House performance by Anderson, Mrs. Roosevelt did not even attend Anderson's Easter concert.
111. Weaver interview.
112. "'God Made No Distinction of Race, Creed, Color,' Ickes Tells Concert Audience," *Pittsburgh Courier*, 15 April 1939, 4.
113. Weaver interview.
114. "Anderson Affair," *Time*, 17 April 1939, 23.
115. Sam Lacy, "Throng Captured by Artistry of Miss Anderson," *Washington Afro-American*, 15 April 1939, 1, 9.
116. Letter to Charles H. Houston from Mary McLeod Bethune, 10 April 1939, Marian Anderson–D.A.R. Controversy Collection, box 1, folder 4.

CHAPTER 4

1. "Base Ball in Washington," *Washington Tribune*, 23 September 1922, 4.
2. A team billed as the "Pittsburgh Homestead Grays" played at American League Park on July 4 and 5, 1921, against the Washington Braves. "Braves to Meet Fast Pittsburgh Grays," *Washington Tribune*, 2 July 1921, 4. An advertisement billed the visiting team as the "Pittsburgh Homestead Grays" and permitted all women who arrived at the park before 10:30 A.M. on July 4 to be admitted free. Id.

    Around the same time, NNL founder Rube Foster had considered operating a black baseball franchise in the nation's capital with black theater impresario S. H. Dudley. Lanctot, *Fair Dealing*, 78–79; "S. D. Dudley Dies," *Washington Tribune*, 9 March 1940, 1.

3. Rob Ruck, the leading historian of black baseball in Pittsburgh, argued that the Grays did not "relocate" to Washington; they merely decided to "expand." Ruck, *Sandlot Seasons*, 173. This may have been true initially, but after 1942 the schedule tilted heavily in Washington's favor. See infra Chapters 5 and 6.

   In 1940, however, the first-half schedule listed five home dates in Washington and five in Pittsburgh; the second-half schedule listed three dates in each city. "Baseball Schedules: Negro National League," *Washington Afro-American*, 30 March 1940, 23; "N.N.L. Schedule," *Pittsburgh Courier*, 9 March 1940, 17; "Nat'l League Schedule," *Pittsburgh Courier*, 6 July 1940, 17.

4. Holway, *Voices*, 258–59.

5. The previous day, the Grays opened their season in Pittsburgh by defeating the Cubans, 7–3, at Forbes Field. The *Afro-American* estimated the Pittsburgh crowd as five thousand. "5,000 Grays Win Opener at Forbes Field," *Washington Afro-American*, 18 May 1940, 25. The hometown *Courier* said only two thousand fans braved the chilly weather to attend the Pittsburgh opener whereas five thousand showed up in Washington. "Cubans Lose 3 to Grays," *Pittsburgh Courier*, 18 May 1940, 16. The *Washington Tribune* estimated that more than four thousand fans attended the D.C. home opener and that Ben Taylor served as the Cuban Stars coach. "Ben Taylor's Cuban Stars Drop 2 Games to Homestead Grays," *Washington Tribune*, 18 May 1940, 12; "Two-Game Bill Features D.C.'s Homestead Grays vs. Cubans," *Washington Tribune*, 11 May 1940, 16.

6. Sam Lacy, "4,800 See Teams Break Even in D.C.," *Washington Afro-American*, 25 May 1940, 21. The *Washington Tribune* reported "4,628 cash customers." "Grays Split Twin Bill with Champion Baltimore Elites," *Washington Tribune*, 25 May 1940, 12. Possibly based on an inflated attendance figure from Posey, the *Pittsburgh Courier* estimated the crowd at 5,900. "Elite Giants and Grays Split," *Pittsburgh Courier*, 25 May 1940, 17.

7. In June, the Grays swept Philadelphia (Leonard tripled twice in the first game) before only 1,500 spectators, and the Grays split with the Elites before only 3,118. "Grays Take Pair from Philly Nine," *Washington Afro-American*, 7 June 1941, 22; Ric Roberts, "Grays Beaten, 6–1, After 7–4 Victory," id., 14 June 1941, 27. In July, a Grays–Newark Eagles doubleheader drew 2,000 fans. Ric Roberts, "Eagles Top Grays on Rookie's Hit," id., 26 July 1941, 27. And in August, another Grays-Stars doubleheader mustered only 2,500. Ric Roberts, "Bob Wright Shuts Out Philly Nine," id., 10 August 1941, 22.

8. "Grays Increase Lead by Scoring Double Victory," *Pittsburgh Courier*, 13 July 1940, 17; "Ray Brown Blanks Elites with Three Hit Performance," id., 3 August 1940, 17. Art Carter estimated the Elks' crowd at Yankee Stadium as only eight thousand. Art Carter, "Ray Brown Blanks Foes for 12th Win," *Washington Afro-American*, 3 August 1940, 21.

9. Ted Poston, "15,000 in N.Y. See Elites and Grays Cop," *Pittsburgh Courier*, 14 September 1940, 16.

10. "Fans, Players Riot as Grays, Bushwicks Split," *Washington Afro-American*, 21 June 1941, 27; Morgen S. Jensen, "Leonard and Brown Slug Out Home Runs," *Pittsburgh Courier*, 5 July 1941, 17; "Grays Swamp Cubans, 20–0; Win N.N.L. Title," id., 27 September 1941, 17.

11. Russ J. Cowans, "Elites and Grays Split Double Bill," *Washington Afro-American*, 9 August 1941, 31.
12. Ruck, *Sandlot Seasons*, 173.
13. Holman had persuaded the Washington Pilots to play under Griffith Stadium's floodlights (or football lights) in 1932 and also promoted games for the Grays. Joe Holman, "Hype," *Washington Post*, 20 April 1980, M4. For a terrific profile of Holman, see William Gildea, "'20s to '80s, Holman Rolls with the Punchlines," *Washington Post*, 19 December 1985, F1.
14. Sam Lacy, "Looking 'Em Over," *Washington Afro-American*, 10 February 1940, 23.
15. "Grays to Play in Washington," *Washington Afro-American*, 10 February 1940, 20.
16. "Grays Beat Stars Twice in DC Bill," *Washington Afro-American*, 24 August 1940, 22; Lanier R. Covington, "Washington Grays Twice Down Philly Stars, 6–4 and 10–1," *Washington Tribune*, 24 August 1940, 13. The Newark Eagles were supposed to play the Philadelphia Stars in the first game, with the winner playing the Grays. The Eagles, however, refused to participate with Gibson, an ineligible player, in the lineup. Joe Sewall, "As Athletes Pass," *Washington Tribune*, 24 August 1940, 12.
17. "Famous Catcher Leaves for $6,000 Salary, Report," *Pittsburgh Courier*, 22 March 1940, 17; "Covington's Comments," *Washington Tribune*, 29 March 1941, 10.
18. Cum Posey, "Posey's Points," *Pittsburgh Courier*, 12 April 1941, 16; "Josh Gibson Sued," *Washington Tribune*, 12 April 1941, 13.
19. Ric Roberts, "Renaissance Seen as Baseball Boom Bestirs Leagues," *Washington Afro-American*, 12 July 1941, 23. A few weeks later, Roberts penned a cartoon titled "Baseball's Greatest Boom," depicting Paige in his high leg kick and the large crowds in his wake. Ric Roberts, "Baseball's Greatest Boom," id., 2 August 1941, 26.
20. Randy Dixon, "The Sports Bugle," *Pittsburgh Courier*, 24 August 1940, 17.
21. John Holway, *Black Diamonds: Life in the Negro Leagues from the Men Who Lived It* (Westport, Conn.: Meckler Books, 1989), 125.
22. Wendell Smith, "'Smitty's' Sports Spurts," *Pittsburgh Courier*, 23 July 1938, 16.
23. Holway, *The Complete Book of Baseball's Negro Leagues*, 387–88; Chester L. Washington, "Sez Ches'," *Pittsburgh Courier*, 23 August 1941, 17 (reprinting Salsinger's comments).
24. "Chicago Tribune and Daily News Writers Praise Playing of Leonard and Patterson," *Pittsburgh Courier*, 12 August 1939, 17.
25. Cum Posey, "Posey's Points," *Pittsburgh Courier*, 14 March 1942, 16.
26. Holway, *Black Diamonds*, 30.
27. Ibid., 137.
28. Chester L. Washington, "Sez Ches'," *Pittsburgh Courier*, 17 August 1940, 16.
29. "East Slams Out Victory Over West," *Washington Tribune*, 24 August 1940, 12.
30. Cum Posey, "Posey's 18th All-American Baseball Team," *Pittsburgh Courier*, 25 October 1941, 16.
31. Wendell Smith, "'Smitty's' Sports Spurts," *Pittsburgh Courier*, 26 July 1941, 17.
32. "Are Sepia Players of Big League Caliber? We'd Bet on These Two!" *Pittsburgh Courier*, 22 July 1939, 17.
33. Sam Lacy, "Looking 'Em Over," *Washington Afro-American*, 6 July 1940, 21.
34. Art Carter, "From the Bench," *Washington Afro-American*, 29 January 1938, 18.
35. "Looking 'Em Over," *Washington Afro-American*, 1 April 1939, 23.

36. Bill Gilbert, *They Also Served: Baseball and the Home Front, 1941–1945* (New York: Crown Publishers, 1992), 42. See also Richard Goldstein, *Spartan Seasons: How Baseball Survived the Second World War* (New York: Macmillan, 1980), 19–23; William Mead, *Baseball Goes to War* (Washington, D.C.: Broadcast Interview Source, Inc., 1998), 36–37; Pietrusza, *Judge and Jury*, 432–34. Spink, *Judge Landis and 25 Years of Baseball*, 279.

37. William Mead and Paul Dickson, *Baseball: The President's Game* (New York: Walker Publishing Company, 1997), 71, 76, 79.

38. Morris Bealle quoted Griffith and reported that the lights cost the Senators $165,000. Bealle, *The Washington Senators*, 164. Shirley Povich said the lights cost Griffith $230,000. Povich, *The Washington Senators*, 219. Jon Kerr, in his book on Calvin Griffith, also reported the $230,000 figure, as well as Calvin's claim that the American League provided the family with a $125,000 interest-free loan. Kerr, *Calvin*, 31.

39. Bealle, *The Washington Senators*, 164.

40. Ibid.

41. Mead and Dickson, *The President's Game*, 79.

42. Mead, *Baseball Goes to War*, 38, 83.

43. Cum Posey, "Posey's Points," *Pittsburgh Courier*, 24 January 1942, 17.

44. Weaver interview.

45. Mead and Dickson, *The President's Game*, 200.

46. Box scores from 1920 confirm that it was a four-game series between Joe Judge's All-Stars and the Brooklyn Royal Giants. "Giants Beaten by Judge's All-Stars," *Washington Post*, 6 October 1920, 13. Sam Lacy, in a detailed account of the Brower incident in a 1933 column, recalled the Negro League team as being the Baltimore Black Sox. Sam Lacy, "Looking 'Em Over with the Tribune," *Washington Tribune*, 13 July 1933, 12. But Lacy's mentor, former *Tribune* sports editor Louis Lautier, wrote in a 1925 column that the team was the "Brooklyn Royals." Louis R. Lautier, "Sports Chatter," *Washington Tribune*, 5 September 1925, 4. After a 1925 contest between a black and a white semipro team scheduled for Griffith Stadium was canceled at the last minute, Lautier wrote: "Clark Griffith is to be reasoned with rather than censured. A fair-minded person cannot conclude that the 'Old Fox' is moved by prejudice. . . . Griffith is wrong, but he is not to be censured." Louis R. Lautier, "Sports Chatter," *Washington Tribune*, 12 September 1925, 4. Obviously, with the Senators reaching the World Series in 1925, the black press (as well as the rest of the black elite) was still infatuated with Griffith's Senators.

47. Both Lautier and Lacy recounted the incident in columns eight years apart. See Louis R. Lautier, "Sports Chatter," *Washington Tribune*, 5 September 1925, 4; Sam Lacy, "Looking 'Em Over with the Tribune," id., 13 July 1933, 12. But Washington's white daily papers, in their brief coverage of the final game between Judge's All-Stars and the Royal Giants, failed to mention the incident. See "Royal Giants Again Down Judge's Stars," *Washington Post*, 9 October 1920, 20; "Royal Giants Take Final," *Washington Evening Star*, 9 October 1920, pt. 1, p. 8; "Giants Get Even Break," *Washington Times*, 9 October 1920, 16. The *Washington Herald* failed to cover the final game. Washington's black newspaper of the day, the *Washington Bee*, did not cover such matters. The *Washington Tribune* did not start until Feb-

ruary 1921. Although Washington's white dailies neglected the incident, Lacy and Lautier's accounts are reliable and accurate.

48. Peter L. Jackson, "Fans Riot as Grays Split with Bushwicks," *Washington Afro-American*, 27 July 1940, 23.

49. Peter L. Jackson, "Fans, Players Riot as Grays, Bushwicks Split," *Washington Afro-American*, 21 June 1941, 27.

50. "Arrest of 13 Follows Riot of Thousands at Griffith Stadium," *Washington Evening Star*, 24 July 1942, A-3; "Stadium Battle of Music Turns to Battle Royal," *Washington Post*, 24 July 1942, 1; Joe Sewall, "Pop Bottles Fly As 'Battle of Music' Turns into Riot," *Washington Tribune*, 25 July 1941, 1.

51. Holway, *Voices*, 259.

52. L. Covington, "Josh Gibson's Slugging Bat Thrills in Split Twin-Bill," *Washington Tribune*, 22 July 1939, 12; Cum Posey, "Posey's Points," *Pittsburgh Courier*, 5 August 1939, 17; "3 Teams to Play in Stadium Bill," *Washington Afro-American*, 17 August 1940, 21.

Gibson's second homer, which came off the Stars' Henry McHenry and broke a 7–7 tie in the ninth inning of the first game, may have been his famous fooled-curveball homer. Gene Benson told John Holway:

> Josh Gibson in Washington did something I can't believe. Henry McHenry had been getting Josh out all day. He got two strikes on Josh in the ninth and threw him a curveball—and he had a good curveball—and fooled Josh. Josh stepped back—you know how you step in the bucket when the ball fools you? He swung with one hand, and it went over my head. All I did was look at it, didn't even turn around. McHenry broke the water cooler! He had a fit. He was high strung, you know.

Holway, *Josh and Satch*, 41. The box score shows Benson playing center field. In the game story, Lanier Covington wrote: "[Gibson] looked at the first pitch for a called strike, fouled the next sharply back of the stands, and swung on the third pitch straight from the shoulders with the fat of the bat, sending the sphere ten rows up in the left field stands." *Washington Tribune*, 22 July 1939, 12.

53. Joe Sewall, "As Athletes Pass," *Washington Tribune*, 1 June 1940, 12.

54. Ibid.

55. Sam Lacy, "Looking 'Em Over," *Washington Afro-American*, 18 May 1940, 27.

56. Ibid., 19 April 1941, 23.

57. Ibid., 3 May 1941, 26.

58. Wendell Smith, "'Smitty's' Sports Spurts," *Pittsburgh Courier*, 14 May 1938, 17; Lester, *Black Baseball's National Showcase*, 110.

59. For a wonderful description of that day at Griffith Stadium, see Richard Ben Cramer, *Joe DiMaggio: The Hero's Life* (New York: Simon & Schuster, 2001), 172–75.

60. Maya Angelou, *I Know Why the Caged Bird Sings* (New York: Bantam Books, 1993), 135.

61. Art Carter, "From the Bench," *Washington Afro-American*, 7 June 1941, 21.

62. Sam Lacy, "Kid Cocoa Decisions McDowell," *Washington Afro-American*, 15 June 1940, 23.

63. "Mrs. Roosevelt Says Lincoln's Plea Is Ignored," *Pittsburgh Courier*, 3 February 1940, 1. A month later, picketers greeted the all-black Lincoln Theater's premiere of "Gone with the Wind" because of the film's racist depiction of slavery.

64. "Ickes Order Opens Golf Links to All," *Washington Afro-American*, 12 July 1941, 21; "Meddlers Makes Golf Costly on District Course," id., 9 August 1941, 28.

65. Sam Lacy, "100 Turned Away from Ice Show," *Washington Afro-American*, 1 February 1941, 22.

66. The Grays, by contrast, lost good young players but not great ones: third baseman Howard Easterling; second baseman Lick Carlisle; outfielders Wilmer Fields and Frank Williams; and pitchers Johnny Wright, Garnett Blair, and Roy Welmaker. *Negro Baseball*, 1945 edition, 23, 27, box 1, folder 24, Art Carter Papers.

67. Leonard, *The Black Lou Gehrig*, 147.

68. Mead, *Baseball Goes to War*, 25–27.

69. Ibid., 100. The Senators lost another player, outfielder Elmer Gedeon, for good. Gedeon, who had played five games for the Senators in 1939, was one of two major leaguers killed while fighting for their country. Gilbert, *They Also Served*, 7.

70. Frazier, *The Negro in the United States*, 250.

71. Bureau of the Census, *Eighteenth Census of the United States—Population: 1960, Characteristics of the Population* (Washington, D.C.: GPO, 1963) vol. I, pt. 10, tbl. 15, p. 10–11.

72. Daniel M. Johnson and Rex R. Campbell, *Black Migration in America: A Social Demographic History* (Durham, N.C.: Duke University Press, 1981), 101–2.

73. The high literacy rate among Southern migrants, according to sociologist Carole Marks, suggested that black North Carolinians first migrated from rural to urban areas in their own state before going to the North. Carole Marks, *Farewell—We're Good and Gone: The Great Black Migration* (Bloomington, Ind.: Indiana University Press, 1989), 43–44. The census supports Marks's theory. In 1940, of the 7,415 black Washingtonians who lived in the nation's capital but had made their residences in North Carolina in 1935, some 4,606 came from urban areas, 1,283 from rural nonfarming areas, and only 1,240 from rural farm areas. Bureau of the Census, *Sixteenth Census of the United States. Population: Internal Migration 1935–1940* (Washington, D.C.: GPO, 1943), 19.

74. By 1950, more than thirty thousand African Americans living in Washington came from North Carolina, and another thirty thousand came from South Carolina. Bureau of the Census, *Seventeenth Census of the United States, Special Reports: State of Birth* (Washington, D.C.: GPO, 1953), tbl. 4A, 37–38.

75. *Washington Tribune*, 3 August 1940, 12.

76. A. C. Braxton, taped interview by author, Seat Pleasant, Md., 18 August 1992; Eddie Dozier, taped interview by author, Washington, D.C., 18 August 1992.

77. Lena Cox interview, 5 August 1992.

78. *Pittsburgh Courier*, 14 February 1942, 1.

79. Sam Lacy, "Comrades Tomorrow . . . Why Not Today?" *Washington Afro-American*, 15 June 1940, 24.

80. Lacy, *Fighting for Fairness*, 45–46.

81. Ibid., 43.

82. *1930 District of Columbia Census*, roll 295, E.D. 110, sheet 18b, lines 57–63. Cardozo Business High School had been formed in 1928 from Dunbar's business department. At Cardozo, Carter started on the basketball and football teams and received the school's James E. Walker Medal for "the highest record in athletics, military activities, and scholarship." Art Carter, "A Review of Cardozo in Athletics,"

The Nautilus: Cardozo Business High School yearbook, Washington D.C., 1931, box 6, Art Carter Papers.

83. Sam Lacy, taped interview by author, Baltimore, Md., 17 May 1994.

84. Carter's first bylined sports article for the *Tribune*, on April 29, 1932, was about a Baltimore marathon. *Washington Tribune*, 29 April 1932, 12. In July 1932, Carter covered the city's Negro League baseball entry, the Washington Pilots, during a night game at Griffith Stadium. Id., 29 July 1932, 12. In October, Carter wrote about Howard University football and authored a column called "Capitol City Sports Scripts." Id., 21 October 1932, 12. Carter's byline appeared less frequently in the *Tribune* sports section in 1933. He wrote several articles in April and May about the controversy about a high school relay race, some of them under a byline emphasizing his middle name, "A. Mantel Carter." Id., 21 April 1933, 12; id., 5 May 1933, 12. In November 1934, Carter published a "Sports Scripts" column, his first byline in months. Id., 24 November 1934, 12. The city directories from 1933 through 1935 list Carter as a "reporter" for the *Tribune*. *1933 City Directory*, 336; *1934 City Directory*, 347; *1935 City Directory*, 352.

 Before writing for the *Tribune* in 1932, Carter worked as an elevator operator in an apartment house. *1930 Census*, roll 295, E.D. 110, sheet 18b, line 59. In 1931, he joined the staff of an obscure newspaper known as the *Washington World*. *1931 City Directory*, 378. An article by Carter in the 1931 Cardozo High School yearbook listed him as the sports editor at the *World*. Art Carter, "A Review of Cardozo in Athletics," *The Nautilus: Cardozo Business High School* yearbook, Washington, D.C., 1931, box 6, Art Carter Papers. The 1932 city directory listed him as an "asst. editor" at the *World*. *1932 City Directory*, 365.

85. Sam Lacy interview, 17 May 1994.

86. On February 19, 1941, the *Washington Daily News* revealed that the Bruins' weekend contests turned out to be so lucrative—even after paying Turner's Arena 20 percent of the gross gate receipts—that Lacy could afford to put up the team's out-of-town stars in Black Washington's first-rate Whitelaw Hotel and to pay for all their meals. "To date I've spent $1486 in salaries alone," Lacy boasted to the reporter. "I've paid around $900 in rent, about $300 in equipment and the same for advertising. So you see we're doing pretty well." *Washington Daily News*, 19 February 1941, 28.

 Lacy's public comments concerned his immediate boss, the editor of the *Washington Afro-American*, Ralph Matthews, and eventually the paper's boss, Dr. Carl Murphy. Lacy, *Fighting for Fairness*, 41–43.

87. Letter from William B. West to Art Carter, box 1, folder 3, Art Carter Papers.

88. "Season's Passes," box 1, folder 13, Art Carter Papers.

89. Janet Bruce, *The Kansas City Monarchs* (Lawrence, Kans.: University of Kansas Press, 1985), 49.

90. Wilmer Fields, taped interview by author, Manassas, Va., 13 August 1992.

91. Kerr, *Calvin*, 13.

92. "Season Passes—1945," box 2, folder 17, Art Carter Papers.

93. Posey hired Clark, the former Pittsburgh Crawfords public relations director, in April 1942 to promote the Grays in Pittsburgh. Cum Posey, "Posey's Points," *Pittsburgh Courier*, 18 April 1942, 17. Posey's brother, See, was the team's traveling secretary.

94. Letter from Art Carter to Clark Griffith, 28 April 1938, box 8, Art Carter Papers.
95. Kerr, *Calvin*, 35.
96. Bill Scott, taped interview by author, Washington, D.C., 5 August 1992.
97. As early as 1937, Posey wrote: "For the past few years Negro National League clubs have played at Griffith Stadium in Washington, D.C., and have received great cooperation and much valuable advice from the Washington American League club owner, Clark Griffith, who predicts a great future for Negro League Baseball." Cum Posey, "Posey's Points," *Pittsburgh Courier*, 17 April 1937, 17. In 1941, Posey also wrote: "The owners of Griffith Stadium, Forbes Field, Yankee Stadium, helped to keep organized Negro baseball alive by allowing them to use these million dollar stadiums. The profits they derive from these rentals is small." Cum Posey, "Posey's Points," *Pittsburgh Courier*, 8 February 1941, 17.
98. Cum Posey, "Posey's Points," *Pittsburgh Courier*, 18 April 1942, 17.
99. Balance Sheet, 19–20 April 1942, Homestead Grays v. Newark Eagles, box 1, folder 9, Art Carter Papers.

CHAPTER 5

1. "Grays letterhead," box 2, folder 4, Art Carter Papers.
2. Twelve thousand in New Orleans attended an exhibition against Paige and the Kansas City Monarchs, and eighteen thousand in Newark saw Gibson's eighth-inning homer defeat the Eagles in the Grays' official season opener. Art Carter, "From the Bench," *Washington Afro-American*, 9 May 1942, 27; "18,000 See Josh Drive in All Runs," id., 9 May 1942, 25; Ric Roberts, "Record Crowd in Offing for Games," id., 9 May 1942, 24. The *Courier* reported the Newark crowd at twelve thousand. "Circuit Clout by Josh Wins for Grays," *Pittsburgh Courier*, 9 May 1942, 17.
3. Only five thousand fans watched the Grays drop both games of an April 19 exhibition doubleheader to the Newark Eagles. Ric Roberts, "Newark Takes Twin Bill from Grays," *Washington Afro-American*, 25 April 1942, 29; "Irwin's Hitting Paces Eagles as Grays Fall Twice," *Pittsburgh Courier*, 25 April 1942, 16.

    Only 4,253 turned out for the team's official Griffith Stadium opener on May 14, a Sunday doubleheader sweep of the New York Black Yankees. The Grays even admitted five hundred soldiers to that game for free. Judge William H. Hastie, a civilian aide to the secretary of war, threw out the first ball. Ric Roberts, "Partlow Blanks Yanks in Nightcap," *Washington Afro-American*, 23 May 1942, 28; "Grays Down Yanks As Elites Defeat 'Stars,'" *Pittsburgh Courier*, 16 May 1942, 17.
4. Joe Sewall, "Sportin' Around," *Washington Tribune*, 23 May 1942, 24; "Elites Stop Grays," *Pittsburgh Courier*, 23 May 1942, 16.
5. Holway, *Josh and Satch*, xii.
6. Robert Gregory, *Diz: The Story of Dizzy Dean and Baseball During the Great Depression* (New York: Viking, 1992), 334–39; Curt Smith, *America's Dizzy Dean* (St. Louis, Mo.: Bethany Press, 1978), 104–5. Dean may have been pitching with a sore arm at the outset of the 1937 season. Vince Staten, *Ol' Diz: A Biography of Dizzy Dean* (New York: HarperCollins, 1992), 181–88. Either way, his career never recovered.
7. Wendell Smith wrote after interviewing Dean that the pitcher "seemed to be proud of [the] fact that he had pitched against Satchell [sic] Paige and one time had struck out Josh Gibson." *Pittsburgh Courier*, 12 August 1939, 16.

8. Howard Martin, "Monarchs, Plus Paige, Beat Stars, Minus Feller, 3 to 1," *Chicago Tribune*, 25 May 1942, sec. 2, p. 1.

9. Several books mistakenly claim that an additional Dean-Paige matchup in 1942 occurred in Pittsburgh. See Mark Ribowsky, *Don't Look Back: Satchel Paige in the Shadows of Baseball* (New York: Simon & Schuster, 1994), 207–8; Pietrusza, *Judge and Jury*, 417. No such game took place, at least according to the accounts in the black press: *Pittsburgh Courier*, 6 June 1942, 16; *Chicago Defender*, 6 June 1942, 20; *Washington Afro-American*, 6 June 1942, 25. That year, Dean and Paige faced each other only in Chicago and Washington, before Judge Landis canceled a June 6 matchup in Indianapolis. See infra text accompanying note 23.

10. Ric Roberts, "Satchel Fans 7 in 5 Innings on Hill," *Washington Afro-American*, 6 June 1942, 25.

11. Jack Munhall, "Paige, Grays Beat Stars, 8–1, Before 22,000," *Washington Post*, 1 June 1942, 17.

12. Ibid.; "22,000 See Grays Top Dean's Stars," *Washington Times-Herald*, 1 June 1942, 15.

13. *Chicago Tribune*, 25 May 1942, sec. 2, p. 1.

14. Wendell Smith, "Paige Brilliant as Grays Wallop Dean and Team," *Pittsburgh Courier*, 6 June 1942, 16; Ric Roberts, "Satchel Fans 7 in 5 Innings on Hill," *Washington Afro-American*, 6 June 1942, 25.

15. Francis E. Stann, "Win, Lose, or Draw," *Washington Evening Star*, 1 June 1942, A-10.

16. Holway, *The Complete Book of Baseball's Negro Leagues*, 315; Holway, *Josh and Satch*, 67–68; Gregory, *Diz*, 239–42; Smith, *America's Dizzy Dean*, 82; Staten, *Ol' Diz*, 171.

17. Holway, *The Complete Book of Baseball's Negro Leagues*, 471. Holway had previously written that of the 436 interracial contests between 1900 and 1950, black teams won 268, and white teams won 168. Holway, *Blackball Stars*, xii.

18. Buck O'Neil, panel discussion, "Baseball Heroes of World War II," World War II Veterans Committee's Third National Conference, 10 November 2000, MCI Center Sports Gallery, Washington, D.C. O'Neil played on Paige's All-Star team that faced Feller's All-Star team in their famous 1946 interracial barnstorming tour. Paige's team won six of those games; Feller's team won seven. Holway, *Josh and Satch*, 188. See also infra note 20.

19. Pietrusza, *Judge and Jury*, 412–14; Jules Tygiel, *Baseball's Great Experiment: Jackie Robinson and His Legacy* (New York: Oxford University Press, 1983; Vintage Books, 1984), 26–27; Holway, *The Complete Book of Baseball's Negro Leagues*, 184.

20. Feller, who had volunteered for the navy shortly after Pearl Harbor and was stationed in Newport, Rhode Island, allegedly had been barred by naval authorities from pitching the previous week in Chicago against Paige and the Monarchs. "Feller . . . sent his regrets earlier in the day because he had been called back to duty by the navy. . . ." *Chicago Tribune*, 25 May 1942, sec. 2, p. 1.

But See Posey, the Grays' traveling secretary, received assurances from the navy and from Feller himself that the erstwhile Cleveland Indians ace would appear in Washington. See Posey said that Feller was not allowed to play in Chicago because the naval relief game involving major league teams had not been played in the Second City. Because the naval relief game had been played in the nation's capital, Posey told the *Afro* that Feller would play in Washington. Feller even wired

345

Posey requesting that the fans be informed that Feller would donate his share of the proceeds to the naval relief fund. "Grays Battle All-Stars in Griffith Stadium Tilt," *Washington Afro-American*, 30 May 1942, 27.

Four days before the game (and two hours after the *Afro's* deadline, according to Art Carter), Feller "was forced to cancel his agreement." Art Carter, "Satchel Paige Called the Joe Louis of Baseball," *Washington Afro-American*, 13 July 1942, 27.

Nearly sixty years later, Feller attributed his absence to several factors. "Some promoter must have misrepresented the whole deal," Feller recalled. "Judge Landis had nothing to do with it. That was the [decision of] the commanding officer at the naval college, Old Red Neck Magruder." Bob Feller, interview with author, Washington, D.C., 10 November 2000. Feller and Paige faced each other in a series of exhibition games in 1946. The two teams, Feller's All-Stars and Paige's All-Stars, flew in planes adorned with their respective teams' names. Bob Feller with Bill Gilbert, *Now Pitching Bob Feller* (New York: Birch Lane Press, 1990), 136–41; Ribowsky, *Don't Look Back*, 233–36; Holway, *Josh and Satch*, 187–88. Paige often referred to Feller as "Bob Rapid." Satchel Paige with Hal Leibovitz, *Pitching Man: Satchel Paige's Own Story* (Cleveland: The *Cleveland News*, 1948), 73–74 . Feller is fiercely proud of those exhibitions, believing that they made it easier for Robinson to integrate the major leagues in 1947 and that they led to Paige's 1971 induction in the Hall of Fame. Bob Feller, panel discussion, Washington, D.C., 10 November 2000; Feller, *Now Pitching*, 140.

Feller, however, embroiled himself in controversy in 1945 by publicly declaring that Jackie Robinson (whose Jackie Robinson's All-Stars faced Feller's team) was not major league caliber because Robinson's "football shoulders" prevented him from hitting Feller's inside fastball. Wendell Smith, "The Sports Beat," *Pittsburgh Courier*, 10 November 1945, 14; Feller, *Now Pitching*, 140–41; Tygiel, *Baseball's Great Experiment*, 76, 160.

21. Ric Roberts, "All Up in Washington," *Washington Afro-American*, 6 June 1942, 25.
22. *Washington Post*, 3 June 1942, 20.
23. Art Carter, "From the Bench," *Washington Afro-American*, 13 June 1942, 25. In July, Carter received no reply to a letter to Judge Landis proposing a major league–Negro League All-Star game to benefit war relief. Letter from Art Carter to Judge Kenesaw Mountain Landis, 3 July 1942, box 8, Art Carter Papers. Landis's role in canceling the third exhibition game between Paige and Dean's All-Stars is well documented and accepted by even the most sympathetic account of the commissioner's racial attitudes. Pietrusza, *Judge and Jury*, 414 ("In 1942, however, we do have solid evidence of the Judge prohibiting in-season games at major league ballparks"), 417.
24. Others included Cardinals pitcher Johnny Grodzicki; Yankees catcher Ken Silvestri; former Phillies second baseman Heinie Mueller; future Dodgers and Reds shortstop Claude Corbitt; former Tigers, Senators, and Browns outfielder George Archie; former Yankees, Browns, and Dodgers outfielder Joe Gallagher; and former Braves pitcher Al Piechota.
25. Francis E. Stann, "Win, Lose, or Draw," *Washington Evening Star*, 1 June 1942, A-10.

26. Ibid. Dave Odom, a stocky right-handed pitcher who shut down the Grays for three innings, would be rewarded by the Boston Braves with an unsuccessful call-up (0–3, 5.27 ERA) in 1943. Pitcher Wedo Martini had failed miserably in his 1935 appearances (0–2, 17.05 ERA, eight hits, 11 walks, 6⅓ innings) with the Philadelphia Athletics. Martini, who relieved Odom in the fifth inning, walked one Grays batter before deciding after two more pitches that his arm was too sore to pitch.

27. There may have been one other exception. Claude Corbitt, who played shortstop for Dean's All-Stars in Chicago, also may have played for Dean's team in Washington. There was someone listed as both "Corbitt" or "Corbett" in various box scores as having played first base at Griffith Stadium. Claude Corbitt was stationed at Camp Wheeler along with Cecil Travis, which probably meant that both players received weeklong furloughs to play with Dean's team. But it is unclear why Corbitt, a top Dodgers shortstop prospect with the Montreal farm club, would have yielded his natural position in order to play first base. At least one newspaper listed Corbitt as scheduled to appear in Washington. "Dean, Travis, Paige Play Here Today," *Washington Post*, 31 May 1942, sports section, p. 2. The "Corbett" listed in some box scores was not Gene Corbett, a Phillies infielder from 1936 to 1938. But see Francis E. Stann, "Win, Lose, or Draw," *Washington Evening Star*, 1 June 1942, A-10 (referring to the player as Gene Corbett but also describing him as playing in his Camp Wheeler uniform along with Travis). Gene Corbett was playing for a minor league team in Salisbury, Maryland, at the time. Gene Corbett, telephone interview by author, Salisbury, Md., 7 November 2000. My best guess is that it was Claude Corbitt, who was taking a breather by playing first base for Dean's team and who played for the Dodgers in 1945.

28. For Williams's comments as well as the best profile of Travis, see Dave Kindred, "Memories Frozen in Time," *The Sporting News*, 2 January 1995, 6.

29. Vincent X. Flaherty, "Straight from the Shoulder," *Washington Times-Herald*, 31 May 1942, 1-B; Vincent X. Flaherty, "Straight from the Shoulder," id., 2 June 1942, 22.

30. "Travis Gets 'Hero' Award," *Washington Times-Herald*, 2 June 1942, 22, 25.

31. Cecil Travis, telephone interview by author, Riverdale, Ga., 4 November 2000.

32. Buck Leonard, taped interview by author, Rocky Mount, N.C., 20 July 1992.

33. Rogosin, *Invisible Men*, 72.

34. Ibid. In the mid- to late 1940s, Grays batboy Billy Coward also wore an old Senators uniform. Billy Coward, taped interview by author, Washington, D.C., 20 August 1992.

35. Holway, *Voices*, 261.

36. Sam Lacy, "Looking 'Em Over," *Washington Afro-American*, 24 August 1940, 23.

37. Mickey Vernon, telephone interview by author, Wallingford, Pa., 10 November 1994.

38. "Never even thought about it," he said. Ibid.

39. Pee Wee Covington, "Covington's Chattering Comments," *Washington Tribune*, 10 August 1940, 10.

40. Edsall Walker, taped interview by author, Secaucus, N.J., 30 May 1992.

41. Joe Sewall, "Sportin' Around," *Washington Tribune*, 27 June 1942, 18.

42. Leonard, *The Black Lou Gehrig*, 141.

43. Ibid.

44. "Dugout Dust," *Washington Afro-American*, 6 June 1942, 25.

45. Gehringer, a famous contact hitter who stood flatfooted at the plate, gave Paige the most trouble. Paige wrote: "I'd rather face a Waner or a DiMaggio or a Williams than a Gehringer." Paige, *Pitchin' Man*, 46.

46. Myrdal, *An American Dilemma*, 771.

47. Art Carter, "Satchel Paige Called the Joe Louis of Baseball," *Washington Afro-American*, 13 June 1942, 27.

48. Robert McNeill, taped interview by author, Washington, D.C., 2 July 1992.

49. "Dugout Dust," *Washington Afro-American*, 6 June 1942, 25.

50. Vincent X. Flaherty, "Straight from the Shoulder," *Washington Times-Herald*, 2 June 1942, 22.

51. Wendell Smith, "'Smitty's' Sports Spurts," *Pittsburgh Courier*, 6 June 1942, 17.

52. Vincent X. Flaherty, "Straight from the Shoulder," *Washington Times-Herald*, 2 June 1942, 22.

53. Cecil Travis interview.

54. Mead, *Baseball Goes to War*, 201; Goldstein, *Spartan Seasons*, 254; Gilbert, *They Also Served*, 226; Frederick Turner, *When the Boys Came Back: Baseball and 1946* (New York: Henry Holt, 1996), 22–23, 83, 85.

55. Kindred, "Memories Frozen in Time," 6.

56. Cecil Travis interview.

57. Jack Munhall, "Paige, Grays Beat Stars, 8–1, Before 22,000," *Washington Post*, 1 June 1942, 17. The *Times-Herald* story was no better, referring to "Russ" Gibson and "Judd" Bankhead. "22,000 See Grays Top Dean's Stars," *Washington Times-Herald*, 1 June 1942, 15.

58. Francis E. Stann, "Win, Lose, or Draw," *Washington Evening Star*, 1 June 1942, A-10.

59. "Dugout Dust," *Washington Afro-American*, 6 June 1942, 25.

60. "Expense Sheet—31 May 1942," box 1, folder 10, Art Carter Papers.

61. Wendell Smith, "Paige Brilliant as Grays Wallop Dean and Team," *Pittsburgh Courier*, 6 June 1942, 16.

62. Francis E. Stann, "Win, Lose, or Draw," *Washington Evening Star*, 1 June 1942, A-10; Vincent X. Flaherty, "Straight from the Shoulder," *Washington Times-Herald*, 2 June 1942, 22; "Satchel Paige Real Iron Man; Pitches 125 Games Year," *Washington Daily News*, 1 June 1942, 27.

63. "Grays Battle All-Stars in Griffith Stadium Tilt," *Washington Afro-American*, 30 May 1942, 27.

64. "Satchelfoots," *Time*, 3 June 1940, 44; Ted Shane, "Chocolate Rube Waddell," *Saturday Evening Post*, 27 July 1940, 20, 79–81; "Satchel Paige, Negro Ballplayer, Is One of Best Pitchers in Game," *Life*, 2 June 1941, 90–92; Ribowsky, *Don't Look Back*, 187–90, 196; Buck O'Neil, *I Was Right on Time* (New York: Simon and Schuster, 1996), 107–8.

65. Paige, *Pitchin' Man*, 28–29.

66. Richard Donovan, "The Fabulous Satchel Paige," *Collier's* (1953) in *The Baseball Reader*, ed. Charles Einstein (New York: Bonanza Books, 1989), 101.

67. Ibid., 77–78; Paige, *Pitchin' Man*, 67–68; John B. Holway, "Introduction" in *Maybe I'll Pitch Forever* by LeRoy "Satchel" Paige with David Lipman (Lincoln, Nebr.: University of Nebraska Press, 1993), vi.

68. Paige, *Pitchin' Man*, 68.

69. Whitey Herzog and Kevin Horrigan, *White Rat: A Life in Baseball* (New York: Harper & Row, 1987), 53–55. Herzog and Paige were teammates in 1957 with the Triple-A Miami Marlins. Ironically, Herzog was sent down to Miami by the Senators.

70. Paige, *Pitchin' Man*, 26–27; Paige, *Maybe I'll Pitch Forever*, 17–18.

71. Traditionally, the "New Negro" is associated with Howard University professor Alain Locke and other black literati who started a cultural revolution during the Harlem Renaissance. Alain Locke, ed., *The New Negro: An Interpretation* (New York: Albert and Charles Boni, 1925), 3–16; Nathan Irvin Huggins, *Harlem Renaissance* (New York: Oxford University Press, 1971), 52–65.

72. Paige, *Maybe I'll Pitch Forever*, 16.

73. Holway, *Voices*, 265.

74. James Overmyer, *Queen of the Negro Leagues: Effa Manley and the Newark Eagles* (Lanham, Md.: Scarecrow Press, 1998), 154–59.

75. O'Neil, panel discussion.

76. Ed Bolden's papers show Paige receiving 15 percent of the gate at a four-team doubleheader in 1950 at Shibe Park against the Philadelphia Stars. Ed Bolden Papers, "balance sheet—July 21, 1950," Moorland-Spingarn Research Center, Manuscript Division, Howard University, Washington, D.C.

77. Holway, *Josh and Satch*, 141.

78. Buck O'Neil wrote in his autobiography: "Satchel Paige was no Stepin Fetchit . . . and if Satchel had ever run into a writer who called him Stepin Fetchit, that man would have had to battle Satchel. . . ." O'Neil, *I Was Right on Time*, 112. Even the black press was guilty of stereotyping Paige. *Pittsburgh Courier* columnist Chester Washington referred to Paige as the "'Stepin Fetchit' of colored baseball." Chester Washington, "Sez Ches'," *Pittsburgh Courier*, 3 April 1937, 17.

79. Paige, *Pitchin' Man*, 26.

80. O'Neil, *I Was Right on Time*, 100–101.

81. Quincy Trouppe, *29 Years Too Soon* (Los Angeles: S and S Enterprises, 1977), 103.

82. Stephen Banker, *Black Diamonds: An Oral History of Negro Baseball* (Washington, D.C.: Tapes for Readers, 1978).

83. Ric Roberts, "Policeman Socks Satchel Paige in Washington," *Pittsburgh Courier*, 18 August 1945, 12; *Washington Afro-American*, 18 August 1945, 27.

84. "Grays Win 2–1," *Pittsburgh Courier*, 27 June 1942, 16. Crowd estimates from the June 18 game varied among the different newspapers: 32,000 in the *Washington Tribune*, 30,000 in the *Pittsburgh Courier*, 28,000 in the *Washington Afro-American*, 26,113 "cash customers" in the *Washington Post*, and 26,000 in the *Washington Times-Herald*. *Washington Tribune*, 20 June 1942, 1; *Pittsburgh Courier*, 27 June 1942, 16; *Washington Afro-American*, 27 June 1942, 26; *Washington Post*, 25 June 1942, 25; Vincent X. Flaherty, "Straight from the Shoulder," *Washington Times-Herald*, 20 June 1942, 33. I went with the *Afro's* 28,000 figure because it is the median number and because the *Afro's* information is most likely to be accurate with Art Carter running the event. Whatever the exact attendance figure, it dwarfed the crowds of 11,000 who would receive free admission to a June 21 game between Bob Feller's All-Stars and the Senators and 10,000 who had contributed to the war relief effort for a match-up between the Senators and the New York Yankees. Ric Roberts, "Grays Outdraw All Sports Events at Griff Stadium; Battle Newark Sunday," *Washington Afro-American*, 27 June 1942, 25.

85. "Satchel Paige to Face NNL Champs," *Washington Afro-American*, 13 June 1942, 24 ("It will mark the first time that two colored nines have ever performed under major league arcs"); "28,000 See Grays Nip Monarchs, 2–1, in First Night Game Under Major League Arc Lights in Washington," id., 27 June 1942, 26.

86. The lower number of $3,253 ($2,772 rent plus $481 expenses) is based on the April 19, 1942, exhibition game between the Grays and Eagles. During that game, which drew 4,714 fans, Griffith received 20 percent of $3,176.66 in gross profits, or $635.33, for stadium rental, plus $62.50 in expenses for ticket sales, ushers, and cleanup. Balance Sheet, 19–20 April 1942, Homestead Grays v. Newark Eagles, box 1, folder 9, Art Carter Papers.

    The higher figure of $4,096 total is based on the $6,337 in park rent and $1,179 in expenses that Griffith received from the 1946 All-Star Classic held at Griffith Stadium. That game drew 15,009 fans and grossed $30,494.40. Balance Sheet, box 1, folder 9, Art Carter Papers. But that was four years later, after substantial wartime inflation and increased ticket prices. Nonetheless, $3,000 to $4,000 is a safe figure for May 31.

    Based on the same balance sheets, on June 18, the lower number comes to $4,140 ($3,528 in rent plus $612) and the higher number comes to $5,214 total. About the grounds crew, see *Washington Afro-American*, 27 June 1942, 26.

87. See Posey told the *Afro* in June 1941 that "progress has been made on a deal that would allow colored teams to play under the new arcs at Griffith Stadium." "Grays Hope to Close Deal for Night Ball," *Washington Afro-American*, 7 June 1941, 22.

88. "Ray Brown Loses Game to Phillies," *Washington Afro-American*, 10 August 1940, 22.

89. An unsigned article found in Art Carter's papers placed the figure at fifteen hundred dollars. This three-page article, written shortly after Jackie Robinson signed with the Brooklyn Dodgers in October 1945, was a wire story from the National Negro Press Association found in Carter's files. Incomplete Typescripts, box 1, folder 31, Art Carter Papers.

    Other Negro League executives, such as Baltimore Elite Giants president Vernon Green, claimed that Cum Posey inflated the cost of the lights to discourage other teams from trying to rent the ballpark. Vernon Green wrote Art Carter in 1949: "I know what the percentage is but don't know the exact cost for the lights. I do know they didn't cost as much as Posey claims they did." Letter from Vernon Green to Art Carter, 22 January 1949, box 1, folder 8, Art Carter Papers.

    An expense sheet from a sparsely attended 1948 game between the Grays and the New York Cubans revealed that the lights cost three hundred dollars. Expense Sheet, 12 August 1948—Grays v. Cubans, box 1, folder 10, Art Carter Papers.

    Griffith initially charged more than that to defray the installation cost of his lights, probably closer to five hundred to one thousand dollars a game. Calvin Griffith placed the figure at one thousand dollars. Calvin Griffith interview.

90. "Satchel Paige to Face NNL Champs," *Washington Afro-American*, 13 June 1942, 24.

91. Advertisement, *Nite Life*, 14 June 1942, box 2, folder 23, Art Carter Papers.

92. Advertisement, undated, box 2, folder 22, Art Carter Papers.

93. Art Carter, "From the Bench," *Washington Afro-American*, 2 September 1940, 27; Wendell Smith, "'Smitty's' Sports Spurts," *Pittsburgh Courier*, 14 September 1940, 16.

94. Ric Roberts, "Renaissance Seen as Baseball Boom Bestirs Leagues," *Washington Afro-American*, 12 July 1941, 23 ("Sir Posey is still dreaming of bringing [Paige] to Washington on a night date at Griffith Stadium, there to pit him and his Monarch buddies against the Grays with Ray Brown bending them across. It may attract 20,000 fans").

95. Ric Roberts, "Record Crowd in Offing for Games," *Washington Afro-American*, 9 May 1942, 24; Ric Roberts, "All Up in Washington," id., 9 May 1942, 25.

96. Bruce, *The Kansas City Monarchs*, 70–72; Holway, *Blackball Stars*, 327–43; Larry G. Bowman, "The Monarchs and Night Baseball," *The National Pastime: A Review of Baseball History* no. 16 (Cleveland: SABR, 1996), 80–84.

97. Paige, *Maybe I'll Pitch Forever*, 130–31, 141–42.

98. O'Neil, *I Was Right on Time*, 132–33.

99. Paige, *Maybe I'll Pitch Forever*, 66. After the game against Dean's All-Stars, Paige said that Gibson was the toughest hitter he had ever faced: "Josh can hit anything you throw him, and I mean hit it hard. He really lays the wood into the ball." Art Carter, "Satchel Paige Called the Joe Louis of Baseball," *Washington Afro-American*, 13 June 1942, 27.

100. Cum Posey, "Posey's Points," *Pittsburgh Courier*, 2 April 1938, 17.

101. Ric Roberts, "All Up in Washington," *Washington Afro-American*, 27 June 1942, 24.

102. Vincent X. Flaherty, "Straight from the Shoulder," *Washington Times-Herald*, 20 June 1942, 33.

103. Ibid.

104. Ric Roberts, "All Up in Washington," *Washington Afro-American*, 27 June 1942, 24.

105. Ric Roberts, "28,000 See Grays Nip Monarchs, 2–1," *Washington Afro-American*, 27 June 1942, 26.

106. Ibid.

107. Covington, "Partlow Outshines Paige in Mound Duel," *Washington Tribune*, 20 June 1942, 17.

108. "Grays Win 2–1," *Pittsburgh Courier*, 27 June 1942, 16.

109. Cum Posey, "Posey's Points," *Pittsburgh Courier*, 27 June 1942, 17.

110. Wilmer Fields, interview by author, Durham, N.C., 16 February 1993.

111. Ric Roberts, "All Up in Washington," *Washington Afro-American*, 27 June 1942, 24.

112. Ric Roberts, "Vic Harris Says Build Own Baseball Leagues," *Washington Afro-American*, 8 August 1942, 26.

113. Ric Roberts, "Grays Outdraw All Sports Events at Griff Stadium; Battle Newark Sunday," *Washington Afro-American*, 8 August 1942, 25.

114. Art Carter, "From the Bench," *Washington Afro-American*, 27 June 1942, 25.

115. Overmyer, *Queen of the Negro Leagues*, 103.

116. Leonard, *The Black Lou Gehrig*, 139.

117. Buck O'Neil interview.

118. Cum Posey, "Posey's Points," *Pittsburgh Courier*, 27 June 1942, 17.

119. Letter from Effa Manley to Art Carter, 19 June 1942, box 1, folder 7, Art Carter Papers.

120. An undated, handwritten expense sheet found in Carter's papers from a game between the Grays and New York Cubans indicates that the Cubans netted $1,519.84, the Grays netted $2,068.12, and Carter received $206.80. Undated expense sheet, box 1, folder 10, Art Carter Papers.

121. "Eagles Nip Grays, 6–5, in 14th," *Washington Afro-American*, 4 July 1942, 25. The *Washington Tribune* estimated the crowd at ten thousand. "Eagles Down Grays, 6–5; Deadlock Nightcap, 1–1," *Washington Tribune*, 4 July 1942, 16; "Grays and Eagles to Clash Here in Halfway Stretch," *Washington Tribune*, 27 June 1942, 17. "Grays Split with Barons," *Washington Afro-American*, 8 August 1942, 27; "Grays, Barons Break Even," *Pittsburgh Courier*, 8 August 1942, 16.

122. "Grays Win Twin Bill at Forbes Field; Cop Matinee Tilt in D.C.," *Pittsburgh Courier*, 4 July 1942, 17.

123. "Monarchs and Paige Face Grays Tuesday," *Washington Afro-American*, 18 July 1942, 17.

124. Chester L. Washington, "Sez Ches'," *Pittsburgh Courier*, 1 August 1942, 16.

125. Chester Washington wrote: "And to top the evening off, he held the mighty jolter, Joshua Gibson, hitless, fanning him at one particular time when the chips were really down and after he had walked Easterling, another good hitter, to get to Josh." Ibid. This is the only account of Paige striking out Gibson after intentionally walking Easterling. In recalling the classic duel a year later, Paige did not mention that it occurred during the World Series. Satchel Paige, "'Satch' Struck Out Josh Gibson for Biggest Thrill," *Pittsburgh Courier*, 8 May 1943, 19. The oral histories and Negro League historians who claim it happened during the World Series must be mistaken. See infra note 140.

126. Satchel Paige, "'Satch' Struck Out Josh Gibson for Biggest Thrill," *Pittsburgh Courier*, 8 May 1943, 19.

127. "Satchel Beaten in 5–4 Game," *Washington Afro-American*, 25 July 1942, 27. The *Afro* account, unlike Chester Washington's column, does not mention Paige intentionally walking Easterling to get to Gibson.

128. Ric Roberts, "Pitching Duel Ends with Monarchs on Short End of 3–2 Score," *Washington Afro-American*, 22 August 1942, 25; Ric Roberts, "All Up in Washington," id., 22 August 1942, 27; "20,000 See Grays Beat 'Satch' in D.C.," *Pittsburgh Courier*, 22 August 1942, 16.

129. Ibid.

130. Ibid.

131. Bill Scott, taped interview by author, Washington, D.C., 5 August 1992.

132. Tygiel, *Past Time*, 126 (discussing the difficulty of staging the 1924 Negro League World Series between the Monarchs and the Hilldale Club because of low weekday crowds).

133. "Grays-Elite Series to Be Broadcast," *Washington Afro-American*, 8 August 1942, 27. Some Negro League historians believe that this game marked the first-known radio broadcast of a Negro League game. Holway, *Josh and Satch*, 156.

134. *Washington Afro-American*, 15 August 1942, 25.

135. Ibid., 5 September 1942, 27.

136. Ric Roberts, "Paige Limits NNL Champs to 2 Hits," *Washington Afro-American*, 5 September 1942, 27.

137. O'Neil, *I Was Right on Time*, 129.

138. Ibid., 3.

139. *Washington Afro-American*, 5 September 1942, 27.

140. Noted Negro League historian Larry Lester discovered a box score in the *Pittsburgh Sun-Telegraph* from the second World Series game filled out by official scorer

Wendell Smith indicating that Paige walked three batters. See Larry Lester with John "Buck" O'Neil, "Satch vs. Josh," *The National Pastime: A Review of Baseball History* no. 13 (Cleveland: SABR, 1993), 30–33. But neither Lester's box score nor the accounts in the *Pittsburgh Courier* and the *Afro* indicate that Paige *intentionally* walked Harris and Easterling to pitch to Gibson. "Kaysees Win 2nd Tilt, 8–4," *Washington Afro-American*, 19 September 1942, 30. Furthermore, Buck O'Neil, Satchel Paige, and others claim that Gibson never took the bat off his shoulder. Lester, "Satch v. Josh," 33; O'Neil, *I Was Right on Time*, 130–36; Holway, *Josh and Satch*, 160–62; Paige, *Maybe I'll Pitch Forever*, 152–53. However, the *Afro* says Gibson fouled off the first two pitches in that game. "Kaysees Win 2nd Tilt, 8–4," *Washington Afro-American*, 19 September 1942, 30; Ribowsky, *The Power and the Darkness*, 248–49.

   Other evidence indicates that the famous Paige-Gibson incident did not happen during the 1942 World Series. A few days after the World Series game in Pittsburgh, Grays public relations director John Clark mailed a box score of the game to Art Carter along with a fairly detailed account of the game. Clark mentioned nothing about Paige walking Harris and Easterling to pitch to Gibson. Letter from John L. Clark to Art Carter, 13 September 1942, box 1, folder 7, Art Carter Papers. Less than a year after the World Series, Paige described his greatest thrill as a strike-out of Gibson the previous season. Paige, however, said nothing about the game occurring during the World Series. Satchel Paige, " 'Satch' Struck Out Josh Gibson for Biggest Thrill," *Pittsburgh Courier*, 8 May 1943, 19. Finally, years later, Monarchs backup catcher Frazier Robinson, who was one of Paige's close friends, conceded that Paige never intentionally walked the bases loaded to pitch to Gibson during the 1942 World Series. Frazier "Slow" Robinson with Paul Bauer, *Catching Dreams: My Life in the Negro Baseball Leagues* (Syracuse, N.Y.: Syracuse University Press, 1999) 93–94 ("It's a great story and Satchel loved to talk about it, but I'm sorry to say it didn't happen—at least not in that Series, and I saw every game from the dugout"). Paige was famous for embellishing his stories. Buck O'Neil was Paige's chief accomplice.

   Given these conflicting accounts and the lack of hard evidence, I believe that Paige intentionally walked Easterling to pitch to Gibson, not during the 1942 World Series game in Pittsburgh, but during the Grays-Monarchs 1942 regular-season meeting in Pittsburgh. Historian Donn Rogosin reported that Paige's two intentional walks to get to Gibson actually happened on July 21, 1942. Rogosin, *Invisible Men*, 97–99. This is consistent with Chester Washington's account in the August 1 *Pittsburgh Courier* that Paige intentionally walked Easterling and then struck out Gibson. See supra text accompanying note 125. This is the only contemporary account that confirms Paige ever pulled such a stunt.

141. Leonard, *The Black Lou Gehrig*, 137.
142. Buck O'Neil interview; O'Neil, *I Was Right on Time*, 127–28, 138.
143. Letter from John L. Clark to Art Carter, 13 September 1942, box 1, folder 7, Art Carter Papers.
144. Ric Roberts wrote: "The secret of the Monarch's [sic] success with the Grays seems to be inherent in the ages of the two clubs." Ric Roberts, "All Up in Washington," *Washington Afro-American*, 26 September 1942, 27.

145. "Homestead Grays Drop Their Opinion on Recent Series," *Washington Tribune*, 10 October 1942, 17, 19; Leonard, *The Black Lou Gehrig*, 135.

146. Holway, *Voices*, 252; Leonard, *The Black Lou Gehrig*, 149. It is entirely possible, however, that Leonard and Gibson's big payday did not come until 1943. That's when the Mexican League began sending officials to the United States to pursue the Grays' players.

147. Vic Harris had played with the Crawfords in 1934. Gibson had played with the Crawfords from 1932 to 1936 and had spent several seasons in Latin America playing only one or two games a week. Ray Brown also had spent time in Latin America.

148. Ric Roberts, "All Up in Washington," *Washington Afro-American*, 11 July 1942, 27.

149. "Dave Whatley Shows Way for Grays in D.C. Games," *Washington Afro-American*, 29 August 1942, 25.

150. "Grays Boast Four .300 Batters for Monarchs," *Washington Afro-American*, 5 September 1942, 25.

151. "Posey's All-American Team for '42," *Pittsburgh Courier*, 7 November 1942, 17.

152. Leonard, *The Black Lou Gehrig*, 143, 160.

153. "Dave Whatley Shows Way for Grays in D.C. Games," *Washington Afro-American*, 29 August 1942, 25.

154. "Grays Boast Four .300 Batters for Monarchs," *Washington Afro-American*, 5 September 1942, 25.

155. "'Dream Game' Box Score," *Pittsburgh Courier*, 22 August 1942, 16; "Posey's All-American Team for '42," id., 7 November 1942, 17.

156. "Gibson in Fold as '41 Champs Launch Drills in Raleigh," *Pittsburgh Courier*, 4 April 1942, 16.

157. Josh Gibson, "Double Award Was Top Event in Josh's Career," *Pittsburgh Courier*, 10 April 1943, 19.

158. Cum Posey, "Posey's Points," *Pittsburgh Courier*, 8 August 1942, 17.

159. W. Rollo Wilson, "Thru the Eyes of W. Rollo Wilson," *Philadelphia Tribune*, 10 June 1944, 12.

160. Ribowsky, *The Power and the Darkness*, 252–54.

161. "Famous Catcher Sent to Hospital," *Pittsburgh Courier*, 9 January 1943, 16; "Gibson's Condition Improved," *Pittsburgh Courier*, 16 January 1943, 17; *Washington Tribune*, 16 January 1943, 11; Harold Jackson, "On the Sports Front," *Washington Afro-American*, 23 January 1943, 23.

162. Cum Posey, "Posey's Points," *Pittsburgh Courier*, 23 January 1943, 16.

163. Cum Posey, "Posey's Points," *Pittsburgh Courier*, 31 October 1942, 17.

164. Art Carter, "From the Bench," *Washington Afro-American*, 5 September 1942, 25.

165. During their ten home dates at Griffith Stadium during the regular season, the Grays drew 102,690 fans. Ibid. This figure was before the first World Series game, which drew 25,000 fans to Griffith Stadium.

166. Reichler, *The Ronald Encyclopedia of Baseball*, 240–41.

CHAPTER 6

1. See text accompanying notes 25–31 in Chapter 2.

2. Peterson, *Only the Ball Was White*, 158.

3. Art Carter first wrote that Gibson was hitting more home runs to left field and center field than the American League was hitting midway through the 1943 season. Art Carter, "Joltin' Josh Helps the Grays Hit the Jackpot," *Washington Afro-American*, 24 July 1943, 26. Several books have repeated the claim that Gibson hit more home runs than the entire American League. Robert Peterson credited Gibson with 11 home runs in 1943 and wrote that Gibson "reportedly" hit more home runs to left field than the AL. Peterson, *Only the Ball Was White*, 170. Michael Benson reported that the feat took place in the "early 1940s" and credited the story to Clark Griffith. Benson, *Ballparks of North America*, 409.

4. Lowry, *Green Cathedrals*, 245.

5. Griffith's favorite major league ballpark was the horseshoe-shaped Polo Grounds, which was only 280 feet down the left-field line and 259 down the right-field line (and 490 feet to dead center). In a question-and-answer session with Gibson, Posey remarked: "No use of asking you why [the Polo Grounds was Gibson's favorite] as I know it is on account of the short left-field stands." Gibson replied: "Right field, too." "Posey's Points," *Pittsburgh Courier*, 2 April 1938, 17. Gibson's response indicated that he could pull the ball but that he liked to hit to all fields.

6. "Clark Griffith to Join League Heads in Appeal to ODT," *Pittsburgh Courier*, 13 March 1943, 18; Cum Posey, "Posey's Points," id. The *Afro* does not mention whether Griffith actually accompanied them to the meeting. "Officials Talk with Eastman," *Washington Afro-American*, 13 March 1943, 27.

7. *Washington Tribune*, 3 April 1943, 11.

8. "Boom Towns Will Save Negro Baseball—Clarke," *Pittsburgh Courier*, 6 March 1943, 18.

9. Edsall Walker, taped interview by author, Secaucus, N.J., 30 May 1992.

10. Art Carter, "Joltin' Josh Helps Grays Hit the Jackpot," *Washington Afro-American*, 24 July 1943, 26.

11. Gatewood, *Aristocrats of Color*, 77.

12. "Recreation and Morale," *Crisis* 50:9 (September 1943), 277.

13. Holway, *Voices*, 261.

14. Art Carter, "Joltin' Josh Helps the Grays Hit the Jackpot," *Washington Afro-American*, 24 July 1943, 26.

15. A Grays average attendance figure of 8,653.8 per game is based on 225,000 (125,000 fans plus 100,000 estimate)/26 games.

16. Edsall Walker interview.

17. Bob McConnell and David Vincent, eds., SABR *Presents the Home Run Encyclopedia: The Who, What, and Where of Every Home Run Hit Since 1876* (New York: Macmillan, 1996), 101. McConnell and Vincent, in discussing the fewest home runs ever hit by a team during the course of a season from 1920 to 1960, noted that Griffith Stadium was the toughest home-run park in the American League and Braves Field in Boston was the toughest in the National League. Id., 9.

18. Ibid., 1140.

19. Ibid., 693, 1228.

20. Spence homered to right field off Chicago White Sox pitcher Buck Ross on September 27 and off Cleveland Indians pitcher Jim Bagby on September 29. Shirley Povich, "Malzberger Twice Star in Relief Role," *Washington Post*, 28 September 1943, 14; Merrell W. Whittlesey, "Wynn Scores 18th Victory in Nightcap," *Wash-*

ington Post, 30 September 1943, 20. Vernon homered to right field off St. Louis Browns pitcher Bob Muncrief on August 1. Shirley Povich, "Nats Wallop Browns Twice, Second, 20–6," *Washington Post*, 2 August 1943, 11. The detailed research on the Griffith Stadium home runs of 1943 was facilitated by the Society of American Baseball Research's Tattersall/McConnell Home Run Log, with the dates of the Griffith Stadium home runs in 1943 compiled by David Vincent.

21. Mickey Vernon, telephone interview by author, Wallingford, Pa., 10 November 1994.

22. Inside-the-park homers (4): Boston Red Sox second baseman Bobby Doerr off Senators pitcher Early Wynn on May 7, Philadelphia Athletics outfielder Elmer Valo off Senators pitcher Dutch Leonard on June 25, Senators second baseman Jerry Priddy off Detroit Tigers pitcher Roy Henshaw on July 22, Tigers outfielder Ned Harris off Senators pitcher Bobo Newsom on October 2. See *Washington Post*, 8 May 1943, 15; *Washington Evening Star*, 26 June 1943, B-4; id., 23 July 1940, A-10; id., 3 October 1943, B-2.

   Right-field homers (10): New York Yankees outfielder Charlie Keller off Wynn on May 2, Senators outfielder Gene Moore off Red Sox pitcher Mace Brown on July 18, Cleveland Indians outfielder Hank Edwards off Senators pitcher Mickey Haefner on July 24, St. Louis Browns outfielder Mike Chartak off Dutch Leonard on July 31, Vernon off Browns pitcher Bob Muncrief on August 1, Browns first baseman George McQuinn off Wynn on August 3, Senators catcher Jake Early off Red Sox pitcher Tex Hughson on September 15, Spence off White Sox pitcher Buck Ross on September 27, Indians outfielder Roy Cullenbine off Wynn on September 29, Spence off Indians pitcher Jim Bagby on September 29. See *Washington Post*, 3 May 1943, 13; *Washington Evening Star*, 19 July, 1943, A-13; id., 25 July 1943, B-1; id., 1 August 1943, B-2; *Washington Post*, 2 August 1943, 11; *Washington Evening Star*, 4 August 1943, A-17; id., 16 September 1943, A-18; *Washington Post*, 28 September 1943, 14; id., 30 September 1943, 20.

23. American League home-run totals: 796 in '39, 883 in '40, 734 in '41, 533 in '42, 473 in '43, 459 in '44, 430 in '45, 653 in '46. McConnell and Vincent, *Home Run Encyclopedia*, 164–69.

24. Gilbert, *They Also Served*, 90–91; Mead, *Baseball Goes to War*, 78–79.

25. "Pyle Sets Back Yankees with Lively Sphere," *Washington Evening Star*, 3 May 1943, A-12; James P. Dawson, "Rookie Overcomes McCarthymen, 4–1," *New York Times*, 3 May 1943, 22; Shirley Povich, "Early Wynn Is Pounded in Opener," *Washington Post*, 3 May 1943, 13.

26. *Negro Baseball*, 1945 and 1946 editions, box 1, folder 24, Art Carter Papers.

27. Holway, *Voices*, 251; Rogosin, *Invisible Men*, 72.

28. Holway, *Voices*, 276. Leonard wasn't the only black player who deemed the Wilson balls to be inferior to the Spalding balls used by the major leagues. So did Judy Johnson and Ted "Double Duty" Radcliffe. Holway, *Josh and Satch*, 34.

29. Expense sheets, box 1, folders 8 and 9, Art Carter Papers.

30. Overmyer, *Queen of the Negro Leagues*, 77.

31. *Washington Afro-American*, 18 July 1942, 27.

32. "Gibson Big Gun as Elites Bow to Grays," *Washington Afro-American*, 22 May 1943, 26; "Grays Down Elite Giants Twice Here Sunday," *Washington Tribune*, 22 May 1943, 11.

33. "Grays Beat Philly in Washington," *Pittsburgh Courier*, 29 May 1943, 18; *Washington Afro-American*, 29 May 1943, 25. The *Washington Tribune* estimated the blast at 422 feet. "Grays Cop Twin-bill from Philly Stars," *Washington Tribune*, 29 May 1943, 10; id., 29 May 1943, 11 (photograph of Gibson crossing home plate).

34. Harold Jackson, "Gibson's 440-Foot Home Run in Second Game Thrills 6,500 Fans," *Washington Afro-American*, 29 May 1943, 25.

35. "Grays Run Amuck in 3rd Game of Series with Elite Giants," *Washington Tribune*, 5 June 1943, 10.

36. "Nats' Hold on Second Maced as Tigers Pound to Victory," *Washington Evening Star*, 4 June 1943, A-14.

37. Shirley Povich, "Nats Defeat Tigers Twice, Hold Second," *Washington Post*, 7 June 1943, 11. Detroit Tigers first baseman Rudy York, who led the American League that year with 34, hit 4 home runs at Griffith Stadium—the most of any hitter besides Gibson. York's accomplishment is perhaps more amazing than Gibson's because not only was he a right-handed batter like Gibson but he also played only eleven games at Griffith Stadium (compared to Gibson's forty). The Alabama-born York had the slight advantage of hitting off fewer pitchers at Griffith Stadium, though the Senators pitching staff gave up the fewest road home runs in the American League and included a young Early Wynn. Gibson, by contrast, faced at least a dozen pitching staffs and perhaps better pitchers, such as Paige and Leon Day. Nonetheless, York's feat of 4 home runs in eleven games at Griffith Stadium in 1943 deserves its due.

38. "Grays, Cubans Split Before 10,000 Fans," *Pittsburgh Courier*, 19 June 1943, 18; *Washington Afro-American*, 19 June 1943, 23; "Cubans Halt Gray's [sic] Local Winning Ways," *Washington Tribune*, 19 June 1943, 11 (describing them as 420 feet and 440 feet).

39. Harold Jackson, "On the Sports Front," *Washington Afro-American*, 19 June 1943, 23.

40. "Wynn, Johnson Share Honors in Night Tilt," *Washington Evening Star*, 27 June 1943, B-1.

41. "Josh Gibson's Home Run Wins Nightcap," *Washington Afro-American*, 10 July 1943, 26; "Gibson's Homer Saves Grays in Thrilling Nightcap," *Pittsburgh Courier*, 10 July 1943, 19; "Gibson's Drive in Bleachers Gives Grays Twin Victory," *Washington Tribune*, 10 July 1943, 17.

42. Art Carter, "10,000 at Mixed Contest," *Washington Afro-American*, 10 July 1943, 26; "Grays Down Bushwicks, 11–3; Play Cleveland Here Sunday," *Washington Tribune*, 10 July 1943, 17.

43. "Double, Homer by Bob Upset Red Sox, Help Put Griffs Second," *Washington Evening Star*, 16 July 1943, A-10.

44. "Nats' Little Men Big in Crises; Tackle Tigers Twice Tonight," *Washington Evening Star*, 22 July 1943, A-16.

45. "Nats Trying to Save Second After Two Losses to Tigers," *Washington Evening Star*, 23 July 1943, A-10.

46. Shirley Povich, "Nats Wallop Browns Twice, Second, 20–6," *Washington Post*, 2 August 1943, 11.

47. "Tour to Be Severe Test; Two More Beatings Handed Browns," *Washington Evening Star*, 4 August 1943, A-17.

48. Ric Roberts, "Gibson, Suttles Smash Decisive Round Trippers," *Pittsburgh Courier*, 14 August 1943, 19; "Suttle's [sic] Pinch Homer Gives Eagles Split," *Washington Tribune*, 14 August 1943, 18.

49. Harold Jackson, "Gibson and Suttles Hit Long Home Runs," *Washington Afro-American*, 14 August 1943, 23.

50. Harold Jackson, "Grays Gain 2–1 Margin," *Washington Afro-American*, 21 August 1943, 26; Harold Jackson, "On the Sports Front," id., 27. Although Harold Jackson recounts the near–home run in great detail, the *Pittsburgh Courier* and *Washington Tribune*'s brief stories failed to mention it. See Ric Roberts, "Cubans, Grays Split Slugfests," *Pittsburgh Courier*, 21 August 1943, 19; "Grays Down Cubans Twice," *Washington Tribune*, 21 August 1943, 17.

51. *1943 Baseball* (Chicago: Office of the Baseball Commissioner, 1943), 647.

52. Harold Jackson, "Josh Gibson Clouts 3 Homers in Series," *Washington Afro-American*, 28 August 1943, 27; Ric Roberts, "Champs Sweep Elites," *Pittsburgh Courier*, 28 August 1943, 18.

53. "Grays Wallop Yankees, 12–4 in Night Tilt," *Washington Afro-American*, 28 August 1943, 26.

54. Harold Jackson, "Grays Capture Twin Bill," *Washington Afro-American*, 18 September 1943, 26.

55. These figures are from the Grays' season-ending won-loss schedule, which was complete through September 12, plus two World Series games against the Birmingham Black Barons. It does not include the North-South All-Star Game. "Record of Games Played by Homestead Grays—1943 Season," box two, folder four, Art Carter Papers.

56. Edsall Walker interview.

57. Lena Cox interview, 5 August 1992.

58. Buck O'Neil interview.

59. Ibid.

60. Harold Jackson, "Josh Gibson Paces Grays in Twin Win," *Washington Afro-American*, 26 June 1943, 26; "Paige Falters as Grays Take Monarchs," *Washington Tribune*, 26 June 1943, 10.

61. "Monarchs Wallop Grays as Paige Again Stars," *Washington Tribune*, 14 August 1943, 16.

62. "Covington's Comments," *Washington Tribune*, 4 September 1943, 17.

63. "Gibson Hits Homer, Doubles Off Paige," *Washington Afro-American*, 4 September 1943, 27; "Josh Clouts Home Run, Double as Monarchs Go Down," *Pittsburgh Courier*, 4 September 1943, 19; "Grays Nip Monarchs; Gibson Beats Paige," *Washington Tribune*, 4 September 1943, 18.

64. Art Carter, "Use of Ineligible Men Belittles World Series," *Washington Afro-American*, 9 October 1943, 26; Wendell Smith, "Smitty's Sports Spurts," *Pittsburgh Courier*, 2 October 1943, 16; Hayward Jackson, "New Orleans Fans Score Cancellation of Series Game," *Pittsburgh Courier*, 16 October 1943, 16.

65. *Washington Afro-American*, 18 July 1942, 27.

66. Haskell Cohen, "Negro Baseball Champs," *Sport*, 14 September 1943, 41–43.

67. "Josh the Basher," *Time*, 19 July 1943, 75–76; Holway, *Josh and Satch*, 166–67.

68. Shirley Povich, "Opener Lost to Chisox by 15–3 Score," *Washington Post*, 27 September 1943, 18.

69. Art Carter, "Joltin' Josh Helps the Grays Hit the Jackpot," *Washington Afro-American*, 24 July 1943, 26.
70. "Clark Griffith Comes Through," *Washington Tribune*, 18 September 1943, 24.
71. Holway, *Voices*, 252. Leonard has told a variation of this story in practically every history of the Negro Leagues. Despite the variations in the dialogue, the gist is the same. See Leonard, *The Black Lou Gehrig*, 99; Rogosin, *Invisible Men*, 192; Peterson, *Only the Ball Was White*, 169; Holway, *Josh and Satch*, 155; Tygiel, *Baseball's Great Experiment*, 40; Brashler, *Josh Gibson*, 132. In his own book, Leonard says the conversation took place in 1938, but it may have been later because it was after Gibson got back from the Mexican League. Leonard, *The Black Lou Gehrig*, 99. Gibson returned from the Mexican League in 1942, the year Leonard originally told historian John Holway the conversation took place. Holway, *Voices*, 252. Given that the Grays did not begin playing in Washington until 1940, Gibson did not come back from Mexico until 1942, and Leonard was out much of the 1942 season, I believe that 1942 or 1943 is the accurate date.
72. Holway, *Voices*, 252. Although Washington's black population was around 200,000 in 1943, Washington was not 50 percent black. It did not become a majority-black city until the early to mid-1950s.
73. Herman Hill, "Jackie Robinson, Nate Moreland Barred at Camp," *Pittsburgh Courier*, 21 March 1942, 16. Several Robinson biographies and Negro League histories mistakenly suggest that Robinson and Moreland actually tried out. Holway, *Voices*, 12; Tygiel, *Baseball's Great Experiment*, 39 (citing Holway); Lester, *Black Baseball's National Showcase*, 173. But see David Falkner, *Great Time Coming: The Life of Jackie Robinson from Baseball to Birmingham* (New York: Simon and Schuster, 1995), 68 (arguing that Robinson failed to mention the tryout because it was organized by the Communist *Daily Worker*; Robinson, however, never mentioned it because it never happened); Arnold Rampersad, *Jackie Robinson: A Biography* (New York: Alfred A. Knopf, 1997), 89 (writing that Robinson was "teased and tantalized by an opportunity to work out in Brookside Park with the Chicago White Sox," but never indicating that a tryout actually occurred). The two players, accompanied by the *Courier's* West Coast correspondent Herman Hill, merely talked with White Sox manager Jimmy Dykes. Dykes mentioned having seen Robinson play in an exhibition game on a previous occasion, but the *Courier* unequivocally reported that the White Sox failed to give him a tryout. *Pittsburgh Courier*, 21 March 1942, 16. This article was reprinted in the *Daily Worker* several days later. In his excellent biographical sketch of Moreland's life, John McReynolds confirmed that no tryout ever occurred. John McReynolds, "Nate Moreland: A Mystery to Historians," *The National Pastime: A Review of Baseball History* no. 19 (Cleveland: SABR, 1999), 57–58.
74. Ric Roberts, "All Up in Washington," *Washington Afro-American*, 25 July 1942, 27; "Commissioner Landis' Emancipation Proclamation—'Negro Players Are Welcome,'" *Pittsburgh Courier*, 25 July 1942, 17; "Landis, Major Baseball Czar, Passes Buck to Club Owners; Denies Bars Exist 'Gainst Negroes," *Washington Tribune*, 25 July 1942, 16.
75. Art Carter, "From the Bench," *Washington Afro-American*, 1 August 1942, 26.
76. Chester L. Washington, "Sez Ches'," *Pittsburgh Courier*, 25 July 1942, 16; Vincent X. Flaherty, "Straight from the Shoulder," *Washington Times-Herald*, 19 July 1942, 1-B.

77. "Griff Says Organize Colored," *Washington Afro-American*, 25 July 1942, 26.
78. Ric Roberts, "Vic Harris Says Build Own Baseball Leagues," *Washington Afro-American*, 8 August 1942, 26.
79. "Ball Players Skeptical of Big Leagues," *Washington Afro-American*, 1 August 1942, 27.
80. Art Carter, "From the Bench," *Washington Afro-American*, 15 August 1942, 25.
81. "'Majors Couldn't Pay Enough,' 'Satchel' Claims," *Pittsburgh Courier*, 15 August 1942, 16.
82. "'Was Misquoted,' Says Satchel," *Pittsburgh Courier*, 22 August 1942, 17.
83. Ibid., 22 August 1942, 26; Art Carter, "From the Bench," *Washington Afro-American*, 22 August 1942, 26.
84. Bob Considine, "On the Line," *Washington Post*, 15 August 1942, 15.
85. Ibid.
86. Holway, *Voices*, 260–61; Buck Leonard interview, 20 July 1992.
87. "H.U. Student Pickets Force Restaurant to Drop Color Bar," *Washington Afro-American*, 24 April 1943, 1, 14. Pauli Murray, *The Autobiography of a Black Activist, Feminist, Lawyer, Priest, and Poet* (Knoxville, Tenn.: The University of Tennessee Press, 1987), 202.
88. "Sidat-Singh Is One of 4 Flyers Killed in Army Plane Mishaps," *Washington Afro-American*, 15 May 1943, 1, 24; "Sidat-Singh Given Up as Lost After Crash." *Washington Tribune*, 15 May 1943, 1. For an excellent recent article on Sidat-Singh, see Luke Cyphers, "Lost Hero: Sidat-Singh a Two-Sport Star, Harlem Renaissance Man," *New York Daily News*, 25 February 2001, 82, and 30 March 2001.
89. Art Carter, "From the Bench," *Washington Afro-American*, 27 March 1943, 25.
90. Harold Jackson, "On the Sports Front," *Washington Afro-American*, 29 May 1943, 26.
91. "Jake Powell Kills Himself as Police Are Questioning Him," *Washington Post*, 5 November 1948, 1. Wendell Smith wrote an embittered farewell column about Powell: "Jake's gone. We feel just like the man who when asked if he were going to Huey Long's funeral said: 'No, but I'm in favor of it.'" Wendell Smith, "Sports Beat," *Pittsburgh Courier*, 20 November 1948, 10.
92. Harold Jackson, "On the Sports Front," *Washington Afro-American*, 28 August 1943, 26.
93. Reichler, *The Ronald Encyclopedia of Baseball*, 240–41.
94. Art Carter, "Joltin' Josh Helps the Grays Hit the Jackpot," *Washington Afro-American*, 24 July 1943, 26.
95. "Fans Honor Josh Gibson in D.C.," *Pittsburgh Courier*, 11 September 1943, 19; "Gibson Honored by Fans," *Washington Afro-American*, 11 September 1943, 27.
96. "Grays Enter World Series with .370 Team Average," *Washington Afro-American*, 18 September 1943, 26.
97. Ribowsky, *The Power and the Darkness*, 254.
98. Leonard, *The Black Lou Gehrig*, 145–48; Brashler, *Josh Gibson*, 133–38; Ribowsky, *The Power and the Darkness*, 261–64; W. Rollo Wilson, "Thru the Eyes of W. Rollo Wilson," *Philadelphia Tribune*, 10 June 1944, 12.
99. Ibid.
100. "Grays Enter World Series with .370 Team Average," *Washington Afro-American*, 18 September 1943, 26.

101. Art Carter, "Satchel Paige Star of Diamond Classic," *Washington Afro-American*, 7 August 1943, 23; "West Downs East, 2–1, Leonard Homers," *Washington Tribune*, 7 August 1943, 12.

102. Harold Jackson, "Jud Wilson Paces Grays to Twin Bill," *Washington Afro-American*, 11 September 1943, 26; Ric Roberts, "Grays Defeat Kansas City 2–1, 8–1," *Pittsburgh Courier*, 11 September 1943, 19.

103. Cum Posey, "Famous Catcher and Pitcher Selected on Posey's 'Dream Team,'" *Pittsburgh Courier*, 27 November 1943, 16.

104. Wendell Smith, "'Smitty's' Sports Spurts," *Pittsburgh Courier*, 25 December 1943, 14.

Chapter 7

1. Young, as Lacy told Jim Reisler, was "rather jealous of his job, a man who made a point that I was not to be writing sports." Reisler, *Black Writers/Black Baseball*, 12. For more on Frank Young, see id., 57–59. Reisler also claims that Young was the first black sportswriter to protest baseball's color barrier, in a 1926 column that said: "the ban against Negro players is a silly one, and one that should be removed." Id., 7.

2. In 1942 and 1943, Lacy's first wife, Alberta, continued to live in their northwest Washington apartment on 722 Park Road along with their young son, Samuel Howe "Tim" Lacy (b: February 8, 1938). *1942 City Directory*, 940; *1943 City Directory*, 867. For the birth of Lacy's son, see Lacy, *Fighting for Fairness*, 27. Alberta Lacy worked as a clerk and had been employed as a waiter at the Woodward and Lothrop department store. Id.; *1938 City Directory*, 741.

3. Sam Lacy, "Looking 'Em Over," *Baltimore Afro-American*, 8 January 1944, 19.

4. In 1955, the group changed the name to the National Newspaper Publishers Association. Armstead S. Pride and Clint C. Wilson III, *A History of the Black Press* (Washington, D.C.: Howard University Press, 1997), 194.

5. Sam Lacy, "Looking 'Em Over," *Baltimore Afro-American*, 8 January 1944, 19.

6. Sheingold, "In Black and White," 58. Eight members of the NNPA officially attended the meeting: Sengstacke, Lewis, and Murphy; *Amsterdam News* publisher C. B. Powell; *Michigan Chronicle* publisher Louis E. Martin; and *Cleveland Call and Post* publisher William O. Walker; as well as two "advisory members," *Amsterdam News* managing editor Dan Burley and *Pittsburgh Courier* city editor Wendell Smith. "Yankee Boss OKs Colored Players," *Baltimore Afro-American*, 11 December 1943, 30; "Big League Moguls Get Plea for Negro Players," *Chicago Defender*, 11 December 1943, 1, 4. Lacy may have overlooked or simply ignored that *Courier* president Ira Lewis was a former sportswriter who along with the *Defender*'s Fay Young sounded the initial calls for the integration of the major leagues among the black press during the 1920s. Fay Young, "Through the Years: Past Present Future," *Chicago Defender*, 1 August 1942, 19.

7. Sam Lacy, "Looking 'Em Over," *Baltimore Afro-American*, 8 January 1944, 19. Lacy did not attend the meeting but could have read the text of Sengstacke and Lewis's speeches and Murphy's recommendations in the black press. *Baltimore Afro-American*, 14 December 1943, 18–19; *Pittsburgh Courier*, 11 December 1943, 14; *Chicago Defender*, 11 December 1943, 1.

8. A month after the December 3 meeting, Lacy wrote:

> For truly, that was a three-base error committed in the conference room at the Roosevelt Hotel. . . . First, Judge Kenesaw M. Landis, the high commissioner of baseball, did NOT invite the delegation to the meeting; second, the delegation should have been an over-all representative body rather than a one-industry declaration; and third, Paul Robeson should have been identified as Landis's guest and Landis's ALONE.

Sam Lacy, "Looking 'Em Over," *Baltimore Afro-American*, 8 January 1944, 19. Other contemporary accounts confirm that Robeson was Landis's guest. See Wendell Smith, "Publishers Place Case of Negro Players Before Big League Owners," *Pittsburgh Courier*, 11 December 1943, 1 (Landis told the owners: "I brought Paul here . . ."); Nat Low, "Major Leagues Pave Way for Negroes," *Daily Worker*, 4 December 1943, 1 ("Robeson was a last-minute addition to the joint meeting of the magnates, coming to speak at the insistence of the aged Landis . . ."); "How New York Sportswriters Viewed Big League Attitude on Admitting Colored Baseball Aces," *Amsterdam News*, 11 December 1943, 4B ("Robeson was there as an invited guest of Landis himself") (quoting Joe Cummiskey, "Plea Received, Contents Noted—Period," *PM*, 5 December 1943, 17).

In his later years, Lacy erroneously blamed Sengstacke for inviting Robeson. Lacy interviews, 15 July 1992 and 17 May 1994; Patrick Ercolano, "He Went to Bat for Blacks," *Baltimore Sun Magazine*, 6 April 1986, 20; Steve Katz, "Sam Lacy Traveled Rough Road with Black Athletes," *Baltimore Sun*, 17 August 1980, C5; Marilyn McCraven, "Writing on the Wall," *Baltimore Sun*, 1 April 1997, F1; Kevin Merida, "Going to Bat for Robinson," *Washington Post*, 11 June 1997, D8; Mark G. Judge, "Writing the Good Fight," *Washington City Paper*, 17 May 1991, 30; Ron Fimrite, "Sam Lacy: Black Crusader," *Sports Illustrated*, 29 October 1990, 93; Larry Whiteside, "It's Lacy's Honor," *Boston Globe*, 26 July 1998, C1; Barry Horn, "As Good as His Word," *Dallas Morning News*, 12 April 1998, 24B; D. L. Cummings, "His Everlasting Power of the Pen," *Austin-American Statesman*, 21 February 1997, C1. Lacy's efforts to blame Sengstacke and the *Defender* also made their way into several book-length accounts of the Robinson/integration story. Tygiel, *Baseball's Great Experiment*, 41; Pietrusza, *Judge and Jury*, 424 (citing Tygiel); Falkner, *Great Time Coming*, 100. The haziness of Lacy's recollections is confirmed by his repeated assertions to newspaper reporters and in his autobiography that the 1943 meeting between Robeson and the owners occurred at Cleveland's Hotel Hollenden. Lacy, *Fighting for Fairness*, 45. The 1943 meeting actually took place at the Roosevelt Hotel in New York; two years later, Lacy addressed the major league owners in Cleveland about forming an integration committee.

In his autobiography, Lacy partially acknowledged that the blame rested with Landis. He wrote that Robeson was invited "apparently at the encouragement of Commissioner Landis. . . ." Lacy continued: "I was not included in the contingent to meet with the owners because it was believed that handing a speaking role to Robeson would have a greater impact on the moguls of baseball. I knew that was a kiss of death because at that time, Paul was considered by many to be a communist." Id.

Wendell Smith, in an oral history with Jerome Holtzman in the early 1970s, claimed that the Roosevelt Hotel meeting with Landis and the owners occurred in 1939, not 1943. Smith said: "Ira Lewis, the publisher of the *Courier*, and Paul Robeson, the famous singer, accompanied me to an owners' meeting at the Roosevelt Hotel in New York. . . . We had written a letter asking if we could make an appearance, if we could make an appeal on behalf of the Negro ballplayers. Robeson, at that time, had a good name. Later, he became controversial. Paul Robeson and Ira Lewis spoke, for twenty minutes to a half hour." Jerome Holtzman, ed., *No Cheering in the Press Box*, rev. ed. (New York: Henry Holt, 1995), 335–36. Cf. Rampersad, *Jackie Robinson*, 121 (relying on several newspaper articles, probably citing Holtzman's book, that Robeson accompanied Wendell Smith to meet with Landis in 1939).

John Sengstacke died at age eighty-four on May 28, 1997. Jennifer Ackerman, "John H. Sengstacke, 84, Civil Rights Activist, Owned Michigan Chronicle," *Detroit News*, 30 May 1997, 2D. To the best of my knowledge, no one ever asked Sengstacke about his version of events.

I am most comfortable relying on contemporary accounts that Landis invited Robeson to speak to the owners at New York's Roosevelt Hotel in 1943. The initiative for the meeting, however, was Lacy's.

9. Wendell Smith, "Publishers Place Case of Negro Players Before Big League Owners," *Pittsburgh Courier*, 11 December 1943, 1. Other accounts have quoted Landis's introduction as follows: "It is unnecessary to introduce Paul Robeson. Everybody knows him as an actor and an artist. I want to introduce him as a man of great common sense." Nat Low, "Major Leagues Pave Way for Negroes," *Daily Worker*, 4 December 1943, 1; Falkner, *Great Time Coming*, 99.

10. Joe Cummiskey, "Plea Received, Contents Noted—Period," *PM*, 5 December 1943, 17. Other contemporary accounts quoted Robeson as saying: "To me, the most indicative thing that has happened in the fight against racial discrimination is the reception that I've been given in Othello. I was told before the play was produced that America is not ready to accept me or such a delicate theme, but I've never appeared before friendlier audiences." "How New York Sportswriters Viewed Big League Attitude on Admitting Colored Baseball Aces" *Amsterdam News*, 11 December 1943, 4b (quoting Stanley Frank, "Negroes Receive Wordy 'Brushoff' from Baseball," *New York Post*, 4 December 1943, 22). For additional accounts of the meeting, see "Big League Moguls Get Plea for Negro Players," *Chicago Defender*, 11 December 1943, 1, 4; John Drebinger, "Harris Is Called by Commissioner," *New York Times*, 4 December 1943, 17; Tygiel, *Baseball's Great Experiment*, 41.

11. Nat Low, "Major Leagues Pave Way for Negroes," *Daily Worker*, 4 December 1943, 1; Martin Bauml Duberman, *Paul Robeson: A Biography* (New York: Ballantine Books, 1989), 283.

12. Sam Lacy, "Looking 'Em Over," *Baltimore Afro-American*, 8 January 1944, 19.

13. Ric Roberts, "Hopes for Colored Players in Major Leagues Fade with Waning '42 Season," *Washington Afro-American*, 26 September 1942, 26.

14. Murray Polner, *Branch Rickey: A Biography* (New York: New American Library, 1982), 150.

15. Wendell Smith, "Publishers Place Case of Negro Players Before Big League Owners," *Pittsburgh Courier*, 11 December 1943, 17.

16. Wendell Smith, "Frick Says Owners Were Impressed," *Pittsburgh Courier*, 11 December 1943, 14.

17. Stanley Frank, "Negroes Receive Wordy 'Brushoff' from Baseball," *New York Post*, 4 December 1943, 22.
18. Ralph Matthews, "Clark Griffith Won't Budge on Use of Colored Players," *Baltimore Afro-American*, 11 December 1943, 1.
19. Bob Considine and Shirley L. Povich, "Old Fox: Baseball's Red-Eyed Radical and Archconservative, Clark Griffith," *Saturday Evening Post*, 13 April 1940, 14–15; id., 20 April 1940, 18–19.
20. Lacy, *Fighting for Fairness*, 45; Sam Lacy interview, 17 May 1994.
21. Frazier, *Negro in the United States*, 514. According to Frazier, the circulation was as follows: *Pittsburgh Courier*—270,812, *Afro-American*—229,812, *Chicago Defender*—161,009, and *Norfolk Journal and Guide*—77,462. Id.
22. "The AFRO Yesterday," *Baltimore Afro-American*, 15 December 1981, special section, pt. 1, p. 2; Roland E. Wolseley, *The Black Press, U.S.A.* 2d rev. ed. (Ames, Iowa: Iowa State University Press, 1990), 31; Pride and Wilson, *A History of the Black Press*, 133–35.
23. Wolseley, *The Black Press, U.S.A.*, 207.
24. Carl Murphy et al., "The Afro: Seaboard's Largest Weekly," *The Crisis* 45:2 (February 1938), 44.
25. Lee Finkle, *Forum for Protest: The Black Press During World War II* (Cranbury, N.J.: Associated University Presses, 1975), 59.
26. From July 1, 1942, to June 20, 1943, the 144 black newspapers (114 weekly) had "a combined average net circulation per issue of 1,613,255." Frazier, *Negro in the United States*, 513–14; Pride and Wilson, *A History of the Black Press*, 153 (discussing the peak year of the black press as being during World War II).
27. Frazier, *Negro in the United States*, 512.
28. Finkle, *Forum for Protest*, 51–52, 60–61.
29. Murphy et al., "The Afro: Seaboard's Largest Weekly," 44.
30. "Did You Know?" *Baltimore Afro-American*, 15 December 1981, special section, pt. 1, p. 2; Wolseley, *The Black Press, U.S.A.*, 75.
31. Myrdal, *An American Dilemma*, 910, 924.
32. Wolseley, *The Black Press, U.S.A.*, 374.
33. For the story of the NNPA and criticism from red-baiting columnist Westbrook Pegler, see Pride and Wilson, *A History of the Black Press*, 185–86, 188; Patrick S. Washburn, *The Federal Government's Investigation of the Black Press During World War II* (New York: Oxford University Press, 1986), 21–22.
34. "Undated Transcript of WBAL Radio Interview—'Afro American War Correspondents,'" box 29, Art Carter Papers.
35. Lacy, *Fighting for Fairness*, 45–46.
36. Sheingold, "In Black and White," 35–36.
37. Sam Lacy, "Looking 'Em Over," *Washington Afro-American*, 1 April 1939, 23.
38. Sam Lacy, "Looking 'Em Over," *Baltimore Afro-American*, 26 February 1944, 14.
39. "Beisboleros," *Newsweek*, 29 May 1944, 90.
40. Sam Lacy, "Looking 'Em Over," *Washington Afro-American*, 8 April 1944, 22. Roberts and Lacy's speculation about Connie Mack as an ardent segregationist turned out to be well founded. During spring training in 1946, Mack "blew his stack" over a Philadelphia writer's suggestion that Rickey would bring Jackie Robin-

son to a Florida spring training game against the Philadelphia Athletics. Ira Berkow, *Red: A Biography of Red Smith* (New York: Times Books, 1986), 109.

41. Sam Lacy, "Looking 'Em Over," *Baltimore Afro-American*, 20 May 1944, 14.

42. Art Carter, "10,000 at Mixed Contest," *Washington Afro-American*, 10 July 1943, 26; "Grays Down Bushwicks, 11–3; Play Cleveland Here Sunday," *Washington Tribune*, 10 July 1943, 17.

43. Ibid.

44. Tygiel, *Baseball's Great Experiment*, 36 ("The efforts of these and other black writers to integrate sports possessed an element of irony. They too were victims of Jim Crow, who held analogous positions to the athletes they covered. Segregation hid their considerable skills from the larger white audience and severely restricted their income earning potential. Yet they rarely mentioned their own plight. Indeed, the barriers for black journalists lasted long after those for athletes disappeared"); Rogosin, *Invisible Men*, 89; Reisler, *Black Writers/Black Baseball*, 1–7 (introducing a terrific anthology of selected stories and biographical sketches).

45. Robert McNeill interview.

46. Sam Lacy interview, 17 May 1994.

47. Reisler, *Black Writers/Black Baseball*, 33. Jim Reisler, in his anthology on the black sporting press, compares W. Rollo Wilson to Red Smith because Wilson's work was "folksy with a certain playfulness." Id., 113. Jules Tygiel wrote: "Smith ranked among the nation's best sportswriters. He could be bitterly sarcastic and vitriolic in his rage against Jim Crow, yet lyrical in his descriptive prose. Although his columns tended to run overlong and belabor a point, they nonetheless offered entertainment and insight." Tygiel, *Baseball's Great Experiment*, 35. For more articles on Smith, see David K. Wiggins, "Wendell Smith, the *Pittsburgh Courier-Journal* and the Campaign to Include Blacks in Organized Baseball," *Journal of Sports History* 10:2 (Summer 1983), 5; Chris Lamb, "Making a Pitch for Equality: Wendell Smith and His Crusade to Integrate Baseball" (paper presented to History Division, 1999 AEJMC national conference, New Orleans, La., August 1999; on file with author). The only in-depth interview of Smith before his death in 1972 appeared in the revised edition of Jerome Holtzman's wonderful collection of interviews with legendary sportswriters. Holtzman, *No Cheering in the Press Box*, 312–24.

48. Holtzman, *No Cheering in the Press Box*, 312.

49. Ibid., 323–24. Tresh's son, Tom, played for the Yankees.

50. J. Wendell Smith, "Blues Set for W. Va. Classic," *Pittsburgh Courier*, 31 October 1936, sec. 2, p. 6; J. Wendell Smith, "Kentucky Will Get 'Warm' Reception at West Va.," id., 7 November 1936, sec. 2, p. 4.

51. Letter from J. Wendell Smith to Robert L. Vann, box 144-30, folder 14, Percival Leroy Prattis Papers, Manuscript Division, Moorland-Spingarn Research Center, Howard University, Washington, D.C.

52. Smith claimed to have been appointed the *Courier's* sports editor in 1938, a year after joining the paper. Holtzman, *No Cheering in the Press Box*, 314. Other sources, however, indicate that Smith did not become sports editor until 1940, when his mentor, Chester Washington, became the city editor. Reisler, *Black Writers/Black Baseball*, 35; Lamb, "Making a Pitch for Equality," 12.

53. Holtzman, *No Cheering in the Press Box*, 314–15.

54. *Pittsburgh Courier*, 5 August 1939, 16.
55. *Pittsburgh Courier*, 22 July 1939, 1.
56. *Pittsburgh Courier*, 15 July 1939, 1, 16 (Cincinnati Reds) ; id., 22 July 1939, 1, 16 (New York Giants); id., 29 July 1939, 16 (Philadelphia Phillies); id., 5 August 1939, 16 (Brooklyn Dodgers); id., 12 August 1939, 16 (Chicago Cubs); 19 August 1939, 16 (St. Louis Cardinals); id., 26 August 1939, 16 (Boston Braves); id., 2 September 1939, 16 (Pittsburgh Pirates).
57. Holtzman, *No Cheering in the Press Box*, 315.
58. Sam Lacy interview, 17 May 1994.
59. Lacy, *Fighting for Fairness*, 98. For more on Lacy's relationship with and admiration for Smith, see id., 97–98.
60. *Washington Afro-American*, 18 March 1944, 22; Sam Lacy, "Looking 'Em Over," *Baltimore Afro-American*, 1 April 1944, 14.
61. Sam Lacy, "Looking 'Em Over," *Washington Afro-American*, 16 September 1944, 30.
62. Wendell Smith, "'Smitty's' Sports Spurts," *Pittsburgh Courier*, 27 February 1943, 18. Smith was not the only other black writer blasting Griffith. In August 1942, the *Defender*'s Fay Young wrote that "Griffith still clings to the jim crow attitude of most of the owners." Fay Young, "Through the Years," *Chicago Defender*, 1 August 1942, 19.
63. Wendell Smith, "An Editorial — Washington's Pennant Chances Gone Because Griffith to Give Americans a Chance," *Pittsburgh Courier*, 22 July 1944, 12.
64. Wendell Smith, "'Smitty's' Sports Spurts," *Pittsburgh Courier*, 18 March 1944, 12.
65. Dan T. Carter, *Scottsboro: A Tragedy of the American South* (Baton Rouge, La.: Louisiana State University Press, 1990), 137–73.
66. Kelly E. Rusinack, "Baseball on the Radical Agenda: The *Daily Worker* and *Sunday Worker* Journalistic Campaign to Desegregate Major League Baseball, 1933–1947," in *Jackie Robinson: Race, Sports, and the American Dream*, eds. Joseph Dorinson and Joram Warmund (Armonk, N.Y.: M. E. Sharpe, 1998), 75–85; Tygiel, *Baseball's Great Experiment*, 36–37; Falkner, *Great Time Coming*, 95–100; Tom Gallagher, "Lester Rodney, the Daily Worker, and the Integration of Baseball," *The National Pastime: A Review of Baseball History* no. 19 (Cleveland: SABR, 1999), 77–80; Peter Duffy, "Red Rodney: The American Communist Who Helped Liberate Baseball," *The Village Voice*, 10 June 1997, 122.
67. *Washington Afro-American*, 5 September 1942, 22.
68. Holway, *Voices*, 268–69.
69. "Here They Are! These Negro Aces Are Major Leaguers," *Daily Worker*, 3 December 1943, 5.
70. "Pirates' Chief Scout to Handle Epochal Try-Outs," *Pittsburgh Courier*, 22 August 1942, 1. Rodney recalled the Pirates' tryout as involving Campanella. Gallagher, "Lester Rodney, the Daily Worker, and the Integration of Baseball," 78.
71. Gallagher, "Lester Rodney, the *Daily Worker*, and the Integration of Baseball," 78. Dick Young, *Roy Campanella: Most Valuable Player Series* (New York: A. S. Barnes, 1952), 95–96.
72. "Sports Editor of Negro Paper Sends Congratulations on Jim Crow Fight," *Sunday Worker*, 20 August 1939, sec. 1, p. 8.
73. Gallagher, "Lester Rodney, the Daily Worker, and the Integration of Baseball," 78–79; Falkner, *Great Time Coming*, 95. See, e.g., Lester Rodney, "Why Do Brook-

lyn's Dodgers Dodge Race Issue, Asks Writer; Says Sepia Stars Would Make Turnstiles Click," *Pittsburgh Courier*, 2 April 1938, 16.

74. Wendell Smith, "Sports Beat," *Pittsburgh Courier*, 23 August 1947, 14; Lamb, "Making a Pitch for Equality," 15.

75. Duffy, "Red Rodney," 122.

76. Sam Lacy, "Looking 'Em Over," *Washington Afro-American*, 8 January 1944, 19.

77. Falkner, *Great Time Coming*, 100.

78. Peterson, *Only the Ball Was White*, 175; Rogosin, *Invisible Men*, 181; Tygiel, *Baseball's Great Experiment*, 34–35. For a study comparing white and black coverage of Jackie Robinson's first spring training, see Chris Lamb and Glen Bleske, "Democracy on the Field: The Black Press Takes on White Baseball," *Journalism History* 24:2 (Summer 1998), 51.

79. Holtzman, *No Cheering in the Press Box*, 317.

80. Ken Denlinger, "Near 90, but Still All Write," *Washington Post*, 30 April 1995, D4. Others agreed with that assessment. "If it hadn't been for his friend Red Smith," Holtzman told Ira Berkow, "Shirley Povich would have been regarded as the best sports columnist in the country." Ira Berkow, "Shirley Povich Dies at 92; Washington Sports Columnist," *New York Times*, 7 June 1998, 30.

81. Berkow, "Shirley Povich Dies at 92," 30.

82. Povich, *All These Mornings*, 11–13; Holtzman, *No Cheering in the Press Box*, 123–24.

83. Shirley Povich, "This Morning," *Washington Post*, 7 April 1939, sec. 3, p. 21.

84. Shirley Povich, "'Josh a $200,000 Catcher,' Claims Famous Pitcher," *Pittsburgh Courier*, 15 April 1939, 17; Sam Lacy, "Looking 'Em Over," *Washington Afro-American*, 15 April 1939, 21.

85. Peterson, *Only the Ball Was White*, 175; Rogosin, *Invisible Men*, 181; Tygiel, *Baseball's Great Experiment*, 34–35.

86. Sam Lacy, "Looking 'Em Over," *Washington Afro-American*, 15 April 1939, 21.

87. Ibid. See, e.g., "Pro and Con on the Negro in Organized Baseball," *Washington Tribune*, 11 June 1938, 13.

88. Sam Lacy, "Looking 'Em Over," *Washington Afro-American*, 15 April 1939, 21.

89. Ibid.

90. Ibid., 19 August 1939, 22.

91. Ibid.

92. Lacy, *Fighting for Fairness*, 100.

93. Lacy interview, 15 July 1992. Lacy may have been referring to his groundbreaking article in the 1945 edition of *Negro Baseball*, promoting Jackie Robinson among a list of "potential" major leaguers but refusing to say that any of them was a surefire major leaguer without the benefit of major league training and facilities. Sam Lacy, "Will Our Boys Make the Grade," *Negro Baseball Pictorial Yearbook*, 1945, p. 9, 28–29, box 1, folder 24, Art Carter Papers. In 1945, New York Yankees president Larry MacPhail quoted Lacy's article out of context to argue against integration. Sam Lacy, "Looking 'Em Over," *Washington Afro-American*, 29 September 1945, 23. Maybe Povich quoted MacPhail quoting Lacy.

94. Lacy interview, 15 July 1992; Judge, "Writing the Good Fight," *Washington City Paper*, 17 May 1991, 30–31.

95. Lacy interview, 15 July 1992.

96. Ibid. Several years later, Wendell Smith gained admission to the organization's Chicago chapter while covering the White Sox for the *Chicago American*. In the past,

Smith had argued unsuccessfully "that if the sports editor of the *Daily Worker*, a Communist paper, was qualified, so was I." Holtzman, *No Cheering in the Press Box*, 317.

97. Judge, "Writing the Good Fight," *Washington City Paper*, 17 May 1991, 30–31.
98. Shirley Povich, taped interview with author, Washington, D.C., 12 January 1993.
99. Shirley Povich, "Mo Siegel, Storyteller," *Washington Post*, 3 June 1994, F8.
100. Shirley Povich interview, 12 January 1993.
101. Lacy, *Fighting for Fairness*, 99–101 (detailing the white writers Lacy liked, disliked, and thought were "ok").
102. Lacy interview, 15 July 1992.
103. Sam Lacy, "400 Miles of 'Red Carpet' — for Me," *Baltimore Afro-American*, 27 June 1998–3 July 1998, A12. Red Smith, although a supporter of integration, never advocated the integration of baseball in his columns and rarely wrote about the Negro Leagues. Berkow, *Red*, 108–9. He certainly did not write about the issues as often as did Povich, who was one of the most outspoken sportswriters about integration.
104. Lacy, *Fighting for Fairness*, 101. When Steadman posthumously received the 2001 Red Smith Award, Lacy said: "John was my No. 1 choice. He had a humane quality unmatched by most writers I've known." Mike Klingaman, "Steadman Wins Red Smith Award; Late *Sun* Columnist 21st Recipient by AP," *Baltimore Sun*, 2 May 2001, 1D.
105. Povich, *All These Mornings*, 88–89.
106. For an excellent account of how Udall and the Kennedy Administration prodded Marshall to integrate the Redskins, see Thomas G. Smith, "Civil Rights on the Gridiron: The Kennedy Administration and the Desegregation of the Washington Redskins," *Journal of Sports History* 14:2 (Summer 1987), 189–208.
107. Povich, *All These Mornings*, 88–89.
108. Ibid., 93–96.
109. Shirley Povich, "A Sporting Life," *Washington Post Magazine*, 29 October 1989, W22.
110. Bob Considine and Shirley L. Povich, "Old Fox: Baseball's Red-Eyed Radical and Archconservative, Clark Griffith," *Saturday Evening Post*, 13 April 1940, 14–15; id., 20 April 1940, 18–19.
111. Shirley Povich, "This Morning," *Washington Post*, 28 October 1955, 46.
112. Shirley Povich, "Can Negro Win Housing Fight in Spring Camps?" *The Sporting News*, 8 March 1961, 10.
113. Shirley Povich interview, 12 January 1993.
114. Ibid.
115. Ibid.
116. Povich, *All These Mornings*, 99–122.
117. Red Smith's biographer, Ira Berkow, wrote that during the 1940s Smith "had written sparingly about blacks in baseball" and "didn't attack the color barrier in print." Berkow, *Red*, 108.
118. Smith told Jerome Holtzman:

> Shirley Povich of the Washington *Post* was another who was very forthright. Shirley was exposed to Negro baseball. The Negro population in Washington was very large and the Negro teams always appeared at Griffith Stadium. I recall once when Shirley,

commenting on the barrier, said that the Washington Senators had a lot of Cubans on their club but no Negroes as such, some of whom were suspect. He wrote that everyone in the ballpark should sing the "Star Spangled Banner" except the Washington squad.

Holtzman, *No Cheering in the Press Box*, 317.

CHAPTER 8

1. *Pittsburgh Courier*, 8 April 1944, 12.
2. Ibid. The photograph in the *Afro* caught Lacy with a grim expression on his face. *Washington Afro-American*, 8 April 1944, 22; *Washington Tribune*, 8 April 1944, 30.
3. Dan Burley, "Confidentially Yours," *Amsterdam News*, 11 December 1943, 4B. The owner was probably the outspoken Newark Eagles boss, Effa Manley. Given the New York location of the *Amsterdam News*, Burley's source also could have been Jim Semler of the New York Black Yankees or Alex Pompez of the New York Cubans. Whoever it was, Burley's source was not off base. In April 1945, the *Washington Afro-American* reported that three out of five Negro League owners opposed integration. *Washington Afro-American*, 7 April 1945, 22.
4. Cum Posey, "Posey's Points," *Pittsburgh Courier*, 1 April 1944, 12.
5. Wendell Smith, "'Smitty's' Sports Spurts," *Pittsburgh Courier*, 18 December 1943, 14.
6. Sam Lacy, "Looking 'Em Over," *Washington Afro-American*, 9 September 1944, 22.
7. Ibid.
8. Ibid., 16 September 1944, 30.
9. Ric Roberts, "Redskins' Owner Ties-Up Stadium," *Pittsburgh Courier*, 23 August 1944, 12.
10. Harold Jackson, "On the Sports Front," *Washington Afro-American*, 7 October 1944, 30.
11. Cum Posey, "Posey's Points," *Pittsburgh Courier*, 17 April 1937, 17 ("For the past few years Negro National League clubs have played at Griffith Stadium in Washington, D.C., and have received great cooperation and much valuable advice from the Washington American League club owner, Clark Griffith, who predicts a great future for Negro League Baseball"); Chester Washington, "Pirates' Owner Would Favor Sepia Players in Organized Baseball; Lauds Gibson, Satchell [sic]," id., 12 February 1938, 17 (detailing meeting with Benswanger, Posey, and Washington); Cum Posey, "Posey's Points," id., 5 September 1942, 16 (denying that the Grays paid an "exorbitant price" to rent Forbes Field for a game against the Kansas City Monarchs).
12. Cum Posey, "Posey's Points," *Pittsburgh Courier*, 27 July 1942, 17.
13. Sam Lacy, "Looking 'Em Over," *Baltimore Afro-American*, 14 January 1944, 19.
14. Cum Posey, "Posey's Points," *Pittsburgh Courier*, 9 November 1940, 18; "Posey Exposes Flaws of Sepia Baseball," id., 23 August 1941, 16; "'Keep Opportunists Out of Organized Baseball'—Posey," id., 30 August 1941, 17; Cum Posey, "Posey's Points," id., 31 October 1942, 17. For the best discussion of white booking agents, see Ruck, *Sandlot Seasons*, 117–22.
15. Sam Lacy, "Looking 'Em Over," *Washington Afro-American*, 17 June 1942, 18.

369

16. "NNL Wars on Saperstein, Raps American League," *Washington Afro-American*, 1 July 1944, 26; Don De Leighbur, "Commissioner of Baseball Colored Leagues' Big Need," id., 8 July 1944, 27.
17. Although Posey admitted that "all the clubs in Negro organized baseball made money in 1943," the bus ban hurt the Grays' bottom line. The Grays spent thousands of dollars on railroad fares and "more money was spent in 1943 on taxicabs alone . . . than was spent for travelling all over the country in their privately owned bus in any previous year." Posey lamented that it cost him eight times as much to operate in 1943 as in 1933, with six times as much in salaries, three times as much for hotel rooms, four times as much for meals, and twenty times as much to travel. Cum Posey, "Posey's Points," *Pittsburgh Courier*, 4 March 1944, 12.
18. "National League Set for Season," *Pittsburgh Courier*, 11 March 1944, 12.
19. Ric Roberts, "Negro Baseball—A $2,000,000 Business," *Negro Baseball Pictorial Yearbook*, 1945, pp. 9, 27, box 1, folder 24, Art Carter Papers.
20. Sam Lacy, "15,000 See Grays Take Inaugural Double Bill," *Washington Afro-American*, 13 May 1944, 18; "Grays Top Yanks in D.C. Lidlifter," *Pittsburgh Courier*, 13 May 1944, 19; "15,000 Watch Grays Win Twin Bill Opener Here," *Washington Tribune*, 13 May 1944, 28; Ric Roberts, "Paige on Mound in First Tilt," *Pittsburgh Courier*, 1 July 1944, 12; "Grays Cop Series from KC Monarchs," *Washington Afro-American*, 1 July 1944, 26.
21. "Homestead Grays Seeking Younger Players, Throw Doors Open to Future Diamond Stars," *Pittsburgh Courier*, 25 March 1944, 12.
22. "Grays Meet Cardinals in Dayton, Easter," *Pittsburgh Courier*, 8 April 1944, 12; "Army Eyes Gibson, Brown; Both Now in 1-A," id., 8 January 1944, 14.
23. "Grays Take NNL Lead by Double Win Over Stars," *Washington Afro-American*, 12 August 1944, 26.
24. Wendell Smith, "'Smitty's' Sports Spurts," *Pittsburgh Courier*, 3 June 1944, 12.
25. Holway, *Blackball Stars*, 200.
26. Sam Lacy, "Two Grays Stars Arouse Bosses' Ire; One Ouster," *Washington Afro-American*, 27 May 1944, 18.
27. Holway, *Blackball Stars*, 213.
28. Wendell Smith, "'Smitty's' Sports Spurts," *Pittsburgh Courier*, 30 September 1944, 12.
29. Harold Jackson, "Sports Front," *Washington Afro-American*, 9 September 1944, 23.
30. "Grays Top Eagles Twice in NNL Exhibition Bill," *Washington Afro-American*, 29 April 1944, 18.
31. Sam Lacy, "Two Grays Stars Arouse Bosses' Ire; One Ouster," *Washington Afro-American*, 27 May 1944, 18.
32. *Washington Tribune*, 3 June 1944, 28; W. Rollo Wilson, "Thru the Eyes of W. Rollo Wilson," *Philadelphia Tribune*, 10 June 1944, 12.
33. Harold Jackson, "On the Sports Front," *Washington Afro-American*, 10 June 1944, 18.
34. "Diamond Dopes," *Pittsburgh Courier*, 17 June 1944, 19.
35. Ibid., 8 July 1944, 12.
36. For more on why the Polo Grounds was Gibson's favorite ballpark, see supra Chapter 6, note 5.

37. "Josh Gibson Hits 3 Home Runs in 3 Days on Trip," *Washington Afro-American*, 22 July 1944, 26; "Josh Hits 2 Homers in N.Y.," *Pittsburgh Courier*, 22 July 1944, 12.
38. "Austin, Philly Rookie Wins NNL Batting Title," *Washington Afro-American*, 16 September 1944, 30.
39. Cum Posey. "The 1944 All-American Baseball Team," *Pittsburgh Courier*, 16 December 1944, 12.
40. Holway, *Voices*, 266.
41. "Leonard Homers as Grays Win 2," *Washington Afro-American*, 6 May 1944, 18.
42. "Grays Top Yanks in D.C. Lidlifter," *Pittsburgh Courier*, 13 May 1944, 19.
43. "Leonard's Homer Wins First Tilt," *Pittsburgh Courier*, 10 June 1944, 12.
44. Ric Roberts, "Grays and Kansas City Split Before 15,000," *Pittsburgh Courier*, 1 July 1944, 12.
45. "Grays and Newark Divide Twin Bill," *Pittsburgh Courier*, 8 July 1944, 12.
46. Holway, *Voices*, 346.
47. Bill Scott interview.
48. Wendell Smith, "'Smitty's' Sports Spurts," *Pittsburgh Courier*, 30 September 1944, 12.
49. Leonard, *The Black Lou Gehrig*, 164–65.
50. "Baseball Owners Talk Trades, But—," *Washington Afro-American*, 23 December 1944, 30.
51. "Composite Box Score of 5-Game World Series," *Washington Afro-American*, 30 September 1944, 31.
52. Lacy speculated that "Buck Leonard's refusal to remain with [the] team for two exhibition games following the Barons series was being interpreted as general dissatisfaction with the conduct of the club." Sam Lacy, "Ousting of Candy Jim Taylor Reported Likely," *Washington Afro-American*, 28 October 1944, 26. Leonard, however, already had left for Rocky Mount and could not be reached for comment. Leonard's autobiography revealed the real reason. Leonard, *The Black Lou Gehrig*, 169.
53. Sam Lacy, "Final Standings in NNL First Half Hinges on Outcome of Eagle Protest," *Washington Afro-American*, 8 July 1944, 27; "NNL Prexy Orders Replay of Grays-Newark Contest," *Washington Afro-American*, 15 July 1944, 26; "Grays Beat Newark, 8–4, for NNL First Half Title," id., 26 August 1944, 27.
54. Sam Lacy, "Looking 'Em Over," *Washington Afro-American*, 30 September 1944, 30.
55. Ibid. The following season, the *Washington Tribune*'s Al Sweeney would take issue with the Grays' manipulation of the league schedule. Al Sweeney, "As I See It," *Washington Tribune*, 23 June 1945, 21.
56. Sam Lacy, "Looking 'Em Over," *Washington Afro-American*, 16 September 1944, 30.
57. "Baseball Owners Talk Much but Do Little," *Washington Afro-American*, 23 December 1944, 30.
58. "Judge Landis Dies; Baseball Czar, 78," *New York Times*, 26 November 1944, 56; Pietrusza, *Judge and Jury*, 449–52; Spink, *Judge Landis and 25 Years of Baseball*, 288–92.
59. "Griffith Turns 75; 57th Year in Game," *New York Times*, 21 November 1944, 18; Pietrusza, *Judge and Jury*, 450.

60. J. G. Taylor Spink, who had a rocky though mostly friendly relationship with Landis, wrote in his biography of the commissioner: "I believe the club owners for whom he had the most affection were men who had played big league baseball, such as Connie Mack and Clark Griffith, frequently one of his winter Florida golfing companions." Spink, *Judge Landis and 25 Years of Baseball*, 74.

61. Wendell Smith, "'Smitty's' Sports Spurts," *Pittsburgh Courier*, 2 December 1944, 12.

62. Sam Lacy, "Looking 'Em Over," *Washington Afro-American*, 20 January 1945, 27.

63. Ibid.

64. Ibid., 3 February 1945, 23.

65. In April, about twenty-four people marched outside a Yankees–Red Sox game at Yankee Stadium with signs that said, "If we can stop bullets, why not balls?" and "If we can pay, why can't we play?" "Pickets Protest Baseball Bigotry," *Washington Afro-American*, 21 April 1945, 23.

66. Sheingold, "In Black and White," 66.

67. For more on Shepard, see Joe Naiman, "Bert Shepard," *The National Pastime: A Review of Baseball History* no. 19 (Cleveland: SABR, 1999) 75–76; Mead, *Baseball Goes to War*, 203–4; Gilbert, *They Also Served*, 209–17. Gilbert, a Senators batboy during the team's 1945 spring training at College Park, Maryland, wrote a particularly moving account. See id., 166–71.

68. "The Sports Note Pad," *Baltimore Afro-American*, 2 April 1945, 22. Two years later, the elder Lacy gave up Senators games altogether because of Griffith's segregationist stance. See Sam Lacy, "From A to Z," *Baltimore Afro-American*, 2 April 1949, sec.1, p. 7; infra Chapter 9.

69. Jimmy Smith, "McDuffie, Thomas First Negroes in Big League Uniforms," *Pittsburgh Courier*, 14 April 1945, 12.

70. Wendell Smith, "Red Sox Candidates Waiting to Hear from Management," *Pittsburgh Courier*, 28 April 1945, 12; "Red Sox Tryouts Given to Trio of Colored Players," *Baltimore Afro-American*, 28 April 1945, 18. For the fullest secondary source account of the tryouts, see Tygiel, *Baseball's Great Experiment*, 43–46. See also Holtzman, *No Cheering in the Press Box*, 320; Polner, *Branch Rickey*, 155–61.

    Smith later told Jerome Holtzman that the city councilman, Muchnick, was seeking reelection in a prominently black district. Holtzman, *No Cheering in the Press Box*, 320. At that time, however, Muchnick's district was 99 percent white. Stephen H. Norwood and Harold Brackman, "Going to Bat for Jackie Robinson: The Jewish Role in Breaking Baseball's Color Line," *Journal of Sport History* 26:1 (Spring 1999), 125.

71. Lacy interview, 15 July 1992.

72. The committee also included: Magistrate Joseph H. Rainey, a former Negro National League president selected by Lacy; and Judge Myles Paige of New York, a consultant selected by Rickey. "AFRO Leads Move to Abolish Major League Baseball Discrimination," *Washington Afro-American*, 16 June 1945, 18; "Club Owners Turned Deaf Ear to AFRO Warning Their Players Might Be Signed," id., 3 November 1945, 31.

73. Tygiel, *Baseball's Great Experiment*, 42; Lacy, *Fighting for Fairness*, 58.

74. For an example of Rickey as card shark, Harold Parrott, the Dodgers' traveling secretary and publicist, recounts how Rickey treated "some of the millionaire own-

ers"—including Clark Griffith—"like children," playing them against each other when selling off some of the Dodgers' minor league players at the end of the 1949 season. Harold Parrott, *The Lords of Baseball: A Wry Look at a Side of the Game the Fan Seldom Sees—the Front Office* (New York: Praeger Publishers, 1976; Atlanta: Longstreet Press, 2001), 284–91.

75. Polner, *Branch Rickey*, 51–52.

76. Tygiel, *Baseball's Great Experiment*, 51; Rampersad, *Jackie Robinson*, 121–23.

77. Tygiel, *Baseball's Great Experiment*, 57–58.

78. "Branch Rickey Says He Might Be Interested in a Franchise in Sepia League," *Pittsburgh Courier*, 14 April 1945, 12; "Brooklyn Franchise Added to League," id., 28 April 1945, 12; "New U.S. League Gets Full Backing of Branch Rickey," *Washington Afro-American*, 12 May 1945, 13; Tygiel, *Baseball's Great Experiment*, 57.

79. "Griff Raps Rickey for USL Activity," *Washington Afro-American*, 19 May 1945, 27; Wendell Smith, "The Sports Beat," *Pittsburgh Courier*, 1 September 1945, 12.

80. Ibid.

81. Wendell Smith, "The Sports Beat," *Pittsburgh Courier*, 26 May 1945, 12.

82. Ibid.

83. Sam Lacy, "Looking 'Em Over," *Baltimore Afro-American*, 19 May 1945, 18.

84. "Club Owners Turned a Deaf Ear to AFRO Warning Their Players Might Be Signed," *Washington Afro-American*, 3 November 1945, 31.

85. Ibid.; "Owners Spurn AFRO Bid to Join in Baseball Study," *Washington Afro-American*, 14 July 1945, 27; Sam Lacy, "Looking 'Em Over," id., 11 August 1945, 26.

86. Fay Young, "Through the Years," *Chicago Defender*, 28 May 1945, 7.

87. Jerome Mehlman, "Try for Big League Jobs Fails, Writer Tells Why," *Amsterdam News*, 14 April 1945, 4B.

88. Holtzman, *No Cheering in the Press Box*, 319.

89. Bruce Adelson, *Brushing Back Jim Crow: The Integration of Minor League Baseball in the American South* (Charlottesville, Va.: The University Press of Virginia, 1999), 55.

90. Cum Posey, "Many Problems League Must Solve," *Pittsburgh Courier*, 5 May 1945, 12.

91. Ibid.

92. Jerome Mehlman, "Mississippi Sports Writer Wants Negro in Big Leagues," *Amsterdam News*, 7 April 1945, 4-B.

93. Sam Lacy, "Looking 'Em Over," *Washington Afro-American*, 15 September 1945, 30.

94. "Grays vs. Stars Tonite," *Washington Afro-American*, 19 May 1945, 27.

95. "A Jinx Maybe?" *Washington Tribune*, 16 June 1943, 30.

96. Trouppe, *29 Years Too Soon*, 150–51; "Buckeyes Top Grays, 5–0, to Sweep World Series," *Washington Afro-American*, 29 September 1945, 30; Wendell Smith, "The Sports Beat," *Pittsburgh Courier*, 22 September 1945, 12; Wendell Smith, "Battling Bucks Win 2 to 1, 4 to 2 in World Series," id., 22 September 1945, 12; Wendell Smith, "The Sports Beat," id., 29 September 1945, 12; "Cleveland Rules Baseball World," id., 29 September 1945, 12.

97. Sam Lacy, "Looking 'Em Over," *Washington Afro-American*, 15 September 1945, 30.

98. "13,000 See Grays Take DC Inaugural Bill from Yanks," *Washington Afro-American*, 19 May 1945, 27; "Grays Sweep Black Yankees," *Pittsburgh Courier*, 19 May 1945, 12.

99. "Thousands Hail War's End," *Washington Afro-American*, 18 August 1945, 1.

373

100. The *Afro* reported 18,000, and the *Pittsburgh Courier* reported "more than 20,000." "Welmaker Bests Paige, Grays Drub KC Before 18,000," *Washington Afro-American*, 30 June 1945, 18; "Grays Beat Kansas City in Twin Bill," *Pittsburgh Courier*, 30 June 1945, 12.
101. "Jackie Robinson to Make D.C. Bow with Monarchs," *Washington Afro-American*, 23 June 1945, 22. The *Washington Tribune* gave Paige a slightly better billing. "Satchel Paige and Jackie Robinson Lead Monarchs Against Grays, Sunday," *Washington Tribune*, 23 June 1945, 22.
102. "Paige Feuding?" *Washington Tribune*, 16 June 1945, 30.
103. "Welmaker Bests Paige, Grays Drub KC Before 18,000," *Washington Afro-American*, 30 June 1945, 18.
104. Leonard, *The Black Lou Gehrig*, 175.
105. Harold Jackson, "Sports Front," *Washington Afro-American*, 25 August 1945, 27.
106. Ibid.
107. Holtzman, *No Cheering in the Press Box*, 313–14, 320–21.
108. Sam Lacy, "Looking 'Em Over," *Washington Afro-American*, 29 September 1945, 23.
109. Ibid.
110. Sam Lacy, "Will Our Boys Make the Grade?" *Negro Baseball Pictorial Yearbook*, 1945, p. 8, box 1, folder 24, Art Carter Papers.
111. Ibid., 29.
112. Ibid., 28–29.
113. Ric Roberts of the *Pittsburgh Courier* even wanted to write an article about Lacy and his early beat on Robinson for the 1946 edition of *Negro Baseball*. Roberts wrote: "Inasmuch as we feel that your Sam Lacy, in pointing up Jackie Robinson's talents in an article written for *NEGRO BASEBALL*, started the ball rolling toward cracking the color line of the major leagues, I feel that I might do a nice piece of copy on the *AFRO* sports department with a nod to Mr. Lacy." Letter from Ric Roberts to Ellison Higginbotham, 22 April 1946, box 1, folder 4, Art Carter Papers.
114. Sam Lacy, "Looking 'Em Over ," *Washington Afro-American*, 18 August 1945, 26.
115. Wendell Smith, "The Sports Beat," *Pittsburgh Courier*, 4 August 1945, 12.
116. Sam Lacy, "Looking 'Em Over ," *Washington Afro-American*, 18 August 1945, 26.
117. "Elites Take 10-Inning Tilt from Homestead Grays, 5–4," *Washington Afro-American*, 28 July 1945, 27.
118. "Champion Grays Twice Down Cubans, 5–0, 3–2," *Washington Afro-American*, 26 May 1945, 18; "DC Grays Repeat; Face Stiff Week," id., 7 July 1945, 26; "Homestead Grays Clinch NNL First Half Crown," id., 7 July 1945, 27; "Grays Twice Down Elites to Win 6th NNL Pennant," id., 8 September 1945, 26; "Vic Harris Calls on Himself, Comes Through in Clutch as Grays Win Two," *Washington Tribune*, 26 May 1945, 30.
119. McConnell and Vincent, *The Home Run Encyclopedia*, 102.
120. "Josh Gibson Wins NNL Batting Title," *Washington Afro-American*, 22 September 1946, 30.
121. "Josh Gibson Back with Sancture [sic]," *Washington Afro-American*, 17 November 1945, 31.
122. "Went Nude," *Chicago Defender*, 9 March 1946, 9. In the picture accompanying the *Defender's* story, Gibson looked like he had gained a massive amount of weight.

123. "His Bat Bears East Hopes," *Washington Afro-American*, 28 July 1945, 26.

124. "Josh Gibson Wins NNL Batting Title," *Washington Afro-American*, 22 September 1946, 30; Sam Lacy, "Looking 'Em Over," id., 18 August 1945, 26; Leonard. *The Black Lou Gehrig*, 172–73.

125. Sam Lacy, "Will Our Boys Make the Grade?" *Negro Baseball Pictorial Yearbook*, 1945, p. 29, box 1, folder 24, Art Carter Papers.

126. "Colored Nine Tops Nat Ace," *Washington Afro-American*, 1 December 1945, 29.

127. Wendell Smith, "The Sports Beat," *Pittsburgh Courier*, 15 December 1945, 16 ("Buck Leonard and Roy Campanella are doing very well," Robinson wrote Smith. "Buck Leonard has two home runs"). Robinson confessed to Gene Benson, his roommate in Venezuela, fears about not making it in the majors. See Holway, *Blackball Stars*, xi.

128. Sam Lacy, "Will Our Boys Make the Grade?" *Negro Baseball Pictorial Yearbook*, 1945, p. 29, box 1, folder 24, Art Carter Papers.

129. Sam Lacy, "Looking 'Em Over," *Washington Afro-American*, 23 June 1945, 23.

130. Wendell Smith, "The Sports Beat," *Pittsburgh Courier*, 12 May 1945, 12.

131. Bill Veeck with Ed Linn, *Veeck—As in Wreck* (New York: G. P. Putnam's Sons, 1962), 171–72. Interestingly, among the many great sportswriters and historians who helped promulgate an early version of Veeck's myth was Shirley Povich. Povich, *All These Mornings*, 129–30.

132. David Jordan, Larry Gerlach, and John Rossi, "A Baseball Myth Exploded," *The National Pastime: A Review of Baseball History* no. 18 (Cleveland: SABR, 1998), 3–13.

133. Wendell Smith, "Sepia Shortstop and Dodgers' Boss Meet in Brooklyn," *Pittsburgh Courier*, 8 September 1945, 12.

134. Michael Carter, "It's a Press Victory, Says Jackie Robinson," *Baltimore Afro-American*, 3 November 1945, 1.

135. Sam Lacy, "Looking 'Em Over," *Baltimore Afro-American*, 10 November 1945, 18.

136. Holway, *Voices*, 267.

137. Ibid.; Leonard, *The Black Lou Gehrig*, 176–77.

138. "Paige OK's Jackie," *Baltimore Afro-American*, 10 November 1945, 18.

139. Paige, *Maybe I'll Pitch Forever*, 173.

140. William Marshall, *Baseball's Pivotal Era: 1945–1951* (Lexington, Ky.: University Press of Kentucky, 1999), 131. For more on Effa Manley and her relationship with Branch Rickey, see Overmyer, *Queen of the Negro Leagues*, 219–22.

141. Wendell Smith, "The Sports Beat," *Pittsburgh Courier*, 3 November 1945, 12; "Montreal Club First to Drop Color Bar," *Baltimore Afro-American*, 3 November 1945, 26.

142. Wendell Smith, "Branch Rickey Tells Courier," *Pittsburgh Courier*, 3 November 1945, 3.

143. "Montreal Club First to Drop Color Bar," *Baltimore Afro-American*, 3 November 1945, 26. See also "Griff Questions Right of Purchase," *Washington Post*, 24 October 1945, 14; "Griff Backs Monarchs in Squawk Against Grabbing Player," *Washington Evening Star*, 24 October 1945, A-18.

144. See, e.g., "Club Heads Give Views," *New York Times*, 24 October 1945, 17; Bus Ham, "Dodgers Should Buy Robinson—Griffith," *Philadelphia Inquirer*, 25 October 1945, 24; "Should Pay Him, Says Griffith," *New York Herald Tribune*, 25 Octo-

ber 1945, 26; "Majors Can't Act as Outlaws—Griffith," *Boston Globe*, 25 October 1945, 8; " 'Should Pay'—Griffith," *Chicago Tribune*, 25 October 1945, 29.

145. Wendell Smith, "Branch Rickey Tells Courier," *Pittsburgh Courier*, 3 November 1945, 3.

146. Sam Lacy, "Looking 'Em Over," *Baltimore Afro-American*, 10 November 1945, 18.

147. For more on Griffith's profits in 1943, see supra Chapter 6, text accompanying note 86.

148. "The Race Question: The Major League Steering Committee (August 27, 1946)," in *The Jackie Robinson Reader: Perspectives on an American Hero*, ed. Jules Tygiel (New York: Dutton, 1997), 129–31; Tygiel, *Baseball's Great Experiment*, 82–86; Polner, *Branch Rickey*, 187–91; Congress, House of Representatives, Judiciary Committee, Study of Monopoly Power, Pt. 6, *Organized Baseball*, Hearings Before the Subcommittee on the Study of Monopoly Power, 82nd Cong., 1st sess., 1951, 484–85.

The origin of the section of the report on the "Race Question" is unclear. Larry MacPhail, the report's probable author, argued against integration—but these sections of the report were not included in the final version unanimously approved by the owners. Tygiel, *Baseball's Great Experiment*, 85–86; Marshall, *Baseball's Pivotal Era*, 134–35. All of the original copies of the draft report—except one—were immediately destroyed, but some of the material made it into the 1951 congressional hearings. Id.

149. Calvin Griffith interview.

150. "Washington American League Base Ball Club, Inc., D/B/A Minnesota Twins Baseball Club—Financial Statement," 30 June 1961, Mr. Calvin R. Griffith, President (on file with author).

151. Kerr, *Calvin*, 137.

152. Holtzman, *No Cheering in the Press Box*, 317.

153. "The Race Question: The Major League Steering Committee (August 27, 1946)," 131.

154. Ibid., 130.

155. Hi Turkin, "Nats Used 'Negroes,' Says Rickey," *Washington Times-Herald*, 25 October 1945, 38; "No Racial Issue in Cubans Is Griff's Reply to Rickey," *Washington Evening Star*, 25 October 1945, A-16; "Griffith Answers Rickey on Use of Cuban Players," *Washington Post*, 26 October 1945, 27; "Rickey's Thrust at Griff Arouses Cuban Embassy," *Washington Daily News*, 26 October 1945, 38.

156. "What 'Name' Writers Wrote About Signing of Jackie Robinson," *Pittsburgh Courier*, 3 November 1945, 12. The *Courier* listed Smith as writing for the *Philadelphia Record*. Smith began writing for the *New York Herald Tribune* on September 24, 1945, but the *Record* soon after began buying Smith's column in syndication. Berkow, *Red*, 95, 101.

157. "The Sport Note Pad," *Baltimore Afro-American*, 3 November 1945, 22. Other white sportswriters reacted differently. Roger Treat, a liberal voice with the *Washington Daily News*, applauded Rickey's move as an act of "courage." Roger Treat, "This Is on Me," *Washington Daily News*, 26 October 1945, 38. Shirley Povich adjudged Rickey's signing of Robinson to be "sincere." Shirley Povich, "This Morning," *Washington Post*, 27 October 1945, 27.

O'Neill's talk of libel was, of course, preposterous. Even before the Supreme Court revolutionized First Amendment law by protecting nonreckless falsehood in the 1964 case of *New York Times v. Sullivan*, truth had been an absolute defense to libel. Calvin Griffith later admitted that the Senators passed off black Latins as "white" major leaguers.

158. Sam Lacy, "Just Clark, That's All (an Editorial)," *Washington Afro-American*, 27 October 1945, 31. The *Washington Tribune*'s Al Sweeney wrote:

> This is the same Clark Griffith upholding Negro organized ball as being insulted, who has been oft quoted that the Negroes should build their own league, first. He had been intimating that Negro organization attempts at baseball were a farce, prior to the signing of Robinson.
>
> All we can say, is Griff, it's got to be this or that. Which is it?

Al Sweeney, "As I See It," *Washington Tribune*, 30 October 1945, 26.

159. Letter to Albert B. Chandler from J. B. Martin, Thomas T. Wilson and C. W. Posey, 9 November 1945, box 2, folder 4, Art Carter Papers.

160. Ibid. Posey's leadership role was well documented. He dominated a meeting of black baseball owners at Harlem's Hotel Theresa in which they discussed their response to Rickey's signing Robinson without compensating the Monarchs. "Negro League Owners Meet to Protest 'Raiding' by Majors; New U.S. League Also Meets," *New York Age*, 17 November 1945, 1, 11.

161. Letter to C. W. Posey from Clark Griffith, 5 November 1945, box 2, folder 4, Art Carter Papers. Both Posey's and Griffith's letters were reprinted in their entirety in the *New York Age*. "Negro League Owners Meet to Protest 'Raiding' by Majors; New U.S. League Also Meets," *New York Age*, 17 November 1945, 1, 11.

162. Ibid.

163. Marshall, *Baseball's Pivotal Era*, 16–17.

164. For a terrific account of how Chandler became commissioner, see ibid., 14–27, 135–36 (discussing Chandler's surprise support of Rickey given his deep Southern roots).

165. Ric Roberts, "Chandler's Views on Player Ban Sought," *Pittsburgh Courier*, 5 May 1945, 12. Roberts told John Holway that Chandler expressed stronger feelings about integration. "'I'm for the Four Freedoms. If a black boy can make it on Okinawa and Guadalcanal, hell, he can make it in baseball,'" Chandler reportedly told Roberts. "The moment Rickey read that in the *Courier*, he began to move. And Chandler paid for it. Mr. Griffith was outraged. He was outraged!" Holway, *Voices*, 14. Roberts may have been embellishing Chandler's quotation, which never appeared in Roberts's May 5 story.

Chandler was much more reserved in his public statements about baseball's color barrier. A week after Roberts's May 5 story, the *Courier* attributed a quote to Chandler that blacks should "'have a chance like everybody else to play major league baseball, and believes that this is a free country, where everyone should have a chance to play his favorite pastime.'" James Edmund Boyack, "Committee Proposed to Study Problem," *Pittsburgh Courier*, 12 May 1945, 12. In that same issue, Chandler expressed his support for a committee on integration. "Chandler Plans Parley on Issue of Negroes in Majors," id.

The black press lauded Chandler for his comments. Fay Young of the *Chicago Defender* wrote that "Rickey . . . didn't seem one-twentieth as fair as Senator Albert 'Happy' Chandler of Kentucky who said he had played with Negroes and that they ought to be given a chance on their ability to play but would have to take that phase

377

of the game up when he came to it." Fay Young, "Through the Years," *Chicago Defender*, 28 May 1945, 7. For more on the initial reaction to Chandler, see Tygiel, *Baseball's Great Experiment*, 42–43.

166. Marshall, *Baseball's Pivotal Era*, 394 (Chandler told *The Sporting News*: "I think every boy in America who wants to play professional baseball should have the chance regardless of race, creed, or color. I have always said—and I repeat it now—that Negro players are welcome in baseball"). During the 1946 season, Chandler signaled stronger support for Robinson's impending major league bid. He described Robinson as a "credit to his race" and paid him various other compliments. "Chandler Praises Jackie Robinson," *Baltimore Afro-American*, 3 August 1946, 16; "Chandler and Wife Laud Robinson," *Pittsburgh Courier*, 21 December 1946, 13. Years later, Robinson thanked Chandler for supporting integration. See Marshall, *Baseball's Pivotal Era*, 150.

167. Tygiel, *Baseball's Great Experiment*, 89–90.

168. "Chandler Sees Martin, Wilson," *Chicago Defender*, 26 January 1946, 9.

169. "Commissioner 'Happy' Chandler Tells Negro Baseball to 'Get Your House in Order,'" *Pittsburgh Courier*, 26 January 1946, 16; Sam Lacy, "Looking 'Em Over," *Baltimore Afro-American*, 30 March 1946, 18 ("It's pitifully sad [or is it?] the Negro National and American league baseball owners don't realize Commissioner A. B. [Happy] Chandler is simply pulling their legs when he tells them to petition his office for admittance to the ranks of organized baseball. He ain't the man"); Tygiel, *Baseball's Great Experiment*, 89–90.

170. Overmyer, *Queen of the Negro Leagues*, 224–26.

171. Over the years, Chandler overstated his role in the integration saga. Chandler claimed that in 1946 the owners voted, 15–1, against integration, and that Chandler and Rickey met in secret and Chandler pledged support for Rickey's experiment. Two historians who have extensively studied this issue doubt that such a vote ever took place. See Marshall, *Baseball's Pivotal Era*, 456, n. 71 (concluding that no vote took place); id., 135–36 (but suggesting that Rickey indeed visited Chandler's home and that Chandler pledged support for Robinson); Tygiel, *Baseball's Great Experiment*, 81–82 (surmising that Chandler "chose the discretion of a mute").

172. "Club Owners Turned a Deaf Ear to *AFRO* Warning Their Players Might Be Signed," *Baltimore Afro-American*, 3 November 1945, 22; Sam Lacy, "Looking 'Em Over," *Baltimore Afro-American*, 10 November 1945, 18.

173. Wendell Smith, "The Sports Beat," *Pittsburgh Courier*, 1 December 1945, 12; Wendell Smith, "The Sports Beat," *Pittsburgh Courier*, 26 January 1946, 16.

174. Wendell Smith, "The Sports Beat," *Pittsburgh Courier*, 2 February 1946, 12.

175. Ibid.

176. Lucius Jones, "Johnny Wright, Ex-Gob, Says He Is 'Very Lucky,'" *Pittsburgh Courier*, 9 February 1946, 16.

177. Wendell Smith, "The Sports Beat," *Pittsburgh Courier*, 1 December 1945, 12. Posey was aware of Rickey's advances toward Wright as early as his November 5 letter to Chandler.

178. Tygiel, *Baseball's Great Experiment*, 103.

179. Sam Lacy, "Looking 'Em Over," *Washington Afro-American*, 2 February 1946, 26.

180. Ibid. See also "Second to Sign," *Chicago Defender*, 9 February 1946, 9.

181. Tygiel, *Baseball's Great Experiment*, 126, 155.

182. Ibid., 155–58.

183. "Partlow First Player Bought from Race Club," *Pittsburgh Courier*, 25 May 1946, 17; W. Rollo Wilson, "Rickey Grabs Partlow; 'Mex' Loop Snatches Ed Stone," *Pittsburgh Courier*, 11 May 1946, 12; Tygiel, *Baseball's Great Experiment*, 127.

184. Sam Lacy, "Looking 'Em Over," *Washington Afro-American*, 2 February 1946, 26.

185. Overmyer, *Queen of the Negro Leagues*, 230.

186. Roberts, who relayed this quote to John Holway, mistakenly attributes it to Cum Posey's older brother, See. But Roberts was definitely referring to Cum because Roberts described Posey as "almost on his way to the hospital." Holway, *Blackball Stars*, 326.

187. Harry Keck, "Late Cum Posey Was Heart of Homestead Grays," *Pittsburgh Sun-Telegraph*, 29 March 1946, 26.

188. "Homestead, Pa. Pays Homage to a Great Sportsman," *Pittsburgh Courier*, 24 September 1949, 23.

189. "What They Said About Cum Posey," *Pittsburgh Courier*, 6 April 1946, 17.

190. Wendell Smith, "'Smitty's' Sports Spurts," *Pittsburgh Courier*, 19 June 1943, 18.

191. Fay Young, "Through the Years," *Chicago Defender*, 13 April 1946, 11. This column also was published in Reisler, *Black Writers/Black Baseball*, 69–70. The *Washington Tribune* described Posey as "unofficial president of the Negro National League" and "one of the most hated, yet most respected, in Negro baseball circles." "'Cum' Posey Buried Monday," *Washington Tribune*, 2 June 1946, 30.

192. Wendell Smith, "The Sports Beat," *Pittsburgh Courier*, 13 April 1946, 14.

193. Overmyer, *Queen of the Negro Leagues*, 264–65.

194. Tygiel, *Baseball's Great Experiment*, 108.

195. Leonard, *The Black Lou Gehrig*, 181–82; "Cum Posey, Co-Owner of Homestead Grays, Dies," *Chicago Defender*, 6 April 1946, 15.

CHAPTER 9

1. Tiemann and Palmer, "Major League Attendance," in *Total Baseball*, eds. Thorn et al., 107.

2. The Senators drew a club-record 1,027,216 fans. Not to be outdone, the Yankees became the first team to draw more than two million fans that season. Ibid.; Reichler, ed., *The Ronald Encyclopedia of Baseball*, 240–41.

3. Brown, who was married to Posey's daughter, probably no longer felt beholden to play for his father-in-law's team.

4. Peterson, *Only the Ball Was White*, 283; "Grays, Boasting 5-Game Win Streak, Play Stars in Finale," *Washington Afro-American*, 21 September 1946, 26.

5. Sam Lacy, "Looking 'Em Over," *Washington Afro-American*, 7 September 1946, 23.

6. Ibid.

7. Season Passes—1945, box 2, folder 17, Art Carter Papers.

8. The All-Star Classic Committee consisted of Grays owner Rufus Jackson as chairman, along with See Posey, New York Cubans owner Alex Pompez, Baltimore Elite Giants president Vernon Green, and the Grays' promoters, John Clark and Art Carter. Letterhead, box 1, folder 7, Art Carter Papers.

9. Letter from J. B. Martin to Rufus Jackson, 8 July 1946, box 1, folder 7, Art Carter Papers. In signaling the NAL's acceptance of the game, Martin wrote: "This game is to be played using the same players we use in the East-West Game here in Chi-

cago August 18th. By no means use the East-West name in your publicity. I hope you will get the publicity going soon." Id.

10. "Expect 30,000 at All-Star Game in D.C.," *Pittsburgh Courier*, 20 July 1946, 17; Wendell Smith, "The Sports Beat," id., 20 July 1946, 16; "Interest Soaring as Moguls Map Plans for Big All-Star Game in Washington," id., 27 July 1946, 16; "Top Stars to Clash Before Record Throng in Washington All-Star Tilt," id., 3 August 1946, 17; "Clash in Capital on August 15," id., 10 August 1946, 16.

11. Art Carter, "25,000 Expected to Watch All-Star Classic at Stadium," *Washington Afro-American*, 17 August 1946, 27; Wendell Smith, The Sports Beat," *Pittsburgh Courier*, 10 August 1946, 16.

12. "All-Star Classic Delayed by West's Pay Demands," *Baltimore Afro-American*, 24 August 1946, 16.

13. Balance Sheet, Negro National League and Negro American League All-Star Game, 15 August 1946, box 1, folder 9, Art Carter Papers.

14. Sam Lacy, "Jackie Answers Baltimore Boos with Stellar Play," *Washington Afro-American*, 3 August 1946, 27; "Montreal Star Spurts to Top with Average of .361 for 86 Loop Games," id., 10 August 1946, 26; "Throng of 28,000 Sets Attendance Mark in Baltimore," *Baltimore Afro-American*, 3 August 1946, 16.

15. Sam Lacy, "Baltimore Elites' Bill Byrd Credited with 6–3 Win Before 16,268 in Capital," *Baltimore Afro-American*, 24 August 1946, 16; "Nationals Victor in D.C. Game," *Pittsburgh Courier*, 24 August 1946, 17.

16. Ibid.

17. "The Sports Notepad," *Baltimore Afro-American*, 24 August 1946, 16.

18. "Major League Scouts 'Eye' Classic Stars," *Pittsburgh Courier*, 10 August 1946, 16.

19. Billy Coward interview.

20. Phil Dixon and Patrick J. Hannigan, *The Negro Baseball Leagues: A Photographic History* (Mattituck, N.Y.: Amereon House, 1992), 259. The seventy-eight-year-old Withers, a Memphis-based photographer, claimed that the photo was the last one taken of Gibson before his death. He recalled the suffering slugger wanting to be left alone that day in Chicago: "I was the only person that Josh Gibson would let come close to him. He didn't know me personally. It was just something psychologically that would allow him to pose for me." Ernest Withers, telephone interview with author, Washington, D.C., 16 April 2002.

21. "Grays to Play Yankees in Easter Sunday Tilt in D.C.," *Washington Afro-American*, 20 April 1946, 29 ("In addition, Double Duty Radcliffe, former Birmingham catcher, will be the champions' catcher, taking over for Josh Gibson, who is ailing at the moment and is not expected back in the lineup for several weeks").

22. "1946 Averages," *Washington Afro-American*, 28 September 1946, 19.

23. Western Union Telegram, Rufus Jackson to Art Carter, 21 January 1947, box 1, folder 4, Art Carter Papers. Wendell Smith, "Grays Home Run King Dies at 36," *Pittsburgh Courier*, 25 January 1947, 1, 5.

24. Brashler, *Josh Gibson*, 146–47. Another Gibson biographer wrote that "the coroner fixed the cause of death as a brain hemorrhage, with hypertension as a contributing factor." Ribowsky, *The Power and the Darkness*, 296.

25. Peterson, *Only the Ball Was White*, 167.

26. Ibid., 168; Brashler, *Josh Gibson*, 189.

27. Leonard, *The Black Lou Gehrig*, 187.

28. Brashler, *Josh Gibson*, 189–91.
29. Robert Peterson initially invoked biblical themes, titling Part Two of his groundbreaking book "Way Down in Egypt Land." Peterson, *Only the Ball Was White*, 52.
30. Lacy, *Fighting for Fairness*, 8, 11.
31. Ibid., 8–10.
32. Ibid., 8–9.
33. Letter from Jackie Robinson to Wendell Smith, October 31, 1945; letter from Wendell Smith to Branch Rickey, 19 December 1945; letter from Rickey to Smith, 8 January 1946; box 1, Wendell Smith Papers, National Baseball Hall of Fame Library, Cooperstown, N.Y.
34. Holtzman, *No Cheering in the Press Box*, 15–16.
35. Jackie Robinson with Wendell Smith, *Jackie Robinson: My Own Story* (New York: Greenberg, 1948).
36. Jackie Robinson with Alfred Duckett, *I Never Had It Made* (New York: G. P. Putnam's Sons, 1972), 41.
37. Rampersad, *Jackie Robinson*, 206–7. Others have discovered evidence of Smith's rift with Robinson. Michael Marsh, "Writer Helped Robinson Along; Smith Played Key Role in Baseball's Integration," *Chicago Sun-Times*, 30 March 1997, 17.
38. Letter from Jackie Robinson to P. L. Prattis, 7 January 1961; letter from P. L. Prattis to Jackie Robinson, 12 January 1961; letter from Jackie Robinson to P. L. Prattis, 17 January 1961; box 144-12, folder 12, Percival Leroy Prattis Papers.
39. Letter from Wendell Smith to P. L. Prattis, 9 January 1961, box 144-13, folder 20, Percival Leroy Prattis Papers.
40. Letter from Wendell Smith to P. L. Prattis, 30 January 1961, box 144-12, folder 12, Percival Leroy Prattis Papers.
41. Lacy, *Fighting for Fairness*, 73. For Robinson's feud with Campanella and Robinson's appearing overweight in 1948, see id., 71–73.
42. Ibid., 73–74.
43. In a May 1946 column about his son, Tim, Lacy wrote: "I'd want him to combine the wisdom of Joe Louis with the courage of Jackie Robinson. . . . I'd hope for him Jackie's ability to hold his head high in adversity, the ability to withstand the butts and digs and meanness of those who envy him." Sam Lacy, "Looking 'Em Over," *Baltimore Afro-American*, 18 May 1946, 14.
44. Ronald A. Smith, "The Paul Robeson–Jackie Robinson Saga and a Political Collision," in *The Jackie Robinson Reader*, ed. Tygiel, 180.
45. Ibid., 183.
46. Rampersad, *Jackie Robinson*, 210–16; Falkner, *Great Time Coming*, 197–203; Duberman, *Paul Robeson*, 360–62; Robinson, *I Never Had It Made*, 94–98; Tygiel, *Baseball's Great Experiment*, 334; Bill Mardo, "Robinson-Robeson," in *Jackie Robinson*, ed. Dorinson and Warmund, 98–106; Smith, "The Paul Robeson–Jackie Robinson Saga and a Political Collision," 169–88.
47. Later in his life, Robinson adopted a more sympathetic view of Robeson:
    That statement was made over twenty years ago, and I have never regretted it. But I have grown wiser and closer to painful truths about America's destructiveness. And I do have an increased respect for Paul Robeson who, over the span of that twenty years, sacrificed himself, his career, and the comfort he once enjoyed because, I believe, he was sincerely trying to help his people.

Robinson, *I Never Had It Made*, 98. Robinson, a lifelong Republican, regretted his 1960 endorsement of Nixon. Id., 147.

48. Robinson, *I Never Had It Made*, 35. Indeed, Harold Jackson claimed that in 1945 he once talked Robinson out of quitting the Monarchs during midseason to become head of a YMCA in Dallas, Texas. Jackson, *The House That Jack Built*, 23. For more on Robinson's unhappiness in the Negro Leagues, see Robinson, *I Never Had It Made*, 35–36; Rachel Robinson with Lee Daniels, *Jackie Robinson: An Intimate Portrait* (New York: Harry N. Abrams, 1996), 33–34; Rampersad, *Jackie Robinson*, 113–19; Falkner, *Great Time Coming*, 92–94; Tygiel, *Baseball's Great Experiment*, 63.

49. Jackie Robinson, "What's Wrong with Negro Baseball," *Ebony*, June 1948, 16–17.

50. Ibid. The article shocked Wendell Smith, who claimed that Robinson had written the article "all by himself"—lest anyone thought Smith wrote it. Rampersad, *Jackie Robinson*, 203.

51. Effa Manley, "Negro Baseball Isn't Dead," *Our World*, August 1948, 27; "Mrs. Manley Flays Jackie for Attack on Baseball," *Washington Afro-American*, 22 May 1948, sec. 2, p. 15; Overmyer, *Queen of the Negro Leagues*, 233–34.

52. "Wright, Thompson Banished by NNL," *Washington Afro-American*, 31 July 1948, sec. 2, p. 11.

53. Leonard, *The Black Lou Gehrig*, 165.

54. Daniel Cattau, "Forgotten Champions," *Washington Post Magazine*, 3 June 1990, 28.

55. "Marquez Paces Grays at Bat," *Washington Afro-American*, 2 August 1947, 19; Leonard, *The Black Lou Gehrig*, 193.

56. "'Ches' Washington—Gray Mainstays Top Nats," *Pittsburgh Courier*, 6 September 1947, 14; "'Ches' Washington . . . Vic Rates the Nationals," id., 31 May 1947, 15; Leonard, *The Black Lou Gehrig*, 194.

57. Wilmer Fields interview, 13 August 1992.

58. Leonard, *The Black Lou Gehrig*, 151–53.

59. Art Carter, "NNL Votes to Limit Club Payrolls to $6,000 Monthly," *Washington Afro-American*, 24 January 1948, 23.

60. Holway, *Voices*, 253.

61. Expense Sheet—9 August 1948, box 2, folder 11, Art Carter Papers.

62. *Washington Afro-American*, 15 May 1948, sec. 2, p. 15; "Diamond Dust," id., 22 May 1948, sec. 2, p. 13.

63. "Heavy Hitting Takes Team to Lead in Pennant Fight," *Washington Afro-American*, 12 June 1948, sec. 2, p. 14.

64. Art Carter, "Easter and Leonard Clout Three Homers in 13–4 Victory," *Washington Afro-American*, 17 July 1948, sec. 2, p. 12.

65. "Going Strong," *Pittsburgh Courier*, 7 August 1948, 12.

66. "Leonard, Easter Pace Loop Hitter with High Scores," *Washington Afro-American*, 31 July 1948, sec. 2, p. 11.

67. "Baseball Scores, Standings and Statistics," *Washington Afro-American*, 11 September 1948, sec. 2, p. 13; Holway, *Complete Book of Baseball's Negro Leagues*, 458.

68. "Baltimore Club Refuses to Complete Disputed Tilt," *Washington Afro-American*, 25 September 1948, sec. 2, p. 14; "Baltimore 'Stalled'; Grays Awarded Flag," *Pittsburgh Courier*, 2 October 1948, 11.

69. Leonard, *The Black Lou Gehrig*, 201–2.

70. "Clowns, Monarchs, Grays on Buck Leonard Day Card," *Washington Afro-American*, 28 August 1948, sec. 2, p. 11; "10,000 Expected to See Bill Honoring Buck Leonard," id., 4 September 1948, sec. 2, p. 13.

71. "6,000 Fans Pay Tribute to Grays' Buck Leonard," *Washington Afro-American*, 11 September 1948, sec. 2, p. 12.

72. Ibid.; Leonard, *The Black Lou Gehrig*, 197–98.

73. Al Sweeney, "As I See It," *Washington Afro-American*, 10 July 1948, sec. 2, p. 8.

74. Advertisement, *Washington Afro-American*, 8 April 1950, 26; "19,000 Watch Dodgers, Orioles to 3–3 Tie, Campanella Clouts Homer," id., 15 April 1950, 23.

75. McNeill interview, 2 July 1992.

76. Kermitt K. Wheeler, "Browns Sign Up Negro Stars," *Pittsburgh Courier*, 26 July 1947, 15; "St. Louis Releases Outfielder, Infielder," id., 30 August 1947, 14.

77. Joseph Thomas Moore, *Pride Against Prejudice: The Biography of Larry Doby* (New York: Greenwood Press, 1988), 168. Paige's breaking curfew and his showing up late to the ballpark and for a team train ride to Boston made headlines in the black press. Wendell Smith, "Sports Beat," *Pittsburgh Courier*, 16 October 1948, 10.

78. Moore, *Pride Against Prejudice*, 169.

79. Paige, *Pitchin' Man*, 92.

80. Tygiel, *Baseball's Great Experiment*, 231–33.

81. Al Sweeney, "As I See It," *Washington Afro-American*, 1 January 1949, sec. 2, p. 10. The *Washington Post's* Morris Siegel confirmed Sweeney's account. Morris Siegel, "Old Satch Shuffles Off to Ovation by 28,058," *Washington Post*, 31 August 1948, 16–17. Satchel's performance garnered the attention of every white daily. See id.; Burton Hawkins, "Paige Draws 265,000 in Five Starts," *Washington Evening Star*, 31 August 1948, A-9; Bob Addie, "28,058 Fans Pack Stadium for Rout," *Washington Times-Herald*, 31 August 1948, 21, 23; Ev Gardner, "Old Satch Demeans Mr. Spink, and How!" *Washington Daily News*, 31 August 1948, 38.

82. Shirley Povich, "Doby Hits 450-Foot Homer; Nats Lose, 6–1," *Washington Post*, 9 May 1948, C-1; Burton Hawkins, "Negro's Wallop Presses Ruth's Record Hit Here," *Washington Evening Star*, 9 May 1948, B-1; Bob Addie, "Nats Baffled by Cleveland Rookie, 6–1," *Washington Times-Herald*, 9 May 1948, sec. 2, pp. 1, 4; Ed McAuley, "Indians Whooping Over Steady Whacking by Keltner, Boudreau," *The Sporting News*, 19 May 1948, 9; Tygiel, *Baseball's Great Experiment*, 237.

83. "Ches" Washington, "Josh, Ruth, or Doby?" *Pittsburgh Courier*, 22 May 1948, 14. Washington erroneously referred to the magazine as the *Saturday Evening Post*, but it was actually *Time*. The article, which came out July 19, 1943, described "a recent doubleheader at Griffith Stadium, he hit three home runs, one for a distance of 485 ft." "Josh the Basher," *Time*, 19 July 1943, 75–76. Although Gibson homered twice in a Griffith Stadium doubleheader in 1943, he never homered three times that season. He accomplished that feat only during a sparsely attended 1939 Griffith Stadium doubleheader. The only contemporary newspaper account of that game does not mention a 485-foot homer. "Josh Gibson's Slugging Bat Thrills in Split Twin-Bill," *Washington Tribune*, 22 July 1939, 12. The national magazines, as usual, most likely exaggerated Gibson's home-run exploits.

84. "Doby Reminisces Over a 450-Foot Homer," *Washington Afro-American*, 15 May 1948, sec. 2, p. 13; Fred Leigh, "Four Sports Highlighted by Interracial Competition," *Washington Afro-American*, 1 January 1949, sec. 2, p. 10.

85. Ric Roberts, "500 Foot Homer at Washington Seen Longer than Record Clouts by Jimmy [sic] Foxx at Chicago," *Pittsburgh Courier*, 4 June 1949, 14; Shirley Povich,

"Doby Hits Super Homer Estimated at 500 Feet," *Washington Post*, 26 May 1949, 4B; Burton Hawkins, "Tribe Is Blasted Before Long Poke Is Hit by Larry," *Washington Evening Star*, 26 May 1949, C1; Bob Addie, "Kuhel Chased After Beef with Umpire," *Washington Times-Herald*, 26 May 1949, 32; Dave Reque, "Missing Doby's Clout Kept Kuhel Warm," *Washington Daily News*, 26 May 1949, 59; "Hit Longer Drive at Capital," *The Sporting News*, 1 June 1949, 3.

86. Sam Lacy, "500-Foot Smash Declared Longest by Clark Griffith," *Washington Afro-American*, 28 May 1949, sec. 2, p. 13; "One of the Longest . . . and Doby Hit It," *Pittsburgh Courier*, 28 May 1949, 1.

87. Sam Lacy, "500-Foot Smash Declared Longest by Clark Griffith," *Washington Afro-American*, 28 May 1949, sec. 2, p. 13

88. Ibid.

89. Veeck, *Veeck as in Wreck*, 210.

90. Tygiel, *Baseball's Great Experiment*, 225.

91. "An Open Letter: Griffs Could Use Colored Players," *Washington Afro-American*, 13 March 1948, 29.

92. "Appearance of Colored Players Cited as Reason," *Washington Afro-American*, 23 July 1949, 26.

93. Adelson, *Brushing Back Jim Crow*, 35. In 1954, the FBI investigated threats to eight nonwhite members of the Senators' Chattanooga farm club during spring training in Winter Garden, Florida. The city officials told the Senators to get their nonwhite players out of the city by sundown. The players in question were moved to Orlando. Id., 141.

94. "Nats Continue to Igg Tan Players," *Washington Afro-American*, 29 July 1950, 24.

95. "Minor Loops Snub Colored Applications," *Washington Afro-American*, 24 January 1948, 23; "Colored Baseball Is Given Rebuff," id., 28 February 1948, 25.

96. Clark and Lester, eds., *The Negro Leagues Book*, 255–60.

97. Sam Lacy, "Ex-Grays Southpaw Ace to Get San Diego Contract," *Washington Afro-American*, 5 March 1949, sec. 2, p. 11.

98. Wendell Smith reported that the Triple-A Oakland Oaks purchased Fields's contract, "but for some strange reason he refuses to report." Wendell Smith, "The Sports Beat," *Pittsburgh Courier*, 16 July 1949, 22. Fields just felt more comfortable playing in the Negro Leagues and in Latin America, turning down five offers from major league teams over the years. Wilmer Fields interview; Holway, *Black Diamonds*, 177; Wilmer Fields, *My Life in the Negro Leagues* (Westport, Conn.: Meckler, 1996), 31–37. After the Grays folded, Fields played in Canada and Latin America rather than take a salary cut to try to work his way up to the majors. Fields, *My Life*, 31.

99. Originally, Marquez signed with the New York Yankees and played with the Double-A Newark Bears, Easter signed with the Indians and initially played with their Triple-A club in San Diego, and Thurman left to play in his hometown for the Kansas City Monarchs. "Bad Weather Halts Drills in Danville Training Camp," *Washington Afro-American*, 16 April 1949, sec. 2, p. 14.

100. "National Circuit Folds Up," *Pittsburgh Courier*, 11 December 1948, 11.

101. "Grays Plan to Continue Local Games," *Washington Afro-American*, 4 December 1948, sec. 2, p. 12.

102. Letter from Seward Posey to Art Carter, 17 December 1948, box 10, Art Carter Papers.

103. Letter from Vernon Green to Art Carter, 22 January 1949, box 1, folder 8, Art Carter Papers.

104. Letter from Seward Posey to Art Carter, 19 January 1949, box 1, folder 7, Art Carter Papers.

105. Art Carter, "Grays' Co-Owner Praised as 'Big Brother to All,'" *Washington Afro-American*, 5 March 1949, sec. 2, p. 14; "Popular Co-Owner of Homestead Grays Dies in Pittsburgh," *Pittsburgh Courier*, 12 March 1949, 12.

106. Ruck, *Sandlot Seasons*, 181.

107. "Grays Join New 8-Team American Association," *Washington Afro-American*, 12 March 1949, sec. 2, p. 12; "Grays Lead American Ass'n," *Pittsburgh Courier*, 25 June 1949, 22.

108. Lena Cox interview, 5 August 1992.

109. "Grays Winning in Spite of Early Handicaps; Face Money Problems on the Road," *Washington Afro-American*, 18 June 1949, sec. 2, p. 13.

110. "Partlow, Southpaw Ace, Bolsters Pitching Staff," *Washington Afro-American*, 30 April 1949, sec. 2, p. 14

111. "Grays to End Season Here Against Philadelphia Stars," *Washington Afro-American*, 17 September 1949, 27.

112. Ibid.; "Partlow's Five-Hit Hurling Triumphs Over Latins, 8–1," *Washington Afro-American*, 6 August 1949, 25.

113. "Cubans, Stars to Play First NAL Bill Sunday," *Washington Afro-American*, 23 July 1949, 25; "Rain Plays Havoc with Grays, 2 Games Delayed," id., 20 August 1949, 13.

114. "Grays Beat Philly Stars, 5–1, in Season's Finale," *Washington Afro-American*, 1 October 1949, 26.

115. Ruck, *Sandlot Seasons*, 181; *Pittsburgh Courier*, 1 September 1951, 1.

116. For example, at a July 2 four-team doubleheader involving the Elite Giants, Stars, Cubans, and Grays at Shibe Park that drew 3,780 fans, each team made only $357.80. Satchel took home $547.50. Balance Sheet—24 July 1950, Ed Bolden Papers, Manuscript Division, Moorland-Spingarn Research Center, Howard University, Washington, D.C.

117. Holway, *Voices*, 15, 271.

118. "Veteran Hurler to Face Grays for Philadelphia Stars," *Washington Afro-American*, 5 August 1950, 23.

119. "Grays Hit the Road After Beating Philly Stars Twice," *Washington Afro-American*, 12 August 1950, 25.

120. "Grays End Season with 100 Wins," *Washington Afro-American*, 16 September 1950, 26.

121. "Grays Have 8–0 Record on Tour," *Washington Afro-American*, 4 November 1950, 29; Leonard, *The Black Lou Gehrig*, 194–95.

122. Leonard, *The Black Lou Gehrig*, 210.

123. The official cause of Charlie's death was carcinoma of the stomach, which had metastasized. North Carolina Death Certificates, Charles Delmont Leonard, 10 October 1952, vol. 11B, p. 517, s.123.378, North Carolina State Archives, Raleigh, N.C.; C. D. Leonard interview.

124. Cattau, "Forgotten Champions," 29.

EPILOGUE

1. Sam Lacy, "Senators Search for Tan Players," *Baltimore Afro-American*, 2 April 1949, sec. 1, p. 1.
2. Sam Lacy, "Looking 'Em Over with the Tribune," *Washington Tribune*, 25 December 1937, 12.
3. Sam Lacy, "Senators Search for Tan Players," *Baltimore Afro-American*, 2 April 1949, sec. 1, p. 1.
4. Ibid. As late as 1950, Leonard had been hearing the same rumors about the Senators' interest in signing him. Leonard, *The Black Lou Gehrig*, 210.
5. Sam Lacy, "Clark Griffith Sees the Light," *Baltimore Afro-American*, 2 April 1949, sec. 1, p. 7.
6. Ibid.
7. Sam Lacy, "From A to Z," *Baltimore Afro-American*, 2 April 1949, sec. 1, p. 7.
   Griffith's sincerity about a finding a black player in 1949 is called into question by Harold Parrott's memoir, which details a 1949 sale of minor leaguers by Branch Rickey. Although Parrott acknowledged that Griffith and other owners felt pressure in 1949 to integrate their teams because of people picketing their ballparks, Griffith did not bid on two black players up for sale—outfielder Sam Jethroe and pitcher Dan Bankhead. Instead, Griffith pursued two of Rickey's white minor league players, shortstop Danny O'Connell and outfielder Irv Noren. When Griffith lost O'Connell to the Pittsburgh Pirates, Rickey sold him on Noren, who was playing for the Senators the following year. Jethroe was sold to the Boston Braves; Bankhead remained with the Dodgers. Parrott, *The Lords of Baseball*, 285–91.
8. Kenesaw M. Landis II, *Segregation in Washington: A Report of the National Committee on Segregation in the Nation's Capital* (Chicago: November 1948), 91.
9. *District of Columbia v. John R. Thompson Co.*, 346 U.S. 100 (1953). For more on the Thompson's Restaurant controversy, see Green, *The Secret City*, 296–98; Kluger, *Simple Justice*, 595.
10. Beverly Washington Jones, *Quest for Equality: The Life and Writings of Mary Eliza Church Terrell, 1863–1954*, vol. 13 (Brooklyn, N.Y.: Carlson Publishing, 1990), 85. For a complete account of Mrs. Terrell's struggle, see id., 73–82.
11. *Shelley v. Kraemer*, 334 U.S. 1 (1948). Houston won his companion case, *Hurd v. Hodge*, 334 U.S. 24 (1948), on behalf of Washington's black home buyers.
12. Kluger, *Simple Justice*, 246–55.
13. For the best account of the grassroots efforts to desegregate the District of Columbia's school system and Houston's alliances with working-class black Washingtonians, see Kluger, *Simple Justice*, 508–23.
14. *Bolling v. Sharpe*, 347 U.S. 497 (1954).
15. *Brown v. Board of Education*, 347 U.S. 483, 494 (1954).
16. Clark Griffith, as told to J. G. Taylor Spink, "At 82, He Prefers to Look Forward," *The Sporting News*, 23 July 1952, 11.
17. Kerr, *Calvin*, 37.
18. Fitzgerald, "Clark Griffith," 42.
19. Shirley Povich, "Griffith Always Played It Hard Until Final Out," *Washington Post*, 28 October 1955, 46, 48; Fitzgerald, "Clark Griffith," 42.
20. Seymour, *Baseball: The Golden Age*, 72.
21. Kerr, *Calvin*, 138.
22. Calvin Griffith interview. A few years after Jackie Robinson broke into the majors, Pittsburgh Pirates owner Bill Benswanger blamed his failure to integrate on Cum

Posey, claiming that Posey refused to sell him Buck Leonard and Josh Gibson. As Wendell Smith pointed out, Benswanger's post hoc excuses rang hollow. Wendell Smith, "The Sports Beat," *Pittsburgh Courier*, 28 January 1950, 22.

23. Holway, *Josh and Satch*, 154.

24. Lacy interview, 15 July 1992.

25. *The Sporting News*, 23 July 1952, 12.

26. A. S. "Doc" Young, "Inside Sports," *Jet*, 2:15 (7 August 1952), 53.

27. Dan Daniel, "Griff Sees Yank Pitching Stalling Fifth Flag Drive," *New York World-Telegram*, 17 April 1953, 34. Despite Griffith's confirmation of the proposed Doby-Jensen swap in the *World-Telegram*, Povich wrote the following week that "the published report of the Indians' offer of Larry Doby for Jackie Jensen was a phoney. . . . It was a hypothetical trade broached to Bucky Harris by a baseball writer, not by the Indians. . . ." Shirley Povich, "Griffs Whip Bosox, 4–0," *Washington Post*, 26 March 1953, 18. Not according to quotes in Dan Daniel's article attributed to Griffith.

28. Dan Daniel, "Griff Sees Yank Pitching Stalling Fifth Flag Drive," *New York World-Telegram*, 17 April 1953, 34.

29. The *Washington Post* mentioned that Paula was the "first Negro ever to play a regular game for the Nats." Bob Addie, "Nats Whip A's, 8–1," *Washington Post*, 7 September 1954, 18; Burton Hawkins, "Paula and Lemon Show Senators Some Promise," *Washington Evening Star*, 7 September 1954, A-20 (not mentioning Paula as the first black Senator but describing him as the "muscular Cuban Negro"); "Debut Impressive," *Baltimore Afro-American*, 18 September 1954, 17 (running a photograph of Paula and a caption about his 2-for-5 debut). The 1955 Senators yearbook noted that Paula had the "distinction" of the being the "first Negro" to play in a major league game with the Senators. 1955 Washington Nationals yearbook, 30.

30. Lacy interview, 15 July 1992. Scull (pronounced "School"), a five-foot six-inch outfielder signed by Joe Cambria, never appeared in a major league game. Yet Scull appeared in the team's 1954 yearbook. 1954 Washington Nationals yearbook, 23.

 The Senators apparently brought two dark-skinned Cuban players to their 1953 spring training, Scull and fellow outfielder Juan Vistuer, neither of whom made the team. Lester, *Black Baseball's National Showcase*, 378. In his coverage of the Senators' spring training, Povich wrote of Scull: "The Nats now have a Negro player being seasoned in the Triple A American Association." Shirley Povich, "Harris Sees Yost Hitting More Homers," *Washington Post*, 31 March 1953, 16. Povich, however, did not explicitly refer to Vistuer as a "Negro." He wrote: "All of the Nats Cubans are now in camp with pitchers Sandy Consuegra and Raul Sanchez and outfielder Juan Vistuer reporting today." Shirley Povich, "A's Burn Nats, 7–1," *Washington Post*, 16 March 1953, 11.

 In February 1953, *Jet* magazine wrote about the Senators trying out a "Negro outfielder." It was referring to Scull, whom Joe Cambria boasted was "'faster than Minnie Minoso' of the White Sox." "Senators to Try Out Negro Outfielder," *Jet* 3:18 (26 February 1953), 48. *Jet* did not mention Vistuer.

31. "'Why No Negro Players?' Dailies in Three Cities Ask," *Pittsburgh Courier*, 29 August 1953, 15; Tygiel, *Baseball's Great Experiment*, 293.

32. Clark Griffith file, National Baseball Library, Cooperstown, New York; Kerr, *Calvin*, 15.

33. For Griffith's ties to Abe Attell, see Seymour, *Baseball: The Golden Age*, 336–37.

34. Povich, *All These Mornings*, 70–71.

35. Henry Whitehead interview.

36. Shirley Povich, "Griffith Always Played It Hard Until Final Out," *Washington Post*, 28 October 1955, 46.

37. "No Tears for Griffith," *Washington Afro-American*, 5 November 1955, 4.

38. Bureau of the Census, *Eighteenth Census of the United States: 1960—Population, Characteristics of the Population—District of Columbia* (Washington, D.C.: GPO, 1963), vol. I, part 10, tbl. 15, pp. 10–11.

39. Calvin B. Griffith, "Griffith Not Happy with Armory Stadium Site," *Washington Post*, 17 January 1958, A-18.

40. Kerr, *Calvin*, 136. A *Chicago Daily News* reporter wrote a contemporaneous account of the meeting by listening through a hotel vent.

41. Shannon and Kalinsky, *The Ballparks*, 239.

42. Gordon Thomas, "Griffith Stadium: 30th Anniversary of the Finale," (September 1991; unpublished article on file with author); John Sherwood, "Last Whistle to Blow Soon for Old Griffith Stadium," *Washington Evening Star*, 10 November 1964, D-1.

43. Dave Brady, "Big Ball Set for Griffith Stadium Finale," *Washington Post*, 28 October 1964, D3; Dave Brady, "TV Writes Requiem to Griffith Stadium," *The Sporting News*, 7 November 1964, 23.

44. Department of Labor and Health, Education, and Welfare Appropriations for 1964, Subcommittee of the Committee on Appropriations, House of Representatives, 88th Cong., 1st sess. (Washington: GPO, 1963). James Nabrit told Congress on March 20, 1963: "That covers the cost of the land, and the estimated cost by the government of what it would require to tear down and get rid of those stands. They are concrete and embedded and it would cost some money." Id.

45. Logan, *Howard University*, 496.

46. Harriet Griffiths, "Wreckers Send Old Stadium Fading into History," *Washington Evening Star*, 13 February 1965, A-24.

47. Michael Lenehan, "The Last of the Pure Baseball Men," *Atlantic Monthly* 248:2 (August 1981), 44; Doug Grow, "The Last Dinosaur," *Inside Sports* vol. 6 (July 1984), 35; Pat Jordan, "Just Some of the Folks Who Ruined Your Summer," *New York Times Magazine*, 18 September 1994, 1, 66, 86, 87, 93.

48. Grow, "The Last Dinosaur," 35.

49. Kerr, *Calvin*, 137.

50. Ibid., 49.

51. Calvin Griffith interview.

52. Ibid.

53. Dick Heller, "Griffith Stadium Lives Again in Memory," *Washington Times*, 26 September 2001, C5.

54. In her study of the Great Migration, Carole Marks wrote: "Returning to [their] place of origin is the dream of many migrants, particularly those who succeed in the host society. It is a logical opinion because of the migrant's familiarity with its language, culture, and custom and because wage disparities between sending and receiving areas provide migrants with a distinct advantage." Marks, *Farewell—We're Good and Gone*, 158.

55. Buck's manager with Durango and Xalapa was the former Negro League pitching and hitting legend (and future Hall of Famer), Martin Dihigo. In 1955, Durango fired Leonard the same week they fired Dihigo. Holway, *Voices*, 273.

56. Leonard, *The Black Lou Gehrig*, 214–16, 221.

57. Ibid., 222; Holway, *Voices*, 272.
58. Holway, *Voices*, 130.
59. Leonard, *The Black Lou Gehrig*, 223.
60. Ibid., 229–30.
61. Ibid., 230, 263.
62. Buck Leonard interview, 12 October 1992.
63. Leonard, *The Black Lou Gehrig*, 230.
64. C. D. Leonard interview.
65. Lena Cox interview, 29 August 1992.
66. Holway, *Josh and Satch*, xiii.
67. Leonard, *The Black Lou Gehrig*, 269.
68. *New York Times*, 29 November 1997, A1, A29.
69. Leonard, *The Black Lou Gehrig*, 263.
70. Chip Alexander, "Celebrating a Full Life," *Raleigh News and Observer*, 3 December 1997, C1.
71. Ibid.
72. Lacy interview, 15 July 1992.
73. Michael A. Fletcher, "The Changes," *Washington Post Magazine*, 1 February 1998, 11.
74. Anderson, "A Very Special Monument," 108.
75. Wolseley, *The Black Press U.S.A.*, 323.
76. Ibid., 71–72.
77. Ross Hetrick, "Newspaper Cuts Back to Once a Week," *Baltimore Evening Sun*, 22 September 1988, C1.
78. Sam Lacy interview, 17 May 1994.
79. Leonard Shapiro, "Post Sports Columnist Shirley Povich Dies," *Washington Post*, 5 June 1998, A1.
80. "Sam Lacy's Hall of Fame Speech," *Baltimore Sun*, 27 July 1998, 7D.
81. Ibid.
82. Linda Wheeler, "A Building of the People," *Washington Post*, 18 January 1999, A1; Jackie Spinner, "Keeping the Best of the True Reformer," *Washington Post*, 1 September 2000, E1.
83. Mary Battiata, "Landscape: U Street," *Washington Post Magazine*, 1 February 1998, 13.
84. Mark Gauvreau Judge, "A Washington Landmark; in a City of Monuments, No Room for the Howard?" *Washington Post*, 25 April 1999, B3; Christine Montgomery, "Next Act in the Wings; New Effort to Save Historic Howard Theatre Would Make It Part of Black Cultural District," *Washington Times*, 22 April 1999, C8.
85. Linda Wheeler, "Recovering a Part of D.C. History," *Washington Post*, 3 October 1998, G1 ("a new wave of home buyers is discovering the area around the U Street NW corridor"); Daniela Deane, "Going Upscale on U St.," id., 24 March 2001, H1; Marc Fisher, "Bringing a New Look to U Street," id., 12 April 2001, B1; Marc Fisher, "Barber Fears Demise in U Street Revival," id., 14 April 2001, B1.

BIBLIOGRAPHY

Manuscript Collections

Afro-American Collection. Enoch Pratt Free Library, Baltimore, Maryland.

Atlantic Coast Line Railroad Records. Southern Historical Collection. Wilson Library, University of North Carolina, Chapel Hill, North Carolina.

Bolden, Ed, Papers. Moorland-Spingarn Research Center, Howard University, Washington, D.C.

Carter, Art, Papers. Moorland-Spingarn Research Center, Howard University, Washington, D.C.

Davidson, Eugene C., Collection. Moorland-Spingarn Research Center, Howard University, Washington, D.C.

Henderson, E. B., Papers. Moorland-Spingarn Research Center, Howard University, Washington, D.C.

Lloyd, John Henry, File. Heston Collection. Atlantic City Free Public Library, Atlantic City, New Jersey.

Logan, Rayford W., Papers. Manuscript Division, Library of Congress, Washington, D.C.

Marian Anderson–D.A.R. Controversy Collection. Moorland-Spingarn Research Center, Howard University, Washington, D.C.

NAACP Papers. Moorland-Spingarn Research Center, Howard University, Washington, D.C.

Negro League Collection. National Baseball Hall of Fame Library, Cooperstown, New York.

North Carolina Collection. University of North Carolina, Chapel Hill, North Carolina.

Player Clipping Files. National Baseball Hall of Fame Library, Cooperstown, New York.

Prattis, Percival Leroy, Papers. Moorland-Spingarn Research Center, Howard University, Washington, D.C.

Smith, Wendell, Papers. National Baseball Hall of Fame Library, Cooperstown, New York.

Washington, D.C., High School Yearbooks. The Charles Sumner School Museum and Archives, Washington, D.C.

Washingtonian Division and the Washington Star Collection. Martin Luther King Memorial Library, Washington, D.C.

Public Documents

Baist, George William. *Baist's Real Estate Atlas of Surveys of Washington, District of Columbia*. Philadelphia: G. W. Baist, 1891–1935.

Marriage Licenses. Edgecombe County Record of Deeds, Tarboro, North Carolina.

Marriage Licenses. Nash County Record of Deeds, Nashville, North Carolina.

Report of the President's Committee on Civil Rights. *To Secure These Rights*. Washington, D.C., 1947.

Rocky Mount City Directories, 1908–09, 1912–13, 1934, 1940.

U.S. Bureau of the Census. *Eighteenth Census of the United States—Population: 1960, Characteristics of the Population*. Vol. I, Pt. 10. Washington, D.C., 1963.

U.S. Bureau of the Census. *Negroes in the United States 1920–1932*. Washington, D.C., 1935.

U.S. Bureau of the Census. *Ninth, Tenth, Twelfth, Thirteenth, Fourteenth*, and *Fifteenth Census of the United States—Population*. North Carolina and Washington, D.C.

U.S. Bureau of the Census. *Seventeenth Census of the United States, Special Reports: State of Birth*. Washington, D.C., 1953.

U.S. Bureau of the Census. *Seventh and Eighth Census of the United States—Population*. Free and slave schedules for 1850 and 1860. Franklin County, North Carolina.

U.S. Bureau of the Census. *Sixteenth Census of the United States: 1940—Population*. Vol. II, Pt. 6. Washington, D.C., 1943.

U.S. Bureau of the Census. *Sixteenth Census of the United States. Population: Internal Migration 1935–1940*. Washington, D.C., 1943.

U.S. Congress. House of Representatives. Department of Labor and Health, Education, and Welfare Appropriations for 1964. Subcommittee of the Committee on Appropriations. 88th Cong., 1st sess., 1963.

U.S. Congress. House of Representatives. Judiciary Committee. *Study of Monopoly Power, Pt. 6, Organized Baseball: Hearings Before the Subcommittee on the Study of Monopoly Power*. 82nd Cong., 1st sess., 1951.

Washington, D.C., City Directories, 1910–1942.

Interviews by Author

Artisst, Paul. Washington, D.C., 25 August 1993.

Awkard, Russell. Silver Spring, Md., 26 August 1993.

Benson, Gene. Secaucus, N.J., 31 May 1992.

Black, Joe. Secaucus, N.J., 31 May 1992.

Bolden, Frank Page. Washington, D.C., 2 July 1992.

Braxton, A. C. Seat Pleasant, Md., 18 August 1992.

Carter, Callie. Washington, D.C., 19 March 1993.

Cash, Bill. Secaucus, N.J., 31 May 1992.

Cohen, Jim. Washington, D.C., 25 June 1992.

Corbett, Gene. Telephone interview. Salisbury, Md., 7 November 2000.

Coward, Billy. Washington, D.C., 20 August 1992.

Cox, Lena. Chillum, Md., 5 August 1992, 29 August 1992, and 21 April 1995.

Crutchfield, Jimmie. Secaucus, N.J., 31 May 1992.

Dandridge, Ray. Secaucus, N.J., 31 May 1992.

Day, Leon. Baltimore, Md., 24 August 1992.

Dozier, Eddie. Washington, D.C., 18 August 1992.

Duckett, Mahlon. Secaucus, N.J., 31 May 1992.

Feller, Bob. Washington, D.C., 10 November 2000.

Fields, Wilmer. Manassas, Va., 13 August 1992 and 20 March 1993.

Franklin, John Hope. Durham, N.C., 21 April 1994 and 14 June 1994.

Gibson, Josh, Jr., Secaucus, N.J., 30 May 1992.

Gilbert, Bill. Potomac, Md., 9 July 1992, and telephone interview, 3 June 1992.

Griffith, Calvin. Indiatlantic, Fla., 10–11 February 1995.

Griffith, Clark, II. Telephone interview. Minneapolis, Minn., 31 May 1994.

Hemond, Roland. Baltimore, Md., 8 June 1992.

Hill, Calvin. Baltimore, Md., 5 June 1992.

Hinton, Chuck. Washington, D.C., 5 August 1992.

Holway, John B. Washington, D.C., 29 May 1992.

Hopkins, Gordon. Washington, D.C., 18 August 1993.

Irvin, Monte. Telephone interview. Homosassa, Fla., 23 February 1995.

Israel, Elbert. Rockville, Md., 26 August 1993.

Jackson, Harold. Telephone interview. New York City, N.Y., 11 May 1994.

Jackson-Cornish, Alyce. Washington, D.C., 26 February 1995.

Jefferson, Buster. Washington, D.C., 24 August 1993.

Johnson, Josh. Secaucus, N.J., 31 May 1992.

Lacy, Sam. Washington, D.C., 15 July 1992 and 17 May 1994.

Leonard, Buck. Rocky Mount, N.C., 20 July 1992, 12 October 1992, 15 June 1994, and 27
   April 1995.

Leonard, C. D. Oxon Hill, Md., 26 December 1994.

Lewis, Dr. Harold O. Washington, D.C., 19 August 1992.

Lincoln, C. Eric. Durham, N.C., 6 May 1994.

Mathis, Verdell. Secaucus, N.J., 31 May 1992.

McNeill, Robert. Washington, D.C., 2 July 1992 and 17 August 1993.

Medley, Wilfred C. Washington, D.C., 8 July 1992.

Moore, Bob and Ophelia. Washington, D.C., 4 August 1992 and 10 August 1992.

Nabrit, James, III. Telephone interview. Washington, D.C., 9 January 1995.

O'Neil, Buck. Washington, D.C., 11 November 2000.

Perry, Geneva. Washington, D.C., 17 August 1993.

Povich, Shirley. Washington, D.C., 12 January 1993.

Powell, Dick. Baltimore, Md., 24 August 1992.

Scott, Bill. Washington, D.C., 5 August 1992.

Siegel, Morris. Baltimore, Md., 6 June 1992.

Stone, C. Sumner. Chapel Hill, N.C., 26 April 1994.

Travis, Cecil. Telephone interview. Riverdale, Ga., 4 November 2000.

Venison, Ernest. Burtonsville, Md., 28 August 1992.

Vernon, Mickey. Telephone interview. Wallingford, Pa., 10 November 1994.

Walker, Edsall. Secaucus, N.J., 30 May 1992.

Walker, James. Washington, D.C., 30 June 1992.

Weaver, Robert C. New York City, N.Y., 30 July 1992.

Whitehead, Henry. Telephone interview. Washington, D.C., 19 January 1995.

Withers, Ernest. Telephone interview. Washington, D.C., 16 April 2002.

Wood, Norman. Washington, D.C., 24 August 1993 and 19 January 1995.

BOOKS

Adelson, Bruce. *Brushing Back Jim Crow: The Integration of Minor-League Baseball in the American South.* Charlottesville, Va.: The University Press of Virginia, 1999.

Alexander, Charles C. *John McGraw.* New York: Penguin Books, 1988.

Angelou, Maya. *I Know Why the Caged Bird Sings.* New York: Bantam Books, 1993.

Anson, Adrian C. *A Ballplayer's Career.* Chicago: Era, 1900.

Bak, Richard. *Turkey Stearns and the Detroit Stars: The Negro Leagues in Detroit, 1919–1933.* Detroit: Wayne State University Press, 1994.

Banker, Stephen. *Black Diamonds: An Oral History of Negro Baseball.* Washington, D.C.: Tapes for Readers, 1978.

Bankes, James. *The Pittsburgh Crawfords: The Lives & Times of Black Baseball's Most Exciting Team.* Dubuque, Iowa: Wm. C. Brown, 1991.

Barlow, William. *Voice Over: The Making of Black Radio.* Philadelphia: Temple University Press, 1999.

Bealle, Morris A. *The Washington Senators: An 87-Year History of the World's Oldest Baseball Club and Most Incurable Fandom.* Washington, D.C.: Columbia Publishing Co., 1947.

Benson, Michael. *Ballparks of North America: A Comprehensive Historical Reference to Baseball Grounds, Yards, and Stadiums, 1845 to present.* Jefferson, N.C.: McFarland, 1989.

Berkow, Ira. *Red: A Biography of Red Smith.* New York: Times Books, 1986.

Birmingham, Stephen. *Certain People: America's Black Elite.* Boston: Little, Brown and Co., 1977.

Borchert, James. *Alley Life in Washington: Family, Community, Religion, and Folklife in the City, 1850–1970.* Urbana, Ill.: University of Illinois Press, 1980.

Brashler, William. *Josh Gibson: A Life in the Negro Leagues.* New York: Harper and Row, 1978.

Brown, Letitia, and Elsie M. Lewis. *Washington in the New Era, 1870–1970.* Washington, D.C.: Smithsonian Institution, 1972.

Bruce, Janet. *The Kansas City Monarchs: Champions of Black Baseball.* Topeka, Kans.: University Press of Kansas, 1985.

Byington, Margaret. *Homestead: The Households of a Mill Town.* New York: Russell Sage Foundation, 1910.

Carter, Dan T. *Scottsboro: A Tragedy of the American South.* Baton Rouge, La.: Louisiana State University Press, 1990.

Clark, Dick, and Larry Lester, eds. *The Negro Leagues Book.* Cleveland, Ohio: SABR, 1994.

Clark-Lewis, Elizabeth. *Living In, Living Out: African American Domestics in Washington, D.C., 1910–1940.* Washington, D.C.: Smithsonian Institution Press, 1994.

Cottrell, Robert Charles. *The Best Pitcher in Baseball: The Life of Rube Foster, Negro League Giant.* New York: New York University Press, 2001.

Cramer, Richard Ben. *Joe DiMaggio: The Hero's Life.* New York: Simon & Schuster, 2001.

Creamer, Robert W. *Babe: The Legend Comes to Life.* New York: Simon and Schuster, 1974.

———. *Baseball in '41: A Celebration of the "Best Baseball Season Ever"—In the Year America Went to War.* New York: Viking, 1991.

Debono, Paul. *The Indianapolis ABCs: History of a Premier Team in the Negro Leagues.* Jefferson, N.C.: McFarland, 1997.

Dixon, Phil S. *The Monarchs 1920–1938: Featuring Wilber "Bullet" Rogan: The Greatest Ballplayer in Cooperstown.* Sioux Falls, S.D.: Mariah Press, 2002.

Dixon, Phil S., and Patrick J. Hannigan. *The Negro Baseball Leagues: A Photographic History.* Mattituck, N.Y.: Amereon House, 1992.

Dorinson, Joseph, and Joram Warmund, eds. *Jackie Robinson: Race, Sports, and the American Dream.* Armonk, N.Y.: M. E. Sharpe, 1998.

Drake, St. Clair, and Horace R. Cayton. *Black Metropolis: A Study of Negro Life in a Northern City.* New York: Harcourt, Brace and Company, 1945.

Duberman, Martin Bauml. *Paul Robeson: A Biography.* New York: Ballantine Books, 1989.

Ellington, Edward Kennedy. *Music Is My Mistress.* New York: De Capo Press, 1973.

Evelyn, Douglas E., and Paul Dickson. *On This Spot: Pinpointing the Past in Washington, D.C.* Washington, D.C.: Farragut Publishing, 1992.

Falkner, David. *Great Time Coming: The Life of Jackie from Baseball to Birmingham.* New York: Simon and Schuster, 1995.

Feller, Bob, with Bill Gilbert. *Now Pitching Bob Feller.* New York: Birch Lane Press, 1990.

Fields, Wilmer. *My Life in the Negro Leagues.* Westport, Conn.: Meckler, 1996.

Finkle, Lee. *Forum for Protest: The Black Press During World War II.* Cranbury, N.J.: Associated University Presses, 1975.

Fitzpatrick, Sandra, and Maria R. Goodwin. *The Guide to Black Washington.* New York: Hippocrene Books, 1990.

Fligstein, Neil. *Going North, Migration of Blacks and Whites from the South, 1900–1950.* New York: Academic Press, 1981.

Franklin, John Hope. *The Free Negro in North Carolina 1790–1860.* New York: W. W. Norton & Company, 1971.

Frazier, E. Franklin. *Black Bourgeoisie.* New York: The Free Press, 1957.

———. *Negro in the United States.* Rev. ed. New York: The Macmillan Company, 1957.

Gatewood, Willard B. *Aristocrats of Color: The Black Elite, 1880–1920.* Bloomington, Ind.: Indiana University Press, 1990.

Gilbert, Bill. *They Also Served: Baseball and the Home Front, 1941–1945.* New York: Crown Publishers, 1992.

Goggin, Jacqueline. *Carter G. Woodson: A Life in Black History.* Baton Rouge, La.: Louisiana State University Press, 1993.

Goldstein, Richard. *Spartan Seasons: How Baseball Survived the Second World War.* New York: Macmillan, 1980.

González Echevarría, Roberto. *The Pride of Havana: A History of Cuban Baseball.* New York: Oxford University Press, 1999.

Graham, Lawrence Otis. *Our Kind of People: Inside America's Black Upper Class.* New York: HarperCollins, 1999.

Gregory, Robert. *Diz: The Story of Dizzy Dean and Baseball During the Great Depression.* New York: Viking, 1992.

Green, Constance McLaughlin. *The Secret City: A History of Race Relations in the Nation's Capital.* Princeton, N.J.: Princeton University Press, 1967.

Haizlip, Shirlee Taylor. *The Sweeter the Juice: A Family Memoir in Black and White.* New York: Simon and Schuster, 1994.

Herzog, Whitey, and Kevin Horrigan. *White Rat: A Life in Baseball*. New York: Harper & Row, 1987.

Holtzman, Jerome, ed. *No Cheering in the Press Box*. Rev. ed. New York: Henry Holt, 1995.

Holway, John B. *Black Diamonds: Life in the Negro Leagues from the Men Who Lived It*. Westport, Conn.: Meckler Books, 1989.

———. *Blackball Stars: Negro League Pioneers*. Westport, Conn.: Meckler, 1988.

———. *The Complete Book of the Negro Leagues: The Other Half of Baseball History*. Fern Park, Fla.: Hastings House Publishers, 2001.

———. *Josh and Satch*. Westport, Conn.: Meckler, 1991.

———. *Voices from the Great Black Baseball Leagues*. New York: De Capo Press, 1975; rev. ed., 1992.

Huggins, Nathan Irvin. *Harlem Renaissance*. New York: Oxford University Press, 1971.

Hundley, Mary Gibson. *The Dunbar Story (1870–1955)*. New York: Vantage Press, 1965.

Jackson, Hal, with James Haskins. *The House That Jack Built*. New York: Amistad Press, 2001.

James, Bill. *The Bill James Historical Baseball Abstract*. New York: Villard Books, 1986.

———. *The New Bill James Historical Baseball Abstract*. New York: The Free Press, 2001.

Johnson, Daniel M., and Rex R. Campbell. *Black Migration in America: A Social Demographic History*. Durham, N.C.: Duke University Press, 1981.

Jones, Beverly Washington. *Quest for Equality: The Life and Writings of Mary Eliza Church Terrell, 1863–1954*. Vol. 13. Brooklyn, N.Y.: Carlson Publishing, 1990.

Jones, William H. *Recreation and Amusement Among Negroes in Washington, D.C.* Washington, D.C.: Howard University Press, 1927; reprint Westport, Conn.: Negro University Press, 1970.

Kerr, Jon. *Calvin: Baseball's Last Dinosaur*. Dubuque, Iowa: Wm. C. Brown Publishers, 1990.

King, LeRoy O. *100 Years of Capital Traction: The Story of Streetcars in the Nation's Capital*. Dallas: Taylor Publishing, 1972.

Kluger, Richard. *Simple Justice: The History of* Brown v. Board of Education *and Black America's Struggle for Equality*. New York: Alfred A. Knopf, 1976.

Kuklick, Bruce. *To Every Thing a Season: Shibe Park and Urban Philadelphia, 1909–1976*. Princeton, N.J.: Princeton University Press, 1991.

Lacy, Sam, with Moses J. Newson. *Fighting for Fairness: The Life Story of Hall of Fame Sportswriter Sam Lacy*. Centreville, Md.: Tidewater Publishers, 1998.

Lanctot, Neil. *Fair Dealing and Clean Playing: The Hilldale Club and the Development of Black Professional Baseball, 1910–1932*. Jefferson, N.C.: McFarland, 1994.

Landis, Kenesaw M. *Segregation in Washington: A Report of the National Committee on Segregation in the Nation's Capital*. Chicago, 1948.

Leonard, Buck, with James A. Riley. *Buck Leonard: The Black Lou Gehrig*. New York: Carroll and Graf, 1995.

Lester, Larry. *Black Baseball's National Showcase: The East-West All-Star Game, 1933–1953*. Lincoln, Nebr.: University of Nebraska Press, 2001.

Lester, Larry, and Sammy J. Miller. *Black Baseball in Pittsburgh*. Charleston, S.C.: Arcadia, 2001.

Lewis, David Levering. *W. E. B. DuBois: Biography of a Race (1868–1919)*. New York: Henry Holt, 1993.

———. *W. E. B. DuBois: The Fight for Equality and the American Century*. New York: Henry Holt, 2000.

Lieb, Fred. *Baseball As I Have Known It*. New York: Coward, McCann & Geoghegan, 1977.

Link, Arthur S. *Wilson: The New Freedom*. Princeton, N.J.: Princeton University Press, 1956.

Locke, Alain, ed., *The New Negro: An Interpretation*. New York: Albert and Charles Boni, 1925.

Logan, Rayford W. *Howard University: The First Hundred Years, 1867–1967*. New York: New York University Press, 1969.

———. *The Negro in American Life and Thought: The Nadir, 1877–1901*. New York: Dial Press, 1954.

Lowry, Philip J. *Green Cathedrals: The Ultimate Celebration of All 271 Major League and Negro League Ballparks Past and Present*. Rev. ed. Reading, Mass.: Addison-Wesley, 1992.

Marks, Carole. *Farewell—We're Good and Gone: The Great Black Migration*. Bloomington, Ind.: Indiana University Press, 1989.

Marshall, William. *Baseball's Pivotal Era: 1945–1951*. Lexington, Ky.: University Press of Kentucky, 1999.

McConnell, Bob, and David Vincent, eds., *SABR Presents the Home Run Encyclopedia: The Who, What, and Where of Every Home Run Hit Since 1876*. New York: Macmillan, 1996.

Mead, William B. *Baseball Goes to War*. Washington, D.C.: Broadcast Interview Source, Inc., 1998.

Mead, William B., and Paul Dickson. *Baseball: The President's Game*. New York: Walker Publishing Company, 1997.

Moore, Joseph Thomas. *Pride Against Prejudice: The Biography of Larry Doby*. New York: Greenwood Press, 1988.

Murray, Pauli. *The Autobiography of a Black Activist, Feminist, Lawyer, Priest, and Poet*. Knoxville, Tenn.: The University of Tennessee Press, 1987.

Myrdal, Gunnar. *An American Dilemma: The Negro Problem and Modern Democracy*. New York: Harper and Brothers, 1944.

1943 Baseball. Chicago: Office of the Baseball Commissioner, 1943.

O'Neil, Buck. *I Was Right on Time*. New York: Simon and Schuster, 1996.

Overmyer, James. *Queen of the Negro Leagues: Effa Manley and the Newark Eagles*. Lanham, Md.: Scarecrow Press, 1998.

Paige, Leroy "Satchel," with David Lipman. *Maybe I'll Pitch Forever*. Lincoln, Nebr.: University of Nebraska Press, 1993.

Paige, Leroy Satchel, with Hal Leibovitz. *Pitching Man: Satchel Paige's Own Story*. Cleveland: The *Cleveland News*, 1948.

Peterson, Robert. *Cages to Jump Shots: Pro Basketball's Early Years*. New York: Oxford University Press, 1990.

———. *Only the Ball Was White*. New York: Oxford University Press, 1970; rev. ed. 1992.

Pietrusza, David. *Judge and Jury: The Life and Times of Judge Kenesaw Mountain Landis*. South Bend, Ind.: Diamond Communications, 1998.

Polner, Murray. *Branch Rickey: A Biography*. New York: New American Library, 1982.

Povich, Shirley. *All These Mornings*. N.J.: Prentice-Hall, 1969.

——. *The Washington Senators: An Informal History*. New York: G. P. Putnam's Sons, 1954.

Pride, Armstead S., and Clint C. Wilson III. *A History of the Black Press*. Washington, D.C.: Howard University Press, 1997.

Rampersad, Arnold. *Jackie Robinson: A Biography*. New York: Alfred A. Knopf, 1997.

——. *The Life of Langston Hughes*. Vol. 1. New York: Oxford University Press, 1986.

Reichler, Joseph L. *The Baseball Encyclopedia: The Complete and Official Record of Major League Baseball*. 7th ed. New York: Macmillan, 1988.

Reichler, Joseph L., ed. *The Ronald Encyclopedia of Baseball*. New York: Ronald Press Co., 1962.

Reisler, Jim. *Black Writers/Black Baseball*. Jefferson, N.C.: McFarland, 1994.

Ribowsky, Mark. *A Complete History of the Negro Leagues, 1884 to 1955*. New York: Birch Lane Press, 1995.

——. *Don't Look Back: Satchel Paige in the Shadows of Baseball*. New York: Simon & Schuster, 1994.

——. *The Power and the Darkness: The Life of Josh Gibson in the Shadows of the Game*. New York: Simon and Schuster, 1996.

Riley, James A. *The Biographical Encyclopedia of the Negro Baseball Leagues*. New York: Carroll & Graf, 1994.

——. *Dandy, Day and the Devil*. Cocoa, Fla.: James A. Riley, 1987.

Ritter, Lawrence S. *Lost Ballparks: A Celebration of Baseball's Legendary Fields*. New York: Viking Studio Books, 1992.

Ritz, David. *Divided Soul: The Life of Marvin Gaye*. New York: De Capo Press, 1985.

Robinson, Frazier "Slow," with Paul Bauer. *Catching Dreams: My Life in the Negro Baseball Leagues*. Syracuse, N.Y.: Syracuse University Press, 1999.

Robinson, Jackie, with Alfred Duckett. *I Never Had It Made*. New York: G. P. Putnam's Sons, 1972.

Robinson, Jackie, with Wendell Smith. *Jackie Robinson: My Own Story*. New York: Greenberg, 1948.

Robinson, Rachel, with Lee Daniels. *Jackie Robinson: An Intimate Portrait*. New York: Harry N. Abrams, 1996.

The Rocky Mount Record. *Rocky Mount: One of the Best, Most Progressive, and Fastest Growing Cities in N. Carolina*. Rocky Mount, N.C., 1906.

Rogosin, Donn. *Invisible Men: Life in Baseball's Negro Leagues*. New York: Atheneum, 1988.

Ruck, Rob. *Sandlot Seasons: Sport in Black Pittsburgh*. Urbana, Ill.: University of Illinois Press, 1993.

Saunders, Frances Wright. *First Lady Between Two Worlds: Ellen Axson Wilson*. Chapel Hill, N.C.: University of North Carolina Press, 1985.

Seymour, Harold. *Baseball: The Golden Age*. New York: Oxford University Press, 1989.

Shannon, Bill, and George Kalinsky. *The Ballparks*. New York: Hawthorn Books, 1975.

Smith, Curt. *America's Dizzy Dean*. St. Louis, Mo.: Bethany Press, 1978.

Spink, J. G. Taylor. *Judge Landis and 25 Years of Baseball*. New York: Thomas Y. Crowell Company, 1947.

Staten, Vince. *Ol' Diz: A Biography of Dizzy Dean*. New York: HarperCollins, 1992.

Terrell, Mary Church. *A Colored Woman in a White World*. Washington, D.C.: Ransdell, Inc., 1940.

Thorn, John, et al., ed. *Total Baseball: The Official Encyclopedia of Major League Baseball*. 6th ed. New York: Total Sports, 1999.

Toomer, Jean. *Cane*. New York: Liveright, 1923, 1975.

Trouppe, Quincy. *29 Years Too Soon*. Los Angeles: S and S Enterprises, 1977.

Tucker, Mark. *Ellington: The Early Years*. Urbana, Ill.: University of Illinois Press, 1991.

Turner, Frederick. *When the Boys Came Back: Baseball and 1946*. New York: Henry Holt, 1996.

Tushnet, Mark. *The NAACP's Legal Strategy Against Segregated Education, 1925–1950*. Chapel Hill, N.C.: University of North Carolina Press, 1987.

Tygiel, Jules. *Baseball's Great Experiment: Jackie Robinson and His Legacy*. New York: Oxford University Press, 1983; Vintage Books, 1984.

———. *Past Time: Baseball as History*. New York: Oxford University Press, 2000.

Tygiel, Jules, ed., *The Jackie Robinson Reader: Perspectives on an American Hero*. New York: Dutton, 1997.

Veeck, Bill, with Ed Linn. *Veeck: As in Wreck*. New York: G. P. Putnam's Sons, 1962.

Webb, Lillian Ashcroft. *About My Father's Business: The Life of Elder Michaux*. Westport, Conn.: Greenwood Press, 1981.

White, Sol. *Sol White's History of Colored Base Ball: With Other Documents on the Early Black Game, 1886–1936*. Lincoln, Nebr., University of Nebraska Press, 1995.

Williams, Juan. *Thurgood Marshall: American Revolutionary*. New York: Times Books, 1998.

Wilson, August. *Fences*. New York: New American Library, 1986.

Wolseley, Roland E. *The Black Press, U.S.A.*. 2d rev. ed. Ames, Iowa: Iowa State University Press, 1990.

Woodward, C. Vann. *The Strange Career of Jim Crow*. 3d rev. ed. New York: Oxford University Press, 1974.

Young, Dick. *Roy Campanella: Most Valuable Player Series*. New York: A. S. Barnes, 1952.

ARTICLES

Allen, George. "Washington: A Capital That Went Boom." *Nation's Business* 25, no. 9 (1937): 33, 99–102.

"Anderson Affair." *Time*, 17 April 1939, 23.

Anderson, Jervis. "A Very Special Monument." *The New Yorker*, 20 March 1978, 91–121.

"Beisboleros." *Newsweek*, 29 May 1944, 90.

Bjarkman, Peter C. "Cuban Blacks in the Majors Before Jackie Robinson." *The National Pastime* no. 12 (1992): 58–63.

Blenko, Jim. "Nick Altrock." *The National Pastime: A Review of Baseball History* no. 18 (1998): 73–77.

Bowman, Larry G. "The Monarchs and Night Baseball." *The National Pastime: A Review of Baseball History* no. 16 (1996): 80–84.

Cattau, Daniel. "Forgotten Champions." *Washington Post Magazine*, 3 June 1990, 22–30.

Considine, Bob. "Ivory from Cuba: Our Underprivileged Baseball Players." *Colliers*, 3 August 1940, 19, 24

Considine, Bob, and Shirley L. Povich. "Old Fox: Baseball's Red-Eyed Radical and Archconservative, Clark Griffith." Parts 1 and 2. *Saturday Evening Post*, 13 April 1940, 14–15; 20 April 1940, 18–19.

Costello, Al. "Griff's Adopted Son Cal Trained to Take Over." *The Sporting News*, 13 August 1952, 11.

Crepeau, Richard. "The Jake Powell Incident and the Press: A Study in Black and White." In *Baseball History*. Westport, Conn.: Meckler, 1986, 32.

Daly, Victor R. "Washington's Minority Problem." *Crisis* 46, no. 6 (June 1939): 170.

Donovan, Richard. "The Fabulous Satchel Paige." In *The Baseball Reader*, edited by Charles Einstein. New York: Bonanza Books, 1989. First published in *Collier's*, 1954.

Dunbar, Paul L. "Negro Life in Washington." *Harper's Weekly*, 13 January 1900, 32.

———. "Negro Society in Washington." *Saturday Evening Post*, 14 December 1901, 9, 18.

Duffy, Peter. "Red Rodney: The American Communist Who Helped Liberate Baseball." *The Village Voice*, 10 June 1997, 122.

Fimrite, Ron. "Sam Lacy: Black Crusader." *Sports Illustrated*, 29 October 1990, 90–94.

———. "His Own Biggest Fan." *Sports Illustrated*, 19 July 1993, 76–80.

Fitzgerald, Ed. "Clark Griffith: The Old Fox." *Sport* 16, no. 5 (May 1954): 45.

Franklin, John Hope. "The Birth of a Nation: Propaganda as History." In *Race and History: Selected Essays 1938–1988*. Baton Rouge, La.: Louisiana State University Press, 1990.

Frazier, E. Franklin. "The Negro Middle Class and Desegregation." *Social Problems* 4, no. 4 (April 1957): 295.

Gallagher, Tom. "Lester Rodney, the Daily Worker, and the Integration of Baseball." *The National Pastime: A Review of Baseball History* no. 19 (1999): 77–80.

Greenlee, Marcia M. "Shaw: Heart of Black Washington." In *Washington at Home: An Illustrated History of Neighborhoods in the Nation's Capital*, edited by Kathryn Schneider Smith. Northridge, Calif.: Windsor Publications, 1988, 119.

Griffith, Clark, as told to J. G. Taylor Spink. "At 82, He Prefers to Look Forward." *The Sporting News*, 23 July 1952, 11.

Griffith, Clark, as told to J. G. Taylor Spink. "Clark Griffith's 50 Golden Years in the American League: Sale of Son-in-Law Cronin 'Nats' Financial Salvation." *The Sporting News*, 30 July 1952, 11.

Grow, Doug. "The Last Dinosaur." *Inside Sports* 6 (July 1984): 35.

Heuer, Robert. "Look What They've Done to My Game!" *Americas*, 1 May 1995, 36.

Holway, John B. "Troy Maxon's Negro Leagues." *Playbill*, June 1990 (Arena Stage, Washington, D.C.), 111.

"Howard University: It Is America's Center of Negro Learning." *Life* 2, no. 21 (18 November 1946): 100.

Hughes, Langston. "Our Wonderful Society: Washington." *Opportunity*, August 1927, 226–27.

Hyman, Sidney. "Washington's Negro Elite." *Look*, 6 April 1965, 60–63.

Jacobs, Barry. "Buck Leonard." *Baseball America*, 1 June 1983, 5.

"Jim Crow Concert Hall." *Time*, 6 March 1939, 33–34.

Johnson, Ronald M. "LeDroit Park: Premier Black Community," In *Washington at Home: An Illustrated History of Neighborhoods in the Nation's Capital*, edited by Kathryn Schneider Smith. Northridge, Calif.: Windsor Publications, 1988, 139–41.

Jordan, David, Larry Gerlach, and John Rossi. "A Baseball Myth Exploded." *The National Pastime: A Review of Baseball History* no. 18 (1998): 3–13.

Jordan, Pat. "Just Some of the Folks Who Ruined Your Summer," *New York Times Magazine*, 18 September 1994, 1.

"Josh the Basher." *Time*, 19 July 1943, 75–76.

Kernan, Michael. "The Object at Hand; Marian Anderson's Mink Coat," *Smithsonian* 24, no. 3 (June 1993): 14.

Kindred, Dave. "Memories Frozen in Time." *The Sporting News*, 2 January 1995, 6.

Lamb, Chris. "L'Affaire Jake Powell: The Minority Press Goes to Bat Against Segregated Baseball." *Journalism and Mass Communication Quarterly* 76, no. 1 (Spring 1999): 21–34.

Lamb, Chris, and Glen Bleske, "Democracy on the Field: The Black Press Takes on White Baseball." *Journalism History* 24, no. 2 (Summer 1998): 51.

Lenehan, Michael. "The Last of the Pure Baseball Men." *Atlantic Monthly* 248, no. 2 (August 1981): 44.

Lester, Larry, with John "Buck" O'Neil. "Satch vs. Josh." *The National Pastime: A Review of Baseball History* no. 13 (1993), 30–33.

Lieb, Frederick G. "Griffith Canny as Hill Star, Pilot, Owner." *The Sporting News*, 2 November 1955, 11.

Logan, Rayford W. "Growing Up in Washington: A Lucky Generation." In *Records of the Columbia History Society of Washington, D.C.*, vol. 48 (1971–1972), edited by Francis Coleman Rosenberger, 506. Charlottesville, Va.: University Press of Virginia, 1973.

Lunardini, Christine. "Standing Firm: William Monroe Trotter's Meetings with Woodrow Wilson, 1913–1914," *Journal of Negro History* 64, no. 3 (Summer 1979): 244–64.

Malloy, Jerry. Introduction to *Sol White's History of Colored Base Ball*, by Sol White. Lincoln, Nebr.: University of Nebraska Press, 1995.

Manley, Effa. "Negro Baseball Isn't Dead." *Our World*, August 1948, 27.

Mardo, Bill. "Robinson-Robeson." In *Jackie Robinson*, edited by Joseph Dorinson and Joram Warmund, 98–106. Armonk, N.Y.: M. E. Sharpe, 1998.

"Marian Anderson at Last Sings in D.A.R.'s Hall." *Life*, 25 January 1943, 102.

McReynolds, John. "Nate Moreland: A Mystery to Historians." *The National Pastime: A Review of Baseball History* no. 19 (1999): 57–58.

Miller, Kelly. "Howard: The National Negro University." In *The New Negro: An Interpretation*, edited by Alain Locke, 312. New York: Albert and Charles Boni, 1925.

Miner, Curtis, and Paul Roberts. "Engineering an Industrial Diaspora: Homestead, 1941." *Pittsburgh History* 72, no. 1 (Winter 1989): 8.

Murphy, Carl, William N. Jones, and William I. Gibson. "The Afro: Seaboard's Largest Weekly." *The Crisis* 45, no. 2 (February 1938): 44.

Naiman, Joe. "Bert Shepard." *The National Pastime: A Review of Baseball History* no. 19 (1999): 75–76.

Norwood, Stephen H., and Harold Brackman. "Going to Bat for Jackie Robinson: The Jewish Role in Breaking Baseball's Color Line." *Journal of Sport History* 26, no. 1 (Spring 1999): 115–41.

Okrent, Daniel. "A Background Check: Was Babe Ruth Black? More Important, Should We Care?" *Sports Illustrated*, 7 May 2001, 27.

Povich, Shirley. "Can Negro Win Housing Fight in Spring Camps?" *The Sporting News*, 8 March 1961, 10.

Pringle, Henry F., and Katherine Pringle. "America's Leading Negro University." *Saturday Evening Post* 221, no. 34 (February 19, 1949): 36.

Rasky, Frank. "Harlem's Religious Zealots." *Tomorrow* 9, no. 3 (November 1949): 12.

"Recreation and Morale." *Crisis* 50, no. 9 (September 1943): 277.

Robinson, Jackie. "What's Wrong with Negro Baseball." *Ebony*, June 1948, 16–17.

Rosengarten, Theodore. "Reading the Hops: Recollections of Lorenzo Piper Davis and the Negro Baseball League." *Southern Exposure* 5 (1977): 62–79.

Rusinack, Kelly E. "Baseball on the Radical Agenda: The *Daily Worker* and *Sunday Worker* Journalistic Campaign to Desegregate Major League Baseball, 1933–1947." In *Jackie Robinson*, edited by Joseph Dorinson and Joram Warmund, 75–85. Armonk, N.Y.: M. E. Sharpe, 1998.

"Satchel Paige, Negro Ballplayer, Is One of Best Pitchers in Game." *Life*, 2 June 1941, 90–92.

"Satchelfoots." *Time*, 3 June 1940, 44.

"Senators to Try Out Negro Outfielder." *Jet* 3, no. 18 (26 February 1953): 48.

Shane, Ted. "Chocolate Rube Waddell." *Saturday Evening Post*, 27 July 1940, 20, 79–81.

Simons, William. "Jackie Robinson and the American Mind: Journalistic Perceptions of the Reintegration of Baseball." *Journal of Sport History* 12, no. 1 (Spring 1985): 39–64.

Small, Connie. "Baseball's Improbable Imports." *Saturday Evening Post* 225, no. 5 (2 August 1952): 90.

Smith, Gary. "A Lingering Vestige of Yesterday." *Sports Illustrated*, 4 April 1983, 110.

Smith, Ronald A. "The Paul Robeson–Jackie Robinson Saga and a Political Collision." In *The Jackie Robinson Reader*, edited by Jules Tygiel, 169–88. New York: Dutton, 1997.

Smith, Thomas G. "Civil Rights on the Gridiron: The Kennedy Administration and the Desegregation of the Washington Redskins." *Journal of Sports History* 14, no. 2 (Summer 1987): 189–208.

Terrell, Mary Church. "Society Among the Colored People of Washington." In *Voice of the Negro*. Vol. 1, 1904. New York: Negro University Press, 1969.

———. "History of the High School for Negroes in Washington." *The Journal of Negro History* 2, no. 3 (July 1917): 252–66.

Tiemann, Robert L., and Pete Palmer. "Major League Attendance." In *Total Baseball: The Official Encyclopedia of Major League Baseball*. 6th ed. Edited by John Thorn et al. New York: Total Sports, 1999.

Tindall, William. "Beginning of Street Railways in the Nation's Capital." *Records of the Columbia Historical Society* 21 (1928): 76–77.

Tygiel, Jules. "Black Ball." In *Total Baseball*, edited by John Thorn and Pete Palmer. New York: Warner Books, 1989.

Waterman, Guy. "The Upstart Senators of 1912–1915." *The National Pastime* no. 13 (1993): 24–27.

White, Alvin E. "Washington Is (Not) a Jimcrow Town." *Our World* 9, no. 1 (January 1954): 23.

Wiggins, David K. "Wendell Smith, the *Pittsburgh Courier-Journal* and the Campaign to Include Blacks in Organized Baseball." *Journal of Sports History* 10, no. 2 (Summer 1983): 5.

Williams, Juan. "14th & U: When Being There Meant Being Somebody." *Washington Post Magazine*, 23 February 1988, 23–31.

Wilson, W. Rollo. "They Could Make the Big Leagues." *The Crisis: A Record of the Darker Races* 41, no. 10 (October 1934): 305.

Young, A. S. "Doc." "Inside Sports." *Jet* 2, no. 15 (7 August 1952): 53.

THESES AND DISSERTATIONS

Angel, Lisa. "The Appointment of a Black Postmaster, Rocky Mount, North Carolina, 1897–98." Senior honors essay, University of North Carolina, 1990.

Boettijer, John W. "Street Railways in the District of Columbia." Master's thesis, George Washington University, 1963.

Coates, James Roland, Jr. "Gentlemen's Agreement: The 1937 Maryland-Syracuse Football Controversy." Master's thesis, University of Maryland, 1982.

Dabney, Lillian G. "The History of Schools for Negroes in the District of Columbia 1807–1947." Ph.D. diss., Catholic University of American, 1949.

Lamb, Chris. "Making a Pitch for Equality: Wendell Smith and His Crusade to Integrate Baseball." Paper presented to History Division, 1999 AEJMC national conference, New Orleans, La., August 1999 (on file with author).

The Northern Shaw-Striver Cultural Resources Survey (1991–1992) (on file with author).

Sheingold, Peter M. "In Black and White: Sam Lacy's Campaign to Integrate Baseball." Undergraduate thesis, Hampshire College, 1992.

ACKNOWLEDGMENTS

The research for and writing of this book have spanned almost a third of my lifetime. It began when I was a twenty-year-old sophomore at Duke University and ended when I was a twenty-nine-year-old lawyer living with my parents. In between, I fulfilled a childhood dream of covering the Baltimore Orioles for the *Baltimore Sun*, went to law school, and clerked for a federal appeals court judge. At the end of my clerkship, I decided to turn my college honors thesis about the Homestead Grays playing in Washington, D.C., into a book. So I moved back home and began writing, enduring good-natured jokes from friends about living at the Holiday Inn and being the only unemployed member of my law school class. For eight months, I churned out a three hundred–page first draft and exhausted my savings account. I began work as a lawyer in April of 2001, moved out of the house (much to my parents' relief), and finished the manuscript.

Over the past ten years, many people have helped me with this project. It would be impossible to thank every single person who has aided my sometimes-quixotic efforts with his or her time, expertise, or words of encouragement. If I have not mentioned you by name, I apologize. All of the errors and mistakes in judgment in this book are my own.

Beyond the Shadow of the Senators exists because of the encouragement of two of Duke University's finest teachers and history professors, Raymond Gavins and John H. Thompson.

Professor Gavins introduced me to Afro-American history during my sophomore year, suggested that I apply for a twenty-five hundred dollar summer research grant to interview black Washingtonians and Negro League players about the Grays, and served as my senior honors thesis adviser. He patiently taught me how to be a historian, and he has always supported my efforts to turn my honors thesis into a book.

Professor Thompson and I met through our love of baseball at the end of my freshman year. Along the way, he suggested that I study Afro-American history and taught me how to write baseball history in a popular style that was grounded in scholarly research. During and after my four years at Duke, Professor Thompson has been my mentor and one of my closest friends. He has endured all of my fits and starts in writing this manuscript.

In addition to Professors Gavins and Thompson, several other scholars at Duke contributed to this project: the late Jack Cell, the late Edward Hill, and Ted Rosengarten.

Numerous archivists, librarians, and historians have aided my research efforts. Thanks go to the following people and organizations: Duke's Center for Documentary Studies (for its research grant in the summer of 1992); the librarians and archivists at Duke's Perkins Library; Donna Wells at Howard University's Moorland-Spingarn Research Center; Esme Bhan, formerly of the Moorland-Spingarn Research Center, who introduced me to the Art Carter Papers and opened numerous doors for me; the librarians at the Moorland-Spingarn Research Center Reading Room at Howard's Founders Library and at the Library of Congress's newspapers and microforms divisions; W. C. Burdick and numerous others at the National Baseball Hall of Fame Library in Cooperstown, New York; Dave Kelly at the Library of Congress; John Vernon at the National Archives; the librarians at the Washingtoniana Division of the Martin Luther King Library in Washington, D.C.; the Enoch Pratt Free Library in Baltimore, Maryland; the *Baltimore Sun* library; the Atlantic City Public Library; the Free Library in Philadelphia, Pennsylvania; Ellen Roney Hughes and Dave Burgevin at the Smithsonian; Judy Capurso at the Charles Sumner School Museum and Archives; Tom Gilbert at AP/Worldwide; Mark Rucker at Transcendental Graphics; Willie B. Cox Prather for her assistance in publishing a Leonard family photo; the archivists at *The Sporting News*; the Society of American Baseball Research, particularly Negro League committee members Dick Clark, John Holway, Larry Hogan, and Jim Riley; authors Neil Lanctot, Jim Overmyer, and Jim Reisler for answering my queries; Alan Feinberg for his knowledge about the Washington Senators; and research librarian Caitlin Lietzan for fielding my last-minute questions.

Many people who lived this story sat down with me for interviews or spoke with me by phone. Most of them have since passed away. Among the most generous with their time were Buck Leonard and his sister, Lena Cox; Calvin Griffith; Shirley Povich; Sam Lacy; and Wilmer Fields. Photographer Robert McNeill deserves special mention, not only for entertaining me on multiple occasions with stories about his extraordinary life and career but also for allowing me to use his wonderful photographs in this book.

Contemporary Books published *Beyond the Shadow of the Senators* thanks to the hard work of many talented people in the publishing world. My agents at Venture Literary, Greg Dinkin and Frank Scatoni, made it happen, from negotiating the contract to providing me with insightful comments on the manuscript. My editor at Contemporary Books, Matthew Carnicelli, championed this project from the outset. I am indebted to him and to the rest of the staff at Contemporary Books including Mandy Huber, Marisa L'Heureux, Michele Pezzuti, and Dawn Shoemaker. On short notice, Andy Knobel proofread and fact-checked the manuscript, lending his keen eye and knowledge of baseball and saving me from many embarrassing mistakes.

Many friends from my childhood, Duke, the *Baltimore Sun*, Yale Law School, and Williams and Connolly LLP heard me talk about this book ad nauseam and encouraged me to hurry up and finish it. You know who you are. Thank you for your moral support. A few people deserve special mention for reading all or part of the manuscript or book proposal or helping me find an agent: Chet Fenster, Abbe Gluck, Julie Hilden, Chris Klatell, Paul McMullen, John Thompson, and Jules Tygiel. I could not have finished the book without your help.

Finally, I want to thank my family for always being there for me. My mother and father, Harry and Linda Snyder, have since sold the house where I grew up (probably to prevent me from ever moving back in again), but they have bought into everything I have ever done. Along with my brother, Ivan, they are my best friends and my biggest fans (and I, theirs). They are the sources of my inspiration. This book is dedicated to them.

INDEX

413